6

WITHDRAWN

CHICAGO AND COOK COUNTY

A GUIDE TO RESEARCH

Loretto Dennis Szucs

D0381369

Ancestry®

Szucs, Loretto Dennis.

Chicago and Cook County : a guide to research / Loretto Dennis
Szucs.

p. cm.

Includes bibliographical references and index.

ISBN 0-916489-62-0 (soft)

1. Chicago (Ill.)—Genealogy—Library resources. 2. Cook County
(Ill.)—Genealogy—Library resources. 3. Chicago
(Ill.)—Genealogy—Archival resources. 4. Cook County
(Ill.)—Genealogy—Archival resources. I. Title.

Z1278.C5S97 1996

[F548.25]

026.929'1'07207731—dc20   95-48440

Copyright © 1996

Ancestry

P.O. Box 476

Salt Lake City, Utah 84110-0476

First printing 1996

10 9 8 7 6 5 4 3 2 1

Printed in the United States of America

Contents

Introduction

No history can be written without a precise knowledge of available original and published resources. Yet, the sheer magnitude, bureaucratic barriers, and geographical distribution of Chicago and Cook County records present such formidable challenges that a complete knowledge of sources is almost impossible. Nonetheless, this guide is designed to shed an inviting light on the abundance of rich Chicago and Cook County sources, and to facilitate research by historians—local, family, and social—and journalists, students, and teachers.

While there are literally hundreds of archives, libraries, churches, cemeteries, and other research possibilities, a researcher who is unfamiliar with the area may overlook important sources. Changes in boundaries and in community, town, and street names can complicate or even block research progress. Locating record sources and knowing where to find answers to changed names and jurisdictions can eliminate hours of wasted time.

Foremost among the problems of locating records in the metropolitan area is its great size. The 1990 census counted 5,105,067 inhabitants in Cook County. The density of its population is multiplied hundreds of times over by the volume of records created each year. Management of these records is no easy task. In fact, the Illinois state-wide Historical Records Needs Survey Assessment *Final Report* (1982) singled out this area as having the most critical records problem in Illinois. No archival program for historical records existed, and no records management system was in place. Cook County has "Home Rule" laws that tend to confuse further those accustomed to research policies of other counties.

Not until late 1993 was the Illinois State Archives awarded a matching grant from the National Historical Publications and Records Commission for the purpose of surveying and scheduling the records of Chicago and Cook County. In 1987 the Illinois Regional Archives Depository-Chicago Branch (IRAD) was opened as a central depository for historic public records in Cook County. While it is a step in the right direction, it would be unrealistic to believe that IRAD can centralize "all" historic records. A new section in this revised guide describes IRAD holdings for this area.

The havoc wrought by the Chicago Fire, which began in Mrs. O'Leary's barn on October 8, 1871, continues to threaten the success of research projects focusing on events previous to that date. Many critical documents and primary sources disappeared in the ashes. The checklist of existing and little-known pre-fire sources included in this guide (see page xx) offers new possibilities for this challenging time period. The same sense of determination that rebuilt Chicago after the fire in 1871 may be equally necessary to reconstruct local or family history.

The County Clerk of Cook County has responsibility for administering records of live births, still births, delayed births, marriages, deaths, coroner's records, and miscellaneous other vital records. More than fifty million records have come under the care of the County Clerk since 1871, when record keeping began anew after the Chicago Fire. The County Clerk's office usually receives more than one thousand requests each day.

Chicago and its more than one hundred incorporated suburbs comprise the major portion of Cook County, and are divided into over 1.5 million parcels of real estate. These figures increase as large portions of farmland are subdivided for residential and other uses. Recorded deeds and tract books hold treasures of information, but tracing property history and locating documents is more difficult than it is in less populated areas. The great number of property transactions in Cook County makes the "grantor-grantee indexing system" impractical. The description of the records, the record-keeping system, and a step-by-step guide to tracing real estate property provided in the Land and Property Records section can eliminate much of the confusion associated with the records.

The Circuit Court of Cook County is the largest trial court in the world. Court files kept over the years number over eighty million and are expanding at more than five million per year. History, recorded in its original form, is stored in a mass of case files. Types of available records, examples of some interesting cases, research potential, and procedures for accessing files are presented in the Court Records section.

As an industrial and transportation center, Chicago attracted millions. It was only a temporary residence for many, however, and some moved so frequently that their presence in the area is difficult to document. Finding records for this transient segment of the population is often the greatest research challenge, and requires reaching beyond the commonly used records. Alternative sources are suggested throughout the text.

Original Chicago-area settlers were predominantly New Englanders and New Yorkers. Germans and Irish came in great numbers from the middle to the late nineteenth century, and Italians, Russian Jews, and Poles flooded into the area early in the twentieth century. A migration of African Americans from the South, Mexicans, and Asians substantially increased Chicago's ethnic diversity in later years. At various times in its history, Chicago has been the largest Lithuanian city, the second largest Bohemian city, the second largest Ukrainian city, the third largest Swedish, Irish, Polish, and Jewish city in the world. Knowing the unique record collections that exist for each of the ethnic groups can mean the difference between success and failure in research; therefore, a primary goal of this guide is to identify the many hard-to-find ethnic sources. One section is devoted to this topic.

Religious records, considered primary sources, are acceptable supplements to civil vital records. These documents fill gaps where official county records are missing, and often include important facts not found in other sources. Finding records of religious congregations in the Chicago metropolitan area is especially difficult because of the great number of churches and synagogues supported by the enormous population for over 150 years. While population, geography, and ethnic differences make searching for religious records difficult enough, over the years some institutions closed, consolidated, and moved as neighborhoods changed. A large section of this book describes available church and religious records.

If researchers are thwarted by problems which are a result of the massive population in one respect, they are compensated at least partially by the fact that the size of the city and county has resulted in the creation of sources not available in less-populated areas. In addition to the original records held by governmental agencies, Cook County has excellent research centers such as the Newberry Library, the National Archives-Great Lakes Region, the Chicago Historical Society, and the Chicago Public Library. These institutions and their holdings are documented in various sections of this guide.

Since *Chicago and Cook County Sources* was first published in 1986, collections have been moved, access policies have changed, some records have become unavailable, and some new sources have been discovered. Among the major changes are:

* The Chicago Public Library consolidated its once-splintered collections and moved into the beautiful new Harold Washington Center in 1992. The Chicago Municipal Reference Library, a victim of budget cuts, closed January 1, 1991. Materials from the Municipal Reference Library were also moved into the Harold Washington Center.

* The Illinois State Archives' seventh regional depository at the University Library of Northeastern Illinois University in Chicago officially opened on October 11, 1990. Since the opening, IRAD-Chicago has allowed researchers access to an ever-growing body of Chicago information.

* The 1920 federal census was released.

* Old Cook County Circuit Court records have become more accessible through the newly-created Circuit Court Archives in the Daley Center.

* Records of Chicago area Catholic churches and of a few of other denominations have been microfilmed; more cemetery records have been microfilmed; Chicago voter registration records (1888-1892) have been found and microfilmed; World War I draft registration cards have been microfilmed, and World War II draft registration cards have become available.

* Policy changes have affected access to Cook County vital records; a number of statewide indexes, such as the *Illinois Death Index 1916-1938* have made this information available at several different sites.

* New ethnic sources have been published and local genealogical societies and historical organizations continue to preserve and publish historically important records and guides at an impressive rate.

* There have been many address, area code, zip code, and telephone number changes.

The list of topics has been modified in this updated guide; however, for quick reference, the topics are arranged alphabetically. The text, wherever possible, acknowledges sources of information and provides additional bibliographical notes and background reading material.

Significant effort has been made to ensure that all information is current at the time of publication. It is advisable, however, to call any and all research facilities in advance to verify access policies and to be sure that needed sources will be available at the time of a planned visit. Ancestry appreciates notification of any information that is in error or additional information that might be added in future reprints.

This book is the result of a prolonged and careful survey of available sources. Further, it is an outgrowth of my work with many others who willingly shared their time, knowledge, and expertise. My experiences in professional research, writing for genealogical journals, working at the National Archives-Great Lakes Region, and becoming fascinated with the rich history of Cook County have all contributed to the compilation of this much needed guide.

Loretto Dennis Szucs

Misprints, Errors and Changes

Ancestry has made every effort to ensure that the thousands of statements of fact in this book are as accurate and up-to-date as possible. Hundreds of experts, professionals, and a wide variety of sources were consulted during the book's compilation, but, as is inevitable in a work of this magnitude and scope, inaccuracies and changes are likely to develop.

Our customers, however, are the real experts, and we need and welcome your feedback. If, while using this book, you discover a factual error or inaccurate statement, please bring it to our attention. We will make verifiable corrections in future printings and editions of the work, thereby assuring the most scrupulous and exact book possible. This is Ancestry's ongoing commitment to our individual customers and the genealogical and historical community at large. Please send your suggestions and corrections to the Editorial Department, Ancestry, P.O. Box 476, Salt Lake City, UT 84110-0476.

Area Code Changes

Chicago is experiencing an explosion in demand for telephone numbers for a wide variety of telecommunications services. As a result, the available numbers in the 708 area code are being rapidly depleted, creating the need for new area codes. Most area codes in effect as this guide goes to press remain unchanged: 312 remains the area code for most of the city of Chicago. However, the existing suburban 708 area code is being divided into three separate area codes: 847, 630, and 708. Some of the changes for the Chicago area have already gone into effect. Suburban Cook County north of the Chicago city limits, most of Lake County, the portion of McHenry County currently under 708, and the northern portion of Kane County came under area code 847 in January 1996. DuPage County, the southern portion of Kane County, and the northern portions of Kendall and Will counties that are now 708 will come under 630 on August 3, 1996. South suburban Cook County, areas around Peotone and Beecher currently in 708, and the near-west Cook County suburbs south of Franklin Park will remain under area code 708.

SECTION ONE

Chicago and Cook County Facts

Chicago Facts

In 1679, the French explorer Rene Robert Cavelier, sieur de La Salle traveled through the area where Chicago now stands and called it *checagou*, an Indian word that has had various translations.

Town of Chicago incorporated . . . . 12 August 1833

Population 350

City of Chicago incorporated . . . . 4 March 1837

Population 4,170

Population (1990) 5,105,067

Six-county metropolitan area (1990) 7,261,173

Geography

Area (square miles) 228,126

Length (miles) 25.0

Figure 1: The Chicago Water Works and Tower—1870
(courtesy The Chicago Historical Society)

Breadth (miles) 15.0

Lake front (miles of shoreline) 29.0

City block (average size) . . . . 330' x 660' or 5 acres

100 street numbers equal one block

Eight city blocks, or 800 street numbers equal one mile.

Five city blocks, or 500 street numbers equal one kilometer.

North and south street numbers are divided by Madison Street.

East and west street numbers are divided by State Street.

Even numbered buildings are on the north and the west sides of the street.

Uneven numbered buildings are on the south and the east sides of the street.

Lake Michigan is always on the East.

The Flag of the City of Chicago

The Chicago Municipal Flag consists of two blue bars, representing the two branches of the Chicago River. These bars enclose a white center bar that represents the west division of the city. The narrower stripe of white above the top blue bar and below the bottom blue bar represent the north and south divisions. The four red, six-pointed, stars on the white center bar represent Fort Dearborn, the Chicago Fire of 1871, the Columbian Exposition of 1893 and the Century of Progress Exposition of 1933.

The Seal of the City of Chicago

The symbolic meaning of the seal:

1. The shield suggests the national spirit of Chicago.

2. The American Indian represents the discoverers of the

site of Chicago and is indicative of the aboriginal contribution which enters into its history.

3. The ship in full sail signifies the approach of civilization and commerce.

4. The sheaf of wheat is typical of activity and plenty, holding the same meaning as the cornucopia.

5. The babe in the shell is the ancient classical symbol of the pearl, and Chicago, situated at the neck of the lake, signifies that it shall be "the gem of the lakes."

6. The motto, "*Urbs in Horto*," means "City in a Garden."

7. The date, "March 4, 1837," is the date of the incorporation of the City.

The Chicago Water Tower

The Chicago Water Tower, designed by William W. Boyington in the "castellated Gothic" style, has played a major role in the city's history since it was built during the years 1867-1869. Rough-faced yellow limestone from quarries near Joliet was used in its construction. After the Great Chicago Fire of 1871, the Water Tower was one of the few buildings to survive without being burned. It came to symbolize the city's ability to overcome calamity. The Tower remains one of the city's most well-known landmarks, and was officially designated as such by the Chicago City Council in 1971. The adaptive redesign of the Water Tower as a Visitor Information Center was coordinated by the Chicago Convention and Tourism Bureau.

Chicago Convention and Tourism Bureau, Inc.
McCormick Place-on-the-Lake
Chicago, IL 60616
(312-567-8500)

Cook County Facts

Named after Daniel P. Cook; member of Congress and the first state's attorney.

Created .... 15 January 1831

Area .... 956 square miles

Suburban cities and municipalities . 444 square miles

Unincorporated areas .... 285 square miles.

Incorporated cities and villages 126

1990 Cook County population .... 5.1 million

Two Chicago buildings constitute the seat of Cook County government. The Richard J. Daley Center (formerly called the Civic Center) is 648 feet high, and towers above the old County Courthouse which is sometimes referred to as the County Building. Together they house the courts, the elective county offices, and many county and city departments. Notable is the famous Picasso sculpture in the courtyard of the Daley Center. Construction of the County Building, with its classic pillars, was begun in 1906 and completed in 1907. Daley Center construction was started in 1963 and completed in 1966.

Cook County Flag

The Cook County flag consists of a white field with red and yellow trim and blue lettering. In the center of the flag is the county seal. The thirty-eight small stars on the circular band of the seal represent the county's thirty suburban townships and the eight townships in Chicago.

The large star at the apex of the circular band represents Chicago, seat of the Cook County government.

The outline in the center of the scroll bears the date "January 1831 " which is the date Cook County was created by an act of the State Legislature.

Symbol of Cook County

The Corporate Seal is the symbol of Cook County. In the center of the seal is a map of Cook County. A scroll bears the date when the county was created. The ship sailing on Lake Michigan, at the lower left of the seal, is symbolic of Cook County's geographical location as a shipping port, as well as a center for all transportation. The group of diversified buildings to the right of the scroll symbolizes government, schools, churches, fine arts, dwellings, and the business and industry which comprise the county. The entire design is encircled by a border with the printed words, "Seal of Cook County-Illinois."

Cook County is the only "Home Rule" county in the State of Illinois; the only county with a directly elected executive officer. It is governed by an elected President and Board of Commissioners, ten from Chicago and five from suburban Cook County.

Cook County may exercise all powers as a local government, unless preempted by the State or limited by the Constitution, as long as its ordinances do not conflict with ordinances of municipalities within the county. It carries out state policy; enforces laws, prosecutes offenders, keeps records (including vital statistics, issues marriage licenses), conducts elections, assesses property and collects and distributes taxes for all taxing bodies within the county.

A Chronology of Chicago and Cook County History

1673 Father Marquette and Louis Joliet are the first known Europeans to explore the region.

1696 Father Pierre Pinet establishes the short-lived Mission of the Guardian Angels.

1779 Jean Baptiste Point DuSable builds a trading post and establishes a permanent settlement on the Chicago River near the current location of the Tribune Tower.

1795 American Indian tribes give the U.S. government land at the mouth of the "Chikago River" as part of the Treaty of Greenville.

1803 Captain John Whistler and Lieutenant James S.

Swearingen, U.S.A., with a company of United States regular infantry, build and establish the first Fort Dearborn.

1804 John Kinzie and his family, the first American civilians, settle in Chicago.

First white child born in Chicago, Ellen Marion Kinzie, daughter of John and Eleanor Kinzie.

1810 First doctor arrives in Chicago, John Cooper, surgeon's mate, U.S.A., detailed for duty at Fort Dearborn.

Illinois Potawatomies begin hostilities against the whites.

Attention of government drawn to scheme of canal connecting Lake Michigan with Mississippi River.

1812 August 15, Fort Dearborn massacre.

August 16, Indians burn Fort Dearborn.

1816 Fort Dearborn rebuilt, Indian agency and warehouse re-established. John Kinzie and family return to Chicago to live.

1817 Schooners *Baltimore* and *Hercules* establish route between Chicago and Mackinac.

1818 Illinois admitted to Union as a state.

First large sailing vessel, the United States revenue cutter *Fairplay*, enters the Chicago River.

1822 First baptism in Chicago, Alexander Beaubien baptized by Rev. Stephen D. Badin.

1823 Illinois and Michigan Canal bill passed by legislature.

First marriage is celebrated in Chicago, that of Dr. Alexander Wolcott and Miss Ellen Marion Kinzie.

1825 New York's Erie Canal is completed, providing immigrants and manufactured goods a greater access to Chicago via the Great Lakes.

1826 First election held in Chicago: gubernatorial and congressional.

1827 First company of state militia organized.

First slaughter-house built on north branch of Chicago River by Archibald Clybourne.

1828 Fort Dearborn re-garrisoned by United States troops.

John Kinzie, first settler, died at Fort Dearborn.

1829 First ferry established, near present site of Lake Street bridge.

"Wolf Tavern," Chicago's first hotel, built by James Kinzie and Archibald Caldwell, at the "forks" of the Chicago River.

1830 Chicago's population is about fifty.

Chicago first surveyed and platted.

First bridge built across Chicago River (south branch) near Randolph Street crossing.

1831 Cook County created and Chicago designated as the county seat.

First county election held.

First public building erected in Cook County.

Jonathan N. Bailey appointed first postmaster.

First county roads established: the present day State Street and Archer Avenue, and Madison Street and Ogden Avenue.

First lighthouse constructed.

1832 First frame building, Robert A. Kinzie's store, on the West Side.

First drug store established by Philo Carpenter in log building at what is now the east end of Lake Street bridge.

Black Hawk war broke out. Four companies of volunteers organized in Chicago go to the front.

First cholera epidemic in Chicago brought by United States troops on steamer *Sheldon Thompson*.

First provisions (meat) packed and shipped by George W. Dole.

First sawmill established.

1833 Village, or town, of Chicago incorporated (350 inhabitants).

First issue of first Chicago newspaper, the *Chicago Democrat*, a weekly, by John Calhoun.

First Roman Catholic priest to establish a permanent parish. Rev. John Mary Ireneus St. Cyr arrived in Chicago and established St. Mary's parish.

First Presbyterian church organized by Rev. Jeremiah Porter, chaplain U.S.A.

First Baptist church erected.

First appropriation for harbor improvements.

First fire marshall, Benjamin Jones, appointed as "fire warden."

First shipment from port of Chicago by Newberry & Dole on Schooner *Napoleon*.

First Tremont house built.

1834 First authorized town loan.

First Protestant Episcopal church, St. James, established by Rev. Isaac W. Hallam.

First mail coach route established by Dr. John T. Temple between Chicago and Detroit.

First professional public entertainment by "Professor" Bowers, fire eater, ventriloquist and prestidigitator, at the "Mansion House."

First drawbridge erected over Chicago River at Dearborn Street.

First vessels navigate Chicago River: steamer *Michigan* in June and schooner *Illinois* in July.

First divorce suit and murder trial.

First piano bought in Chicago.

1835 First bank established in Chicago known as the "Chicago Branch of the Illinois State Bank."

Opening of United States land office: great land craze.

First board of health organized.

Volunteer fire department organized.

First courthouse erected, corner Clark and Randolph Streets.

After the American Indians' defeat in the Black Hawk War of 1832, and because of the treaties of 1833 and 1835, the Potawatomies, and other Indian tribes, begin leaving for lands promised to them west of the Mississippi River.

1836 First spadeful of earth thrown out in digging Illinois and Michigan Canal, July 4.

First sailing vessel, *Clarissa*, launched May, 1836.

First house built from architectural designs, for William B. Ogden.

First Chicago railroad chartered, Galena and Chicago Union Railroad.

First water mains laid, two miles wooden pipe.

1837 City of Chicago created.

First city election held. William B. Ogden becomes the Chicago's first mayor.

First census taken, population 4,107.

First great financial panic.

First theater opened.

1838 First steam fire engine bought by Chicago.

First Chicago steamer, the *"James Allen,"* built.

First invoice of wheat, exported from Chicago.

1839 First great fire in Chicago.

A steamship makes the round trip between Chicago and Buffalo, New York, in sixteen days.

1840 Reorganization and permanent establishment of free public schools.

1841 Office of City Marshal created.

1843 First book compiled, printed, bound, and issued in Chicago (1843 Chicago directory).

1844 First university (St. Mary's of the Lake), established.

1845 Cook County Court established.

First permanent school (Dearborn School) building erected.

First power printing press brought to Chicago by "Long John Wentworth" and used by him in printing the *Chicago Democrat*.

1847 First county hospital opened in "Tippecanoe Hall."

First law school opened.

McCormick, inventor of the reaper, starts making farm implements.

1848 Illinois and Michigan Canal opens.

First United States Court opens.

Chicago and Galena Union Railroad built.

First telegram received in Chicago (from Milwaukee).

First smallpox epidemic and first vaccination.

Chicago Board of Trade founded.

1849 Third cholera epidemic.

Bank panic.

Great storm and flood; over $100,000 damage to vessels, wharfs, etc.

Chicago's second big fire; twenty buildings destroyed.

1850 Chicago's population is 29,963. Fifty percent are immigrants from foreign countries.

City first lighted by gas.

First opera performed in city.

Stephen A. Douglas delivered his great speech in Chicago.

1851 Chicago, Rock Island and Pacific and Chicago, Milwaukee and St. Paul railroads organized.

1852 City waterworks operated for first time.

First through train from the East enters Chicago over the Michigan Southern Railroad, February 20.

First railroad wreck: passenger trains on Michigan Central and Michigan Southern railroads collide at Grand Crossing; eighteen killed.

Office of superintendent of schools created.

Northwestern University located.

1853 First labor strike.

A horse-drawn omnibus service becomes the city's first form of mass transit.

1854 Cholera epidemic claimed nearly 1,500 lives. (1,424 dead).

1855 "Beer riot."

Main line of Illinois Central Railroad completed, and with ten major lines, Chicago has become a prominent railroad center.

Police department created.

Direct drainage into river inaugurated.

The city began raising level of streets up to twelve feet to fill in swampy areas and improve drainage.

1856 First steam tugs in river.

First suburban trains.

First high school opened.

First sewers laid.

First iron bridge built at Rush Street.

1857 Destructive fire; twenty-three lives lost, and $500,000 in property loss.

Great financial panic.

1858 First streetcar run in State Street.

Paid fire department organized.

1859 Street car franchises granted by state legislature.

The first horse drawn railway began operation.

1860 Chicago's population is 112,172.

Loss of steamer *Lady Elgin*; 203 deaths.

1861 Outbreak of Civil War and establishment of Camp Douglas at current location of 31st and King Drive. Used as a prison for Confederate soldiers until the Civil War's conclusion in 1865.

1862 First internal revenue collector appointed.

1863 City limits extended to include Bridgeport.

1864 Work commenced on first lake tunnel.

1865 First lake crib placed. Union Stockyards were established to consolidate all slaughterhouses into one area.

Fire alarm telegraph inaugurated.

1867 Lake tunnel completed.

New waterworks building and tower erected.

A sanitary water system was installed.

1869 Washington Steel tunnel, first under river, completed.

Park act passed.

1870 Chicago's population is 298,977.

1871 The Great Chicago Fire of October 8-10 destroys an area nearly five miles long and one mile wide. About 300 people die and almost 100,000 are left homeless. A newspaper report promotes the idea that Catherine O'Leary and her cow were responsible for starting the fire, but no evidence is found to support that accusation. Loss of property amounts to $280,000,000.

City reincorporated under general law.

1872 Ordinance outlawing wooden buildings in downtown area.

1873 United States Subtreasury established.

Second serious financial panic.

As a symbol of Chicago's growth after the Great Fire, an Inter-State Industrial Exposition is held.

1877 Saving bank crash.

Chicago's first telephones are installed.

1880 Chicago's population is 503,185.

George Pullman built his car shop and the town of Pullman.

1882 Cable cars first operated by Chicago City Railway Company.

1883 Courthouse and City Hall completed.

1885 The nine-story Home Insurance Building is erected. Its skeletal construction of iron and steel beams leads the way to future.

1886 Anarchists riots in the Haymarket.

1889 Sanitary district of Chicago created.

Jane Addams and Ellen Gates Starr open Hull House to aid immigrants.

1890 Chicago's population is 1,099,850.

The city has 2,048 miles of streets, but only 629 miles are paved. About half are paved with wooden blocks.

1892 First elevated road built.

Ground broken for Drainage Canal.

University of Chicago founded.

Electric streetcars (trolleys) and a steam powered, elevated railway system (the "el") began widespread service. The "el" system is converted to electric power in 1897. Horse cars and cable cars are not used after 1906.

Telephone lines connect Chicago to New York and Boston.

1893 World's Columbian Exposition held. Mayor Carter H. Harrison, So. assassinated.

1894 Third financial panic.

Pullman car plant strike led to a railroad strike.

1897 Chicago Loop encircled by new "el" lines.

1898 Union Elevated Loop built.

1899 Drainage Canal opened.

Cornerstone of new Federal Building laid, "Chicago day," Oct. 9, by President William McKinley.

The number of automobiles rises from three to more than 300. By 1901, an eight-mph speed limit is established.

1900 Chicago's population is 1,698,575.

Chicago Sanitary and Ship Canal opened; flow of Chicago River reversed so that sewage no longer flows into Lake Michigan.

1902 Prince Henry of Prussia, visited Chicago.

1903 Chicago Centennial celebration.

Iroquois Theater fire with loss of 602 lives.

1905 Chicago Association of Commerce organized.

1906 Municipal Court of Chicago established eliminating old justice court system.

1907 New Cook County Courthouse (County Building) completed at a total cost of $5,000,000.

New street railway ordinances passed and work of rebuilding lines begun.

1908 William H. Taft nominated for President at the National Republican Convention held in Coliseum.

City Hall razed, preparatory to erection of new structure.

1909 The Chicago Plan was originated by Daniel Burnham and streets were renumbered.

1910 Chicago's population is 2,185,283.

1911 Present day City Hall and County Building completed.

Carter H. Harrison, Jr. elected mayor for a fifth term.

1914 A freight subway system beneath the Loop relieves traffic congestion by transporting merchandise, coal, and garbage through sixty-two miles of tunnels.

1915 The excursion steamer *Eastland* overturned in the Chicago River killing 812 people.

1916 Municipal Pier, later called Navy Pier, is completed for passenger and freight vessels.

1917 Motor coaches (buses) began operations in the city.

1919 A violent race riot leaves fifteen whites and twenty-three blacks dead.

1920 Chicago's population is 2,701,705.

Michigan Avenue bridge completed.

1924 Despite prohibition, there were at least fifteen breweries and 20,000 retail alcoholic beverage outlets operating illegally in Chicago.

1927 Chicago's first municipal airport, later called Midway Airport, opened.

1929 Gangsters machine-gun seven of Al Capone's enemies in the St. Valentine's Day Massacre.

1930   Chicago's population is 3,376,438.

1932   Due to the nationwide depression, more than 750,000 Chicagoans (nearly one-fourth of the city's population) are out of work.

Only fifty-one of the city's 228 banks are open.

1933   Century of Progress Exposition opens.

1940   Chicago's population is 3,396,808.

1942   The world's first controlled atomic reaction is achieved at the University of Chicago.

1943   Chicago's first passenger subway opened beneath State Street.

1950   Chicago's population reaches all-time high of 3,620,962. The population of the entire six county metropolitan area is 5,177,868.

1953   Chicago became the world's steel capital.

1955   Richard J. Daley elected mayor. He served six consecutive terms until his death in 1975.

O'Hare Airport opened and eventually becomes one of the world's busiest airports.

1956   The Congress Expressway, later called the Eisenhower Expressway, was the first high-speed automobile route to open in the city.

1959   St. Lawrence Seaway opened.

1960   Chicago's population is 3,550,404.

1968   Riots and fires occurred in parts of Chicago's West Side following news of the assassination of Dr. Martin Luther King, Jr.

1970   Chicago's population is 3,369,357.

1971   Union Stockyards closed.

1974   World's tallest building, the 110-story Sears Tower, erected.

1979   Jane M. Byrne elected Chicago's first woman mayor.

1980   Chicago's population is 3,005,072. The population of the entire six-county metropolitan area is 7,102,328.

Further details about the people and events highlighted in this chronology, and about ethnic groups, politics, industry, labor, and architecture can be found in sources mentioned in the bibliography at the end of this section.

Chicago Fire and Pre-Fire Source Checklist

The Great Chicago Fire of 1871 began Sunday, October 8, in a barn behind the Patrick O'Leary home at 137 (now 558 West) De Koven Street. Although the actual cause of the Fire is unknown, over a dozen theories have been advanced, the most common being that Mrs. O'Leary's cow kicked over a lighted lantern.

At that time, Chicago, a city built almost entirely of wood, was experiencing a severe drought. During the week preceding the Great Fire, there had been many serious fires. The Great Fire that began the following evening quickly spread north and east from the O'Leary barn, ironically sparing their home but rapidly destroying houses, fences, sidewalks, and other structures-almost entirely constructed of dry, resinous pine.

The Fire spread rapidly, at a rate of about six miles an hour or fifteen feet a minute. The wind carried flaming debris which ignited new fires as they settled in new spots.

Although the Fire had begun west of the South Branch of the Chicago River, most of the damage was concentrated east of the river's North and South branches. The burned area—4 ¾ miles long and averaging a mile wide—covered 3.32 square miles or 2,124 acres, including the entire central business district. Lost were 17,450 buildings and much of the city's industrial capacity. About 98,500 people were left homeless by the conflagration. There is no record—not even a partial list—of people killed. It is estimated that at least 300 people lost their lives. The Chicago Fire Academy now stands on the site of the O'Leary home.

A Checklist of Pre-Fire Sources

* Archives and Manuscript Collections: Some history survives only in the form of original manuscripts housed in special archives collections (see section 20).

* Cemetery records.

* Census records.

* Church records (some burned).

* City directories.

* Court records, especially probates and divorce records which, though filed after the Fire, may contain vital statistics and other dates of events previous to the Fire. Land disputes were frequent, and resulting lawsuits often provide pre-fire deeds, testimony, and other important information.

* Post-Fire death certificates which provide pre-fire birth dates and parent's names.

* Fraternal organization records often provide pre-fire birth dates and residences.

* Genealogical societies have collected and indexed records from various public and private sources. These records often include documented proof of dates, places, and relationships.

* Historical societies.

* Illinois State Archives (see information which follows this list) and the Illinois Regional Archives Depository (IRAD) section (section 21).

* Land and property records, particularly those at Chicago Title and Trust Company, and a few documents which were re-recorded as part of the "Burnt Record Series" (section 13).

* Military records.

* Newspapers (some survived in collections outside Cook County).

* Occupational records.

Figure 2: Chicago—10 October 1871
(courtesy The Chicago Historical Society)

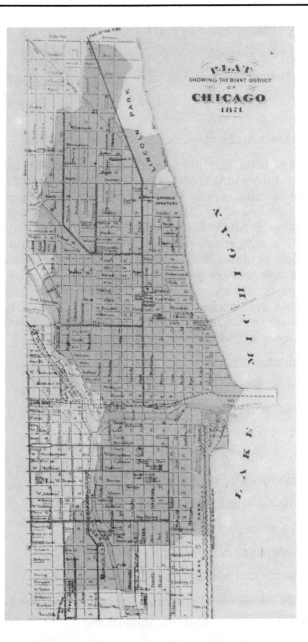

Figure 3: Map Showing the Burnt District
(courtesy The Chicago Historical Society)

* Published histories and biographies.

* School records.

* Vital records indexed from Chicago Newspapers (section 34).

Illinois State Archives—Chicago Records Accession

In April of 1984, the Illinois State Archives accessioned 584 bound volumes and 1075 cubic feet of loose papers from the office of the Chicago City Clerk. Included in the accession are records generated by Chicago city government as well as by several towns and villages which were annexed by it at the end of the eighteenth century. A significant portion of the accession predates the Great Fire of 1871; because these records were previously believed to have been destroyed, they are of particular value. Most of the loose records consist of Chicago City Council Proceedings Files, 1833-1942. The records are the Council's working papers, which in summary form appear in the minutes, and include:

committee reports

orders

assessment rolls

appointments

official oaths and bonds

ordinances and resolutions

poll books and tally sheets

licenses

officials' reports

contracts and specifications

communications

citizens' petitions and remonstrances

The remaining loose records consist of council or trustees' proceedings from the various annexed towns and villages. A comprehensive description of the Chicago Records Accession was published in: *For the Record, Newsletter of the Illinois State Archives* 8, no. 2 (Winter 1986).

Refer also to information about the Illinois Regional Archives Depository (IRAD) in section 21.

A Selected and Annotated Bibliography of Chicago and Cook County History

Abbot, Edith. *The Tenements of Chicago, 1908-1935*. Chicago: The University of Chicago Press, 1936.

A documented study of this serious urban problem.

Addams, Jane. *Twenty Years at Hull House*. New York: Macmillan, 1910.

Ahern, Michael Loftus. *Political History of Chicago*. Chicago, 1886.

Contains biographical notes on several individuals who were prominent in politics.

Allswang, John Myers. *The Political Behavior of Chicago's Ethnic Groups 1918-1932*. New York: Arno, 1980.

Andreas, Alfred T. *History of Chicago*. 3 vols. Chicago, 1884-86.

One of the most often cited of the nineteenth century histories of Chicago.

Andreas, Alfred T. *History of Cook County, Illinois*, Chicago: A. T. Andreas, 1884.

The South Suburban Genealogical and Historical Society added an every-name index to his volume and sponsored its reprinting by Unigraphic Press in 1976.

Andrews, Wayne. *Battle for Chicago*. New York: Harcourt, Brace and Company, 1963.

Angle, Paul M., ed. *The Great Chicago Fire, Described in Seven Letters by Men and Women Who Experienced its Horrors*. Chicago, 1946.

Asbury, Herbert. *Gem of the Prairie*. Garden City: Garden City Publishing Co., Inc., 1942.

Association of Illinois Museums and Historical Societies. *Historical and Cultural Agencies and Museums in Illinois*. Springfield, IL: Phillips Brothers, 1993.

Bach, Ira J. *Chicago on Foot*. Chicago: Follet Publishing Company, 1977.

Barton, Elmer. *A Business Tour of Chicago, Depicting Fifty Years of Progress*. Chicago, 1887.

Beadle, Muriel. *The Fortnightly of Chicago: The City and its Women, 1873-1973*. Chicago: Henry Regnery Co., 1973.

Beijbom, Ulf. *Swedes in Chicago: A Demographic and Social Study of the 1846-1880 Immigration*. Stockholm, 1971.

Bennett, Fremont O. *Politics and Politicians of Chicago, Cook County and Illinois*. Chicago, 1886.

A detailed narrative with lists of officials and excerpts from documents.

Birmingham, George A. *From Dublin to Chicago: Some Notes on a Tour of America*. New York, 1914.

Bishop, Glenn A., and Paul T. Gilbert. *Chicago's Accomplishments and Leaders*. Chicago: Bishop Publishing Company, 1932.

Blanchard, Rufus. *Discovery and Conquests of the North-West with the History of Chicago*. Wheaton, IL, 1881.

A long history of Chicago with a substantial amount of primary material. Some of the information was compiled from original records and part was solicited by Blanchard from early settlers. A second edition was published in 1898-1903 in two volumes which carried the history another two decades. The two volumes are different, making it necessary to consult both editions.

The Book of Chicago. Chicago: Chicago Evening Post, 1911.

Bronstein, Don. *Chicago, I Will.* Text by Tony Weitzel. Cleveland, 1967.

Photographic essay.

Bross, William. *History of Chicago.* Chicago, 1876.

Burg, David F. *Chicago's White City of 1893.* Lexington,KY, 1976.

Burns, Walter N. *The One Way Ride: The Red Trail of Chicago Gangland from Prohibition to Jake Lingle.* New York, 1931.

Butt, Ernest. *Chicago Then and Now.* Chicago, 1933.

Campbell, Edna F., Fanny R. Smith, and Clarence F. Jones. *Our City-Chicago.* New York, 1930.

Chamberlain, Everett. *Chicago and Its Suburbs.* Chicago, 1874.

Chapin, Louella. *Round About Chicago,* Chicago, 1907.

Chatfield-Taylor, Hobart C. *Chicago.* Boston, 1917.

Chicago, Department of Development and Planning. *Historic City: The Settlement of Chicago.* Chicago: Chicago, Department of Development and Planning, 1976.

A survey of the settlement and growth of the city with emphasis on the ethnic groups that made the city, with a set of fold-out maps.

The Chicago Fact Book Consortium. *Local Community Fact Book Chicago Metropolitan Area.* Chicago: The Chicago Fact Book Consortium, 1984.

A convenient compilation of a variety of information on local communities within the metropolitan area embracing the entire nine-county Chicago-Gary-Kenosha Standard Consolidated Statistical Area. Data presented for 131 incorporated communities of 10,000 or more population in the area as well as for seventy-seven community areas in Chicago. Includes brief histories of each community and statistical tables based on the 1970 and 1980 censuses.

Chicago and Northwestern Railway Company. *Yesterday and Today: A History*. Chicago, 1905.

A study of the role played by the railroad in the development of Chicago and the West.

Chicago Association of Commerce, eds. *Chicago. The Great Central Market*. Chicago, 1923.

Chicago Bureau of Statistics and Municipal Library. *The Chicago City Manual*. Chicago, 1908.

Contains a list of the executive and other city officers, and descriptions of their duties. There are also lists of aldermen and committees of the City Council, and the rules that regulated the City Council. This book also provides information on other matters that related to city government or were of municipal concern.

Chicago Historical Society. Documents. *History of Communities, Chicago*. Research under the direction of Vivien M. Palmer. 6 vols. Chicago, 1925-1930. Typescript.

The documents consist of oral histories, excerpts from newspapers, pamphlets, and scrapbooks regarding Rogers Park, West Rogers Park, Uptown, Ravenswood, North Center, Hamlin Park, Lake View, Lower (Near) North Side, Near South Side, Armour Square, Douglas, Oakland, Grand Boulevard, Washington Park, Woodlawn, Grand Crossing, West Englewood, Bridgeport, Canaryville (Fuller Park), Riverdale, and East Side.

Chicago History (Published quarterly by the Chicago Historical Society).

Chicago Plan Commission. *Forty-four Cities in the City of Chicago*. Chicago: Chicago Plan Commission, 1942

Chicago's First Half Century: The City as it was Fifty Years Ago and As It Is Today. Chicago, 1883.

City of Chicago, Department of Development and Planning. *Historic City: The Settlement of Chicago*. Chicago: City of Chicago, Department of Development and Planning, 1976.

Cleaver, Charles. *Early Chicago Reminiscences*. Chicago, 1882.

Colbert, Elias. *Chicago: Historical and Statistical Sketch of the Garden City*. Chicago, 1868.

Colbert, Elias, and Everett Chamberlain. *Chicago and the Great Conflagration*. Chicago, 1871.

Firsthand account of the great fire.

Cook, Frederick F. *Bygone Days in Chicago: Recollections of the "Garden City of the Sixties."* Chicago: A. C. McClurg & Co.,1910.

Coyne, F. E. *In Reminiscence: Highlights of Men and Elements in the Life of Chicago*. Chicago, 1941.

Colorful study containing a number of interesting anecdotes.

Cressey, Paul Frederick. "The Succession of Cultural Groups in the City of Chicago." Ph. D. diss., University of Chicago, 1930.

One of the most important works on ethnics.

Cromie, Robert. *The Great Chicago Fire*. New York: McGraw-Hill, 1958.

_____. *A Short History of Chicago*. San Francisco, CA: Lexikos, 1984.

Currey, Josiah S. *Chicago: Its History and Its Builders: A Century of Marvelous Growth*. Chicago, 1912.

Currey, Josiah Seymour. *Manufacturing and Wholesale Industries of Chicago*. 3 vols. Chicago, 1918.

Sketches of many businessmen and businesses.

Cutler, Irving. *Chicago: Metropolis of the Mid-Continent*. Dubuque, Iowa: Kendall/Hunt Publishing Company, 1976.

Davis, Allen F. *Spearheads For Reform: The Social Settlements and the Progressive Movement, 1890-1914*. New York, 1967.

A descriptive, detailed study of the founding and work of the various settlement houses in the nation with major emphasis on Chicago.

Dedmon, Emmett, *Fabulous Chicago*. Chicago: Random House, 1953.

Drake, St. Clair, and Horace Cayton. *Black Metropolis: A Study of Negro Life in a Northern City*. New York, 1935.

Drury, John. *Old Chicago Houses*. Chicago, 1941.

Duis, Perry. *Chicago: Creating New Traditions*. *Chicago*: Chicago Historical Society, 1976.

Duncan, Otis D., and Beverly Duncan. *The Negro Population of Chicago: A Study of Residential Succession*. Chicago, 1957.

Well documented work dealing with the growth and mobility of African-Americans in Chicago.

Farr, Finis. Chicago: *A Personal History of America's Most American City*. New Rochelle, NY: Arlington House, 1973.

Ffrench, Charles, ed. *Biographical History of the American Irish in Chicago*. Chicago, 1897.

Fiske, Barbara Page, ed. *Key to Government in Chicago and Suburban Cook County*. Chicago: The University of Chicago Press, 1989.

Flinn, John Joseph. *History of the Chicago Police*. New York, 1973.

Furer, Howard B. ed. *Chicago: A Chronological and Documentary History 1784-1970*. Dobbs Ferry, NY: Oceana Publications, Inc., 1974.

Gale, Edwin O. *Reminiscences of Early Chicago*. Chicago: F. H. Revell Company, 1902.

Gates, Paul. *The Illinois-Central Railroad and Its Colonization Work*. Cambridge, 1934.

A Detailed study of the influence of this railroad in the development of Chicago.

German Press Club of Chicago. *Prominent Citizens & Industries of Chicago*. Chicago, 1901.

Gilbert, Frank. *Centennial History of the City of Chicago: Its Men and Institutions*, Chicago, 1905.

Gilbert, Paul T., and Charles L. Bryson. *Chicago and Its Makers*, Chicago, 1929.

Gossnell, Harold F. *Negro Politicians: The Rise of Negro Politics in Chicago*. Chicago, 1935.

Greene, Victor. *For God & Country: The Rise of Polish & Lithuanian Ethnic Consciousness in America, 1860-1970*. Madison, 1975.

Grossman, Ron. *Guide to Chicago Neighborhoods*. Piscataway, NJ: New Century Publishers, Inc., 1981.

Gutstein, Morris A. *A Priceless Heritage: The Epic Growth of Nineteenth Century Chicago Jewry*. New York: Block Publishing Co., 1953.

Guyer, Isaac D. *History of Chicago: Its Commercial and Manufacturing Interests—with Sketches of Manufacturers and Men Who Have Most Contributed to Its Prosperity*. Chicago, 1862.

Hamilton, Henry R. *The Epic of Chicago*, 1932.

Hansen, Harry. *The Chicago*. New York, 1942.

A detailed study of the Chicago River, its influence and importance in the growth of Chicago.

Harper, William H., ed. *Chicago: A History and Forecast*. Chicago, 1921.

Hayes, Dorsha. *Chicago, Crossroads of American Enterprise*. New York: J. Messner, 1944.

Hayner, Don, and Tom McNamee. *Metro Chicago Almanac: Fascinating Facts and Offbeat Offerings About the Windy City*. Chicago: Chicago Sun-Times, Inc., 1991.

Heimovics, Rachel Baron. *Chicago Jewish Sourcebook*. Chicago, 1981.

Hletka, Peter. "The Slovaks of Chicago." *Slovakia* 19, no. 42 (Oct. 1969): 32-63.

Hirsch, Arnold R. *Making the Second Ghetto: Race and Housing in Chicago 1940 to 1960*. Cambridge: Cambridge University Press, 1983.

Hoffman, Charles Fenno. *A Winter in the West: Letters Descriptive of Chicago and Vicinity in 1833-34.* Chicago, 1882.

Hofmeister, Rudolph A. *The Germans in Chicago.* Urbana: University of Illinois Press, 1976.

Holli, Melvin G., and Peter d'A. Jones. *Ethnic Chicago.* Grand Rapids: William Eerdmans, 1984.

Holt, Glen E., and Dominic A. Pacyga. *Chicago: A Historical Guide to the Neighborhoods. The Loop and South Side.* Chicago: Chicago Historical Society, 1979.

Hoyt, Homer. *One Hundred Years of Land Values in Chicago, 1830-1933.* Chicago, 1933.

Hull House Residents. *Hull House Maps and Papers.* New York, 1895.

    Invaluable collection of records and documents of the first and most important Chicago Settlement House.

Hurlbut, Henry Higgins. *Chicago Antiquities.* Chicago, 1881.

    Letters, extracts, and other documents with annotations.

Illinois. *For the Record, Newsletter of the Illinois State Archives* 6, no. 2 (Winter 1984); 7, no. 2 (Winter 1985); 8, no. 2 (Winter 1986).

Illustrated History of Chicago. Chicago: Chicago Herald, 1887.

Inglehart, Babette, ed. *Walking With Women Through Chicago History.* Chicago: Salsedo Press, 1981.

Jewell, Frank. *Annotated Bibliography of Chicago History.* Chicago: Chicago Historical Society, 1979.

Johnson, Charles B. *Growth of Cook County* 2 vols. Chicago: Board of Commissioners of Cook County, Illinois, 1960.

Johnston, W. Wesley. *Researcher's Guide to the Pre-Fire Records of Chicago and Cook County.* Springfield, IL: Wesley W. Johnston, 1982.

Kinze, Juliette A. *Wau-Bun.* Chicago: Rand McNally Company, 1901.

Kirkland, Joseph. *The Story of Chicago*. 3 vols. Chicago: Dibble Publishing Company, 1892-1894.

Koenig, Harry C., ed. *A History of the Parishes of the Archdiocese of Chicago*. 2 vols. Chicago: Archdiocese of Chicago, 1980.

Kogan, Herman, and Rick Kogan. *Yesterday's Chicago*. Miami: E. A. Seeman, 1976.

Kogan, Herman, and Lloyd Wendt. *Chicago: A Pictorial History*. New York: Bonanza Books, 1958.

Lane, George A. *Chicago Churches and Synagogues: An Architectural Pilgrimage*. Chicago: Loyola University Press. 1981.

Lepawsky, Albert. *Home Rule For Metropolitan Chicago*. Chicago, 1932.

Lewis, Lloyd, and Henry J. Smith. *Chicago, the History of Its Reputation*. New York: Harcourt Brace, 1929.

Lindberg, Richard. *Chicago Ragtime: Another Look at Chicago 1880-1920*. South Bend: Icarius Press, 1985.

Longstreet, Stephen. *Chicago 1860-1919*. New York: David McKay Co., 1973.

MacMillan, Thomas C. "The Scots and Their Descendants in Illinois." *Transactions, Illinois State Historical Society* 26 (1919): 31-85.

Mason, Edward G., ed. *Early Chicago and Illinois*. Chicago, 1890.

Mayer, Harold M. *Chicago: City of Decisions*. Chicago, 1955.

Mayer, Harold M., and Richard C. Wade. *Chicago: Growth of a Metropolis*. Chicago: The University of Chicago Press, 1969.

> A narrative of Chicago's growth to 1969. It is recognized as one of the most important books on Chicago, and was among the first books to use photographs and other images as a principal source of information. There are nearly 1,000 photographs and fifty maps.

McCarthy, Kathleen D. *Noblesse Oblige: Charity and Cultural Philanthropy in Chicago 1849-1929.* Chicago: The University of Chicago Press, 1982.

McClellan, Larry A. *Local History South of Chicago: A Guide for Research in the Southern Suburbs.* University Park, IL: Northeastern Illinois Planning Commission and Governors State University, 1987.

McClure, James. B., ed. *Stories and Sketches of Chicago: An Interesting, Entertaining, and Instructive Sketch History of the Wonderful City "By the Sea."* Chicago, 1890.

McIlvaine, Mabel. *Reminiscences of Chicago During the Civil War.* New York: Citadel, 1967.

McIntosh, Arthur T. *Chicago*, 1921.

A popular history of Chicago, laden with anecdotal material.

Meites, Hyman, ed. *History of the Jews of Chicago.* Chicago. 1924.

Divided into three main sections: narrative account of the Jewish community; accomplishments in the arts, professions, politics, labor, finance, industry, and athletics; major Jewish organizations and institutions. All sections have biographical sketches interspersed.

Moses, John, and Joseph Kirkland. *History of Chicago.* 2 vols. Chicago, 1895.

Nelli, Humbert S. *The Italians in Chicago,1880-1930.* New York: Oxford University Press, 1970.

Nelson, Otto M. "The Chicago Relief and Aid Society, 1850-1874." *Journal of the Illinois State Historical Society* 59, 1 (Spring 1966): 48-66.

Pacyga, Dominic A., and Ellen Skerrett. *Chicago: City of Neighborhoods. Histories and Tours.* Chicago: Loyola University Press, 1986.

The history and present of Chicago neighborhoods are explored in a volume which is enhanced with numerous photographs and maps.

Palickar, Stephen J. "The Slovaks of Chicago." *Illinois Catholic Historical Review* 4, no. 2 (Oct. 1921): 180-96.

Palmer, Vivien M. *Social Backgrounds of Chicago's Local Communities.* Chicago, 1930.

Pasley, Fred D. *Al Capone: The Biography of a Self-Made Man.* New York: Ives Washburn, 1930.

Phillips, George S. *Chicago and Her Churches.* Chicago, 1868.

Pierce, Bessie L. *A History of Chicago.* 3 vols. New York: Knopf, 1937,1940,1957.

This massive study is one of the best single works on the history of Chicago.

Poles of Chicago, 1837-1937. Chicago: Polish Pageant, Inc., 1937.

Proba, Daniel. *Czech and Slovak Leaders in Metropolitan Chicago.* Chicago, 1934.

Putnam, James Williams. *The Illinois and Michigan Canal: A Study in Economic History.* Chicago: The University of Chicago Press, 1918.

Quaife, Milo M. *Checagou: From Indian Wigwam to Modern City, 1673-1835.* Chicago,1935.

_____. *Chicago and the Old Northwest, 1673-1835: A Study of the Evolution of the Northwestern Frontier, together with a History of Fort Dearborn.* Chicago, 1913.

_____. *Chicago's Highways Old and New: From Indian Trails to Motor Road.* Chicago: D. F. Keller & Company, 1923.

Randall, Frank A. *History of the Development of Building Construction in Chicago,* Urbana, Illinois, 1949.

Reichman, John J., ed. *Czechoslovaks in Chicago.* Chicago, 1937.

Riley, Elmer. *The Development of Chicago and Vicinity As A Manufacturing Center prior to 1880.* Chicago: McElroy Publishing Co., 1911.

Riley, Thomas James. *The Higher Life of Chicago.* Chicago, 1905.

Robb, Frederic H. ed. *The Negro in Chicago, 1779-1929*, 2 vols. Chicago, 1927-1929.

Schiavo, Giovanni E. *The Italians in Chicago: A Study in Americanization.* Chicago, 1928.

Seeger, Eugene, *Chicago, the Wonder City.* Chicago 1893.

Sentinel Publishing Company. *The Sentinel's History of Chicago Jewry, 1911-1961.* Chicago, 1961.

Shackleton, Robert. *The Book of Chicago.* Philadelphia, 1920.

Siegel, Arthur, ed. *Chicago's Famous Buildings.* Chicago, 1965.

Sinclair, Upton. *The Jungle.* New York. 1906.

Devastating classic of the Chicago meat-packing industry.

Skogan, Wesley G. *Chicago Since 1840: A Time Series Data Handbook.* Urbana, 1976.

Smith, Henry J. *Chicago's Great Century, 1833-1933.* Chicago, 1933.

Solomon, Ezra, and Zarko G. Bilbija. *Metropolitan Chicago: An Economic Analysis,* Glencoe, Illinois, 1959.

Spear, Allan H. *Black Chicago: The Making of a Negro Ghetto, 1890-1920.* Chicago, 1967.

Strand, Algot E., comp. *A History of the Norwegians of Illinois.* Chicago, 1905.

A long narrative of Norwegian settlement in Illinois includes many references to Chicago. In addition, there is an entire section on Chicago. Essays treat Norwegian churches, organizations, industry, and leading citizens.

Thorn, W. & Co. *Chicago in 1860: A Glance at Its Business Houses.* Chicago, 1860.

Thrasher, Frederic M. *The Gang.* Chicago: The University of Chicago Press, 1927.

Townsend, Andrew J. *The Germans of Chicago.* Chicago, 1932.

University of Chicago Center of Urban Studies. *Mid-Chicago Economic Development Study.* 3 vols. Chicago: Mayor's Committee for Economic and Cultural Development, 1966.

Vanderbosch, Amry. *The Dutch Communities of Chicago.* Chicago, 1927.

Waterman, A. N. *Historical Review of Chicago and Cook County and Selected Biography.* 3 vols. Chicago: The Lewis Publishing Co., 1908.

Wrigley, Kathryn, ed. *Directory of Illinois Oral History Resources.* Springfield: Sangamon State University, 1981.

Writer's Program. Illinois. *Selected Bibliography: Illinois, Chicago & Its Environs.* Chicago, 1937.

Zorbaugh, Harvey W. *The Gold Coast and the Slum.* Chicago, 1929.

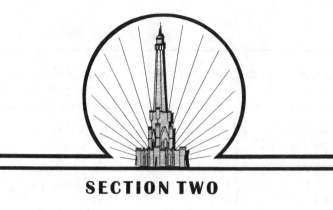

SECTION TWO

Adoption Records

As you conduct your genealogical or historical research, you may need to have some knowledge of adoption laws, records and agencies. The intent of this section is to provide you with some knowledge of adoption laws, records, and agencies. There is some general information to give you some jurisdictional background, an address list of some important agencies, and a selected bibliography of potentially helpful guides. It is beyond the scope of this book to provide comprehensive information about how to conduct adoption research.

The Circuit Court has jurisdiction over adoption proceedings in Illinois. Adoption records in Cook County are impounded by the Clerk of the Court, and the files may be opened for examination only on the specific order of the court (see section 20 for additional information).

On June 3, 1985, all files, dockets, and other papers concerning adoptions, formerly part of the records of the superior, county, and family courts of Cook County, were transferred to the County Division of the Circuit Court of Cook County (8th Floor of the Daley Center) by Special Order 85-208. At the time of the transfer, all ledger entries pertaining to adoptions in the former courts were obliterated from all indexes in other court divisions, and information on file must now be obtained from the county division.

One helpful guide to older records, the "Orphan Court Ledgers," were transcribed by June B. Barekman, and published in the *Chicago Genealogist* 2, no. 1 (September 1969) through 9, no. 4 (Summer 1977). Included in Barekman's work are names of adopting parents, name of child, general number, and filing date. The entries begin in 1871 and end in 1899.

For more recent adoptions, new legislation offers some hope to researchers seeking adoption information. The Illinois Legislature passed bills in 1985 (House Bills 0765 and 1853) which allow for an official registry to help consenting adults who were adopted and their biological parents find each other. The registry is maintained by the Illinois Department of Public Health. Adoption records remain confidential unless a birth parent and an adoptee, who has reached age 21, register with the state, and both consent to the exchange of information. The bills require that background information regarding medical history, excluding any identifying information, be given to all adoptive parents at the time of adoption.

There are several adoption support groups in the Chicago area which meet regularly, offer suggestions, and exchange information. One such group is:

Adoption Triangle
c/o P.O. Box 96
South Holland, IL 60473

Beginning some time before the year 1935 (exact date unknown), adoptees' birth certificates have been amended. A section in the Illinois Annotated Statutes (Chapter III-½, Sec. 73-17(4) Supp. 1972) was amended August 1971 to permit the use of a false birthplace on amended birth certificates.

Searching in Illinois by Beckstead and Kozub is a reference guide to public and private records. This reference lists addresses for state and independent agencies, maternity homes, hospitals, orphanages, cemeteries, colleges and universities, libraries, and governmental agencies. Each list is broken down by Illinois counties.

Bibliography

Askin, Jayne. *Search: A Handbook for Adoptees and Birthparents.* New York, NY: Harper & Row, 1982.

Beckstead, Gayle, and Mary Lou Kozub. *Searching in Illinois.* Costa Mesa, CA: ISC Publications, 1984.

Niles, Reg. *Adoption Agencies, Orphanages and Maternity Homes.* Garden City, NY: Phileas Deigh Corporation, 1981.

Rillera, Mary Jo. *The Adoption Search Book.* Huntington Beach, CA: Triadoption Publications, 1981 (Revised 1991).

Addresses

Adoption Information Center
  201 North Wells Street
  Chicago, IL 60602.
  (Toll Free Hotline 800-572-2390).
Adoption Research Forum
  P.O. Box 2517
  Chicago, IL 60690.
Alliance for Adoption Reunions
  63 West 540 Lake Drive
  Clarendon Hills, IL 60514.
Alma Chapter (Adoptees Liberty Movement Association)
  P.O. Box 59345
  Chicago, IL 60659.
Catholic Charities of Chicago
  126 N. Des Plaines Street
  Chicago, IL 60606
  (312-236-5172).
Children's Home and Aid Society of Illinois
  1122 N. Dearborn Street
  Chicago, IL 60610
  (312-944-3313).
Concerned United Birthparents
  156 W. Burton
  Chicago, IL 60610.

The Cradle Society
  2049 Ridge Avenue
  Evanston, IL 60204
  (312-475-5800).
Illinois Department of Children and Family Services
  510 North Dearborn Street, Suite 400
  Chicago, IL 60601
  (312-793-6800)
Jewish Children's Bureau
  1 South Franklin
  Chicago, IL 60606
Lutheran Social Services of Illinois, Chicago Metropolitan Services
  4840 W. Byron
  Chicago, IL 60641
  (312-282-7800).
Truthseekers in Adoption
  P.O. Box 286
  Roscoe, IL 61073.
Yesterday's Children
  P.O. Box 1554
  Evanston, IL 60204.

Architectural and House History Sources

Have you ever wondered when a house was constructed, who built it, or who else has lived there over the years? Most houses have rich histories which may be reconstructed by using the many collections of research materials available in the Chicago area. A project is enhanced by treating it as though you were collecting biographical information on a long-deceased ancestor. A house can take on a distinct personality as discoveries give it identity and a place in the history of the community.

Researching the History of a House

Begin by searching printed sources for information on what architectural records are available. The bibliography at the end of this section, and the Land and Property section, includes some of the standard and most helpful works. An especially well detailed, step-by-step handbook for architectural research in the Cook County area is: *Architectural Records in Chicago* by Kathleen Roy Cummings.

There are many approaches you can take to develop a house history including:

Figure 4: Chicago's Oldest House—The Clarke House

Previous Research

It is possible that research has already been done on the house of interest. It may have been designated as a landmark or included in a landmark district. Houses which have been placed on National Register of Historic Places have been researched, and copies of nomination forms for Chicago houses are on file at the Burnham Library of the Art Institute and at the Commission on Chicago Landmarks. The Commission on Chicago Landmarks has created a useful pamphlet, *Your House Has A History*, which is available from this commission.

Surveys of Historic Houses

There may be surveys of historic houses and neighborhoods that were conducted by local preservation groups. Consult the city's Commission on Chicago Landmarks, the Landmarks Preservation Council of Illinois, or a local commission to determine if a house has been included in a survey. The Chicago Historical Society has a wealth of information on houses, and local community historical societies should not be overlooked.

Locating a Property

Determine the location of the property in question. A legal description of the address will be needed; refer to section 23 for more details. You can also get legal descriptions by searching title insurance policies, mortgage papers, deeds, Torrens Certificates, and probate records. If you are the owner of the property in question, the Permanent Index Number can be found on your tax bill. Be aware that the street number of a nineteenth-century house may have changed since the house was constructed.

Using Building Permits

The Department of Inspectional Services issues permits to construct, add to, alter, or wreck houses in Chicago. Permit applications (accompanied by plans, specifications, lot surveys, and house number certificates) are filed with:

Department of Inspectional Services
Room 800, City Hall
121 North LaSalle Street
Chicago, IL 60602

Applications, permits, and supporting documents are microfilmed soon after permit issuance and placed on file in the:

Department of Inspectional Services
Records Section, Room 903
City Hall, 121 North LaSalle
Chicago, IL 60602
(312-744-3452)

Viewing of permit records is restricted. Researchers must write or call for an appointment. Unfortunately, these records are by no means complete and are particularly spotty for the years 1880-1900. Take proof of ownership to look at property records.

If a building permit record can't be found, it could be because:

1. If the house was built before 1872 (building permits were not issued) or between 1872 and 1891 (records are not available).

2. The house was built without a permit.

3. The records were misfiled or lost.

4. The property was not located within the Chicago city limits as they existed at the time of construction.

5. Some 1923 permit applications were lost in a fire.

Construction Dates

Construction dates can be estimated from tax assessment records. You'll need a tax index number for this. If you do not know the number, call the Cook County Maps Department (312-443-6253). You can look at the complete history of the assessments for a property by going to the Assessor's Vault on Floor 3-½ of the County Building (118 North Clark Street). A substantial increase in the assessment for a property often reflects construction of a house.

Atlases

Atlases of the city published for fire insurance companies by various publishers show the original and later outlines of a house and its height; information on the materials used in the construction is also provided. These maps can be used to estimate construction dates. If you trace a particular lot back through preceding editions of these atlases until the outline of a building no longer appears on the site, you'll have some idea of when it was built. The Chicago Historical Society Library has a large collection of Fire Atlases.

Newspapers and Periodicals

Old issues of newspapers and periodicals sometimes contain reports of building permits issued. These can give you the architect's name if you weren't able to find it on the building permit application. Architectural magazines, construction trade publications, and real estate journals also published information about construction projects.

Architect

If a house was designed by a well-known architect, there's a chance you will find some biographical information about him, and the names of other houses designed by that individual. The Burnham Library at the Art Institute has a card catalog on locally prominent architects and biographical directories of architects which are useful for those who were nationally prominent.

City Directories, Community Histories

Early city directories can be helpful in tracking down the earlier residents of a house (see section 14). In addition, there are several books on community history that can help you relate a house to a neighborhood (see bibliography in section 12).

Court Records

Don't overlook the possibility that the property of interest may have been involved in a local or a federal court case. Property line disputes, insurance lawsuits, and a multitude of other events, resulted in court records which usually included detailed house and property descriptions. The courts were flooded with lawsuits against fire insurance companies after the Chicago Fire of 1871. The testimony provided in many of these cases yields first-hand accounts which cannot be found in any other source.

Bibliography

The Art Institute of Chicago. *The Plan of Chicago: 1909-1979.* Chicago, IL, 1979.

Block, Jean F. *Hyde Park Houses: An Informal History, 1856-1910.* Chicago: The University of Chicago Press, 1978.

Condit, Carl W. *The Chicago School of Architecture: A History of Commercial and Public Building in the Chicago Area, 1875-1925.* Chicago: The University of Chicago Press, 1964.

Cummings, Kathleen Roy. *Architectural Records in Chicago.* Chicago: The Burnham Library of Architecture, The Art Institute of Chicago. 1981.

Drury, John. *Old Chicago Houses.* Chicago: The University of Chicago Press, 1941.

Randall, Frank Alfred. *History of the Development of Building Construction in Chicago.* Urbana, IL: University of Illinois Press, 1949.

Schulze, Franz, and Kevin Harrington, ed. *Chicago's Famous Buildings,* 4th ed., Chicago: The University of Chicago Press, 1993.

Sharp, Ed. *The Old House Handbook for Chicago and Suburbs*. Chicago, IL: Chicago Review Press, 1979.

Tallmadge, Thomas Eddy. *Architecture in Old Chicago*. Chicago, IL: The University of Chicago Press, 1975.

Addresses

The Art Institute of Chicago
  Burnham Library of Architecture
  Michigan Avenue at Adams Street
  (312-443-3666)
  Mail to:
      111 South Michigan Avenue
      Chicago, IL 60603-6110
  Note: Membership in the Art Institute is required to use the Library.

Chicago Historical Society
  Clark Street at North Avenue
  Chicago, IL 60614
  (312-642-4600)

SECTION FOUR

Biographies (Collected)

The biographical sketch of an individual you may find in a county, city, ethnic or neighborhood history is often the beginning of an exciting research project. Who's Who publications, occupational collections, and obituaries offer additional sources to search for personal information. Biographies, usually based on the testimony of the subject of the sketch, generally include information which would be difficult, if not impossible to obtain elsewhere. These printed sources are a means of learning about a person's birth, parentage, spouse, children, occupation, military service, prior residence, and political and religious affiliations. They can be especially valuable in the study of an immigrants, or the descendants of immigrants, since these publications frequently name the specific town of origin in a foreign country.

Most biographical materials deal with persons who have achieved some degree of prominence in one area or another. For this reason, you may overlook biographical materials if you assume your subject was of common stock and no information would be found in these biographies. However, there is a multiplier factor in this type of source which makes it much more useful than it might first appear. If your search for details on the life of a particular ancestor is often disappointing, remember that sometimes other family members may have achieved prominence, and there may be biographical information on them. Since the origins of these people are the same, the value of the biographical sketch will be essentially the same. Important clues on migrational patterns, ethnic communities, religious affiliation and occupational can be gleaned from a biographical sketch of a member of a group to which an ancestor belonged. These clues may provide a starting place to look for records of the less prominent members of a particular group.

A situation which illustrates the value of this approach is illustrated by the case of an Irish servant girl. Family tradition preserved the fact that a grandmother had been employed by a prominent Chicago citizen who happened to have come from her own hometown in Ireland. While the name of the town was not remembered, nor could it be found in ordinary channels of research, a biographical sketch of her employer divulged the name of the town, and research could continue.

Some of the disadvantages of biographical works are immediately obvious. First, a person had to be living and prominent at the time a publication was printed. The popularity of the biographical sketch in histories was greatest around the turn of the century; a search for people of that time period will often be most productive.

Genealogists continually emphasize the importance of facts, documentation, and accuracy; consequently, these secondary or hearsay accounts must be judged with some degree of skepticism. Biographical sketches are noted for being "richly embroidered" so they portray the subject in saintly light. You must examine the motives of the publisher when considering the accuracy of the material. Much biographical information was included in special local histories which were usually produced on a subscription basis. To be included in one of these publications, the "leading citizen" could be anyone who had the desire and the money to pay for the subscription. Despite the rather exaggerated nature of the sketches, they are generally accurate when it comes to religious, political or fraternal affiliation, and former residences. Basic information regarding a family is usually fairly reliable and may provide an outline, but you should verify the information by using other sources. These accounts should never be accepted as totally accurate even though the subject may have provided the information for the article. Consider the father who was so displeased with a son's activities that he disinherited him and refused to even acknowledge his existence when submitting data for inclusion in a biographical publication.

The following extraction is a typical example of a biographical sketch found in Charles Ffrench's *Biographical History of the American Irish in Chicago* (Chicago: American Biographical Publishing, 1897):

FRANCIS T. MURPHY

This great Western metropolis contains a great many able men who have made the law the profession of their lives. That all should be equally successful in such a career, would be an impossibility; the prizes in life's battle are few and far between, and the fortunate must be gifted with qualifications of a diverse character, exceptional legal ability, good judgement, ready perception, and also personal charm of manner or power of intellect sufficient to dominate and control their fellowmen. Among the representative lawyers of the west, there are but a few who possess these necessary characteristics in a higher degree than the subject of the present sketch, the big, genial-natured, open-hearted young lawyer, Francis T. Murphy.

He was born in this city, where he was destined to make himself so well known, January 25th, 1863, his father, Thomas Murphy being a native of County Meath, Ireland, and his mother from West Meath. It is from his father unquestionably that Francis T. inherits his perseverance and energy, for Thomas Murphy left the dear old land as a mere boy of twelve, traveled all alone to the far country beyond the seas, where he possessed neither kith nor kin, friend nor acquaintance, and when the big ocean journey was finished, set off once more across the continent to Chicago, determined to seek a living and possible fortune in the boundless West. In this city he fought his way, married, and in 1894 died at the comparatively premature age of fifty-seven.

Mr. Murphy was married April 11th, 1893, in Chicago, to Mary V. Halpin, the daughter of one of Chicago's best known citi-

zens. *A man of intensely social nature, the chief delight of Frank Murphy—as he is generally known—is to be surrounded with his friends and to dispense the historical hospitality. For fast horses he admits a decided partiality, and is fortunate in the possession of several that can show a good pace.*

For persons who lived in the Chicago metropolitan area, there is a considerable amount of biographical material you can consult. The size and diversity of the urban population generated an abundance of materials to draw from. Besides the many well known standards such as A.T. Andreas' *History of Cook County Illinois (1884)*, and his three volume *History of Chicago (1884-1886)*, there were those which focused on particular ethnic groups and occupations as well. In addition, there were books published that covered ethnic, political and social groups for the entire state of Illinois, the entries for Chicago citizens frequently forming the largest portion of the biographical section. Many biographical sketches are buried in hard to find volumes which frequently contain partial or no indexes. It should be noted that many of the biographical histories have only partial indexes, and a page by page search may be necessary to be thorough. There is no single reference containing all the biographical sources, but there are some important indexes and collections which are worthy of mention; they are the most logical starting places for a biographical search.

An especially valuable source for biographical information is *Biography and Genealogy Master Index* by Barbara McNeil which contains a consolidated index to more than 3,200,000 biographical sketches in over 350 current and retrospective biographical dictionaries.

The Newberry Library's Chicago and Cook County Biography and Industry File

The following description of the Newberry Index has been extracted from an article by David Thackery as it appeared in a newsletter published by the Local and Family History Section and the Family and Community History Center at the Newberry Library (*Origins* 1, no. 3 [April 1985]):

> *For the last several years the Newberry's Local and Family History section has been compiling a card index to all the biographical sketches appearing in a number of selected Chicago and County—as well as Illinois-collective biographies and mug books published before 1930. In all, seventeen titles, some of them in two or three editions, have been indexed in this fashion. The project is ongoing and will ultimately index twenty-five titles. Historical sketches of industries are also included in this file, but the bulk of the entries refer to individuals.*

The diversity of Chicago is well reflected in the titles that have been indexed. WASP "big wigs" are well represented by such titles as:

> Wood, David Ward. *Chicago and Its Distinguished Citizens.* Chicago: M. George & Co., 1881.

Chicago's ethnic communities are represented by sketches taken from such books as:

> Ffrench, Charles. *Biographical History of the American Irish in Chicago.* Chicago: American Biographical Publishing, 1897.

> *Chicago und Sein Deutschthum.* Cleveland: German-American Biographical Pub. Co., 1902.

> Strand, A.E. *History of the Norwegians of Illinois.* Chicago: John Anderson, 1905.

Books representing particular occupations include:

> *History of Chicago and Souvenir of the Liquor Interest.* Chicago: Belgravia, 1891.

> Taylor, Charles H. *History of the Board of Trade of the City of Chicago.* Chicago: Robert O. Law, 1917.

> Flinn, John Joseph. *History of the Chicago Police.* Chicago, 1887.

Cutting across occupational lines are the sketches contained in:

Memorials of Deceased Companions of the Commandery of the State of Illinois. 3 vols., 1901, 1912, 1923.

Contains obituaries for the Civil War officers belonging to this veterans' group.

The index file is located with the card catalogues at the Newberry Library. Correspondents may ask a staff member in the Local and Family History section to consult the file as long as such requests are limited to no more than three per letter. Library patrons are free to consult the file in person.

The Chicago Historical Society Library

The main card catalog of the Chicago Historical Society Library is an important source for locating biographical material on individuals who have resided in the Chicago metropolitan area. It is not an inclusive index to the printed collection, but a surprising number of citizens are represented in the card catalog. As one might expect, the majority of the entries are for prominent citizens, but some entries can lead to the library's clipping file or provide citations for obituaries for less famous individuals. Many of the card catalog entries refer to veterans who died in earlier and more recent wars; additional information can be obtained by referring to the source cited on the card.

Collective Bibliography *Bench and Bar of Chicago.* Chicago, 1883.

Bennett, Frances Cheney, ed. *History of Music and Art in Illinois Including Portraits and Biographies.* Philadelphia, 1904.

Biographical Sketches of the Leading Men of Chicago, Written by the Best Talent of the Northwest. Chicago, 1868.

Black Book Directory. Chicago 1970.

The Chicago, Rock Island and Pacific Railway. *The Chicago Rock Island and Pacific Railway System and Representative Employees.* Chicago, 1900.

Flinn, John J. *Handbook of Chicago Biography*. Chicago, 1893.

McNeil, Barbara. *Biography and Genealogy Master Index*. Detroit: Gale Research Company, 1995.

    This is a multiple volume work, with annual supplements, and is updated regularly.

Notable Men of Chicago and Their City. Chicago, 1910.

Poole, Ernest. *Giants Gone: Men Who Made Chicago*. New York, 1943.

Portraits and Biographies of the Fire Underwriters of the City of Chicago. Chicago, 1895.

Society of Medical History of Chicago. *Bulletin*. 5 vols. Chicago, 1911-1940.

Sparks, Esther. "A Biographical Dictionary of Painters and Sculptors in Illinois 1808-1945." Ph.D. diss., Northwestern University, 1971.

Thackery, David. "Collected Biography." *Ancestry* 13, no. 4 (July-Aug 1995).

Waterman, Arba Nelson. *Historical Review of Chicago and Cook County and Selected Biography*. 3 vols. Chicago, 1908.

Who's Who in Chicago. *The Book of Chicagoans, a Biographical Dictionary of Leading Living Men and Women of the City of Chicago and Environs*. Chicago: A.N. Marquis, 1905 - 1950.

    Note: The title varies.

Cemeteries in Metropolitan Chicago Area

Some entries in this list of cemeteries in the Chicago area are missing information (for example, a zip code). Since there may no longer be any office associated with a particular cemetery, there is no formal mailing address (or telephone number).

Name		Town	Phone
Address			Zip Code
County	Township		Area
Acacia Park			312-625-7800
7800 Irving Park Rd.		Chicago	60634
Cook	Norwood Park		**NORTH**
All Saints			708-298-0450
700 N. Des Plaines River Rd.		Des Plaines	60016
Cook	Maine		**NORTH**
All Saints Polish Natl. Cath.			708-825-3701
9201 Higgins Rd.		Chicago	60631
Cook	Leyden		**NORTH**
Allerton Ridge			708-627-0070
Highland & Butterfield Rds.		Lombard	60148
DuPage	York		**WEST**

Name Address County	Township	Town	Phone Zip Code Area
Archer Woods Memorial Park			708-839-8800
Keane Ave & 83rd St.		Willow Springs	60480
Cook	Lyons		**WEST**
Arlington Heights			N/A
Euclid Ave.		Arlington Heights	N/A
Cook	Wheeling		**NORTH**
Arlington			708-832-2599
Lake St. & Frontage Rd.		Elmhurst	60126
DuPage	Addison		**WEST**
Ascension			708-362-1247
1920 Buckley Rd.		Libertyville	60048
Lake	Libertyville		**NORTH**
Assumption			708-758-4774
19500 So. Cottage Grove		Glenwood	60425
Cook	Bloom		**SOUTH**
B'nai B'rith			312-545-0044
6600 Addison St.		Chicago	60634
Cook	Jefferson		**NORTH**
Bachelor's Grove			N/A
Midlothian Turnpike		Crestwood	60445
Cook	Bremen		**SOUTH**
Barrington Center			N/A
Old Dundee & Sutton Rds.		Barrington	60010
Cook	Barrington		**NORTH**
Barrington Union			N/A
Algonquin Rd.		Barrington	60010
Cook	Barrington		**NORTH**
Bartlett			N/A
North Ave.		Bartlett	60103
Cook	Hanover		**NORTH**
Berger			N/A
1485 Sibley Blvd.		Dolton	60419
Cook	Thornton		**SOUTH**
Bethania			708-458-2270
7701 Archer Ave.		Justice	60458
Cook	Lyons		**WEST**

Name Address County	Township	Town	Phone Zip Code Area
Bethany Lutheran			N/A
123rd St.		Lemont	60439
Cook	Lemont		**WEST**
Bethel			708-588-6128
5800 No. Pulaski Rd.		Jefferson	60646
Cook	Jefferson		**NORTH**
Beverly			708-385-0750
Kedzie Ave. at 120th St.		Blue Island	60406
Cook	Worth		**SOUTH**
Bloom Evangelical Lutheran			N/A
Volmer Rd.		Chicago Heights	60411
Cook	Bloom		**SOUTH**
Blue Island American Legion			N/A
127th St. & Highland Ave.		Blue Island	60406
Cook	Worth		**SOUTH**
Bluff City			N/A
Wright Ave. & Bluff City Rd.		Elgin	60120
Cook	Hanover		**NORTH**
Bohemian National			312-539-8442
5255 No. Pulaski Rd.		Chicago	60630
Cook	Jefferson		**NORTH**
Bronswood			708-323-0185
3805 Madison St.		Oak Brook	60521
DuPage	York		**WEST**
Brown, M.J. (private)		N/A	
Between Division & Logan Sts.		Lemont	60458
Cook	Worth		**WEST**
Burr Oak			708-233-5676
4400 W. 127th St.		Alsip	60658
Cook	Worth		**NORTH**
Cady			N/A
Ela Rd.		Palatine	60067
Cook	Palantine		**NORTH**
Calumet Park			219-769-8803
2305 W. 73rd Ave.		Merrillville, IN	46410
Lake	Ross		**SOUTH**

Name Address County	Township	Town	Phone Zip Code Area
Calvary Steger Rd. Cook	 Bloom	 Steger	N/A 60475 **SOUTH**
Calvary 301 Chicago Ave. Cook	 Evanston	 Evanston	312-864-3050 60202 **NORTH**
Calvary Cemetery & Crematory 2701 J. Willowdale Rd. Porter	 Portage	 Portage, IN	219-762-8885 46368 **SOUTH**
Cass (aka St. Patrick's) Poppelreiter Rd. N/A	 N/A	 Argonne Nat'l Lab.	708-767-4644 60439 **WEST**
Catholic Cemeteries Office 1400 So. Wolf Rd. Cook	 Proviso	 Hillside	708-378-7373 60162 **N/A**
Cedar Park 12540 So. Halsted St. Cook	 Calumet	 Chicago	312-785-8840 60643 **SOUTH**
Central Cemetery Co. of Ill. Harrison & Ridge Rds. Cook	 N/A	 Niles	N/A 60648 **NORTH**
Chapel Hill Gardens (South) 5501 W. 111th St. Cook	 Worth	 Worth	708-238-7062 60482 **SOUTH**
Chapel Hill Gardens (West) Rt. 83 & Roosevelt Rd. DuPage	 York	 Elmhurst	708-261-1585 60126 **WEST**
Chapel Lawn Memorial Gardens ½ mi. So. of US 30 on Cline Lake	 St. John	 Schererville, IN	219-322-4441 46375 **SOUTH**
Chicago Burr Oak 4400 W. 127th St. Cook	 Worth	 Alsip	708-233-5676 60658 **SOUTH**
Chicago Cemetery Association 123rd & Kedzie Ave. Cook	 Worth	 Blue Island	708-445-6429 60406 **SOUTH**

Name Address County	Township	Town	Phone Zip Code Area
Christ-Lutheran			708-349-0431
82nd Ave. & 147th St.		Orland Park	60462
Cook	Orland		**SOUTH**
City Cemetery (aka Lincoln Park)			N/A
North Ave. at Clark St.		Chicago	N/A
Cook	N/A		**NORTH**
Clarendon Hills			708-968-6590
6900 So. Cass Rd.		Westmont	60559
DuPage	Downers Grove		**WEST**
Con. Kneseth Israel Cem. Fund			219-931-1312
7105 Hohman Ave.		Hammond, IN	46324
Lake	N/A		**SOUTH**
Concordia			708-287-0878
7900 Madison St.		Forest Park	60130
Cook	Proviso		**WEST**
Concordia (Hammond)			219-932-7437
6551 Calumet Ave.		Hammond, IN	46324
Lake			**SOUTH**
Cong. A.D. Beth Hamedresh Hagadol			N/A
71st & Ellis Ave.		Chicago	60619
Cook	Hyde Park		**SOUTH**
Cong. Anshe Sholan (East Jewish)			N/A
71st & Ingleside Ave.		Chicago	60619
Cook	Hyde Park		**SOUTH**
Cooper's Grove (aka St. John's)			708-798-4131
183rd St.		Tinley Park	60477
Cook	Rich		**SOUTH**
Danish			N/A
127th St.		Lemont	60439
Cook	Lemont		**WEST**
Dutton			N/A
Euclid Ave.		Arlington Heights	N/A
Cook	Elk Grove		**NORTH**
Ebenezer			N/A
162nd & Cicero Ave.		Oak Forest	60452
Cook	Bremen		**SOUTH**

Name Address County	Township	Town	Phone Zip Code Area
Eden Memorial Park 9851 Irving Park Rd. Cook	Leyden	Schiller Park	708-678-1631 60176 NORTH
Elk Grove Cemetery Association State Rd. Cook	Elk Grove	Arlington Heights	N/A N/A NORTH
Elm Lawn 401 E. Lake St. DuPage	Addison	Elmhurst	708-833-9696 60126 WEST
Elmwood 2905 Thatcher Rd. Cook	Leyden	River Grove	708-625-1700 60171 NORTH
Elmwood (Hammond) 1413 - 169th St. Lake	N/A	Hammond, IN	219-844-7077 46324 SOUTH
Evangelical Lutheran Telegraph Rd. Cook	Niles	N/A	N/A N/A NORTH
Evangelical Lutheran (Immanuel) Schaumburg Rd. Cook	Schaumburg	N/A	N/A N/A NORTH
Evang. Luth. Church of Blue Island 127th St. Cook	Worth	Alsip	N/A 60658 SOUTH
Evangelical Lutheran Immanuel 1850 W. Lake St. Cook	Northfield	Glenview	N/A 60025 NORTH
Evergreen Hillside & Dundee Aves. Cook	Barrington	N/A	N/A N/A NORTH
Evergreen W. 87th St. & So. Kedzie Ave. Cook	Worth	Evergreen Park	708-776-8434 60642 SOUTH
Fairmount Hills 9100 So. Archer Ave. Cook	Palos	Willow Springs	708-839-8500 60480 WEST

Name Address County	Township	Town	Phone Zip Code Area
Fairview Memorial park			708-455-2714
900 No. Wolf Rd.		Melrose Park	60160
Cook	Leyden		WEST
First Evangelist Lutheran			708-388-3377
4135 W. 127th St.		Alsip	60658
Cook	Worth		SOUTH
First Reformed Church of Lansing			N/A
Ridge Rd. & Burnham Ave.		Lansing	60438
Cook	Thornton		SOUTH
Forest Home			708-287-0772
863 Des Plaines Ave.		Forest Park	60130
Cook	Proviso		WEST
Free Sons			708-366-1190
1600 Des Plaines Ave.		Forest Park	60130
Cook	Proviso		WEST
Gary Oak Hill			219-887-7339
4450 Harrison St.		Gary, IN	46408
Lake	Calumet		SOUTH
German Lutheran			312-525-4038
3963 N. Clark St.		Chicago	60613
Cook	Lakeview		NORTH
German Luth. - St. Paul & Emanuel			N/A
3963 N. Clark St.		Chicago	60613
Cook	Lakeview		NORTH
Glen Oak			708-344-5600
Roosevelt & Oakridge Ave.		Hillside	60162
Cook	Proviso		WEST
Glen View			N/A
Lake Ave.		Glenview	60025
Cook	Northfield		NORTH
Graceland			312-525-1105
4001 No. Clark Ave.		Chicago	60613
Cook	Lakeview		NORTH
Greenland			219-874-5800
153 Tilden Ave.		Michigan City, IN	46360
LaPort	Michigan		SOUTH

Name Address County	Township	Town	Phone Zip Code Area

Haas Park (see Forest Home)

Hazel Green			708-388-2328
115th St. & 52nd Ave.		Alsip	60658
Cook	Worth		SOUTH
Hazelwood			N/A
Ridge Rd. & Halsted St.		Homewood	60430
Cook	Thornton		SOUTH
Hebrew Benevolent Society			312-348-6276
3919 N. Clark St.		Chicago	60613
Cook	Lakeview		NORTH
Highland Memorial Park, Inc.			708-362-5260
Hunt Club Rd. & Rt. 120		Libertyville	60048
Lake	Warren		NORTH
Holy Cross			708-862-5398
Michigan City Rd. & Burnham Ave.		Calumet City	60409
Cook	Thornton		SOUTH
Holy Sepulchre			708-445-2022
6001 W. 111th St.		Worth	60482
Cook	Worth		SOUTH
Homewood Memorial Gardens			708-798-0055
600 Ridge Rd.		Homewood	60430
Cook	Thornton		SOUTH
I.O.O.F.			N/A
127th St.		Lemont	60439
Cook	Lemont		WEST
Immanuel Church			N/A
Kenilworth Ave.		N/A	N/A
Cook	Northfield		NORTH
Immanuel Evangelical Lutheran			N/A
Schaumburg Rd.		N/A	N/A
Cook	Hanover		NORTH
Immanuel Evangelical Lutheran			N/A
Saulk Trail & Cicero Ave.		Richton Park	60471
Cook	Rich		SOUTH

62   Cemeteries in Metropolitan Chicago Area

Name Address County	Town Township	Phone Zip Code Area
Immanuel Evangelical Lutheran 22nd St. & Wolf Rd. Cook	Hinsdale Proviso	N/A 60521 WEST
Immanuel Lutheran 1850 W. Lake St. Cook	Glenview Northfield	N/A 60025 NORTH
Independent (Jewish) (Keiger) Main (btw. Waukegan & Telegraph) Cook	Niles N/A	N/A N/A NORTH
Irving Park 7777 Irving Park Rd. Cook	Chicago Leyden	312-625-3500 60634 NORTH
Jewish Graceland 3919 No. Clark St. Cook	Chicago Lakeview	312-348-6276 60613 NORTH
Jewish Waldheim 1800 So. Harlem Ave. Cook	Forest Park Proviso	708-366-4100 60130 WEST
Jewish Oakridge Roosevelt & Oak Ridge Ave. Cook	Hillside Proviso	708-344-5600 60162 WEST
Joseph Barnett & Son, Inc. 1400 So. Des Plaines Ave. Cook	Forest Park Proviso	708-366-2445 60130 WEST
Kneseth Israel 5246 Hohman Ave. Lake	Hammond, IN N/A	219-931-5380 46320 SOUTH
La Grange Fifth Ave. & 27th St. Cook	La Grange Park Proviso	N/A 60525 WEST
Lake Street Memorial Park Rte. 1, Box 121 Cook	Elgin Hanover	708-741-4040 60120 NORTH
Lebovitz Co., Inc. Des Plaines & Roosevelt Rd. Cook	Forest Park Proviso	708-366-1008 60130 WEST

Name Address County	Township	Town	Phone Zip Code Area
Lincoln			708-445-5400
12300 So. Kedzie Ave.		Blue Island	60406
Cook	Worth		**SOUTH**
Lithuanian National			708-458-0638
Kean Ave. & 82nd St.		Willow Springs	60480
Cook	Lyons		**WEST**
Lower Cass (see Cass)			
Lutheran (Ebenezer)			N/A
165th & Cicero		Oak Forest	60452
Cook	Bremen		**SOUTH**
Lutheran Home for the Aged			N/A
Euclid Ave.		Arlington Heights	N/A
Cook	Wheeling		**NORTH**
Lyons, M.D.			N/A
3652 W. Irving Park Rd.		Chicago	60618
Cook	Jefferson		**NORTH**
Lyonsville Cong. Church			N/A
Joliet & Wolf Rds.		N/A	N/A
Cook	Lyons		**WEST**
Maryhill			708-823-0982
8600 No. Milwaukee Ave.		Niles	60648
Cook	Maine		**NORTH**
Matteson			N/A
Lincoln Hwy.		Matteson	60443
Cook	Rich		**SOUTH**
Memorial Estates, Inc.			708-455-2714
Wolf Rd. at Fullerton		Northlake	60164
Cook	Leyden		**NORTH**
Memorial Park			708-583-5080
9900 Gross Point Rd.		Skokie	60076
Cook	Niles		**NORTH**
Memory Gardens			763-8860
2501 E. Euclid Ave.		Arlington Heights	60004
Cook	Wheeling		**NORTH**

Name Address County	Township	Town	Phone Zip Code Area
Menorah Gardens, Inc.			708-344-1094
2630 So. 17th Ave.		Broadview	60153
Cook	Proviso		**WEST**
Montrose			312-478-5400
5400 No. Pulaksi Rd.		Chicago	60630
Cook	Jefferson		**NORTH**
Mount B'nai B'rith			312-545-0044
6600 Addison St.		Chicago	60634
Cook	Jefferson		**NORTH**
Mount Carmel			708-378-7373
1400 So. Wolf Rd.		Hillside	60162
Cook	Proviso		**WEST**
Mount Emblem			708-626-1332
Grand Ave. & County Line Rd.		Elmhurst	60126
DuPage	Addison		**NORTH**
Mount Glenwood (South)			708-758-5663
18301 Glenwood-Thornton Rd.		Glenwood	60425
Cook	Bloom		**SOUTH**
Mount Glenwood (West)			708-839-8800
8301 Kean Ave.		Willow Springs	60480
Cook	Lyons		**WEST**
Mount Greenwood			708-233-0136
111th St. & California Ave.		Blue Island	60406
Cook	Worth		**SOUTH**
Mount Hope			312-371-2818
115th St. & Fairfield Ave.		Chicago	60655
Cook	Worth		**SOUTH**
Mount Isaiah Israel			312-545-0044
6600 Addison St.		Chicago	60634
Cook	Jefferson		**NORTH**
Mount Mayriv			312-545-0001
3600 No. Narragansett Ave.		Chicago	60634
Cook	Jefferson		**NORTH**
Mount Mercy			219-980-2750
4401 W. Ridge Rd.		Gary, IN	46408
Lake	Calumet		**SOUTH**

Name / Address / County	Township	Town	Phone / Zip Code / Area
Mount Olive 3800 No. Narragansett Ave. Cook	Jefferson	Chicago	312-286-3770 60634 NORTH
Mount Olivet 2755 W. 111th St. Cook	Worth	Chicago	312-238-4435 60655 SOUTH
Mount Prospect N/A Cook	Wheeling	Mount Prospect	N/A 60056 NORTH
Mt. Auburn Memorial Park 4101 Oak Park Ave. Cook	Stickney	Stickney	708-749-0022 60402 WEST
Mt. Olivet Memorial Park, Ltd. 1436 Kenosha Rd. Lake	Benton	Zion	708-872-5476 60099 NORTH
Mt. Vernon Memorial Estates, Inc. 119th St. & Archer Ave. Cook	Lemont	Lemont	708-257-7711 60439 WEST
New Bachelor's Grove 195th St. & Oak Park Ave. Cook	Bremen	N/A	N/A N/A SOUTH
New Light 6807 E. Prairie Rd. Cook	Niles	Lincolnwood	708-673-1584 60645 NORTH
North Northfield Dundee Rd. Cook	Northfield	N/A	N/A N/A NORTH
North Side Cemetery N/A Cook		Chicago	N/A N/A NORTH
Northfield Union Church Milwaukee Ave. Cook	Northfield	N/A	N/A N/A NORTH
Norwood Park 6505 Northwest Highway Cook	Jefferson	Chicago	312-631-3133 60631 NORTH

Name Address County	Township	Town	Phone Zip Code Area
Oak Forest (aka Potter's Field) 159th & Cicero Ave. Cook	Bremen	Oak Forest	N/A 60452 SOUTH
Oak Hill 11900 So. Kedzie Ave. Cook	Worth	Chicago	312-445-5401 60655 SOUTH
Oak Hill (Hammond) 227 Kenwood St. Lake	N/A	Hammond, IN	219-932-0206 46324 SOUTH
Oak Ridge (Jewish) Roosevelt Rd. Cook	Proviso	Hillside	708-344-5600 60162 WEST
Oak Woods N/A Cook	Wheeling	Northfield	N/A 60093 NORTH
Oak Woods 1035 E. 67th St. Cook	Hyde Park	Chicago	312-288-3800 60637 SOUTH
Oakglen Ridge Rd. Cook	Thornton	Lansing	N/A 60438 SOUTH
Oakland Memory Lanes 15200 Lincoln Ave. Cook	Thornton	Dolton	708-8415800 60419 SOUTH
Oaklawn Ridge Rd. & Halsted St. Cook	Thornton	Homewood	N/A 60430 SOUTH
Oakridge Jewish Roosevelt & Oakridge Ave. Cook	Proviso	Hillside	708-344-5600 60162 WEST
Oakridge-Glen Oak Roosevelt & Oakridge Ave. Cook	Proviso	Hillside	708-626-4200 60162 WEST
Old Settlers St. Charles & Taft Rds. Cook	Proviso	N/A	N/A N/A WEST

Name Address County	Township	Town	Phone Zip Code Area
Order of Knights of Joseph 17th & Des Plaines Ave. Cook	Proviso	Forest Park	N/A 60130 **WEST**
Orland German M.E. Church 84th Ave. & 171st St. Cook	Orland	Tinley Park	N/A 60477 **SOUTH**
Orland Memorial Park 143rd St. Cook	Orland	Orland Park	N/A 60462 **SOUTH**
Our Lady of Sorrows 1400 So. Wolf Rd. Cook	Proviso	Hillside	708-449-6100 60162 **WEST**
Palo Hills Memorial Gardens 119th St. & Archer Ave. Cook	Lemont	Lemont	708-257-7711 60439 **WEST**
Palos Oak Hill 8901 W. 131st St. Cook	Palos	Palos Park	708-448-0606 60464 **SOUTH**
Parkholm 2501 No. LaGrange Rd. Cook	Proviso	LaGrange Park	708-352-4143 60525 **WEST**
Plum Grove Plum Grove Rd. Cook	Palatine	N/A	N/A N/A **NORTH**
Potter's Field (see Oak Forest)			
Presbyterian Chicago Rd. at 21st St. Cook	Bloom	Chicago Heights	N/A 60411 **SOUTH**
Progressive Order of the West 16th St. & Des Plaines Ave. Cook	Proviso	Forest Park	N/A 60130 **WEST**
Proviso Lutheran Wolf Rd. & 22nd St. Cook	Proviso	La Grange	N/A 60525 **WEST**

Name Address County	Township	Town	Phone Zip Code Area
Queen of Heaven			708-378-7373
1400 So. Wolf Rd.		Hillside	60162
Cook	Proviso		**WEST**
Randhill Park			708-274-2236
Rand Rd. (US12) & Rt. 53		Palatine	60067
Cook	Wheeling		**NORTH**
Reformed Church of Northfield			N/A
Pfingstan Rd.		N/A	N/A
Cook	Northfield		**NORTH**
Restvale			708-236-4077
115th St. & Laramie Ave.		Worth	60482
Cook	Worth		**SOUTH**
Resurrection			708-767-4644
7200 So. Archer Ave.		Justice	60458
Cook	Lyons		**WEST**
Ridgelawn			708-824-4145
9900 No. Milwaukee Ave.		Des Plaines	60016
Cook	Maine		**NORTH**
Ridgelawn Beth El			312-673-1584
5736 No. Pulaski Rd.		Chicago	60646
Cook	Jefferson		**NORTH**
Ridgelawn (Gary)			219-980-2750
4401 W. Ridge Rd.		Gary, IN	46408
Lake	Calumet		**SOUTH**
Ridgewood			N/A
9900 N. Milwaukee Ave.		Des Plaines	60016
Cook	Maine		**NORTH**
Rosehill			312-561-5940
5800 Ravenswood Ave.		Chicago	60660
Cook	Lakeview		**NORTH**
Rosemont Park			312-736-2553
6758 W. Addison St.		Chicago	60634
Cook	Jefferson		**NORTH**
Sacred Heart			N/A
905 Burr		Winnetka	60093
Cook	New Trier		**NORTH**

Name Address County	Township	Town	Phone Zip Code Area
Sag Bridge (aka St. James) Archer Rd. Cook	Lemont	N/A	N/A N/A SOUTH
Saint Adalbert 6800 No. Milwaukee Ave. Cook	Niles	Niles	708-545-1508 60648 NORTH
Saint Benedict 4600 W. 135th St. Cook	Worth	Crestwood	708-238-4435 60446 SOUTH
Saint Boniface 4901 No. Clark St. Cook	Lakeview	Chicago	312-561-2790 60640 NORTH
Saint Casimir Lithuanian 4401 W. 111th St. Cook	Worth	Chicago	312-239-4422 60655 SOUTH
Saint Henry 1929 W. Devon Ave. Cook	Lakeview	Chicago	312-561-2790 60660 NORTH
Saint James at Sag Bridge Rts. 83 & 171 Cook	Lemont	Lemont	708-257-7000 60439 WEST
Saint John (Hammond) 1547 - 167th St. Lake	N/A	Hammond, IN	219-884-9475 46324 SOUTH
Saint Joseph Cumberland & Belmont Ave. Cook	Leyden	River Grove	708-625-8416 60171 NORTH
Saint Joseph (Hammond) 167th St. & Indianapolis Blvd. Lake	N/A	Hammond, IN	219-844-5762 46320 SOUTH
Saint Lucas 5300 No. Pulaski Rd. Cook	Jefferson	Chicago	312-588-0049 60630 NORTH
Saint Mary W. 87th & So. Hamlin Ave. Cook	Worth	Evergreen Park	708-238-3351 60642 SOUTH

Name Address County	Township	Town	Phone Zip Code Area
Saint Michael 159th St. & Will Cook Rd. Will	 Homer	 Orland Park	708-445-2022 60462 **SOUTH**
Saint Michael the Archangel Algonquin & Roselle Rds. Cook	 Palatine	 Palatine	708-397-3284 60067 **NORTH**
Salem Evang. Church of N. Am. Plum Grove & Kirchoff Rds. Cook	 Palatine	 Rolling Meadows	N/A 60008 **NORTH**
Schaumburg Lutheran Schaumburg Rd. Cook	 Schaumburg	 N/A	N/A N/A **NORTH**
Schwarzbach's 1700 So. Des Plaines Ave. Cook	 Proviso	 Forest Park	708-366-4541 60130 **WEST**
Shalom Memorial Park Rand Rd. (US12) & Rt. 53 Cook	 Wheeling	 Palatine	708-274-2236 60067 **NORTH**
Silverman & Weiss 1303 So. Des Plaines Ave. Cook	 Proviso	 Forest Park	708-378-2838 60130 **WEST**
Skyline Memorial Park US 54 (¼ mi S. of Junc. 50) Will	 Monee	 Monee	708-534-8256 60449 **SOUTH**
Sleepy Hollow Memorial Park 111th St. & Central Ave. Cook	 Worth	 Worth	N/A 60482 **WEST**
Solomon C. Kelsy 119th St. & Will-Cook Rds. Cook	 Palos	 N/A	N/A N/A **WEST**
Sons and Daughters of Joseph 1303 S. Des Plaines Ave. Cook	 Proviso	 Forest Park	N/A 60130 **WEST**
SS. Cyril & Methodius Hwy 4A Cook	 Lemont	 Lemont	708-767-4644 60439 **SOUTH**

Name Address County	Township	Town	Phone Zip Code Area
St. Alphonsus			N/A
212 Custer St.		Lemont	60439
Cook	Lemont		**SOUTH**
St. Andrew's Ukrainian Orthodox			708-893-2827
22W 347 Army Trail Rd.		Addison	60101
DuPage	Bloomingdale		**NORTH**
St. Anne's			N/A
Saulk Trail & Kedzie Ave.		Richton Park	60471
Cook	Rich		**SOUTH**
St. Gabriel's			N/A
165th & Cicero Ave.		Oak Forest	60452
Cook	Bremen		**SOUTH**
St. James (Strassburg)			N/A
3430 S. Halsted		Steger	60475
Cook	Bloom		**SOUTH**
St. Johannes Evang. Lutheran			N/A
Church Rd.		N/A	N/A
Cook	Elk Grove		**NORTH**
St. John's Church			N/A
La Grange Rd. at 69th St.		Hodkins	60527
Cook	Lyons		**WEST**
St. John's Evang. Lutheran			N/A
Chicago, Elgin & Ridenberg Rds.		N/A	N/A
Cook	Schaumburg		**NORTH**
St. John's Evang. Lutheran			N/A
Algonquin & Rosell Rds.		Palatine	60067
Cook	Palatine		**NORTH**
St. Mary's			N/A
Old Buffalo Grove at Lake-Cook Rd.		N/A	N/A
Cook	Wheeling		**NORTH**
St. Mary's Mission			N/A
Lee Rd.		N/A	N/A
Cook	Northfield		**NORTH**
St. Mary's Training School			N/A
Waukegan & Willow Rds.		N/A	N/A
Cook	Northfield		**NORTH**

Name Address County	Township	Town	Phone Zip Code Area
St. Matthew's Evang. Luth.			N/A
129th St.		Lemont	60439
Cook	Lemont		**WEST**
St. Nicholas Ukrainian Cath.			312-825-1854
Higgins Rd. (E. of River Rd.)		Chicago	60631
Cook	Leyden		**NORTH**
St. Paul's Sedem Prairie			N/A
Volmer Rd.		N/A	N/A
Cook	Rich		**SOUTH**
St. Paul's Evang. Lutheran			N/A
Russel & Henry St.		Mount Prospect	60056
Cook	Wheeling		**NORTH**
St. Paul's Evang. Lutheran			N/A
Harms Rd.		N/A	N/A
Cook	Niles		**NORTH**
St. Peter's			N/A
8116 Niles Center Rd.		Skokie	60076
Cook	Niles		**NORTH**
St. Peter's Evang. Lutheran			N/A
N/A		Northbrook	60062
Cook	Northfield		**NORTH**
St. Peter's Evang. Lutheran			N/A
Harris Rd.		N/A	N/A
Cook	Niles		**NORTH**
St. Peter's Evang. Lutheran			N/A
Irving Park Blvd.		N/A	N/A
Cook	Schaumburg		**NORTH**
Stressler			N/A
Long Grove Rd.		N/A	N/A
Cook	Palatine		**NORTH**
Sunset Memorial Lawns			708-724-0669
3100 Shermer Rd.		Northbrook	60062
Cook	Northfield		**NORTH**
Swan Lake Memorial Gardens			219-874-7520
5700 East US Rt. 20		Michigan City, IN	46360
La Porte	Michigan		**SOUTH**

Name Address County	Township	Town	Phone Zip Code Area
Thornton Township			N/A
Ridge Rd.		Thornton	60476
Cook	Thornton		SOUTH
Tinley Park (aka Zion Luth.)			N/A
167th St.		N/A	N/A
Cook	Bremen		SOUTH
Tinley Park Memorial			N/A
84th Ave. & 171st St.		Tinley Park	60477
Cook	Orland		SOUTH
Town of Maine			708-823-3546
Dee Rd. & Touhy Ave.	Park Ridge	60068	
Cook	Maine		NORTH
Trinity Evangelical Lutheran			N/A
159th St. & Oak Park Ave.		N/A	N/A
Cook	Bremen		SOUTH
Trinity Lutheran			N/A
83rd St.		N/A	N/A
Cook	Lyons		SOUTH
Union			N/A
Smith St. & Kenilworth Ave.		Palatine	60067
Cook	Palatine		NORTH
Union Ridge			312-631-0900
6700 Higgins Rd.		Chicago	60656
Cook	Jefferson		NORTH
Waldheim (see Forest Home)			
Washington Memory Gardens			708-798-0645
701 Ridge Rd.		Homewood	60430
Cook	Thornton		SOUTH
Westlawn			312-625-8600
7801 W. Montrose Ave.		Chicago	60634
Cook	Norwood Park		NORTH
Wheeling			N/A
W. Dundee Rd.		Wheeling	60090
Cook	Wheeling		NORTH

Name Address County	Township	Town	Phone Zip Code Area
Whites Waukegan Rd. & Main St. Cook	Niles	Niles	N/A 60648 **NORTH**
Wilmer's Old Settlers Bryn Mawr Ave. Cook	Leyden	N/A	N/A N/A **WEST**
Woodlawn 7600 W. Cermak Rd. Cook	Proviso	Forest Park	708-442-8500 60130 **WEST**
Wunders 3963 No. Clark St. Cook	Lakeview	Chicago	312-525-4038 60613 **NORTH**
Zion Church (aka Evang. Luth) Lincoln Hwy. Cook	Rich	Matteson	N/A 60443 **SOUTH**

SECTION SIX

Cemetery Records

By Brian Scott Donovan

Cemetery, and other records generated by a death, are often the logical starting point for the researcher who applies good genealogical procedure—by working from the present to the past. Records generated when a person dies often contain references to important events in the individual's life and identify family relationships. You should examine all of these records carefully for the different types of information they may contain.

With over 200 cemeteries in Cook County (see section 5), the first priority is to determine where a burial occurred. There is no single source that lists all the burials in Cook County, but the most comprehensive records of burials are contained in the certificates of death available from the County Clerk, Bureau of Vital Statistics, 118 North Clark Street, Chicago, Illinois 60602 (see section 34). The destruction of all vital records in the Great Chicago Fire makes it necessary to check other sources for deaths prior to October 8-10, 1871. Additionally, unknown death dates, and deaths which may have occurred outside Cook County, make searching the vital records of other counties impractical or too expensive. In these instances there are some alternatives.

Rolls of Honor

The burial places of veterans are listed in rolls of honor:

Lewis, E. R., comp. *The Roll of Honor. The Honorable Board of Cook County*, Illinois, 1922.

This roll of honor contains information about deceased veterans from the Revolution to World War I. Under each listed cemetery, the following information is given for a veteran: name, rank, company, U.S. regiment state organization or vessel, date of death, grave number, lot number, block and section. Besides listing the burials in Cook County, and burials in state (outside Cook County), the roll also lists burials outside of the state and unknown burial places. However, neither the cemeteries, nor the veterans buried therein are listed in alphabetical order. This problem was resolved with the recent publication of:

Index to the Roll of Honor, Cook County, Illinois. Salt Lake City, UT: Markam Publications, 1986.

This index covers burials prior to July 1, 1955, and includes veterans of World War II, Korea, veterans listed in the previous reference, and those who died in the intervening years.

Honor Roll, Cook County, Illinois. Springfield, IL: Illinois Veterans' Commission, 1956.

The information in this roll of honor (in twelve volumes), covers all Illinois counties, but there is no index. The first three volumes cover Cook County. The first volume contains cemetery names that begin with the letters A through J, the second volume K through O, and the third   volume P through Z. If the place of burial is unknown, this information is indicated in the list. The names of veterans are arranged alphabetically under each cemetery, and the following information is given: name, war, rank, branch, unit of organization, date of death, grave number, lot number, block, section, and headstone.

Camp Douglas Prisoners

Approximately 5,000 Confederate soldiers died as prisoners of war in Camp Douglas, and were buried at Oakwoods Cemetery (often referred to as Confederate Mound Cemetery). Two sources list the names of soldiers buried there:

Ingmire, Frances Terry. *Confederate P.O.W.s: Soldiers and Sailors Who Died in Federal Prisons & Military Hospitals in the North.* Nacogdoches, TX: distributed by Ericson Books, 1984.

Pompey, Sherman Lee. *Burial Lists of the Confederate Federal Infantry.* Kingsbury, CA: Pacific Specialties, 1972.

Early Cemeteries

Of the original dozen cemeteries within the city limits of Chicago, not a single one remained by the late 1870's. All were closed for public health reasons, and the bodies moved to cemeteries outside the city. It was not until the annexation of 1889 that any cemetery land was again within the city limits. John Kinzie, the first white settler of Chicago, was buried four times: on his property, the City Cemetery, the North Side Cemetery (in what is now the south end of Lincoln Park), and finally, the Graceland Cemetery.

To trace a body removed from early city cemeteries, you will need to examine the Calvary, Graceland, Rose Hill, Oak Woods, Wunder, and Hebrew Benevolent cemetery records. These cemeteries were opened in the late 1850's and early 1860's outside the city limits of Chicago. A good history of the early development of cemeteries in Chicago can be found in:

Denemark, B. *Early Chicago Cemeteries.* Reference Report, Chicago Historical Society (March 3, 1971).

Grossman, Ron. "Cemetery Trove Brings Early Chicago to Life." *Illinois State Genealogical Society Quarterly* 1, no. 4 (Winter 1991): 194-95.

Potter's Field

Several different cemeteries have been used by Cook County to bury unclaimed bodies and those of the indigent:

January 1980 to present

The Garden of the Good Samaritan section of Homewood Memorial Gardens

December 1970 through December 1979

Archer Woods Cemetery (now Mount Glenwood West Cemetery)

1910 through November 1970

Oak Forest Cemetery (which became Cook County Cemetery)

Records of burials in all three cemeteries have been maintained. Cook County cemetery records are kept by the Medical Records Department of Oak Forest Hospital, 159th and Cicero Avenue, Oak Forest, IL 60452 (312-687-7200).

Transcriptions

Transcriptions from cemetery monuments are very useful sources of information, but relying on the work of others has its limitations. The variety of information inscribed varies from dates of birth and death, place of birth and death (especially where far removed from place of burial), maiden name, parents' names, spouse's name, siblings, relationships, occupations, military service, biographical information, fraternal symbols, photographs or signatures. The lack of uniformity in this information makes an orderly compilation of inscriptions difficult, and details may be lost in the transcription. Family relationships, especially between in-laws, may be lost in the alphabetization of transcriptions. Additionally, everyone memorialized on a stone is not necessarily buried in the plot. The best transcriptions include the monument inscriptions, and, when available to the compilers, cross references to cemetery records or obituaries. Transcriptions for Cook County may be found in:

Barekman, June B. "Mt. Olive Cemetery, Jefferson Township, Cook County, Illinois." *Chicago Genealogist* 11, no. 1 (Fall 1978): 15-17.

Bodett, Tom. *Reading of the Gravestones of St. Mary's Cemetery, Located on River Road, on the Grounds of Maryville Academy, Des Plaines, IL.* reading done July 10, 1985.

Golay, Myrna, and Joan Huff. *Elk Grove Cemetery, Early 1840s-1976.*, 1976.

Koss, David, Louis D. Melnick, and Michael A. Melnick. "Inscriptions from Cady Cemetery, Palatine Township, Cook County, Illinois." *Newsletter of the North Suburban Genealogical Society* 2, no. 2 (March 1977): 10-12.

Jacyna, Sister Josephine. "Partial List of St. Henry's Catholic Cemetery at Devon near Damen Avenue, Chicago IL." *Holograph*, Salt Lake City, 1977.

> Available from the Genealogical Department of The Church of Jesus Christ of Latter-day Saints, microfilm 1,036,723, item 6.

Jensen, Mary Ann, John Gifford, and Mary Ellen Gifford. *St. Patrick's Cemetery of Lemont, Illinois.* South Holland, IL: South Suburban Genealogical & Historical Society, 1978.

Johnson, Jo Ellen, ed. *Research Series Volume 3: An Inventory of Cemeteries in South Cook County, Illinois.* South Holland, IL: South Suburban Genealogical & Historical Society, 1991.

Leonard, Craig, and Debbie Craig. *Tombstone Inscriptions from St. John's Cemetery, West Lake Street, Northbrook, Illinois.*, Summer, 1975.

Lundberg, Gertrude W. *Some German Name Cemeteries, Cook County, Illinois.* Homewood, IL: Root & Tree Publications, 1967.

> The transcription includes these cemeteries: Immanuel German Lutheran, Glenview; St. Paul's Lutheran, Skokie;

Old Immanuel Lutheran, Des Plaines; St. John's Lutheran, Northfield Township, Lutheran Home & Service for the Aged.

_____. *St. John's Lutheran Church Cemetery, Mt. Prospect, Illinois, Cook County.* Homewood, IL: Root & Tree Publications, 1970.

_____. "Glenview Area Burial Places, Northfield Township, Cook County, Illinois." *Chicago Genealogist* 7, no. 1, (Fall 1974): 5-12.

This article includes a transcription of St. John's Lutheran Church Cemetery, first recorded in 1966, and revised to 1973.

_____. *Cook County Tombstones, Cemetery #3. St. John's Lutheran, Elk Grove Township.* Homewood, IL: Root & Tree Publications, 1970.

Gertrude Lundberg has also transcribed and indexed a number of other cemeteries:

Arlington Heights Cemetery (#4), Wheeling Township

Sacred Heart Cemetery, Northbrook, Northfield Township

St. Joseph's Catholic Cemetery, Wilmette, New Trier Township

St. John's Lutheran Cemetery, Elk Grove Township

St. Peter's Lutheran Cemetery (#2), Wheeling Township

St. Peter's United Church of Christ Cemetery (#13), Skokie, Niles Township

McHarg, Christopher G. *Tombstone Inscriptions, Arlington Heights Wheeling Township Cemetery, Cook County, Illinois.*, 1976.

Santroch, Gail, ed. *A Transcription of Wunder's Cemetery, Chicago, Illinois.* Chicago: Chicago Genealogical Society, 1985.

Scheskie, Debra Lynn, and James Scheskie. "Inscriptions from the Cemetery Located on Rand Road at Seegers Road, Des Plaines, Illinois Affiliated with Emanuel Lutheran

Church, Des Plaines, Illinois." *Chicago Genealogist* 10, no. 4, (Summer 1978): 139-44.

Scheskie, James, Beverly Scheskie, Debra Scheskie, and Susan Scheskie. *St. Joseph's Cemetery at Lake and Gross Point Roads. Wilmette, Illinois.*, June 1974.

The South Suburban Genealogical and Historical Society has transcribed and indexed these cemeteries:

Bloom Presbyterian Cemetery, Bloom Township, Cook County, Illinois

Oak Glen Cemetery, Lansing, Cook County, Illinois

Old Thornton Township Cemetery, Cook County, Illinois

St. James Cemetery, Bloom Township, Cook County, Illinois

St. Patrick's Cemetery, Lemont, Illinois

Trinity Lutheran Church Cemetery, Tinley Park, Bremen Township

Wunders Cemetery (located at Clark St. and Irving Park Rd.), Chicago, Illinois

Zion Lutheran Cemetery, Tinley Park, Bremen Township

Information about the cemeteries listed may be found in booklets sold by:

South Suburban Genealogical & Historical Society,
P.O. Box 96
South Holland, IL 60473-0096
(312-333-9474)

Arlington Heights Wheeling Township Cemetery, 1840-July 1968 is a pamphlet that includes a history taken from the Minute Books and transcriptions by Joan Allen. Her work, and an article that appeared in the September 3, 1948 *Arlington Heights Herald*, with transcriptions by Dr. Bruce T. Best, are available in the pamphlet file of the Arlington Memorial Library.

Records from the First Record Book of Graceland Cemetery, 1860-1866, Chicago, Illinois is a typescript of 114 leaves, is indexed (1945) and available from the Genealogical Department of The Church of Jesus Christ of Latter-day Saints, microfilm 843,587, item 5.

Transcriptions in Progress

Currently, the Chicago Genealogical Society, and several other suburban groups, have cemetery projects in progress. For up-to-date information on the status of cemetery records and transcriptions, contact the appropriate genealogical society (listed in section 18).

The following organizations maintain lists of Cook County cemetery surveying and transcribing projects in progress and completed:

The Association for Gravestone Studies
  46 Plymouth Road
  Needham, MA 02192
The Illinois State Genealogical Society
  Cemetery Committee
  P.O. Box 10195
  Springfield, IL 62791-0195
Chicago Genealogical Society
  Cemetery Project Committee
  P.O. Box 1160
  Chicago, IL 60690-1160
  (312-725-1306)

Transcribing Methods: References

There are several useful booklets on methods used to transcribe cemetery information:

Jones, Mary Ellen. Photographing Tombstones: Equipment and Techniques. Technical Leaflet no. 92. Nashville: American Association for State and Local History, 1977.

Newman, John J. *Cemetery Transcribing: Preparations and Procedures.* Technical Leaflet no. 9. Nashville: American Association for State and Local History, 1971.

Paddock, Shirley, and Christine Walsh Angelos. *Symbols in Stone.* Northbrook, IL: The Printing Post, Inc., 1982.

Death Indexes

You may have found it difficult to obtain a certificate of death because the date of death is unknown, the decedent had a very common or easily misspelled name, or other reason. There are two death indexes available through the family history centers of the Genealogical Department of The Church of Jesus Christ of Latter-day Saints that may prove very useful in obtaining the correct death record from the Bureau of Vital Statistics. The two indexes are on microfilm or microfiches:

Microfilms (Chicago Deaths 1871-1933)

These microfilms cover the period 1871 to 1933 and include the following information: name, place of death, date, and register number (see section 34 for list of film numbers). The inclusion of addresses is very useful in revealing possible relationships between decedents, and to use with city directories. However, this index only covers deaths that occurred in Chicago. The index also has burial information for the time period when a burial permit was on the certificate of death.

Microfiches (number 6016533, fiches 0001-0070)

These microfiches cover only the period 1871 to 1916, but encompass all of Cook County. Information includes the individual's name, death date, age at death, death place (restricted to Chicago or Cook County; no addresses outside of Chicago), and the identification number (equivalent to the register number; see section 34). The microfiches have two limitations: the time period covered is smaller, and there are no complete addresses.

Newspaper Death Notices and Obituaries

Death notices and obituaries are a particularly useful source for determining the place of interment for the period prior to the Great Chicago Fire of 1871. Families and friends paid for death notices to notify others of these events. Look for additional death notices placed by fraternal organizations. Because obituaries were news stories, they may or may not contain information concerning funeral services or burials. For a brief time, the *Chicago Tribune* ran an "Official Death Record" taken from the County Clerk's records, and the *New World* ran a list of burials in Catholic cemeteries. These lists were usually more comprehensive than the death notices, but they also tended to be printed after the burial had occurred. Accidental, violent, or otherwise notable deaths may appear in other sections of the newspaper besides the obituary section. Death notices were often scattered throughout early newspapers as fillers. Consequently, it is important to make a thorough search.

The following sources are useful in locating death notices and obituaries:

Sam Fink's *Index* (BGL microfilm 1,321,939). This microfilm contains indexes of death notices and obituaries printed in ten different newspapers between 1833 and 1889.

The Chicago Genealogical Society published seven volumes of *Vital Records from Chicago Newspapers* covering the period from 1833 to 1848.

The Chicago Historical Society Library clipping file and card catalog.

Adjacent Counties

Burials occurred often enough in adjacent counties to justify mentioning them here. Cemeteries in adjacent counties were included in the list of cemeteries in section 5 if they appeared on a list, from the Wilbur Vault Company, of frequently called telephone numbers. The list, distributed to funeral directors, served as an indicator of how often these cemeteries were used for burial of late Cook County residents.

Sources for information on burials and cemeteries in adjacent counties include:

The Cemetery Committee, Lake Co. (IL) Genealogical Society. *A Guide to Cemetery Names and Locations in Lake County, Illinois*. Waukegan, IL: Sir Speedy, 1980.

Price, Clarence, and Florence Price. *Lombard Cemetery Records*. Lombard IL: DuPage County Genealogical Society.

Thomas, Nancy Roeser, ed. *Genealogical Sources: Du Page County, Illinois*. Lombard, IL: DuPage County Genealogical Society, 1993.

The Kane County, Illinois *Master Every Name Index* includes forty-seven cemeteries. Contact:

Kane County Genealogical Society
P.O. Box 504
Geneva, IL 60134-0504
(708-695-5893)

Census Records

Federal Population Census

The *Census of Population* from the U.S. Bureau of the Census is the most popular information source available to the American genealogist. Population censuses were taken in 1790 and every 10th year thereafter. The census schedules for 1790 through 1920 are open to the public and available on microfilm. Unfortunately, the 1890 schedules were almost entirely destroyed by fire. This section provides addresses of archives and libraries that have census collections.

Census schedules for Chicago and Cook County are available on the following microfilms at the National Archives:

Year	U.S. Census Schedules	Microfilm Number
1820	Chicago (As part of Clark County, IL)	M33,12
1830	Chicago (As part of Putnam County,IL)	M19,24
1840	Chicago and all of Cook County, IL	M704, 57
1850	Cook County including City of Chicago	M432, 102 & 103
1860	Cook County including City of Chicago	M653, 164-170

1870	Cook County including City of Chicago	M593, 198-213
1880	Cook County including City of Chicago	T9, 184-202
1890	Not available	
1900	Cook County including City of Chicago	T623, 244-295
1910	Cook County including City of Chicago	T624, 237-283
1920	Cook County including City of Chicago	T625, 305-363

1930+ The schedules from 1930 on are confidential by law for 72 years.

Many individuals do not have birth certificates and may use a transcript of population census records to: qualify for social security or retirement benefits; obtain passports; prove citizenship or relationships; satisfy other requests for a birth certificate. The U.S. Bureau of the Census releases information only to the person, his or her heirs, or a legal representative. Census transcripts cannot be furnished for use in tracing missing persons.

The Bureau maintains files from 1900 through 1990 for transcription purposes. These files are administered by the Personal Census Services. Transcripts may be ordered by completing form BC-600. For applications and help in completing them write or call:

Personal Census Services
Census Service Branch
Bureau of the Census
P.O. Box 1545
Jefferson, IN 47131

In the Chicago area call (312-353-0980) for general information.

Where to Find U.S. Population Census Records

The National Archives-Great Lakes Region

7358 South Pulaski Road
Chicago, IL 60629
(312-581-7816)

The National Archives-Great Lakes Region has all of the censuses on microfilm for all available states for the years 1790 to 1920 including the Soundex. There are other indexes which are helpful for locating individuals within the actual census schedules.

The Newberry Library

60 West Walton
Chicago, IL 60610
(312-943-9090)

The Newberry Library has microfilms of all extant census schedules for Illinois up to, and including, 1920. A detailed set of maps serves as a finding aid for locating Chicago addresses. The Newberry Library also has census schedules for several other counties and states.

Chicago Public Library

Harold Washington Library Center
Social Sciences Division, Floors 5 & 6
400 South State Street
Chicago, IL 60605
(312-747-4600)

The Chicago Public Library has only the census schedules for Chicago and Cook County from 1850 to 1920 inclusive. It does not have the Soundex, Miracode, or other indexes, but does have some ward and enumeration district maps to assist in locating street addresses.

The Chicago Historical Society

Clark Street at North Avenue
Chicago, IL 60614
(312-642-4600)

The Chicago Historical Society has the 1840, 1850, 1860, 1870, 1880, and 1900 census schedules for Chicago and Cook County, but does not have any indexes for those schedules. The 1810 and 1820 census schedules for Illinois were published in *Collections of the Illinois State Historical Library*, (volumes 24 and 26, respectively). Volume 24 also contains the 1818 Illinois Territory census schedules. The Chicago Historical Society and the Newberry Library have copies of the publication. The Chicago Historical Society does not have Soundex, Miracode, or other indexes, but does have some ward maps to assist in locating street addresses.

If you live outside of the Chicago area, there are other regional branches of the National Archives, and some large libraries that have census information. One such library is:

The Allen County Public Library
900 Webster Street
Ft. Wayne, Indiana 46802
This library has complete collections of census schedules for the entire United States.

The Archives Building
Springfield, IL 62756-0001
The Illinois State Archives have all available Illinois censuses, but do not participate in interlibrary loan. Paper printouts can be provided.

The Illinois State Library
Centennial Building
Springfield, IL 62701-1703
You can borrow Illinois census films from the Illinois State Library through the standard interlibrary loan process.

Films for the 1790-1920 censuses may be borrowed directly or purchased from:

American Genealogical Lending Library
Box 329
Bountiful, UT 84010-0329
(801-298-5358)
In some instances a poor microfilm copy of a particular census will not be legible nor will it provide a good paper copy. You should explore the possibility of getting a better copy from another library, or the National Archives in

Washington since microfilm quality will often differ from copy to copy.

Indexes and Finding Aids

The Illinois State Archives has an index that covers state and federal census records for Illinois for the years 1810 to 1855. The 1860 census index is separated from the 1810-1855 census index, and Cook County is filed with other counties in that index. A limited amount of research will be performed in reply to mail requests. Please ask only for one or two specific items at a time. Designate the specific census to be searched, provide the complete name of the person to be searched, and do not submit a second request until you have received an answer to your first request.

1830 U.S. Census Index

Jackson, Ronald Vern, David Schaefermeyer, and Gary Ronald Teeples. *Illinois 1830 Census Index*. Bountiful, UT: Accelerated Indexing Systems, Inc. 1976.

1840 U.S. Census Indexes

Smith, Marjorie. "Index to the 1840 U.S. Census of Cook County." *Chicago Genealogist* 2, no. 1 (1970): 14-19; no. 2 (1970): 39-42; no. 3 (1970): 80-83; no. 4 (1970): 75-78.

Jackson, Ronald Vern, and Gary Ronald Teeples. *Illinois 1840 Census Index*. Bountiful, UT: Accelerated Indexing Systems, Inc., 1977.

1850 U.S. Census Indexes

The 1850 census index at the Illinois State Archives has every name, including children, on a separate cardis. This index is part of the *Name Index 1810-1855*, and is particularly helpful when parents' names are unknown. Printed indexes contain only the names of heads of families.

Barekman, June B., Gertrude Lundberg, and Bernice C. Richard. *Surname Index to the 1850 Federal Census of Chicago, Cook County Illinois*. Chicago: June B. Barekman Genealogical Services and Publications, 1976.

Daughters of the American Revolution-Dewalt Mechlen Chapter. *Old Settlers of Chicago 1850-70*. Chicago: by the editors, 1956.

Contains transcription of census records for southwest Chicago and Cook County (including the communities of Worth, Beverly Hills, Morgan Park, Brainerd, Chicago Ridge, Blue Island, Evergreen Park, Oak Lawn, Roseland, Mt. Greenwood and Washington Heights). Not all communities are covered for all of the census years.

Lundberg, Gertrude. *1850 Census of Cook County Illinois Outside of Chicago*. Chicago: Chicago Genealogical Society, 1985.

Note: *Old Settlers of Chicago 1850-70* and *1850 Census of Cook County Illinois Outside of Chicago* are available from:

Chicago Genealogical Society
P.O. Box 1160,
Chicago, IL 60690-1160
(312-725-1306)

Jackson, Ronald Vern, and Gary Ronald Teeples. *Illinois 1850 Census Index*. Bountiful, UT: Accelerated Indexing Systems, Inc., 1976.

The South Suburban Genealogical and Historical Society has indexed the 1850 Census for the townships of Bloom, Bremen, Lemont, Palos, Rich, Thornton and Worth in quarterly publications of *Where the Trails Cross* (1970-74). For further information write to:

South Suburban Genealogical and Historical Society
320 East 61st Place
P.O. Box 96
South Holland, IL 60473-0096
(312-333-9474)

Other references that may be of use in your research are:

Adams, James N., comp. *Illinois Place Names*, Occasional Publications, no.54. (Springfield, IL: Illinois State Historical Society, 1968).

Parker, J. Carlyle. *City, County, Town and Township Index to the 1850 Federal Census Schedules*. Detroit, MI: Gale Research Company, 1979.

A helpful source for locating townships and some towns which are no longer in existence.

1860 U.S. Census Index

The entire 1860 federal census for Cook County, Illinois was transcribed and indexed by Bernice C. Richard of the Chicago Genealogical Society. The original card index has been integrated into the census index at the Illinois State Archives. Microfilm copies are available for purchase from the Illinois State Archives.

The 1860 Federal Census for Illinois has been indexed in three volumes.

Jackson, Ronald Vern. *Illinois 1860 Census Index, North.* 2 vols. Bountiful, UT: Accelerated Indexing Systems, Inc., 1987.

An index of Chicago and Cook County names.

The National Archives-Great Lakes Region and the Newberry Library also have microfilm copies of this 1860 census index for Cook County.

The South Suburban Genealogical and Historical Society has indexed the 1860 census for the townships of Lemont, Orland, Palos, Thornton, and Worth in quarterly publications of *Where the Trails Cross*. (1973-79)

1870 U.S. Census Indexes and Finding Tools

Steuart, Bradley W., ed. *Chicago, IL 1870 Census Index.* Bountiful, UT: Precision Indexing, 1990.

In addition to providing an alphabetical list of personal names, this index provides the age, sex, color, and birthplace of each individual listed, along with the Chicago ward number or the name of the Cook County town of residence, the National Archives series roll and page number on which each name can be found. Despite a cover title inferring that the volume is limited to Chicago, this important reference also includes the many other townships and communities that were within the boundaries of Cook County in 1870.

While Precision's 1870 index has been found to be remarkably accurate, all census indexes are prone to omissions. Probably no index is error free because names were misspelled, some handwriting was difficult to decipher, and some original census schedules were of poor quality.

When the names of individuals, presumed to be living in Chicago, do not appear in the census index, you are faced with the prospect of searching page-by-page through 15 rolls of microfilm. There is another approach devised by historian Keith Schlesinger that may work.

The geographical arrangement of the census schedules makes finding aids vital when searching for urban residents. Schlesinger's system may help locate individuals overlooked by Soundex and other indexing processes. In his system, addresses are gleaned from city directories (which he found both accurate and accessible). The addresses are plotted on maps of census enumeration districts, which normally followed the boundaries of voting precincts in most cities. Narrowing the search for the nonindexed individual to one or two enumeration districts enables you to bypass the Soundex. The technique is described in:

Schlesinger, Keith, and Peggy Tuck Sinko. "Urban Finding Aid for Manuscript Census Searches." *National Genealogical Society Quarterly* 69 (Sept.1981): 171-80.

The Illinois State Archives has a surname (only) index for 1870. However, each ward is indexed separately which makes it difficult to use.

The 1871 Edwards *Census Directory for Chicago* (actual title: *The Chicago Census Report and Statistical Review*) compliments the use of the 1870 ward index at the State Archives since each entry provides ward numbers as well as street addresses. Additionally, this unique directory lists the occupation of the head of house; number of males; number of females; and total number in residence at the address. The birthplace of the head of house is also provided. The Edwards directory is essentially an alphabetically arranged city directory with the addition of statistical information. It was compiled from a canvassing requested by the mayor, city council, business firms and others in Chicago who were not satisfied with the results of the 1870 federal census.

The Newberry Library 1870 Chicago Census Finding Aid

The staff at the Newberry Library has developed a finding aid for the 1870 census for the city of Chicago. The census enumerators' routes have been plotted on a city map so that a specific address can be located by approximate enumeration date. Addresses may be determined by consulting an 1870 or 1871 city directory for the individual or household being sought in the census schedules. The maps are available in the Local and Family History section of the library.

1870 Indexes for Southern Cook County Townships

The South Suburban Genealogical and Historical Society has indexed the 1870 Census for the townships of Bremen, Calumet, Orland and Palos in quarterly publications (1982-84) of *Where the Trails Cross*.

1880 U.S. Census Index

The 1880 Soundex index to the federal census for Illinois is a significant aid for locating individuals or households in the census schedules. Unfortunately, the 1880 Soundex is only a partial index which includes only households where children ten years of age or younger were in residence. This partial index was compiled in the 1930s under the auspices of the Works Projects Administration (WPA) to determine how many people would be eligible for benefits under the proposed Social Security Act. Often names were misspelled or completely omitted in transcription from the original census schedules. Another limitation of the 1880 Illinois Soundex microfilm publication is the omission of over 1,000 cards for the last names beginning with the letter "O." However, this information was later transcribed from the original Soundex cards and published in book form by Nancy Gibb Frederick (1208 Maple Avenue, Evanston, Illinois 6010). Copies of her index are available at the National Archives-Great Lakes Region, the Newberry Library, and several other area libraries. The original 1880 Soundex cards for Illinois are now housed at the Northwestern Memorial Hospital Group Archives, 329 West 18th Street, Suite 901, Chicago, IL 60616. The Illinois State Archives has the Soundex indexes for 1880, and the Illinois State Library makes it available through the interlibrary loan service.

Chicago 1880 Cook County, IL Federal Census Index, a printed every-household index edited by Ronald Vern Jackson, et al. (North Salt Lake, Utah: Accelerated Indexing Systems International, 1989), is available at the Family History Library in Salt Lake City. The printed index covers all of Cook County. The Newberry Library has the CD-ROM version: *U.S. Census Index, 1880 Cook County, IL* (Orem, UT: Automated Archives, 1994).

The Newberry Library 1880 Chicago Census Finding Aids

The staff at the Newberry Library has developed a system to locate people omitted by the Soundex by using enumeration descriptions, ward and precinct maps. Street addresses for individuals sought in the census schedules should first be determined by consulting an 1880 Chicago Directory. Addresses then become the key to locating individuals or households in exact enumeration districts within the census schedules. The 1880 census finding aids are available in the Local and Family History section of the library.

1900 U.S. Census Index

Although there are no special 1900 census indexes for Chi-

cago or Cook County, the 1900 Soundex for Illinois is probably the most complete of any of the census indexes. Because
the 1900 Soundex is so reliable, it is often the suggested
starting point to begin census and other genealogical and
historical projects. Individual Soundex cards provide the
name of the head of household (or persons of different surnames in the household), race, month and year of birth, age,
birthplaces of parents, occupation, citizenship status, place
of residence by state and county, civil division, city name,
house number, and street number. The cards also list the
volume number, enumeration district, page, and line numbers of the original schedules from which the information
was taken.

The Newberry Library 1900 Chicago Census Finding Aids

The staff at the Newberry Library has developed a system
similar to the one used for the 1880 census to help locate
individuals in the 1900 Chicago census.

The Chicago Public Library Finding Aids

The Social Science and History Division at the Chicago Public
Library has a set of maps to help locate households or individuals by address in the 1900 census in Chicago.

The National Archives-Great Lakes Region Finding Aids

The National Archives-Great Lakes Region has an enumeration district finding aid for the 1900 census for Chicago. This
finding aid was developed by former staff member David S.
Weber. Even though the 1900 Soundex is the most complete
index, occasionally there were transcription omissions or
misspellings which necessitates using maps as finding aids.

The Illinois State Archives has the Soundex for the 1900
federal census, and the Illinois State Library makes it available on interlibrary loan.

1900 U.S. Census Schedules for Cook County, National
Archives Microfilm Reel Numbers:

T623-244 = Ward 1	T623-245 = Wards 1 & 2
T623-246 = Wards 2 & 3	T623-247 = Wards 3 & 4
T623-248 = Wards 4 & 5	T623-249 = Wards 5 & 6

T623-250 = Ward 6

T623-251 = Wards 6 & 7

T623-252 = Ward 7 & 8

T623-253 = Ward 8 & 9

T623-254 = Ward 9 & 10

T623-255 = Ward 10

T623-256 = Ward 10

T623-257 = Ward 10 & 11

T623-258 = Ward 11 & 12

T623-259 = Ward 12

T623-260 = Ward 12 & 13

T623-261 = Ward 13 & 14

T623-262 = Ward 14

T623-263 = Ward 14 & 15

T623-264 = Ward 15

T623-265 = Ward 15 & 16

T623-266 = Ward 16

T623-267 = Ward 16 & 17

T623-268 = Ward 17, 18 & 19

T623-269 = Ward 19

T623-270 = Ward 19,20 and 21

T623-271 = Ward 21 & 22

T623-272 = Ward 22 & 23

T623-273 = Ward 23 & 24

T623-274 = Ward 24 & 25

T623-275 = Ward 25

T623-276 = Ward 25 & 26

T623-277 = Ward 26 & 27

T623-278 = Ward 27 & 28

T623-279 = Ward 27 & 28

T623-280 = Ward 28 & 29

T623-281 = Ward 29

T623-282 = Ward 30

T623-283 = Ward 30-31

T623-284 = Ward 31

T623-285 = Ward 31 & 32

T623-286 = Ward 32

T623-287 = Ward 32 & 33

T623-288 = Ward 33 & 34

T623-289 = Ward 34

T623-290 = Ward 34

T623-291 = Ward 34 & 35

T263-292= Townships of Cook County, including Calumet, Schaumburg, Elk Grove, Evanston, and others.

T263-293 = Hanover, Lemont, Leyden, New Trier and others

T263-294 = Northfield, Orland, Palatine, Palos, Proviso, Thornton, Rich, and others.

1910 U.S. Census Index

The 1910 Soundex and Miracode for Illinois should be the quickest way to locate persons in Chicago or Cook County census schedules. However, there are some problems. Many individuals who were actually enumerated in the census were missed in the transcription to the Miracode cards or names were misspelled in the original census in such a way as to be thrown into the wrong Soundex code. Street addresses are not provided on Miracode cards as they are in previous census years so it is not always as easy to identify individuals with similar names by the index alone. Nevertheless, the Soundex/Miracode is the best starting place to locate persons in the 1910 Census.

An index to city streets and census enumeration districts for 39 cities in the 1910 federal census is reproduced on 50 sheets of microfiche. Chicago is one of the cities which is indexed in this fashion. Entries in the index give a list of Chicago streets and house numbers (new and pre-1909 numbering) and the appropriate enumeration district needed to locate individuals in the census. Named streets, arranged alphabetically, are listed first, followed by numerical streets. Immediately preceding the index portion of each volume is a table listing the enumeration districts covered in that volume with a cross reference to the corresponding volume of the original population schedules. The Chicago street index is contained on microfiche publication M-1283:

Fiche

6   A Street thru Curtis Street
7   Curtis thru Ingraham Ave.
8   Institute Place thru Ogden Ave.
9   Ogden Ave thru Wabash Ave.
10 Wabash Ave. thru 38th Place E.
11 38th Place E. thru 87th Street W.
12 87th Street W. thru 138th Street E.

The Newberry Library and the Chicago Public Library have the 1910 finding aids (maps) that operate on the same principles as do the 1880 and 1900 census finding aids. The Illinois State Archives has the 1910 Miracode for Illinois and the Illinois State Library makes this index available through interlibrary loan service.

1920 U.S. Census Index

The 1920 Soundex for Illinois is usually the most direct route to locating individuals listed on the 58 rolls of microfilm that contain the 1920 census schedules for Chicago and Cook

County. Not everyone enumerated in the census schedules will be found in the Soundex due to omissions, misspelled names, and microfilming flaws.

Questions asked in the 1920 census were:

1. Street, avenue, road, etc.
2. House number or farm
3. Number of dwelling in order of visitation
4. Number of family in order of visitation
5. Name of each person whose place of abode was in this family
6. Relationship of person enumerated to head of the family
7. Home owned or rented
8. If owned, free or mortgage
9. Sex
10. Color or race
11. Age at last birthday
12. Single, married, widowed, or divorced
13. Year of immigration to United States
14. Naturalized or alien
15. If naturalized, year of naturalization
16. Attended school any times since September 1, 1919
17. Whether able to read
18. Whether able to write
19. Person's place of birth
20. Mother tongue
21. Father's place of birth
22. Father's mother tongue
23. Mother's place of birth
24. Mother's mother tongue
25. Able to speak English
26. Trade, profession, or particular kind of work done
27. Industry, business, or establishment in which at work
28. Employer, salary or wage worker, or working on own account

29. Number of farm schedule

1920 U.S. Census and Soundex

The 1920 census for Chicago and Cook County and the 1920 Soundex for Illinois are available at the National Archives-Great Lakes Region, the Newberry Library, and the Chicago Public Library.

Mortality Schedules

Mortality schedules list deaths for the twelve months (June 1st through May 31st) prior to the census for the years 1849, 1859, 1869, and 1879. They provide the deceased person's name, sex, age, color, marital status, place of birth, month of death, profession or occupation, cause of death, and number of days ill.

The 1850 mortality schedule for Illinois is integrated into the census index at the Illinois State Archives. Lowell M. Volkel has published *Illinois Mortality Schedule 1850* in three volumes. Volume I covers Adams through Iroquois counties (and includes Cook County).

The 1860 mortality schedule for Illinois is not included in the census index at the Illinois Archives. However, the schedule has been indexed and is available in book form. Lowell M. Volkel has published *Illinois Mortality Schedule 1860* in five volumes. Volume I covers Adams through Effingham counties (and includes Cook County). Although no specific addresses were given for those who died in Chicago in the original schedules, decedents were enumerated by wards.

An index for the 1870 mortality schedule for Illinois is in progress, but the schedules for all counties beginning with the letters *A* through *Ka* are missing. That, of course, includes Cook County. Other Illinois counties have been indexed by Lowell M. Volkel.

Volkel, Lowell M., transcriber/indexer. *Illinois Mortality Schedule 1850.* 3 vols. Indianapolis, IN: Heritage House (vols. 2-3), 1972

Volkel, Lowell M., transcriber/indexer. *Illinois Mortality Schedule 1860.* 5 vols. Indianapolis, IN: Heritage House, 1979.

Volkel, Lowell M., transcriber/indexer. *Illinois Mortality Schedule 1870.* 2 vols. Indianapolis, IN: Heritage House, 1985

The Newberry Library has mortality schedules for Illinois 1850-1880 on 7 reels of microfilm. (Call # Microfilm 118).

Agriculture Schedules

Agriculture schedules, though primarily useful in statistical studies, help: fill gaps when land and tax records are missing or incomplete; distinguish between men with the same name; and document land holdings, movement and economic changes. The originals for these special schedules for Illinois are at the Illinois State Archives (they have also microfilmed them). The records are not indexed. The Illinois State Archives numbers for Cook County agriculture schedules are: 1850 (31-1); 1860 (31-5); 1870 (31-45); 1880 (31-65).

The Newberry Library has agriculture schedules for Illinois on microfilm (unindexed):

> 1850 Cook County is included on Microfilm 111, Reel 1.
>
> 1860 Cook County is included on Microfilm 112, Reel 2.
>
> 1870 (1865) Cook County is included on Microfilm 113, Reel 4.
>
> 1880 Cook County is included on Microfilm 116, Reel 4.

Manufacturers Schedules

Manufacturers schedules tabulated a variety of information about a business: the owner's name; the establishment location; the number of employees; kind and quality of machinery; capital invested; articles manufactured; annual production; general remarks on the business; and the demand for the products.

The Illinois State Archives has microfilm copies of manufacturers schedules (unindexed) for Illinois. Numbers for Cook County are: 1850 (31-97); 1860 (31-60); 1870 (31-60); 1880 (31-54).

The Newberry Library has 1880 nanufacturers schedules on 6 reels of microfilm.

(Cook County is Call # Microfilm 114, Reel #1)

Illinois State Censuses

Census of the Territory and State of Illinois were taken in the years 1810, 1818, 1820, 1825, 1830, 1835, 1840, 1845, 1855, and 1865. Only a transcript of a portion of the 1810 census has been found. The records of most of the 1818 supplementary census, of the 1825 and 1830, and most of the 1835 and 1840 censuses are missing from the state archives. The 1855 census has been integrated into the census index at the Illinois State Archives. The staff will search this index for two specifically named individuals, including both first and last names, for one census year in a designated county location. The state censuses listed only names of the heads of families. Other family members were represented only by numerical totals in various age categories. The 1865 census is unindexed.

1934 Chicago Census

Upon recommendation to the city council, an ordinance was passed December 12th, 1933, providing for the taking of a census of Chicago beginning January, 1934. Prior discussions made clear that the facts and data of the 1930 federal census were considerably out of date for the purpose of planning needed public works and services.

The census taking project used the services of more than 2,800 unemployed men and women. These workers were recruited from the ranks of unemployed clerks and semi-professionals who were not otherwise provided for in the usual types of Civil Works Administration projects.

The ordinance provided for an official body, designated as the Chicago Census Commission, to be composed of seven members to organize and supervise the taking of census. Edward J. Kelly, the mayor of Chicago was the chairman and Charles S. Newcomb served as director of the special census.

The task of enumerating the population of the second largest city in the United States, with only a few weeks for preparation, was a tremendous undertaking. Unfortunately, all that has been found of the 1934 census is the statistical data. The data was published by Newcomb and Lang, and according to them, the census was completed. Attempts to locate the original manuscripts have been unsuccessful, and it is believed that the originals were destroyed.

Newcomb, Charles S. and Richard O. Lang, eds. *Census Data of the City of Chicago, 1934* Chicago: The University of Chicago Press, 1934.

A Selected Bibliography of Census Information Sources

Eakle, Arlene, and Johni Cerny. *The Source: A Guidebook of American Genealogy.* Salt Lake City: Ancestry, 1984.

> A comprehensive chapter on census records, availability and use.

Kirkham, E. Kay. *A Handy Guide to Record Searching in the Larger Cities of the United States.* Logan, UT: Everton, 1974.

> Includes 1850-1855, and 1878 Ward Maps of Chicago.

National Archives Trust Fund Board. *Federal Population Censuses, 1790-1890.* Washington, DC, 1979.

_____. *The 1910 Federal Population Census.* Washington, DC, 1982.

_____. *The 1920 Federal Population Census.* Washington, DC, 1991

National Archives and Record Service, *1900 Federal Population Census.* Washington, DC, 1978.

The preceding four references are catalogs which provide census roll numbers and prices for microfilm copies. Catalogs are available for purchase from the:

National Archives Trust Fund
  NEPS Dept. 735
  P.O. Box 100793
  Atlanta, GA 30384

United States. Department of Commerce, Bureau of the Census. *Twenty Censuses—Population and Housing Questions 1790-1980.* Washington, DC, 1978.

United States. Department of Commerce, Bureau of the Census. *Age Search Information.* Washington, DC, 1979.

Volkel, Lowell. Indexes compiled by Lowell Volkel are published and available from:

Ye Olde Genealogie Shoppe
9605 Vandergriff Road
P.O. Box 39128
Indianapolis, IN 46239
(317-862-3330)

SECTION EIGHT

Chicago Historical Society Library (CHS)

"History teaches everything, even the future." This conviction, attributed to Lamartine, was shared by twelve men who, under the leadership of William Barry, formed the Chicago Historical Society (CHS) in 1856. Their goal was to create an organization whose purpose was, "to institute and encourage historical inquiry, to collect and preserve materials of history, and to spread historical information, especially concerning the Northwestern States." Accordingly, a large portion of the materials collected during the early years concerned general American history as well as the history of other localities. Through the years, the CHS has placed increasing emphasis on Chicago as the predominant, though not exclusive, subject for its collections. Conscious of the importance of obtaining recent materials, Barry criticized some historical societies for being interested primarily in "olden relics." His preference was for, "the broad and teeming harvest of the present." The CHS curators still reflect this concern as they acquire the documents of contemporary social, political, and economic institutions.

For the first few years, the CHS rented rooms in various buildings, but as collections grew, the founders had to make plans for a permanent home. The first home for the CHS opened on November 19, 1868 in a building on the northwest

corner of Ontario and Dearborn. Three years later, the structure, and all of its contents, were destroyed in the Great
Chicago Fire. Collecting began again, and the CHS rebuilt a
new and massive Romanesque building (now a nightclub) on
the original site in 1896. In 1920, the CHS purchased the
fabulous collection of Charles H. Gunther, a Chicago candy
manufacturer. Gunther had acquired a wide variety of objects
including fifteenth-century books, an entire Civil War prison,
Lincoln's carriage, and a printer's typesetting stick used by
Ben Franklin. The sizeable Gunther collection required a
much larger facility to house it. In 1932 the CHS moved to its
present location in Lincoln Park.

Location and Hours

You can contact or visit the CHS at this address:

The Chicago Historical CHS
Clark Street at North Avenue
Chicago, IL 60614-6099
(312-642-4600; FAX: 312-266-2077)

The exhibition galleries are open Mon-Sat. from 9:30 A.M. to
4:30 P.M. and Sun noon to 5:00 P.M. The research collections
are open Tues-Sat from 9:30 A.M. TO 4:30 P.M.

The CHS has a store on the premises. In addition to a wide
assortment of books on subjects related to the CHS's collections, the store has one of the best collections of Chicago and
Illinois books for sale.

Chicago Historical CHS Collection

The CHS collection is contained in seven curatorial departments:

*   The Charles F. Murphy Architectural Study Center
*   Decorative and Industrial Arts
*   The Hope B. McCormick Costume Center
*   Paintings and Sculpture

* The Library
* Archives and Manuscripts
* Prints and Photographs

The CHS collection includes more than 12,000 costume items, 1,500 paintings and sculptures, and 10,000 artifacts.

From a waistcoat worn by George Washington to the extensive Civil War and Lincoln collections, American history is represented at the CHS by a variety of artifacts, exhibitions and publications. The oldest Chicago-related item in the manuscript collection is a letter written by Robert Cavalier de La Salle from "Checagou" and dated September 1, 1683.

Because the CHS is devoted to the preservation of all aspects of Chicago's rich heritage, its collection of artifacts and writings span a period of time that ranges from the Fort Dearborn period to contemporary Chicago. The Chicago History Galleries provide a glimpse of the city's tumultuous past through its exhibits of costumes, photographs, and objects from everyday life. These exhibits allow you to "meet" personalities like Al Capone, Richard J. Daley, Walter Payton, and others who have made Chicago famous.

Research Collections

Almost all of the exhibits, educational programs, and publications created by the CHS are based on its research collections. All aspects of life in Chicago, from the early 19th century to the present, are represented including business and industry, labor, social welfare, politics, architecture, and music. There is a diverse assortment of objects; Chicago directories, trade catalogs, architectural drawings, and TV news film are a few examples.

The CHS does not collect genealogical material per se, its holdings can be of great value to a genealogical researcher. The resources that are the most useful are likely to be found in the Library, Archives and Manuscripts, and Prints and Photographs departments.

The Library

The Library Department at the CHS includes more than 120,000 books and pamphlets, 20,000 volumes of newspapers and periodicals, and 10,000 maps and atlases. While Chicago dominates the library collection, other areas of Cook County and Illinois are well represented. The collection includes the basic sources: general histories of the state, counties and towns; traveler's journals and descriptions; accounts of important organizations and agencies; and similar materials. The library does acquire, on a selective basis, some materials concerning the Civil War and Abraham Lincoln.

Many Chicago publications were lost in the Great Fire of 1871. Some of these (and copies lost in other fires) were replaced with duplicates which survived outside of the city. Chicago newspapers and directories are examples of the replacements.

Most of the holdings are stored in closed-stacks. You need to request items of interests from one of the staff in the Reading Room, and the requested materials will be retrieved for you.

The Library Reference Collection

The extensive Library Reference Collection contains books and articles assembled to answer basic questions about Chicago history. The collection is located in the CHS's main Reading Room for easy access, and the card catalog is still the primary finding aid.

The CHS's Library has some unique sources for researchers interested in biographical information: membership directories and yearbooks from Chicago clubs and associations, high school yearbooks, Civil War regimental histories for Illinois, newsletters from Chicago companies, anniversary (centennial, jubilee, etc.) publications from various organizations, and others. All can be located by using the card catalog.

Newspapers

Files of Chicago newspapers are very extensive, but not complete. The newspaper collection has Chicago's first newspaper, the *Chicago Democrat*, from its inaugural issue in 1833 until it ceased publication in 1861. Many other now extinct newspapers and ethnic and foreign-language newspaper files are there. A list of the newspaper microfilm holdings is available on each table in the Reading Room. There is also a clipping file which consists of about forty-four file drawers of clippings selected from the major Chicago newspapers and arranged by subject. Articles in the clipping file date from the 1930s, and clippings are added to the file on a regular basis. A list of the subject headings used to organize the file is available on each table in the Reading Room.

Directories

City directories from 1839 to 1917 are kept in the Reading Room; these directories attempted to list every individual and every business in Chicago. The city directories ceased consecutive publication after 1917; however, directories were published in 1923 and 1928-29. Many of the original books are crumbling due to time, paper content, and heavy use; consequently, they have been replaced with microfilm versions. For directory information after 1917 you must rely on the telephone directories which are available on microfilm or microfiche.

The CHS holds reverse or "criss-cross" directories arranged by address for the years 1928, 1950, 1952, 1953, 1978 to the present. Also located on the open shelves are the Who's Who in Chicago and the Chicago Blue Books which provide information on Chicago's more prominent residents.

Many directories are not located in the Reading Room. These holdings can be identified by looking in the card catalog under the name of a city or county and noting those with the subheading "Directories" (for example, Evanston, Illinois).

First Facts File

The First Facts file is a compiled list of some of Chicago's "firsts." This file can be found in drawer 559 of the card catalog.

Maps and Atlases

The map and atlas collection contains about 150 Illinois county atlases. There are also approximately, 4,000 nineteenth-and twentieth century maps; half of the maps cover Chicago and the other half cover Illinois counties. Special maps for Chicago show the boundaries for wards, school districts, park district land, cemeteries. Maps that show boundary changes for wards, the city, and surrounding areas were published annually; these maps are listed chronologically. The collection of fire insurance atlases for Chicago is one of the largest in the area; there are also fire insurance atlases for several suburbs and other Illinois towns.

The library has a bibliography (*Checklist of Printed Maps of the Middle West to 1900.* Vol. 4, Chicago: Chicago Historical Society) which lists the library holdings of nineteenth century published maps. In addition, a notebook in the Reading Room lists the nineteenth and twentieth century unpublished Chicago maps available in the library.

Archives and Manuscripts

The Archives and Manuscripts Department at the CHS contains 50,000 pieces of printed ephemera such as theater and concert programs, 14,000 broadsides and posters, and 10,000,000 manuscripts which include correspondence, and other records of individuals, institutions, and organizations. The CHS's extensive holdings of manuscripts constitute one of its most valuable research resources. These collections contain the correspondence, memoranda, internal reports, and other unpublished files accumulated through the years by Chicago organizations, institutions, firms and individuals.

The collection contains documents that originated from quite diverse sources; Senator Paul H. Douglas, the Illinois Manufacturers Association, the United Charities of Chicago, Welfare Council of Metropolitan Chicago, Jewish Community Centers of Chicago, Afro-American Police League, and the Polish-American Democratic Organization are examples.

Among the treasures in this collection are:

* Documents dated as early as 1635 that are related to French explorations and settlements near the Great Lakes and the Native Americans in the Chicago area.

* Records of the Illinois and Michigan Canal and the early Galena and Chicago Union Railroad.

* Records of contemporary institutions and organizations.

Because manuscript collections provide the first-hand accounts in much more detail than most publications, they are in great demand by serious researchers. You should call for information about access to the research materials in this department.

Prints and Photographs

The Prints and Photographs Department is open by appointment only (312-642-5035 ext. 325). The collection in this department contains over 50,000 prints, 900,000 photographs, and 9,900 reels of microfilm. There are over a million images, in the form of photographs, prints (engravings, lithographs, etc.), broadsides, and motion picture films which relate to Chicago history from the early nineteenth century to the present. There are significant holdings related to American history in general. The collection is the largest source for pictorial information concerning the history of Chicago and the surrounding area.

The Prints and Photographs collection includes:

The Hedrich-Blessing Collection of negatives from 1930-1970 (national scope)

The Raymond Trowbridge Collection of negatives—1920s & 1930s (local scope)

The J. W. Taylor Photograph Collection—1880-1890 (local scope)

Kaufmann and Fabry Company photographs of Chicago area—1920-1930

Aerial views of Chicago to each decade since the 1930s

SECTION NINE

Chicago Landmarks

Chicago landmarks are those buildings, areas, and objects officially designated by the Chicago City Council upon recommendation of the Commission on Chicago Historical and Architectural Landmarks and endorsement by the Council's Committee on Cultural Development and Historical Landmark Preservation. The Commission insures the preservation of these landmarks by reviewing applications for building permits to make sure that no adverse changes are made.

These landmarks include:

Jane Addams' Hull-House and Dining Hall: The best known social settlement in the nation was founded here in 1889.

Alta Vista Terrace District: These forty row houses were built about 1900 by Samuel Eberly Gross, a real-estate developer.

Astor Street District: The heart of the Gold Coast where millionaires built some of the city's most elaborate townhouses.

Auditorium Building: The first major commission of Adler and Sullivan was a combined theater, hotel, and office block.

Emil Bach House: A late Prairie school design by Frank Lloyd Wright in which he applied that style to a small urban residence.

Carson Pirie Scott & Company Building: Louis Sullivan's last major commission, considered by many to be his masterpiece.

Chapin and Gore Building: Schmidt and Garden designed this building with its superb brickwork and terra-cotta ornamentation.

James Charnley House: This modern design by Adler and Sullivan changed the face of residential architecture.

Chicago Board of Trade Building: One of the city's most striking and best Art Deco skyscrapers.

Chicago Public Library Cultural Center: Civic pride created this monument; it has fabulous mosaics and Tiffany domes.

City Hall-County Building: Since 1853 the city and county have shared a building on this site, once called Courthouse Square.

Henry B. Clarke House: Chicago's oldest building, built in 1836, and its only example of Greek revival architecture.

Dearborn Street Station: One of the oldest train stations in the country, this one dates from 1885.

Francis J. Dewes House: A wealthy Prussian-born brewer built this house recalling the land of his youth.

Stephen A. Douglas Memorial: The site of this tomb was once part of the Douglas estate, Oakenwald.

Melissa Ann Elam House: An imposing 1903 structure, it became a residence for single black working women in 1930.

Fine Arts Building: Built for the Studebaker carriage company and later a major center of Chicago's artistic life.

First Baptist Congregational Church: Gurdon P. Randall, one of the city's first architects, designed this 1870 church.

Fisher Building: Gothic details, mythical creatures, and marvelous animals decorate this essentially modern structure.

Getty Tomb: Louis Sullivan was the architect for this graceful and dignified mausoleum.

Glessner House: Chicago's first designated landmark and its last surviving design by Henry Hobson Richardson.

Walter Burley Griffin Place District: Chicago's largest concentration of Prairie school houses.

Isidore H. Heller House: An important early work by Frank Lloyd Wright, the house was built in 1897.

Holy Trinity Orthodox Cathedral and Rectory: Louis Sullivan here used traditional Russian forms.

Hutchinson Street District: Two blocks that show the changes in residential architecture around 1900.

Jackson Boulevard District: A one-block stretch is virtually all that remains of the once fashionable Near West Side.

Jewelers' Building: The oldest surviving design by Adler and Sullivan is a small loft building from 1882.

K.A.M.-Isaiah Israel Temple: The style of this 1924 synagogue derives from ancient Byzantine architecture.

Kenwood District: The "Lake Forest of the South Side" boasts some of the city's grandest homes.

Krause Music Store: Louis Sullivan designed the facade of this small store which sits like a jewel box on Lincoln Avenue.

Bryan Lathrop House: The New York firm of McKim, Mead and White designed this fine Georgian revival house in 1882.

Longwood Drive District: Grand homes set on large lots along a high ridge make this one of Chicago's most pleasant streets.

Albert F. Madlener House: An elegant Prairie school design of 1902 by Hugh Garden and Richard Schmidt.

Manhattan Building: Chicago's oldest building with skeleton construction, the basis of the skyscraper.

Marquette Building: Holabird and Roche's 1894 design strongly influenced the form of office buildings that came after it.

McCormick Row House District: Built as part of the seminary endowed by reaper inventor Cyrus Hall McCormick.

Mid-North District: Tall and narrow brick houses march in rows down the tree-lined streets of this district.

Monadnock Block: Its north half marked the end of tall masonry buildings; its south half used skeleton construction.

Navy Pier: The pier was built between 1913 and 1916 to be a shipping and recreational facility.

Samuel M. Nickerson House: This early Chicago mansion is stately outside and lavish within.

Old Chicago Water Tower District: Chicagoans have a special fondness for this survivor of the 1871 fire.

Old Colony Building: Its rounded projecting corners were once a common feature of early skyscrapers.

Old Town Triangle District: Chicago's Greenwich Village resembles a village with blocks of small Chicago cottages.

Pilgrim Baptist Church: Adler and Sullivan produced a striking design for this structure, originally a synagogue.

Prairie Avenue Historic District: A handful of houses survive from the period when this was the city's Gold Coast.

Quinn Chapel: The oldest black congregation in Chicago, founded in 1844, built this church in 1892.

Reid, Murdoch and Company Building: This structure houses the Landmarks Commission and other city departments.

Reliance Building: Its glass facades proclaim its skeleton construction; probably the most advanced structure of its day.

Frederick C. Robie House: Frank Lloyd Wright once referred to this 1909 house as his best residential design.

Robert W. Roloson Houses: The only row houses designed

by Frank Lloyd Wright known to have been constructed.

Rookery Building: A rugged nineteenth-century building, bold in its form and graceful in its ornamentation.

Rosehill Cemetery Entrance: Designed in the castellated Gothic style that Boyington later used for the Water Tower.

George Washington-Robert Morris-Haym Salomon Memorial: The last sculpture designed by Lorado Taft.

Carl Schurz High School: Dwight Perkins combined the Chicago and Prairie styles in the design of this outstanding school.

Second Presbyterian Church: Built in 1874 and reconstructed after a fire in 1900, this church is particularly noted for its stained-glass windows.

James A. Sexton School: This 1882 building was one of the first high schools in the city and is now one of the oldest school buildings in Chicago.

Site of the First Self-sustaining Controlled Nuclear Chain Reaction: A sculpture by Henry Moore recalls the inauguration of the atomic age in 1942.

Site of Fort Dearborn: Built in 1803 and rebuilt after the Massacre of 1812, Fort Dearborn made possible the settlement of Chicago.

Site of the Origin of the Chicago Fire of 1871: A sculpture and the Chicago Fire Academy mark the site where the terrible fire began.

South Pullman District: In the 1880's, Solon Beman designed America's first completely planned company town; in 1898, it became part of the City of Chicago.

Theurer/Wrigley House: The house is one of Lake View's last remaining free-standing mansions facing Lincoln Park.

Three Arts Club: Young women studying the arts have found a home at the club since 1914.

Union Stock Yard Gate: This stone gate with its carved bull's head for many years marked the main entrance to Chicago's Union Stock Yards.

Chicago Public Library

In 1834, a year after Chicago was founded, the predecessor of the Chicago Public Library was established as a subscription library. The library's collection had grown to 30,000 volumes when the Chicago Fire of 1871 destroyed it entirely. Following the fire, an appeal was made in British Parliament to British authors, publishers, and societies to contribute their works to a new library for Chicago. In response to the plea, over 8,000 volumes were shipped to Chicago. Following the passage of the Free Public Library Act of Illinois by the legislature in 1872, the City Council enacted an ordinance establishing the Chicago Public Library on April 3, 1872. For several years, the library's collection was housed in various temporary locations, including inside an old water tank on the site now occupied by the Rookery Building. In 1883, the City Council chose Dearborn Park as the site for a library building which would also house a Civil War museum. Construction on the library began in 1892 as Chicago was coming of age culturally. The building is a monumental structure based on classical Greek and Italian Renaissance precedents with a magnificently decorated interior. The Tiffany Company created the intricate mosaics of colored stone, mother-of-pearl, and favrile glass, and the two large stained-glass domes within the building.

By 1922, there was concern that the expanding library collection would outgrow the space in the building and a new or expanded facility would be needed. However, nothing was done until the late 1980s when construction of a new library building began. The new library, named for former mayor Harold Washington, opened in October 1991.

The old library building was restored and is the Chicago Public Library Cultural Center which is used for special exhibits, functions, and to house a portion of the library's permanent collections. The Cultural Center was designated as a Chicago Landmark in 1976.

In 1895, the Chicago Public Library entered into an informal agreement with the Newberry Library and the John Crerar Library. The two privately endowed institutions were to collect rare and scholarly materials in their respective fields of specialization (humanities by the Newberry Library and science and technology by the John Crerar Library). The Chicago Public Library assumed the responsibility of fulfilling the diverse reading and informational requirements of the general public. However, it is developing an extensive collection in the Social Sciences, an area not covered by any other public library in the city.

As the major public library in the metropolitan area, the Chicago Public Library serves as one of the research and reference centers established under the Illinois Library Act of 1965. Under this Act, the Chicago Public Library and its branches constitute a consolidated library system.

Location and Hours

The Chicago Public Library
Harold Washington Library Center
400 South State Street
Chicago, IL 60605
Hours: Monday-Thursday: 9:00 A.M.—7:00 P.M.; Friday: 9:00 A.M.—6:00 P.M.; Saturday: 9:00 A.M.—5:00 P.M.

General Information Services Division—3rd floor (747-4300)

Social Sciences Division—5th & 6th floors (312-747-4600)

Government Publications Department—5th floor (312-747-4500)

Special Collections Department—9th floor (312-747-4960)

General Information Services Division

Newspapers and General Periodicals

Located in the Newspapers and General Periodical Center in this division are the library's collections of newspapers, periodicals, indexes, and almanacs covering a broad range of subjects in many different languages. The newspaper collection has approximately 300 current papers from every state in the U.S. and papers from more than 40 foreign countries. Many U.S. and Chicago ethnic newspapers are received as well as community newspapers from Chicago and the suburbs.

Retrospective newspaper holdings include full microfilm runs of the major Chicago newspapers, the *New York Times* and the *Times of London*. Indexes for the *New York Times* from 1851, the *Times of London* from 1790, and the *Chicago Tribune* from 1972 can also be found in this unit. There are complete holdings (some dating back to the mid-nineteenth century) of many general magazines, including the various weekly news magazines. Complete runs of almanacs (the *World Almanac, Year Book,* and others) provide valuable tables, charts, and statistical data.

Special research materials are available. For example, there is the Foreign Language Press Survey, the Underground Newspaper Microfilm Collection, and the micro-card collection of early American newspapers, 1704-1820.

Social Sciences Division

The Social Sciences Division on the 5th and 6th floors has resources on microfilm to help trace the movements of ancestors.

Chicago Ancestors

There are microfilm resources to help trace family members from Chicago:

Chicago City Directories, 1839, 1843-1917, 1923, 1928/29.

Chicago Telephone Directories, 1878-1971.

U. S. Personal Name Census, Chicago, 1850, 1860, 1870, 1880, (1890 census records were destroyed in a fire in Washington and are not available), 1900, 1910, and 1920. (1920 for all of Illinois.)

Soundex 1900 Population Schedule: Illinois.

Miracode 1910 Population Schedule: Illinois.

Soundex 1920 Population Schedule: Illinois.

U. S. Ancestors

The *United State Guide to Family Records: Where and How to Write for Family Records in the U. S. and Outlying Areas* is available at the Social Sciences reference desk. It provides information on where to locate sources for birth, marriage, divorce, and death records. You may also want to examine *Genealogies in the Library of Congress Bibliography* (call number: 016929 Un3g) and its supplement (Z5319. U53). This reference lists family histories that have already been written.

Ancestors From Other Countries

If you are researching your family back to their country of origin, be aware that record keeping was quite variable from century to century and from country to country. The Social Sciences Division has information and a number of publications on genealogical searching in other countries. Examples of helpful titles include:

Passengers to America, call number: CS68. P37 1977.

Ship Passenger Lists, call number: CS68. R37 1978.

Passenger and Immigration Lists Index, 3 vols. call number CS68. F54.

Index to Passenger Lists of Vessels Arriving at Baltimore, Maryland, 1833-1866, microfilm.

Index to Passenger Lists of Vessels Arriving at Baltimore, Maryland, 1820-1897, microfilm.

Index to Passenger Lists of Vessels Arriving at Boston, Massachusetts, 1849-1891, microfilm.

Index to Passenger Lists of Vessels Arriving at Philadelphia, Pennsylvania, 1800-1906, microfilm.

Government Publications Department

The Government Publications Department on the 5th floor has United States government publications that are related to military affairs or public office. There are no archival records.

Census Information

The *Census Records Guide,* U. S. Census Bureau. Age Research Information, 1981 is a reference that explains how the Census Bureau's population census records can be used to furnish personal data about individuals.

Family, Employment, and Public Service Records

After WWI, Congress provided funds so that mothers and widows might view the final resting place of their sons and husbands:

Pilgrimage for the Mothers and Widows of Soldiers, Sailors, and Marines of the American Forces Now Interred in the Cemeteries of Europe. Call number: H. doc 71-140 (Serial Set 9225).

In addition to the name and address of the woman qualified to make the pilgrimage, this reference gives the name of the deceased, the rank and organization of the deceased, and the cemetery in which the individual is buried.

Registers of Public Employees, *Official Register of the United States*, Call number: S1. 11 (1832-1859); I1. 25 (1861-1905); C3. 10 (1919-1932); CS1. 31 (1933-1959), also on microfilm (1817-1959).

Included in this register are the civil, military, and judicial officials in the United States government, their office, where employed, and sometimes the state of birth. Earlier editions also listed the names of postmasters.

Military Records

Historical Register of the United State Army, from its Organization. Call number: W3. 11 (1789-1889)

This reference provides information about officers in all branches of military service, including the volunteer staff, as well as enlisted men. Includes state where born (if known), state where appointment was made, brief listing of promotions and appointments, and date of death. A second edition, compiled by Francis Bernard Heitman, covering the years 1789-1903, is part of the Special Collections Department on the 9th floor.

War of the Rebellion: Official Records of the Union and Confederate Armies. Call number: W45. 8. Located in Reference Area.

This study includes an index to assist in locating individuals. The records place an individual in a certain time and location during the Civil War.

Maps and Gazetteers

The U. S. Board of Geographic Names and gazetteers are located in the Reference Area.

Each gazetteer covers either a single country or a group of countries. Place names, including those which have changed, are listed along with the latitude and longitude of the site.

Located in the Map Area are the U. S. Geological Survey Topographical Maps (7. 5' series). The Chicago Public Library has maps of each state and a quadrangle index to accompany them. Maps show location of most cemeteries and churches, as well as cities, towns, and villages.

General Indexes

Located in the Reference Area, the *Checklist of United States Public Documents, 1789-1909*, provides annotations and call numbers for documents issued by the various departments of the U. S. government. The documents are arranged by issuing agency, but there is not a subject index. This reference includes many registers and listings of personnel in the military and government departments.

Also located in the Reference Area is the *CIS U. S. Serial Set Index, 1789-1969* from the Congressional Information Service. Included in this index to Congressional reports and documents are references to petitions by individuals requesting funds, military pensions, or other types of assistance from the U. S. government. Entries are listed by individual's name or by subject heading.

State of Illinois Documents

There are two resources that may be of interest to you:

Illinois. Secretary of State, State Archives. *Archives Marriage Record Index.* 1987. 26 microfiche.

> This index provides an alphabetical listing of names (including the name of the spouse), and where applicable, the license number, date of license, county where applied for, and archival record control number.

Illinois. Secretary of State, State Archives. *Public Domain Sales Land Tract Record Listing.* 1984. Each section contains 144 microfiche.

This second resource has several sections. The first section is an alphabetical listing by name of the purchaser followed by a brief description of the location of the land, the number of acres bought, the price per acre, total price, the date purchased, and a reference to the volume and page in archives records. The second section is arranged by country and then purchaser's name. The third section is arranged by geographical location (county, meridian, range, township, and section). Most listings are for sales before 1870.

City of Chicago Documents

The *City Council, Proceedings*, 1861-Present; Volumes from 1921 to present are located in the Reference Area. In addition to city business, these volumes include memorials or congratulatory remarks to persons residing in Chicago who attained some measure of achievement. Also included are claims of individuals against the city. There is often a subject index for a particular volume including the names of the individuals mentioned.

The manuals, *Bureau of Statistics, City Manual, 1908-1916*, are a compendium of information on city government and politics. Each volume includes the names of officers of city agencies, political party committees, presidents of ward clubs, superintendents of wards, and officers of clubs, such as the Union League and Iroquois Club. Some names are listed in a typescript index to the set of manuals.

Education

Chicago Board of Education, *Annual Report*, 1867-1868 to 1925-1926.

In the volumes up through 1894-1895, the reports include names of high school graduates and the high school graduated from. The names of the members of the Board of Education are also included.

Special Collections Department

The Special Collections Department on the 9th floor contains resources on the World's Columbian Exposition in 1933, book arts, book collecting, Chicago authors, Chicago history, Chicago theater, the Chicago Public Library Archives, and the Mayor Harold Washington Archives, as well as the collections listed below.

The Reading Room is open:

Monday, Tuesday, and Thursday—Noon—6:00 P.M.

Wednesday, Friday, and Saturday—Noon—4:00 P.M.

Neighborhood History Research Collection

The Neighborhood History Research Collection contains manuscripts, printed material, and over 6,000 photographs. Most of the material was collected by neighborhood historical societies that flourished during the 1930s and 1940s. Biographical information files are in almost every sub-collection. These biographical files are accessed by non-published guides available in the Reading Room.

The Westside and Southside neighborhoods included are: Austin, Belmont-Cragin, Calumet, East Garfield Park, Lawndale-Crawford, Logan Square, Lower West Side, North Lawndale, Portage Park, Pullman, Roseland, South Chicago, South Lawndale, South Shore, West Garfield Park, West Side, West Town, and Woodlawn.

Similar collections for Chicago's Northside neighborhoods are located at the Sulzer Regional Library

4455 North Lincoln Avenue
Chicago, IL 60625
(312-728-8652)

Civil War Research Collection

The Civil War and American History Research Collection was formally established in 1975 with the assistance of the Chicago Civil War Round Table. The Grand Army of the Republic research material was the basis of the collection, and included a rich variety of exhibit and research materials: manuscripts, documents, broadsides, photographs, sheet music published, reminiscences, official records, and other contemporary and retrospective accounts of the Civil War. The Grand Army of the Republic collections also included a rich collection of historic artifacts: firearms, swords, military accessories, military uniforms, medical and musical instruments. This collection presents a very personal look at the Civil War: letters from young recruits to their families, diaries, and personal narratives. Portions of the Civil War and American History Research Collection are on display twice a year in a rotating permanent exhibition entitled "A Nation Divided: The War Between the States, 1861-1865."

Special Collections holds a large regimental history collection from all states which participated in the war. Many regimental histories include complete rosters of their soldiers. Some examples of references related to the Civil War are:

Official Records of the Union and Confederate Navies in the War of the Rebellion. An indexed 30-volume set.

Official Army Register of the Volunteer Forces of the United States Army. An indexed 8-volume set.

Index to Compiled Service Records of Volunteer Union Soldiers. Provides an alphabetical listing, state by state, of all volunteer Union soldiers who served in the war, including African-Americans. (microfilm)

Chicago Authors and Imprints Collection

The Chicago Authors and Imprints Collection features early and private press editions of major Chicago authors (Sandburg, Dreiser, Hecht, Farrell, Starrett, and others) together with related manuscripts, advance copies, and page proofs, as well as works by lesser known authors. Pre-1900 imprints and private press productions provide additional resources for studying Chicago's literary and publishing history.

Chicago Theater Arts and History Collection

The Chicago Theater Arts and History Collection includes the Goodman Theater archives (1925-present), theater scrapbooks, thousands of programs, playbills, and broadsides for the legitimate theater, vaudeville, and other amusements (1847-present).

The World's Columbian Exposition Collection is a significant and heavily used research collection of several hundred pamphlets, photographs, published volumes, and manuscript papers of Fair officials James Ellsworth and George Woodbury. There is also a small collection on the Century of Progress Exposition.

Chicago Public Library Archives

The Chicago Public Library Archives constitute the basic source of information on the institution itself, comprising of over 600 linear feet of official and unofficial records created since its founding in 1872.

Book Arts, History and Collecting

The resources in this field include current and back issues of major out-of-print guides, leading antiquarian book and manuscript serials, sales catalogs issued by major dealers and auction houses, and catalogs of major private libraries. The monograph collection includes major works on the history of printing, publishing, antiquarian book selling, bookmaking, and conservation.

Church and Religious Records

Church records are acceptable supplements to civil vital records and are considered primary sources in their own right. These sources fill gaps where official records are missing or were never kept, and they often include important facts not recorded in any other source.

Finding the records of the religious congregation to which an ancestor belonged in the Chicago metropolitan area is especially difficult because of the great number of churches and synagogues supported by the enormous population for over 150 years. Chicago, like the rest of the country, has been a mixture of national and ethnic groups since the beginning. Consequently, there are great differences in their philosophies and religious affiliations.

Population, geography, and ethnicity are confusing enough; but to complicate matters further, different denominations kept different types of records. For example, presbyteries transferred membership records with the departure of the member. Immigrants commonly chose to worship in their own tongues and often went far out of their neighborhoods to find the congenial atmosphere of the national parish. Churches, as well as people, responded to the dynamics of the city, some closing, consolidating, or moving as neighborhoods changed, while others shifted from their ethnic orientation to accommodate new circumstances. Thus, if you are having difficulty tracing the church or synagogue of an ancestor, you might save time by backtracking to study the history of that particular religion in the locale of interest. Though finding religious records may be difficult, it usually repays the time and effort spent. Church records generally predate civil records and often supply valuable information such as birth dates, names of parents, names of sponsors, and sometimes even the town of origin from which individuals emigrated.

An invaluable guide for research in this area is the Historical Records Survey of the Works Progress Administration (WPA). WPA workers inventoried church and public records extant in the 1930s for many areas in the United States. Their lists for urban churches are especially valuable. For the Chicago area, consult: *Guide to Church Vital Statistics Records in Illinois*, prepared by the Historical Records Survey, Chicago, Illinois, 1942. It is available at the Newberry Library (Call # D2896.41).

Although dated, this source still serves to identify churches and records that survived the Chicago Fire of 1871 and outlines existing collections. A typical entry for church vital records would contain the name and address of the institution at the time of the publication, ethnic orientation, and comprehensive dates for each type of vital record. If the organization housed documents from other congregations, the survey noted this and gave a range of dates. A summary of baptisms, marriages, and death records follows for each. In most cases founding dates are listed.

In cases where a church affiliation is not known, other records may serve to locate them. A marriage license from Cook County, for example, will note the name and sometimes the address of the person officiating at the marriage. By consulting a Chicago directory for the same year, the residence of the clergyman may be established, thereby connecting him to a particular congregation. Likewise, religious affiliation can often be determined by death information. If an individual is buried in a cemetery of a particular denomination it is probable that he or she was a member of that denomination. Often that information can be taken a step further when cemetery or obituary information reveals the name of a clergyman which may link the deceased to a church.

Even probate records have been known to provide clues to church affiliation. It is not unusual for people to leave property to their favorite charitable institutions and mention of this is often included in a will. Accountings of funeral expenditures are frequently included in a probate file, and may also provide invaluable clues which lead to church records. Funeral director's bills, for example, are often quite detailed and frequently note that carriages were hired for a named minister for a graveside ritual or that carriages were hired for the trip from a particular church to the cemetery. The clues mentioned are not consistently found in these unlikely sources, but an awareness that the possibility of determining religious affiliation by use of these other records makes them worthy of mention.

There are an increasing number of indexes being created for church records. Area genealogical societies are continually working to preserve and make available church records by means of their indexing projects. These indexes and other printed sources relating to religious communities, such as histories published to commemorate the anniversary of a congregation, will also be a means of identifying the place of worship and respective record collections.

Early county histories, ethnic histories, and biographical sketches also provide other background on religious institutions in the local area. Through these descriptions you can trace the church, its development, and ethnic makeup. Modern studies also are a tremendous help, and their bibliographies enhance their utility. In the book, *Chicago Churches and Synagogues* (Chicago: Loyola University Press, 1981) compiled by George Lane and Alginantes Kezys, 125 houses of worship, with architectural, historical, or social significance, are singled out. Lane and Kezys also provide a detailed description and history of each building, its congregation, ethnic classification, architectural attributes, and locality by exact address and area of city. The acknowledgements and notes contain numerous sources you can use to locate denominational repositories.

Even though there is no comprehensive guide to American church records, two major works that deal with church records are: August B. Suelflow's, *A Preliminary Guide to Church Records and Repositories*, a standard reference of denominational archives; and, for those with a Roman Catholic interest, the *Official Catholic Directory*, published annually since 1886 by P. J. Kenedy and Sons, which lists American dioceses, parishes, institutions, and their addresses. In some instances, successor repositories for closed churches are given. Major libraries and Catholic churches are likely to maintain copies of these volumes. For churches that changed names and denominated affiliation, consult Julia Pettee, *List of Churches: Official Forms of the Names for Denominated Bodies with Brief Description and Historical Notes* (Chicago: American Library Association, 1948).

Some church records are available in book or microform. The Newberry Library in Chicago has a large collection of sources from the eastern United States as well as from local institutions. Area genealogical society publications, which often include church information and indexes, are usually placed at the Newberry Library as soon as they become available. The Genealogical Society of Utah of The Church of Jesus Christ of Latter-day Saints (LDS Church) has filmed church registers from numerous localities including the Cook County area, and its branch library system allows access in every state to these records.

The Newberry Library has been designated as a repository for microfilms of Catholic church registers which are available as a result of a program sponsored by the Genealogical Society of Utah and the Council of Northeastern Illinois Genealogical Societies. The program placed microfilm copies of the registers of the Catholic parishes of the Archdiocese of Chicago as well as other large denominational collections at the Newberry Library. Also available at family history centers (LDS Church) and the Newberry Library is the International Genealogical Index (IGI) which is rich in church registers.

Used in combination with other sources, church vital records may help illuminate even the most perplexing problems. For example, Karl Johnson was known to have lived at a certain address in Chicago for several years near the beginning of the twentieth century, but his death date was unknown. *The Works Progress Administration Index to Chicago Deaths* indicated that he died at that address in 1911. This death year led to a certificate which in turn pointed to the cemetery records. The cemetery gave the officiating minister's name, and a directory search identified him as belonging to the Swedish Covenant Church. It had since moved, but inquiries at another congregation of the same denomination pinpointed the new location of the records. Not only did the church have many records on the family, it had a jubilee book with biographical sketches which included Karl Johnson as a founding member. The biography gave his exact birthplace, his date of arrival in this country, and his prior residence before settling in Chicago in 1884.

Selected Bibliography: Church Sources

Andreas, Alfred T. *History of Cook County, Illinois*. Chicago, 1884.

Eakle, Arlene, and Johni Cerny, eds. *The Source: A Guidebook of American Genealogy*. Salt Lake City: Ancestry, 1984.

Greenwood, Val D. *The Researcher's Guide to American Genealogy*. Baltimore: Genealogical Publishing Co., 1975.

Helge, Jan, and Paula Malak, comps. *Churches of the Greater Roseland (Chicago) Area*. South Holland, IL: South Suburban Genealogical and Historical Society, 1988.

Johnson, Martin William. "Swenson Research Center and ELCA Synod Archives." *Chicago Genealogist* 24, no. 1 (Fall, 1991).

List of microfilm collections of church records in both archives.

Otto, Ronald. "Early South Suburban Area Churches." *Source Book*. South Holland, IL: South Suburban Genealogical and Historical Society, 1982.

Phillips, George S. *Chicago and Her Churches*. Chicago, 1868.

Schnirring, E. Cheryl. "Church Collections in the Illinois

State Historical Library Manuscript Section." *Illinois Libraries* 74, no. 5 (November 1992).

White, Elizabeth P., C. G. "Report on the Illinois Church Records Card File Project." *Chicago Genealogist* 7, no. 4 (Summer, 1975).

Wright, Norman Edgar. *Preserving Your American Heritage*. Provo, UT: Brigham Young University Press, 1981.

Specific Religious Denominations

A census of religious denominations taken in 1916, after the influx of immigrants to America, revealed the following membership statistics for Chicago:

720,000 Roman Catholic

60,000 Lutheran

30,000 Methodist Episcopal

30,000 Jewish

30,000 Presbyterian

30,000 Baptist

The remainder of this section on church and religious records focuses on the major religious denominations listed above; however, some useful addresses for other denominations are provided.

Roman Catholic Records

The laws of the Catholic Church, the Code of Canon Law, requires that each parish maintain a parochial archives in which are preserved, with care, the parish sacramental registers. The III Plenary Council of Baltimore required that the archives be an iron safe; today this may be a separate room or a fireproof vault. There is no central file for all parish records in the Archdiocese of Chicago which has jurisdiction over of Cook and Lake Counties, Illinois. All records are obtained from the parish in which a sacramental event took place. The first step to obtain a record is to locate the correct parish. If the name of the family parish is not immediately known, there are several useful sources to help you locate the needed registers.

For general information contact:

Archdiocese of Chicago, Archives and Records Center
5150 Northwest Highway
Chicago, IL 60630
(312-736-5150)

Genealogical and sacramental records research must be carried on by mail. The Archives and Records Center staff will do a limited amount of genealogical research from the sacramental registers of closed parishes which are held by the archives, but they will reply to mail requests only. The normal request is for an abstract of the record. Non-genealogical research can be conducted by appointment only. Contact the Archives and Records Center for more details on ordering and records availability.

The *Official Catholic Directory*

Previous directories, dated as early as 1833 and under various titles and publishers, can be found. The *Official Catholic Directory* is the single-most important source for identifying parishes in the United States. Parishes having a resident pastor, including the 444 parishes of the Archdiocese of Chicago, are listed by diocese. Diocesan hierarchy and appropriate offices are shown with addresses and telephone numbers for each. American missionary activities and religious orders of men and women are listed with their addresses. Parish entries include the address, telephone number, name of resident pastors, and information regarding any parochial school (student enrollment numbers and the responsible teaching order). Catholic high schools, colleges, and hospitals as well as residences for the aged, child caring institutions, residences for the blind, and other special service institutions are also listed under each diocese. In some cases where a parish or other Catholic institution has been closed, the year of closing and the address of the parish or archives holding records are provided.

Addresses for the chancery offices of all of the archdioceses and dioceses are included. When special problems in locating a parish are encountered, an inquiry directed to the chancery may provide additional help. Chancery (Archdiocesan office) personnel do not make searches of individual parish registers, but may be able to answer questions of a general nature. The back of the *Official Catholic Directory* contains an alphabetical list of the cardinals, archbishops, bishops, abbots, regular and secular priests and their residences. A necrology of the religious who have died during the past year is also included. Copies of the *Official Catholic Directory* are available at almost every Catholic parish and institution, major libraries, and the Newberry Library has copies dating back to about 1880, as do most of the major Catholic libraries in the area.

Selected Bibliography

Archdiocese of Chicago. *Official Directory of the Archdiocese of Chicago.* Chicago: Archdiocesan Pastoral Center.

> A yearly publication, similar to the larger *Official Catholic Directory*, that focuses and elaborates on the Archdiocese of Chicago, its parishes and institutions. One of the most important features is a listing of the location of records of closed parishes. It is available for reference at most parishes.

Bochar, Jack. *Locations of Chicago Roman Catholic Churches 1850—1990.* Geneva, IL: Jack Bochar, 1990.

> Out of print, but available at the Newberry Library, some local libraries, and at the Family History Library of The Church of Jesus Christ of Latter-day Saints in Salt Lake City, Utah. This publication is a church-locating guide for Chicago. To use this guide, you must know the address or approximate location where your ancestor lived during an approximate period of time. The guide is based on present Chicago city boundaries only, using current street names. Since boundaries and

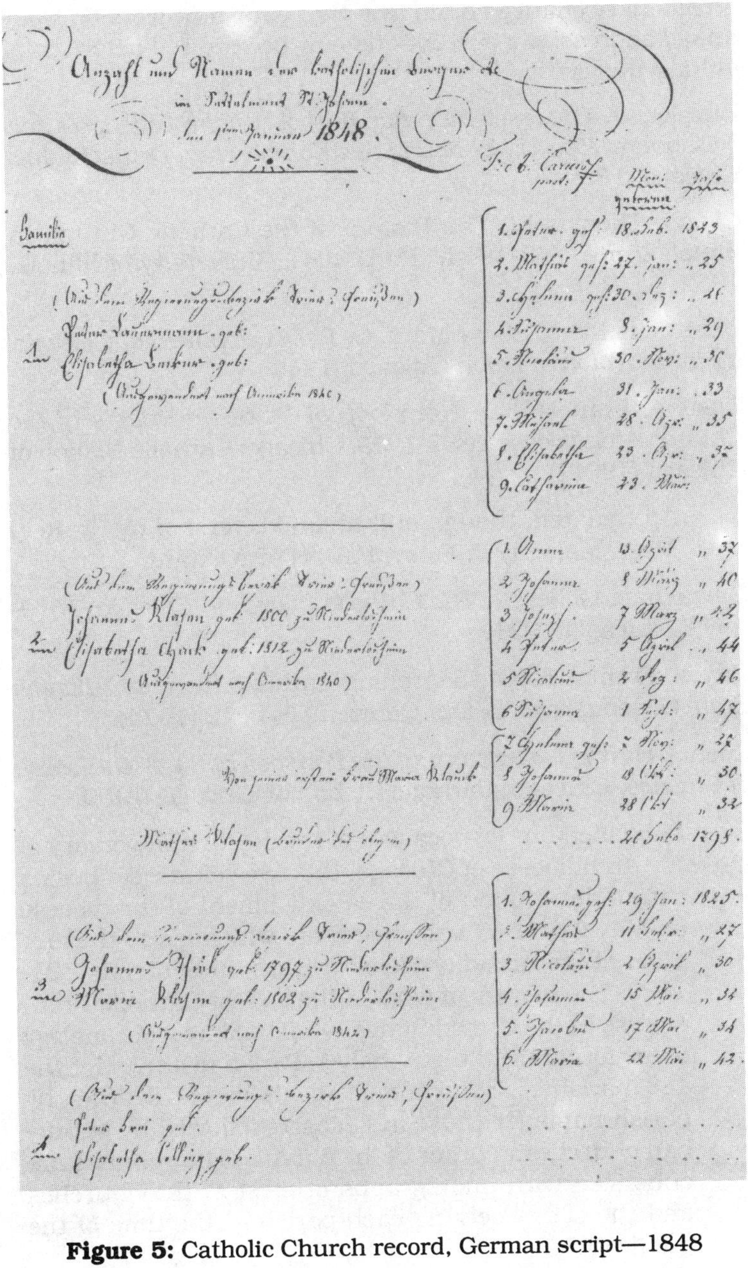

Figure 5: Catholic Church record, German script—1848

streets have changed often over the years, a conversion from an old address to a current one may be required before consulting this guide.

Burgler, J. C. *Geschichte der Kathol. Kirche Chicago's mit Besonderer Berucksichtigung des Katholischen Deutschtums.* Chicago, 1889.

Cleary, Thomas F. "The History of the Catholic Church in Illinois from 1763-1844." Ph.D. diss., University of Illinois, 1932.

Doretheus Ryan, Sister Mary, O. P. *Development of Catholicity in the Town of Lake.* Chicago, 1942.

Epstein, Francis J. *A Necrology of Diocesan Priests of the Chicago Archdiocese 1837-1959.* Chicago: Catholic Bishop of Chicago (1906?).

> An updated, though still undated, version by Rt. Rev. Msgr. Malachy P. Foley, P.A., is also extant.

Garraghan, Gilbert J. *The Catholic Church in Chicago, 1673-1871.* Chicago, 1921.

Hayes, Francis R. O. "Searching Catholic Records." *Illinois State Genealogical Society Quarterly* 6, no. 2 (1974).

Koenig, Harry C. *A History of the Parishes of the Archdiocese of Chicago.* Chicago: Catholic Bishop of Chicago, 1980.

> Published on the occasion of the 100th anniversary of the Archdiocese of Chicago, this two volume set begins with a description of the establishment of the diocese on May 22, 1843 and the events which led to the creation of the Archdiocese of Chicago on September 21, 1880. The history of what is the largest Catholic Archdiocese in the United States is followed by a chronology of the founding of the parishes. Parish histories for the 444 parishes are arranged in alphabetical order by parish name for those in Chicago, followed by suburban churches in order of town name. The volumes are enhanced with photographs of most of the churches and the clergy serving each parish at the time of the publication.

Koenig, Harry C. *Caritas Christi Urget Nos: A History of the Offices, Agencies & Institutions of the Archdiocese of Chicago.* Chicago: Catholic Bishop of Chicago, 1981.

Parot, Joseph John. *Polish Catholics in Chicago, 1850-1920: A Religious History.* Dekalb,IL: Northern Illinois University Press, 1981.

Sanders, James W. *The Education of an Urban Minority: Catholics in Chicago, 1833-1965.* New York: Oxford University Press, 1977.

Shanabruch, Charles H. *The Catholic Church's Role in the Americanization of Chicago's Immigrants, 1833-1928.* 2 vols., Ph.D. diss., University of Chicago, 1975.

South Suburban Genealogical and Historical Society. *Index to Where the Trails Cross.* South Holland, IL: The Society, 1984.

Thomas, Sister Evangeline, ed. *Women Religious History Sources: A Guide to Repositories in the U. S.* New York: Bowker, 1983.

Thompson, Rev. Joseph J. *The First Chicago Church Records, 1833-44.* Baltimore: Gateway Press, 1988.

Index and introduction by Nancy C. Thornton.

Chicago Catholic Parishes to 1875

If nationality is shown in parentheses, it indicates the ethnic group served by the parish at the time of its founding — this may not reflect the current composition of the parish. The Diocese of Chicago, at this time, included the northern half of Illinois. The only parishes listed are those within the City of Chicago.

All Saints (1875)
All Saints (St. Anthony of Padua), 518 W. 28th Pl., 60616
Annunciation (1866), 1650 N. Paulina, 60622
Holy Family (1857), 1019 S. May, 60607
Holy Name Cathedral (1845), 730 N. Wabash, 60611
Holy Trinity (Polish,1873), 1118 N. Noble, 60622

Immaculate Conception (1859), 1415 N. North Park, 60610

Nativity of Our Lord (1868), 653 W. 37th St., 60609

Notre Dame (French, 1864), 1335 W. Harrison, 60607

Our Lady of Sorrows (1874), 3121 W. Jackson Blvd., 60612

Sacred Heart (1865), records at Providence of God, 717 W. 18th, 60616

St. Adalbert (Polish, 1873), 1650 W. 17th, 60608

St. Anne (1865), records at St. Charles Lwanga, 153 W. Garfield, 60621

St. Anthony of Padua (German, 1873), see All Saints—St. Anthony of Padua

St. Boniface (German, 1864), 921 N. Noble, 60622

St. Bridget (1850), 2928 S. Archer, 60608

St. Columbkille (1859), 1648 W. Grand, 60622 (Closed (records at Holy Innocents, 743 N. Armour)

St. Francis Assissi (1853), 813 W. Roosevelt, 60608

St. Henry (1851), 6335 N. Hoyne, 60645

St. James (1855), 2942 S. Wabash, 60616

St. Jarlath (1864), records at St. Patricks (on Adams)

St. John Nepomucene (1870), 2953 S. Lowe, 60616

St. John (1857), records at St. James

St. Josesph (German) (1846), 1107 No. Orleans, 60610

St. Margaret of Scotland (1874), 9837 S. Throop, 60643

St. Mary (1883), Old St. Mary's Chapel, 21 E. Van Buren, 60605

St. Michael (German, 1852), 1633 N. Cleveland, 60614

St. Patrick (1846), 718 W. Adams, 60606

St. Patrick (1857), 9525 S. Commercial, 60617

St. Peter (German, 1846), 110 W. Madison, 60602

St. Pius V (1873), 1909 S. Ashland, 60608

St. Stanislaus Kostka (1867), 1351 W. Evergreen, 60622

St. Stephen (1869), records at St. John Cantius, 825 N. Carpenter, 60622

St. Thomas the Apostle (1865), 5472 S. Kimbark, 60615

St. Wenceslaus (1863), 1224 W. Lexington, (records at Our Lady of Pompeii)

Neighborhood Parishes

Andersonville—St. Gregory, St. Ita

Altgeld Gardens—Our Lady of the Gardens

Austin—St. Lucy (records at St. Catherine of Sienna)

Avondale—St. Wenceslaus, St. Hyacinth

Beverly—St. Therese, Christ the King, St. Margaret of Scotland, St. Barnabas

Bridgeport—St. George, St. Mary of Perpetual Help, Immaculate Conception B. V.M.(Aberdeen), St. Barbara, St. Bridget, Nativity of our Lord (37th St.), St. David, St. John Nepomucene, All Saints-St. Anthony of Padua

Brighton Park—St. Agnes, Immaculate Conception (44th), St. Joseph and St. Anne, St. Pancratius, Five Holy Martyrs

Chicago Lawn—St. Rita, St. Adrian, Nativity B.V.M., St. Nicholas of Tolentine

Edgebrook—Queen of All Saints, St. Mary of the Woods

Gage Park—St. Simon, St. Clare de Monte Falco, St. Gall

Hegewisch—Anunciata, St. Florian, St. Columba

Humbolt Park—St. Fidelis, St. Mark

Hyde Park—St. Thomas the Apostle, St. Ambrose

Jackson Park—St. Clara-St. Cyril, St. Lawrence

Lakeview—Our Lady of Mt.Carmel, St. Sebastian, St. Ephrem

McKinley Park—Our lady of Good Counsel, SS.Peter and Paul (Paulina), St. Maurice

Merrionette Park—St. Christina

North Greektown—Queen of Angels, St. Matthias, Transfiguration (Lincoln Sq./Ravenswood)

Newtown—St. Vincent de Paul

Oldtown—St. Michael, Immaculate Conception (North Park)

Pullman—Holy Rosary, St. Anthony, St. Salomea, St. Louis, St. Willibrod

Riverview—St. Francis Xavier, St. Veronica

Rogers Park—St. Margaret Mary, St. Jerome

Roseland—All Saints/St. Nicholas/Holy Rosary/St. Louis, St. Catherine of Genoa

South Greektown—St. Patrick (Adams)

Summerdale—St. Eugene

Locating Records For Closed, Predominantly Irish, Parishes

All Saints, 25th Place and Wallace, (Records at All Saints-St. Anthony, 518 W. 28th Place, 60616).

St. Anne, 55th and Wentworth, (Records at St. Charles Lwanga, 153 W. Garfield, 60621).

Annunciation, Wabansia Ave.& Paulina, (Records at St. Mary of the Angels, 1825 N. Wood, 60622).

St. Cecilia, 45th and Wells, (Records at St. Charles Lwanga, 153 W. Garfield, 60621).

St. Charles Borromeo, Roosevelt Rd.& Hoyne Ave.(Records at Holy Trinity, 916 Wolcott Ave., 60622).

St. Columbkille, Grand Ave.& Paulina St. (Records at Holy Innocents, 743 N. Armour St., 60622)

St. Cyril, 64th and Dante (Records at St. Clara-St. Cyril, 6415 S. Woodlawn, 60637)

St. Finbarr, 14th and Harding St. (Records at Our Lady of Lourdes, 1444 S. Keeler Ave., 60623)

St. Jarlath, Jackson Blvd and Hermitage Ave. (Records at St. Patricks, 718 W. Adams St., 60606)

Old St. John, 18th and Clark St. (Records at St. James, 2942 S. Wabash, 60616)

St. Louis, Polk and Sherman (Records for this French parish include many Irish names and are currently held by Old St. Marys, 21 W. Van Buren St., 60605)

St. Lucy, Lake St. and Mayfield Ave.(Records at St. Catherine of Siena-St. Lucy, 38 N. Austin Blvd., Oak Park, IL 60302)

St. Matthew, Walnut St. and Albany (Records at Our Lady of the Angels, 3808 Iowa St., 60651)

St. Paul, Lexington and Clinton St. (Records perished in the Chicago Fire of 1871)

Sacred Heart, 19th and Peoria St. (Records at Providence of God, 717 W. 18th St., 60616)

Old St. Stephen, Ohio and Sangamon St. (Records St. John Cantius, 825 N. Carpenter St., 60622)

St. Theodore.62nd and Paulina St. (Records at St. Brendan, 6714 S. Racine, 60636

National (Ethnic) Parishes in Chicago

Belgian

St. John Berchmans (1903), 2517 W. Logan Blvd., 60647

Bohemian

Blessed Agnes (1904) (Moravian Czech) 2651 S. Central Park, 60623 Our Lady of Good Counsel (1889), 916 N. Western, 60622]

Our Lady of Lourdes (1892), 1444 S. Keeler, 60623

St. Cyril and Methodius (1891), 5009 S. Hermitage, 60609

St. John Nepomucene (1870), 2953 S. Lowe, 60609

St. Ludmilla (1891), 2408 S. Albany, 60623

St. Procopius (1876), 1641 S. Allport, 60623

St. Wenceslaus (1863) (Records at Our Lady of Pompeii, 1224 W. Lexington, 60607)

St. Vitus (1888), 1818 S. Paulina, 60608

Croatian

Assumption (1901), 6005 Marshfield, 60636*

Holy Trinity (1914), 1850 S. Throop, 60608*

St. Jerome (1912), 2823 S. Princeton, 60616*

Sacred Heart (1913), 2864 E. 96th, 60617*

St. George (1903) Croatians attended St. George until Sacred Heart was founded in 1913.

*Records have been microfilmed by the Genealogical Society of Utah.

Dutch

St. Willibrod (1900), 11406 S. Edbrooke, 60628

French

Notre Dame (1864), 1335.W. Harrison, 60607

Sacred Heart (1911), 11652 S. Church (Records at Holy Name of Mary, 11159 S. Loomis, 60643)

St. John the Baptist (1892), 911 W. 50th Place, 60609

St. John the Baptist (1882), 33rd and Paulina (Records at St. Joseph and St. Anne, 2751 W. 38th, 60632)

St. Joseph and St. Anne (1889), 2751 W. 38th, 60632

St. Louis (1850), Sherman and Polk Sts. (Records at Old St. Mary's, 21 East Van Buren St, 60605)

St. Louis (1886), 117th Street (Records at All Saints, 10809 S. State, 60628)

German

Holy Ghost (1896), St. Mel-Holy Ghost, 22 N. Kildare, 60624

Holy Trinity (1885), 916 S. Wolcott, 60612

Immaculate Conception (1883), 3111 S. Aberdeen, 60621

Our Lady of Perpetual Help (1898), 1300 S. St. Louis (Closed, records at St. Agatha, 3147 W. Douglas, 60623)

Sacred Heart (1894), 7020 S. Aberdeen, 60621

St. Aloysious (1884), 2300 W. LeMoyne, 60622

St. Alphonsus (1882), 1429 W. Wellington, 60657

St. Anthony of Padua (1873), All Saints-St. Anthony of Padua, 518 W. 28th Place, 60616

St. Augustine (1879), 5045 S. Laflin, 60609

St. Benedict (1901), 2215 West Irving Park, 60618

St. Boniface (1864), 921 N. Noble, 60622

St. Clara (1894) (Records at St. Clara-St Cyril, 6415 S. Woodlawn, 60637)

St. Francis Xavier (1888), 2840 W. Nelson, 60618

St. Francis Assissi (1853), 813 W. Roosevelt, 60608

St. George (1884), Wentworth Ave. (Records at St. Charles Lwanga, 153 Garfield Blvd., 60621)

St. Henry (1851), 6335 N. Hoyne, 60659

St. Joseph Church (1846), 1107 North Orleans, 60610

St. Martin (1886), 5842 S. Princeton, 60621

St. Matthias (1887), 2310 W. Ainslie, 60625

St. Maurice (1890), 3615 S. Hoyne, 60609

St. Michael (Redemptorist)(1852), 1633 N. Cleveland, 60614

St. Nicholas (1890) (Records at All Saints, 10809 S. State, 60628)

St. Paul (1876), 2127 W. 22nd, 60608

St. Peter (1846), 110 W. Madison St., 60602

St. Philomena (1888), 1921 N. Kedvale, 60639

St. Raphael (1901), 6012 S. Laflin, 60636

St. Teresa (1889), 1037 W. Armitage, 60614

St. William (1916), 2600 N. Sayre, 60635

Hungarian

Our Lady of Hungary (1904), 9237 S. Avalon, 60619

St. Stephen, King of Hungary (1934), 2015 W. August Blvd, 60622

Italian

Assumption B.V.M. (1881), 323 W. Illinois, 60610

Holy Guardian Angel (1899) (Records at Our Lady of Pompeii)

Holy Rosary (1904), 612 N. Western, 60612

Our Lady of Pompeii (1910), 1224 W. Lexington, 60604

Santa Maria Addolorata (1903), 528 N. Ada, 60622

Santa Maria Incornata (1899),—Santa Lucia 3022 S. Wells, 60616

Santa Michael the Archangel (1903), 2325 W. 24th Place, 60608

St. Anthony (1904), 11533 S. Prairie, 60628

St. Callistus (1919), 2167 W. Bowler, 60612

St. Frances Cabrini (Mission of St. Callistus. and also known as Mother Cabrini, 1936-1940; parish established in 1940), 743 S. Sacramento St., 60612

St. Francis de Paula (1911), 7822 S. Dobson, 60619

St. Mary of Mt.Carmel (1892), 6722 S. Hermitage, 60636 (Closed, records at St. Justin Martyr Church, 1818 W. 71st St., 60636)

St. Philip Benizi (1904), 357 W. Locust, 60610 (Records at St. Joseph, 1107 N. Orleans)

Latvian

Our Lady of Algona 2543 W. Wabansia, 60647

Lithuanian

All Saints (1907), 10809 S. State, 60628

Holy Cross (1904), 4557 S. Wood, 60609

Immaculate Conception (1914), 2745 W. 44th St., 60632

Nativity, BVM (1927), 6812 S. Washtenaw, 60629

Our Lady Of Vilna (1904), 2327 W. 23rd Pl.60608

Providence of God (1900), 717 West 18th St., 60616

SS. Peter and Paul (1914), 12433 S. Halsted, 60628

St. Anthony (1911), 1515 S. 50th, 60650 (Cicero)

St. Bartholomew (1893), 730 S. Lincoln Waukegan, 60085

St. Casimir (1910), 283 E. 14th St. Chicago Heights, 60411

St. George (1886), 3230 S. Lithuanica, 60608

St. Joseph (1905), 8801 S. Saginaw, 60617

St. Michael (1904), 1644 W. Wabansia (records at Annunciation 1650 N. Paulina, 60622)

Polish

Assumption B.V.M.(1903), 544 W. 123rd, 60628

Good Shepherd (1907), 2719 S. Kolin, 60623

Holy Innocents (1905), 743 North Armour, 60622

Holy Trinity (1873), 1118 N. Noble, 60622

Immaculate Conception (1883), 2944 E. 88th, 60617

Immaculate Heart of Mary (1912), 3824 N. Spaulding, 60618

Sacred Heart (1910), 4600 S. Honore, 60609

SS. Peter and Paul (1895), 3745 S. Paulina, 60609

St. Adalbert (1873), 1650 W. 17th, 60608

St. Ann (1902), 1814 S. Leavitt, 60608

St. Barbara (1910), 2859 S. Throop, 60608

St. Bronislava (1928), 8708 S. Colfax, 60617

St. Casimir (1890), 2226 S. Whipple, 60623

St. Constance (1916), 5843 W. Strong, 60630

St. Florian (1905), 13145 S. Houston, 60633

St. Francis Assissi (1909), 932 N. Kostner, 60651

St. Hedwig (1888), 2226 N. Hoyne, 60647

St. Helen (1913), 2315 W. Augusta Blvd.60622

St. Hyacinth (1894), 3636 W. Wolfram, 60618

St. James (1914), 5730 W. Fullerton, 60639

St. John of God (19060 1234 W. 52nd, 60609

St. John Cantius (1893), 825 N. Carpenter, 60622

St. Josaphat (1884), 2311 N. Southport, 60614

St. Joseph (1887), 4821 S. Hermitage, 60609

St. Ladislaus 5346 W. Roscoe, 60641

St. Mary of Perpetual Help (1882), 1039 W. 32nd, 60608

St. Mary Magdalene (1910), 8424 S. Marguette, 60617

St. Michael (1892), 8237 South Shore, 60617

St. Salomea (1897), 11824 S. Indiana, 60628

St. Stanislaus B and M (1893), 5352 West Belden, 60639

St. Stanislaus Kostka (1867), 1351 W. Evergreen, 60622

St. Stephen (1869), (records at St. John Cantius 825 N. Carpenter, 60622)

St. Wenceslaus (1863), formerly at Halsted and DeKoven (records at Our Lady of Pompeii, 1224 W. Lexington, Chicago, 60607)

St. Wenceslaus (1912), 3400 N. Monticello, 60618

Transfiguration (1911), 2609 W. Carmen, 60625

Slovak

Assumption B.V.M.(1903), 2434 S. California, 60608

Holy Rosary (1907), 100 W. 108th Place (Records at All Saints Church, 10809 S.State, 60628)

Sacred Heart (1914), 721 N. Oakley, 60612

St. Cyril and Methodius (1914), 4244 W. Walton, 60651

St. John the Baptist (1909), 9129 S. Burley, 60617

St. Joseph Church 720 W. 17th Place (records at Providence of God Church, 717 W. 18th Street, 60616)

St. Michael the Archangel (1898), 4821 S. Damen, 60609

Slovenian

St. George (1903), 9546 S. Ewing, 60617

St. Stephen (1898), 1852 W. 22nd Place, 60608

Eastern Rite Churches

Christ the Redeemer (a Byzantine church serving Byelorussians) 3107 West Fullerton, 60647

Nativity of the B.V.M. (1911, a Byzantine church serving mainly Ukrainians), 4952 S. Paulina, 60609

Our Lady of Lebanon (1959, an Antiochian church of the Maronite Rite serving mainly Lebanese and Syrians) 425 N. Hillside, Hillside, IL 60162

SS. Peter and Paul (1905, a Byzantine church of the Ruthenian Rite serving mainly Croations) 3048 S. Central Park., 60623

SS. Volodymyr and Olha (a Byzantine church serving mainly Ukrainians) 739 N. Oakley, Blvd.(office: 2247 W. Chicago, 60622)

St. Basil Mission (1943, a Byzantine Rite church serving mainly Ukrainians, attended by St. Michael) 740 E. 91st St., 60619

St. Ephrem (1911, a Chaldean Rite Church serving Syrians and others from the Middle East) 2537 West Bryn Mawr, 60659

St. John the Baptist (1910, a Byzantine church of Melkite Rite, formerly at 1249 S. Washtenaw), 200 E. North Ave., Northlake, IL 60164

St. Joseph (1956, a Byzantine church serving mainly Ukrainians) 5016 N. Cumberland, 60656

St. Mary (1905, a Byzantine church of the Ruthenian Rite serving Hungarians and Czechs.Liturgy in Old Slavonic) 4949 S. Seeley, 60609

St. Michael (1917, a Byzantine church serving mainly Ukrainians) 12205 S. Parnell, 60628

St. Nicholas (1906, a Byzantine church serving mainly Ukrainians) 2238 W. Rice, 60622

Lutheran Church Records

Earliest German "Lutheran" Churches in the Chicago Area
by Ronald Otto.

Lutheranism came to Chicago area communities as it came to other American communities-via the German speaking immigrants who longed for the comfort of their church in their language. True, Lutheran churches existed earlier in the eastern portions of the United States, but as this "Lutheran" church moved westward, it did so with English language congregations. For additional information about the predecessors to this "Lutheran Church in America" organization in

Illinois, see the article "The American Roots of German Lutheranism in Illinois" by E.Duane Elbert in *Illinois Historical Journal* (Summer 1985). Each of the churches listed at the end of this article began as German speaking congregation.

According to Robert Wiederaenders in "A History of Lutheranism in Chicago" found in the *Chicago Lutheran Planning Study* (Vol. 2, Chicago: National Lutheran Council, 1965), the first German Protestant minister who came to these parts was the Rev. Jacob Boas (at the time in charge of the Miami, Ohio Circuit of the Evangelical Association). In August 1837, he preached the first German sermon in Chicago, but no congregation was organized, and he returned to Ohio. In 1838, a Prussian, Ludwig Cachend-Ervenberg, became Pastor of a German congregation at Dunklee's Grove (today, Addison Township, DuPage County) with missions at Long Grove, Arlington Heights and Bensenville. This last named place emerged as the home of Zion Lutheran, Bensenville. The earliest registers maintained by the Rev. Cachend Evernberg have been translated by Dr. David Koss (Illinois College, Jacksonville, IL) and published in the *Illinois State Genealogy Society Quarterly* 17, no. 1.

Factionalism among German Protestants in Germany carried over in America. To this date, you will find in Illinois "Lutheran" Churches belonging to the Missouri Synod, the Wisconsin Synod, the American Lutheran Church, and the Lutheran Church in America. In addition to the early Lutheran Churches now organized under the above umbrella organizations, you should also look for Illinois German Protestant Churches that were members of the German United Evangelical Synod of North America.

Why so much factionalism? For starters, during the mid-19th century, the early Lutherans (18th century immigrants) were established in the east in English speaking churches, and more recent immigrants were not comfortable in this "foreign" atmosphere. Simplistically, factionalism here was an extension of factionalism in Germany compounded by the fact that each church here was financially supported by the individual parishioners and not by the state. It was quickly learned that he who pays the fiddler selects the music.

On September 27, 1817, King Friedrich Wilhelm III of Prussia promulgated by court proclamation the "Union" of the Lutheran and Reformed Churches there. Thus the Evangelical Church, The Church of the Prussia Union, came into existence. Vigorous opposition immediately emanated from many sources, such as Klaus Harms, the vehement pastor in Kiel. Opposition to this Union Church continued for decades and resulted in certain migrations by "Old Lutherans" (and others) to the United States and Australia for the purpose of religious freedom. For more information about the "Old Lutherans" consult:

Smith, Clifford Neal. *Nineteenth Century Emigration of "Old Lutherans" from Eastern German (Mainly Pomerania and Lower Silesia) to Australia, Canada and the United States.* McNeal, AR: Westland Publications, 1980.

While the "Old Lutherans" settled mainly in Southeastern Wisconsin, another group, the Saxon Lutherans formed the nucleus of the Missouri Synod. For a thorough discussion of the political ramifications of the "Union" Church within Prussia, refer to:

Bigler, Robert M. *The Politics of German Protestantism: the Rise of the Protestant Church Elite in Prussia, 1815-1848.* Berkeley, CA: University of California Press, 1972.

The German United Evangelical Synod of North America was formed in 1872 by the merger of three factions:

> Evangelical Synod of the West
>
> Evangelical United Synod of the East
>
> United Evangelical Synod of the Northwest

The United Evangelical Synod of the Northwest was the synod for most of the Evangelical "Union" churches in the Chicago area, and its repository is located at Elmhurst College in Elmhurst, Illinois. In 1934, the German United Evangelical Synod became the United Evangelical Synod, and when it merged with the Reformed Church it became the Evangelical and Reformed Church.

Published sources about the Evangelical United Synod include:

Dunn, David, et al. *A History of the Evangelical and Reformed Church.* Philadelphia: The Christian Education Press, 1961.

Schneider, Carl Edward. *The German Church on the American Frontier.* St. Louis: Eden Publishing House, 1939.

———."The Origin of the German Evangelical Synod of North." *Church History* 4, no. 4 (December 1935).

In 1957, the Evangelical and Reformed Church and the Christian Congregational Church merged to form the United Church of Christ. To learn about the existing churches whose heritage goes back to the "Union" church, consult a current *United Church of Christ Yearbook* available at the nearest United Church of Christ church and at many regional repositories.

In 1988, the Evangelical Lutheran Church in America was formed from the merger of the Lutheran Church in America and the American Lutheran Church.

Repository Addresses

Addresses for the repositories of the Evangelical and Reformed Church (now the United Church of Christ) are:

Edens Archives
   475 E. Lockwood Ave.
   Webster Groves, MO 63119 (the E and R Archives)
Illinois Conference U.C.C.
   302 S. Grant
   Hinsdale, IL 60521.
      For information on area United Church of Christ churches.
Philip Schaff Memorial Library
   Lancaster Theological Seminary
   Lancaster, PA 17603.

Addresses for other Lutheran repositories:

Archives of the Evangelical Lutheran Church in America
8765 Higgins
Chicago, IL 60631.

> The archives contain many microfilmed records of Evangelical Lutheran Church in America churches throughout the Midwest. Some of the microfilmed records for Chicago churches remain at the Evangelical Lutheran Church in America Regional Archives in Dubuque, Iowa. Consult with the Evangelical Lutheran Church in America Archives in Chicago before visiting to be sure the records you seek are there.

Archives of the (former) American Lutheran Church

Wartburg Theological Seminary
333 Wartburg Place
Dubuque, IA 52001.

> Synods that merged with the American Lutheran Church include: Iowa, Ohio, Hauge, Norwegian, United Norwegian, and Danish (Blair). As of 1988, the archives became a regional repository for the Evangelical Lutheran Church in America archives.

Archives of the Lutheran Church in America

Lutheran School of Theology
1100 E. 55th Street
Chicago, IL 60615.

> Synods that merged with the Lutheran Church in America include: Wartburg, Augustana, Chicago, Northern Illinois, and Danish Evangelical.

Concordia Historical Institute
801 DeMun
St. Louis, MO 63105.

> The general archives of the Missouri Synod are located here. The archives for the Northern District are located at 2301 Wolf Road, Hillside, IL.

Wisconsin Lutheran Seminary
11831 N. Seminary Drive, 65
Mequon, WI 53092.

The archives of the Wisconsin Synod are located here.

The names of merged synods were provided by Robert Wiederaenders, Archivist for the American Lutheran Church. For additional information about the Missouri Synod Churches listed, and for information about other Northern Illinois Churches of this Synod, consult:

Schwartzkopf, Rev. Louis J. *The Lutheran Trail* St. Louis: Concordia Press, Inc., 1950.

This book is available on interlibrary loan.

For information on Chicago churches as of 1893, consult the listing in the *Chicago Genealogist* 14, no.3.

The following is a list of existing and defunct Chicago area German "Lutheran" churches from earliest days:

MS = Missouri Synod

UCC = United Church of Christ

    Addison-St Paul Lutheran, 1849, (MS)

    Arlington Park-St. Peter's Lutheran, 1860, (MS)

    Beecher-St. Paul's Lutheran, 1865, (MS)

    Bensenville-St. John, 1849, (UCC)

    Blue Island-First Ev.Lutheran, 1862, Ann and Grove Sts.

    Burr Ridge-Trinity Ev.Lutheran, 1862, German Church Rd (MS)

    Chicago—First St. Paul Lutheran, 1846, (MS)

    Chicago—St. Paul UCC, 1843, Fullerton Pkwy and Orchard (UCC)

    Chicago—First Immanuel Lutheran, 1854, Roosevelt and Ashland (MS)

    Chicago—First Trinity Lutheran, 1865, (MS)

    Chicago—Salem UCC, 1861, 9717 Kostner, Oak Lawn (UCC)

    Chicago—St. Peter UCC, 1864, 5450 W. Diversey (UCC)

Coopers Grove-St. John's, 1849, 4231 W. 183, Country Club Hills (MS)

Creek-Trinity Lutheran, 1849, (MS)

Dolton-St. Paul Lutheran, 1858, (MS)

Dunklee's Grove, 1838, (Addison) Zion Lutheran, Bensenville (MS)

Eagle Lake-St. John's, 1854, Washington Twp, Wisconsin (MS)

Elk Grove-St. John's, 1848, (MS)

Glencoe-Trinity Lutheran, 1847, (MS)

Green Garden Twp.-St. Peter's Ev., 1862, now merged with St. Paul UCC, Sauk Trail, Frankfort (UCC)

Harlem—St. John Lutheran-today, 1865, Forest Park (MS)

Hillside—Immanuel Lutheran, 1858, (MS)

Joliet—St. Peter's Lutheran, 1857, (MS)

Lansing—Trinity, 1864, (MS)

Long Grove—Long Grove UCC, 1846, Long Grove Road (UCC)

Mokena—Immanuel Lutheran, 1850, (MS)

Mokena—St. John UCC, 1862, 11100 Second St (UCC)

Monee—St. Paul UCC, 1858, 207 Margaret Street (UCC)

Naperville—St. John, 1857, (UCC)

Niles—St. John's Lutheran, 1859, (MS)

Northbrook: St. Peter UCC, 1845, 2700 Willow Road (UCC)

Palatine—St. John, 1846, (UCC)

Richton Park—Immanuel Lutheran, 1852, Cicero and Sauk Trail (MS)

Roselle—St. John Lutheran, 1851, (MS)

Schaumburg—St. Peter's Lutheran, 1840

Seiden Prairie—St. Paul Lutheran, 1862, Vollmer Rd, Matteson

Streamwood—Immanuel, 1852, (UCC)

Thornton—St. Peter Lutheran, 1859, (MS)

Tinley Park—Trinity Lutheran, 1859, 159th and Oak Park (MS)

Records for the Kimball Avenue United Evangelical Church of Chicago (1900-1958) have been microfilmed by the Genealogical Society of Utah using the original records at the United Congregational Church, Valencia, Pennsylvania.

The following list of Lutheran churches was submitted to the *Chicago Genealogical Society Newsletter* (September 1983) by Ronald Otto. Information appears in the following order: name of church, date of origin, location as of 1900 and current location:

Bethany, 1891, Humbolt Pk Blvd and Rockwell, now: 1701 N. Narragansett, 60639

Bethel, 1894, 1076 Hirsch, Hirsch and Springfield

Bethlehem, 1874, 103rd Ave G, now: 10261 S. Ave H, 60617

Christ, 1885, N. Humbolt and McLean, now 2018 N. Richmond, 60651

Concordia, 1891, W. Belmont and N. Washtenaw, 2645 W. Belmont, 60618

Emmaus, 1888, N. California and Walnut, 5440 W. Gladys, 60644

First Immanuel, 1854, Ashland Blvd.& W. 12th, now: 1124 S. Ashland, 60607

First Bethlehem, 1871, N. Paulina and McReynolds, now: 1645 W. LeMoyne, 60622

First Zion, 1868, W. 19th and Johnson

First Trinity, 1865, S. Canal and 25th, now: 643 W 31st St., 60616

First St. John, 1867, W. Superior and Bickerdike, Closed

Gethsemane, 1889, 49th and Dearborn, 2735 W 79th, 60652

Holy Cross, 1886, S. Centre and 31st, now: 3116 S. Racine, 60608

Immanuel, 1872, Colehour (S. Chicago), now: 9031 S. Houston, 60617

St. Mark's, 1887, 1114 S. California

St. Philip, 1893, Lawrence and N. Hoyne, now: 2500 Bryn Mawr, 60625

St. Stephens, 1889, Englewood and Union, 910 W. 65th, 60621

St. Andrew, 1888, 3650 Honore, now: 3650 S. Honore, 60609

St. Luke, 1884, Belmont and Perry, now: 1500 W. Belmont, 60657

St. John, 1875, 1704 W. Montrose, 4939 W. Montrose, 60641

St. Matthew, 1871, S. Hoyne between W. 20th and 21st, 2108 W. 21st St, 60608

St. James, 1869, Fremont and Garfield, now: 2048 N. Fremont, 60614

St. Paul, 1848, Superior and N Franklin, now: 1301 N. LaSalle, 60610

St. Paul's, 1886, 846 N. Menard, now: 846 Menard, 60651

St. Martini, 1884, W. 51st and S. Marshfield, 1624 W. 51st, 60629

St. Peter, 1871, Dearborn south of 39th, now: 7400 S. Michigan, 60619

Trinity, 1887, Hegewisch, now: 13200 Burley, 60653

Zion, 1870, Washington Heights, now: 9901 S. Winston, 60643

Zion's, 1882, 113th and Edbrooke, 10858 S. King Dr., 60628

Swedish Lutheran

The Emigrant Institute of Vaxjo, Sweden began microfilming Swedish-American church records in the United States in 1968. The Lutheran portion of this film is from the Augustana Evangelical Lutheran Church (1860-1962). The filming covers records up through 1930, and copies of the entire set are at the Emigrant Institute of Vaxjo and the Swenson Swedish Immigration Research Center, Augustana College (Box 175, Rock Island, IL 61201). A microfiche listing of holdings is available from the Swenson Swedish Immigration Research Center. Other local and ethnic repositories in the United States have partial sets of these films. See:

Wittman, Elisabeth, "The Evangelical Lutheran Church in America Churchwide Archives." *Illinois Libraries* 74, no. 5 (November 1992).

St. James Evangelical Lutheran Church Records, Chicago, Illinois

The Newberry Library has records for St. James Evangelical Church on two reels of microfilm. Reel I lists confirmations from 1871-1895, baptisms from 1870-1931, marriages from 1870-1923, and burials from 1870-1880. Reel II is a record of burials from 1881-1951.

Methodist Church Archives

The archives of the United Methodist Church, including its predecessor denominations, is now located at Madison, New Jersey. For a fee, the archives accepts genealogical requests pertaining to clergy, but does not have any local church records, such as membership or baptismal lists. For further information write:

General Secretary
General Commission on Archives and History
United Methodist Church
P.O. Box 127
Madison, NJ 07940

For records of the United Methodist Church, and its predecessors (Methodist Episcopal, Methodist Protestant, Evangelical United Brethren), contact the Garrett-Evangelical Theological Seminary Library; it has a joint library with Seabury-Western Theological Seminary (Episcopal).

Garrett-Evangelical Theological Seminary Library
2121 Sheridan Rd.
Evanston, IL 60201

The 1871 *Chicago Directory* listed the following Methodist Churches (and pastors):

First

Clark and Washington (W.H. Daniels)

Wabash Avenue & Harrison (R.M. Hatfield)

Trinity

Indiana Ave. at 24th — new church (J.H. Bayliss)

Indiana Ave. between 31st and 32nd (Robert D. Sheppard)

St. Johns' Oakland (Chas. D. Mandeville)

Grace

N. LaSalle and Chicago Ave. (N. M. Parkhurst)

Centenary

Monroe west of Morgan (C. H. Fowler)

Ada Street, between Lake and Fulton (Thomas R. Stobridge)

Park Avenue and Robey (H. W. Thomas)

Blockson, Charles L., and Ron Fry. *Black Genealogy*. Englewood Cliffs, NJ: Prentice-Hall, 1977.

Cerny, Johni, "Black Ancestral Research." In *The Source: A Guidebook of American Genealogy*, edited by Arlene Eakle and Johni Cerny. Salt Lake City: Ancestry, 1984.

Drake, St. Clair. *Churches and Voluntary Associations in the Chicago Negro Community*. Chicago, 1940. Mimeograph.

Drake, St. Clair, and Horace Cayton. *Black Metropolis: A Study of Negro Life in a Northern City*. New York, 1945.

Frazier, Edward Franklin. *The Negro Family in Chicago*. Chicago, 1932.

Gossnell, Harold Foote. *Negro Politicians: The Rise of Negro Politics in Chicago*. Chicago: The University of Chicago Press, 1935.

Grossman, James R. *Land of Hope: Chicago, Black Southerners, and the Great Migration*. Chicago: The University of Chicago Press, 1989.

Harris, Isaac Counselor. *The Colored Men's Professional and Business Directory of Chicago and Valuable Information of the Race in General*. Chicago: I. C. Harris, 1885.

Henritze, Barbara K. *Bibliographic Checklist of African American Newspapers*. Baltimore: Genealogical Publishing Co., 1995.

Hoobler, Dorothy, and Thomas Hoobler. *The African American Family Album*. New York: Oxford University Press, 1995.

Husband, Lori. "African-American Genealogy Research in the 1990s." *Illinois Libraries* 74, no. 5 (November 1992).

Miller, Robert. "Genealogy Resources at the Vivian G. Harsh Research Collection of Afro-American History and Literature." *Illinois Libraries* 74, no. 5 (November 1992).

Rose, James, and Alice Eicholz. *Black Genesis*. Detroit: Gale Research Company, 1978.

Simm's Blue Book and National Negro Business and Professional Directory. Chicago: James N. Simms, 1923.

Spear, Allan H. *Black Chicago*. Chicago: The University of Chicago Press, 1967.

Thackery, David T. "Native and African-American Genealogical Resources at the Newberry Library." *Illinois Libraries* 74, no. 5 (November 1992).

———. *A Bibliography of African American Family History at the Newberry Library*. Chicago: The Newberry Library, 1993.

Washington, Lucious William. *The Chicago Negro Business Men and Women and Where They are Located*. Chicago: L. W. Flanders Printing Company, 1912.

Native American Sources

The Newberry Library
   Edward E. Ayer Collection of Americana and American Indians and Center for the History of the American Indian
   60 West Walton, Chicago, IL 60610
   (312-943-9090)
The National Archives-Great Lakes Region
   7358 Pulaski Road, Chicago, IL 60629
   (312-581-7816)

Selected Bibliography

American Indians: A Select Catalog of National Archives Microfilm Publications. National Archives Trust Fund Board. U. S. General Services Administration, 1984.

Nixon, George J. "Records Relating to Native American Research." In *The Source: A Guidebook of American Genealogy*, edited by Arlene Eakle and Johni Cerny. Salt Lake City: Ancestry, 1984.

Strong, William Duncan. *The Indian Tribes of the Chicago Region*. Chicago: The Field Museum of Natural History, 1926.

Bohemian Sources

Bohemian-American Hospital Association. *Directory and Almanac of the Bohemian Population of Chicago.* Chicago, 1915.

Goldsborough, Robert. *The Bohemians.* 6, no. 1 (Spring 1969): 46-52.

McCarthy, Eugene Ray. "The Bohemians in Chicago and Their Benevolent Societies, 1875-1946." Master's thesis, University of Chicago, 1950.

Canadian Sources

Baxter, Angus. *In Search of Your Canadian Roots.* Rev. ed. Baltimore: Genealogical Publishing Co., 1994.

DuPage County (IL) Genealogical Society. *Genealogy and Canadian Sources.* The Society, 1984.

> One of the best compilations of Canadian materials available.

Kennedy, Patricia, and Janine Roy. *Tracing Your Ancestors in Canada.* Public Archives of Canada. Revised in 1984.

Chinese Sources

Chicago Public Library
  Chinatown Branch
  2314 S. Wentworth, Chicago, IL 60616
  (312-326-4255)
Ling Long Museum
  2238 S. Wentworth, Chicago, IL 60616
  (312-225-6181)

Selected Bibliography

Fan, Ting C. *Chinese Residents in Chicago.* San Francisco: R & E Research Associates, 1974.

Fang, John T. C. *Chinatown: Handy Guide: Chicago.* Chicago:

The Chinese Publishing House, 1959.

Hoobler, Dorothy, and Thomas Hoobler. *The Chinese American Family Album.* New York: Oxford University Press, 1995.

Li, Peter S. *Occupational Mobility and Kinship Assistance: A Study of Chinese Immigrants in Chicago.* San Francisco: R & E Research, 1977.

Liang, Yuan. "The Chinese Family in Chicago." Master's thesis, University of Chicago, 1951.

Wilson, Margaret Gibbons. "Concentration and Dispersal of Chinese Population of Chicago, 1870 to the Present." Ph. D. diss., University of Chicago, 1969.

Czechoslovakian Sources

Chicago Public Library
  Toman Branch
  4005 W. 27th Street, Chicago, IL 60623
    Has a special collection with focus on Czech community.

The Chicago Genealogical Society
  P. O. Box 1160
  Chicago, IL 60690-1160
  (312-725-1306)
    100th Anniversary Book of Bohemian National Cemetery
    Association.

Czechoslovak Society of America and Museum
  122 W. 22nd Street
  Oak Brook, IL 60521
  (708-795-5800)
    Museum and library, folk costumes, handicrafts, arts, Czech language newspapers, and periodicals published in Chicago.

Selected Bibliography

Bicha, Karel D. "The Survival of the Village in Urban America:

A Note on Czech Immigrants in Chicago to 1914."
International Migration Review 1 (Spring 1971): 72-74.

Chorvat, Lillian K. "Genealogy Collection of the CSA Fraternal
Life in the Czechoslovak Heritage Museum Library and
Archives." *Illinois Libraries* 74, no. 5 (November 1992).

Droba, Daniel. *Czech and Slovak Leaders in Metropolitan
Chicago: A Biographical Study of 300 Prominent Men and
Women of Czech and Slovak Descent.* Chicago, 1974.

Arranged by occupations.

Hletka, Peter. "The Slovaks of Chicago." *Slovakia* 19, no. 42
(October 1969): 32-63.

Lists Slovak institutions and leaders with a list of Slovaks
known to have been Chicago residents 1890-1900.

Horak, Jakub. "Assimilation of Czechs in Chicago." Ph. D.
diss., University of Chicago, 1920.

Hruban, Zdenek, and June Pachuta Farris. "Archives of
Czechs and Slovaks Abroad, University of Chicago Library."
Illinois Libraries 74, no. 5 (November 1992).

International Exposition Chicago 1933, Incorporated. *World's
Fair Memorial of the Czechoslovak Group.* Chicago, 1933.

History of the Czech community and biographical sketches of leaders, with photographs. Available at the
Chicago Public Library.

Palickar, Stephen J. "The Slovaks of Chicago." *Illinois
Catholic Historical Review* 4, no. 2 (October 1921): 180-196.

Reichman, John J., ed. *Czechoslovaks of Chicago.* Chicago,
1937.

Vraz, Vlasta, ed. *Panorama: A Historical Review of Czechs
and Slovaks in the United States of America.* Cicero, IL:
Czechoslovak National Council of America, 1970.

Dutch Sources

The South Suburban Genealogical and Historical Society Library
P. O. Box 96, South Holland, IL 60473
(333-9474)
    Has a considerable amount of material for the area of
    Dutch settlement in Chicago.

The Chicago Public Library (Special Collections and
Preservation Division) has material on predominantly Dutch
neighborhoods and settlements such as Roseland.

Selected Bibliography

DeJong, Gerald F. *The Dutch in America, 1609-1974*. The
Immigrant Heritage of America Series. Boston: Twayne
Publishers, 1975.

Epperson, Gwenn F. *New Netherland Roots*. Baltimore:
Genealogical Publishing Co., 1995.

Ettema, Ross. *The Dutch in South Cook County Since 1847*.
South Holland, IL: Park Press, 1984.

Nijhoff, Martinus. *The Hollanders in America*. San Francisco:
R & E Research Associates, 1972.

Sliekers, Hendrik. "The Dutch Heritage Center." *Illinois
Libraries* 74, no. 5 (November 1992).

Vanderbosch, Amry. *The Dutch Communities of Chicago*.
Chicago, 1927.

Schlyter, Daniel M. *A Handbook of Czechoslovak Genealogical
Research*. Provo, UT: Press America, 1985.

English Sources

The Newberry Library
    60 West Walton, Chicago, IL 60610
    (312-943-9090)

Has a particularly strong collection of British material, guides, maps and transcriptions.

The Chicago Genealogical Society and the DuPage Genealogical Societies have British special interest groups.

Selected Bibliography

Filby, P. William. *American & British Genealogy & Heraldry*, 3rd ed., Boston: New England Historic Genealogical Society, 1983.

Irvine, Sherry. *Your English Ancestry: A Guide for North Americans*. Salt Lake City: Ancestry, 1993.

Moulton, Joy Wade. *Genealogical Resources in English Repositories*. Columbus, OH: Hampton House, 1992.

Finnish Sources

Arra, Esa. *The Finns in Illinois*. Translated by A. I. Brask. Mills, MN, 1971.

Vincent, Timothy Laitila, and Rick Tapio. *Finnish Genealogical Research*. New Brighton, MN: Sampo Publishing, Inc., 1994.

German Sources

Angele, Elisabeth. "Information on the Goethe-Institut Library in Chicago." *Illinois Libraries* 74, no. 5 (November 1992).

Bullard, Thomas. "Distribution of Chicago's Germans 1850-1914." Master's thesis, University of Chicago, 1969.

Chicago und sein Deutschthum. Cleveland, 1901-1902.

German Press Club of Chicago. *Year Book of Chicago*. Chicago, 1933.

Published to commemorate the twentieth anniversary of
its organization.

Gross, Jacob. "A German Family in Chicago: 1856." *Chicago
History* 4, no. 10 (Winter 1956-57).

Hofmeister, Rudolph A. *The Germans of Chicago*. Champaign,
IL, 1976.

Jentz, John B. "Bread and Labor: Chicago's German Bakers
Organize." *Chicago History* 12, no. 2 (Summer 1983): 24-.

Keil, Hartmut, and John B. Jentz. *German Workers in
Industrial Chicago, 1850-1910: A Comparative Perspective*.
DeKalb, IL: Northern Illinois University Press, 1983.

Less, Virginia. "Germans from Russia Research." *Illinois
Libraries* 74, no. 5 (November 1992).

Otto, Ronald L. "Finding Genealogical Sources for Illinois
German-American Ancestors." *Illinois Libraries* 74, no. 5
(November 1992).

Smelser, Ronald M. *Finding Your German Ancestors*. Salt
Lake City: Ancestry, 1991.

Townsend, Andrew Jacke. *The Germans of Chicago*. Chicago,
1932.

Wellauer, Maralyn A. *German Immigration to America in the
Nineteenth Century: A Genealogist's Guide*. Milwaukee, WI:
Roots International, 1985.

German Research

By Ronald L. Otto

To research a German ancestor in Cook County, you need to
begin, as you would for any other genealogical endeavor, with
family records. You would then proceed to vital statistics,
court records, and U.S. census records. With the major
exception of church (and possibly fraternal organization)
records, don't expect to find separate Cook County records
for individuals of German descent. Many Cook County vital
and probate records are on microfilm available at family

history centers of The Church of Jesus Christ of Latter-day Saints (LDS Church). If the ancestor was here in 1900, you should start with a review of the 1900 Illinois Soundex to find the specific entry for the ancestor, and then extract all others of the same surname in Cook County or elsewhere in Illinois. Sooner or later you will use this surname information. If the surname has too many listings, select other entries of the same generation as the ancestor and of the parents. The 1900 Soundex (and the full census data) will provide a specific location, names, and approximate ages of wife and children, and the approximate year of immigration. This will be useful for future research.

German-American church records in Cook County are probably the most valuable records for researching a German born ancestor. Fortunately, most German-American religious organizations kept the European tradition of maintaining detailed church records. Prior to the year 1880, congregational records often included names of German villages. However, 1880 is merely a rule of thumb. You need to consult the individual church records because by the 1870s, German born and educated ministers were being replaced by German-American educated ministers. The effect was a decreased emphasis on the origins of the parishioners.

The church records most used by genealogists are baptismal, marriage, and burial. These, of course, are useful if the family you seek is detailed therein. Again, include everyone of the same surname in your extracts. Sooner or later, you will use this information. *Extract, don't abstract.* Eventually, all the details will prove useful. When you later return to complete abstracts, the records may no longer be available to you. Be sure to include sponsors at baptisms and witnesses at marriages. Although half were neighbors, the other half were relatives. Which were which? Surnames do not always answer the question.

Do not forget confirmation records. One experienced researcher noted that, in his research, the baptism of a certain ancestor was not in the church records. From a burial record he knew the year of birth. By checking the confirmation records 13 years after the birth year, he found the name of his ancestor and the names of the parents. Yes,

...ach seiner Rückkehr im Mai 1868 betrieb Herr
...ried einen Handel mit Faßdauben und im Au...
...1870 brachte er die Saladin'sche Brauerei an der
...der Archer und Stewart Avenue läuflich an sich.
...ungeheuren Schwierigkeiten, welche sich ihm an...
...lich entgegenstellten, überwand er mit Fleiß und
...ter Energie und seine Kundschaft vergrößerte sich
...derartig, daß er zwei große Eishäuser bauen
...te. Im Frühjahr 1884 errichtete er westlich von
...bisherigen Brauerei ein großes fünfstöckiges Ge...
...welches mit allen modernen Verbesserungen,
...sondern mit seinen eigenen werthvollen Erfin...
...gen, ausgestattet wurde. Einen schweren Kampf
...Herr Gottfried mit fast allen Brauereien des
...es zu bestehen, welche sein Patent auf eine Pich...
...hine ausnützten, ohne ihm eine Entschädigung
...zu bezahlen. Er gewann in allen Instanzen
...es wurde ihm eine bedeutende Entschädigungs...
...me zugesprochen. Im Juni 1881 wurde die Fir...
...ter dem Namen „Gottfried Brewing Company"
...erirt.

...err Gottfried war nicht nur ein tüchtiger und
...reicher Geschäftsmann, sondern spielt auch im
...gen Leben eine hervorragende Rolle. Er ist
...ied der Lessing Loge der Freimaurer, der Hoff...
...Loge J. D. O. F., der Knight Templars, Py...
...Ritter, des Germania Männerchors, des Chi...
...Schützenvereins und Mitglied und Gründer des
...vereins „Vorwärts". Seine bedeutenden Erfolge
...Herr Gottfried nicht nur seinen geschäftlichen
...igkeiten und seinem ehrenwerthen Charakter,
...ern auch seinem liebenswürdigen Wesen, seiner
...igkeit und seiner offenen Hand für wohlthätige
...e und gemeinnützige Bestrebungen zu danken.
...Gattin, welche ihm acht Kinder schenkte, war
...ets eine treue und intelligente Gehülfin.

...dolph und Ferdinand, der Erste der älteste,
...der jüngste Sohn, starben jung; Karl, der
...älteste Sohn, jetzt Sekretär der Gottfried Brew...
...Company, verheirathete sich vor fünf Jahren mit
...Hedwig Brand, einer Tochter des Herrn Ru...
...Brand. Febronia, die älteste Tochter, ist die
...in des Herrn Karl Reiffschneider, welcher in Au...
...wohnt; Ida, die zweite, ist die Wittwe des vor
...gen Jahren verstorbenen Herrn Karl Ortmeyer;
...erese, die dritte Tochter, ist die Gattin des
...John H. Weiß, Präsidenten der Gottfried Brew...
...ng Company; Mathilde, die vierte Tochter, ist
...Herrn A. G. Elcod, von der Firma Hanfell-El...
...Foundry Company verheirathet; und Maud, die
...e, heirathete kürzlich Herrn Philipp Brand, ei...
...Sohn des Herrn Rudolph Brand.

Fridolin Madlener.

Als Fridolin Madlener am 25. Januar 1897 seine Augen für immer schloß, verlor das Deutschthum Chicago's einen Vertreter, der in geschäftlichen und

Fridolin Madlener.

geselligen Kreisen sich eines ebenso allgemeinen als wohlverdienten Ansehens erfreute und dessen zu frühes Hinscheiden nicht nur ein herber Schlag für seine Familie war, sondern auch in der ganzen Stadt aufrichtiges Bedauern erregte. Seines gütigen Herzens, seiner stets offenen Hand wegen war er bei Reichen und Armen gleich beliebt und sein sonniges, stets heiteres Temperament erwarb ihm sowohl im Geschäftsleben, als auch im geselligen Verkehr zahlreiche Freunde.

Fridolin Madlener wurde am 3. Mai 1836 in Ueberlingen, am Bodensee, Baden, geboren. Hier lebten und starben seine Eltern Michael und Margaretha Madlener. Die Familie war eine angesehene und alte, und der Vater, welcher das Geschäft eines Müllers betrieb, bestimmte seinen Sohn Fridolin für die kaufmännische Laufbahn. Im Jahre 1856 kam der junge Madlener nach Chicago und verlegte sich vor allen Dingen auf die Erlernung der englischen Sprache und da er sich auch zugleich mit den hiesigen Geschäftsmethoden bekannt machen wollte, besuchte er das Dyrenfurth'sche Business College, das erste derartige Institut in Chicago. Er erlangte eine Anstellung

Figure 10: Chicago und Sein Deutschthum—1902
(courtesy The Newberry Library)

some of these early Chicago area church records are in German (or Latin in Catholic Churches). However, if the information therein is important to you, you will learn to read these records. For help, consult:

How To Read German Church Records Without Knowing Much German by Arta F. Johnson.

If I Can You Can Decipher Germanic Records by Edna M. Bentz.

Both are available at most genealogical book vendors. It is most important, if at all possible, to do the searching yourself. No one else has your interest in your family or your knowledge of the family names.

If you are not in Cook County, most churches will respond to written inquiries. But all churches have staff limitations, and may be unable to provide much, if any, research. You should always include a modest contribution with each request. Remember, research that produces negative results takes as much time as research that produces positive results. Neither party is satisfied if the desired information was not found. If you cannot do the research yourself, consider hiring a professional researcher from the area to do the search for you, especially when you seek information on more than a few events. Whoever does the search must deal with the temperament of the one who controls the records.Tact and diplomacy are essential not only foryour effort, but also for that of those who follow.

Where are the early church records for Cook County? Most are located at the church itself or at a nearby successor to a defunct church. A few of the records have been microfilmed and some are found in archives. For example, the archives of the Missouri Synod (Concordia Historical Institute, 801 DeMun Avenue, St. Louis, MO 63105) hold microfilmed copies of the registers of the earliest Lutheran Churches in Chicago: First Saint Paul and First Immanuel. The Concordia Historical Institute also offers useful pamphlets on German research, and on the use of the archives. A local repository for the Northern Illinois District of the Missouri Synod is located in Hillside (2301 Wolf Road, Hillside, IL 60167). It currently holds the registers for St. Matthew Lutheran which is still open and located at 2108 West 21st Street in Chicago.

Until recently, the local archives held the registers of various closed Missouri Synod Lutheran Churches; these registers have been transferred to the Concordia Historical Institute.

Archives for Lutheran Churches in Chicago also exist at the Evangelical Lutheran Church in America located in Rose- mont, IL (the mailing address is 8765 W. Higgins Road, Chicago, IL 60631). The registers of St John's Lutheran (Cooper's Grove) in the south Cook County community of Country Club Hills have been microfilmed, and are located in the Grande Prairie Library in Hazel Crest, IL. Microfilmed records for St. James Evangelical Lutheran Church, which was organized in 1869 and then located at Fremont and Garfield in Chicago, are at the Newberry Library.

The best method to locate the Cook County church which holds the records you seek is to review a denominational directory of current churches and addresses, and then compare such addresses to a current map of Chicago or your area or interest in Cook County. The best map for this purpose is *Geographia's Complete Street Atlas of Chicago and Vicinity* available at most Chicago book stores. Because street names changed you will occasionally need to refer to a 19th century map. Usually a denominational directory will provide the date of commencement of each church. However, the commencement date is not always the date the extant records begin. If you are not living in Cook County, visit a nearby church of the denomination you seek to look at the current directory. Remember the modest contribution. A current telephone book is a second choice for locating the church you seek. For Cook County, several telephone directories must be considered.

Another method is to review publications of Cook County genealogical societies. For example, the *Chicago Genealogist* (14, no. 3, 1982) has a listing of Chicago churches of all denominations as of the year 1892. It is a reprint of the list in Martin's *World's Fair Album-Atlas*. For south Cook County, the South Suburban Genealogical and Historical Society has a separate publication listing churches by township.

Information about Chicago churches will be found in the 19th century (and early 20th) Chicago directories. Usually the name of the church pastor is given. This is useful information to locate the specific church you seek when you have a marriage license that includes the name of the pastor. The Chicago Public Library and the Chicago Historical Society Library each hold Chicago city directory collections.

To gain a broad perspective of the location of the early Cook County churches of various denominations, all published Cook County histories will provide some information. These histories and genealogical publications are listed elsewhere in this book. City directories, where available, are also a good source. Other sources to consult are:

Schwab and Thoren. *History of the Illinois Conference of the Evangelical Church 1937*. Harrisburg, PA: Evangelical Press, 1937.

Note: These Evangelical Churches became Evangelical United Brethren and today are United Methodist.

Schwartzkopf, Louis J. *The Lutheran Trail.* St. Louis: Concordia Press, 1950.

Note: This covers only Missouri Synod churches.

Wiederaenders, Robert C. *Chicago Lutheran Planning Study*. Vol. 2, *A History of Lutheranism—Beginning to 1893*. National Lutheran Conference, 1965.

Mielton, J. Gordon. *Log Cabins to Steeples—The United Methodist Way in Illinois 1824-1974*. Nashville, TN: Parthanon Press, 1974.

Elbert, E. Duane. "The American Roots of German Lutheranism in Illinois." *Illinois Historical Journal* 97 (Summer 1985).

As mentioned before, all Cook County histories should be considered; however, for German research, two are particularly useful histories:

Hofmeister, Rudolf A. *The Germans in Chicago*. Champaign, IL: Stipes Publishing Co., 1976.

Has an extensive bibliography.

Chicago und Sein Deutschum. Cleveland: German American Press, 1902.

The sole limitation of this reference is that it is written in German.

For south Cook County ancestry (German or other), consider the manuscript *"Southern Cook County and History of Blue Island Before the Civil War"* by Ferdinand Schapper. This manuscript is several hundred pages long, and includes personal dates (unavailable elsewhere) on hundreds of south Cook County families. It is available at the Chicago Historical Society Library.

There is one Lutheran denomination that can cause some confusion for researchers. In Chicago, Cook County, and northeast Illinois during the 19th century, a number of German Protestant congregations associated with the United Evangelical Synod of the Northwest. Its archives were located at its seminary at Elmhurst College, Elmhurst (DuPage County), Illinois. In 1872, this Synod merged with others to form the German Evangelical Synod of North America. In 1934 a merger of this Synod with the Reformed Church resulted in the Evangelical and Reformed Church, and the designation of "E & R" for its individual congregations. In 1957 the E & R Church merged with the Christian Congregational to form the United Church of Christ ("U.C.C."), and today most of these former Evangelical , then E & R, churches are now designated "U.C.C." Consult a *United Church of Christ Yearbook* for dates of commencement of area E & R churches. A useful history of the Evangelical (Union) Church is:

Schneider, Carl Edward. *The German Church on the American Frontier.* St. Louis: Eden Publishing House, 1939.

The archives of the Evangelical E & R Church remain at their original location (Eden Archives, 475 E Lockwood Avenue, Webster Groves, MO 63119).

Some local information can be found at the Elmhurst College Library, but no defunct church registers are there (apparently). Remember to distinguish the Evangelical (Union) churches, later E & R, from   (today's United

Methodists) churches. The archives for the Illinois Conference of the Evangelical Association was formerly located at the Garrett-Evangelical Theological Seminary (2121 Sheridan Road, Evanston, IL 60201). On its way to becoming United Methodist, the Evangelical Association merged with the United Brethren Church to form the Evangelical United Brethren ("E.U.B") Church.

Some Cook County family information can be found in: "Index to the Subjects of Obituaries" abstracted from *Der Christliche Botsshafter of the Evangelical Church 1836-1866* by Mrs. E. R. Seder of Naperville, Illinois. A copy of this book can be found at the Newberry Library.

German Catholic Churches have extensive records of baptisms, confirmations, marriages and burials. Although there were no congregations whose members were all of German descent, records of these events can be found in a nearby Catholic Church regardless of its ethnic composition. Useful information can be found in *Finding Your Chicago Ancestor* by Margaret O'Hara (1982; out of print), and n *A History of the Parishes of the Archdioceses of Chicago* (1980). For additional information about Catholic Church records, see section 11.

I wrote a regular column, "German Interest Group News." for the *Newsletter of the Chicago Genealogical Society.* Occasionally I received correspondence from someone just beginning their German-American research. For the beginner, a useful introduction to Germanic research will be found in:

Konrad, J. *German Family Research Made Simple.* Monroe Falls, OH: Summit Publications.

This book has an excellent section for locating a village of origin. (The address of the publisher is: Summit Publications, P. O. Box 222, 44282.)

To further assist you in locating an elusive village, consider:

Otto, Ronald L. "Locating the Village of Origin for an Immigrant Ancestor." *Chicago Genealogist* 14, no. 1 (Fall 1981).

A more thorough publication is:

Research Guide to German-American Genealogy. St. Paul, MN: Germanic Genealogy Society.

This publication is available from the Germanic Genealogy Society (P. O. Box 16312, St. Paul, MN 55116-0312. The newsletter of this organization is one of the most informative available on the subject of German-American genealogy.

The two volume set by Larry Jensen, Genealogical Handbook of German Research provides an introduction to many aspects of German research, and is keyed to the microfilm collection of the Genealogical Society of Utah (LDS Church). This set is available from most genealogical book vendors, and from the author (P. O. Box 441, Pleasant Grove, UT 84062).

A society without geographic boundaries that can assist your research is the German Research Association (P. O. Box 11293, San Diego, CA 92111). They publish The German Connection three times yearly. Another national society, with both a quarterly publication and a newsletter), is Palatines to America, Capital UniversityBox 106, Columbus, OH 43209. A separate newsletter (six times a year) is published by the Illinois Chapter of Palatines to America (P. O. Box 3884, Quincy, IL 62301-3884, 309-342-0790). Do not be misled by the name Palatines, it is generic and includes all German speaking people regardless of period of immigration.

Local society publications are helpful to both the beginner and the experienced German researcher. Cumulative subject indexes for the Chicago Genealogist and for Where The Trails Cross have recently been published. Write to the Chicago Genealogical Society and the South Suburban Genealogical and Historical Society.

The Illinois State Genealogical Society Quarterly publishes articles about Cook County and German research. You may find this two-part article on finding German ancestors helpful:

Otto, Ronal L. "Finding Your German Ancestor's Church in Chicago." *Illinois State Genealogical Society Quarterly* 24, no. 1 (1992): 27-31; no. 2 (1992): 66-69.

The earliest Lutheran Church registers for the Cook County area were published in the *ISGS Quarterly* (17, no. 1, Spring 1985). These were the registers kept in 1838 and 1839 by the Rev. Cachend Ervenberg. A 15 year subject index for the *ISGS Quarterly* can be found in volume 15, no. 3 (Fall 1983).

Both the beginning, and the advanced researcher of German genealogy, must develop an ability to use gazetteers. They are essential to furthering your research. Suppose you know the name of your ancestor's village of origin. You have looked at the various geographic indexes, but they hold no records for your village of interest. Had you consulted a gazetteer, you would have learned that the Evangeliches (or Katholiches) Kirche for your ancestors was not in "your village" but in the adjoining village of "—." A search of the geographical indexes would inform you that the records of this church are available on microfilm. Or, perhaps wills are available once you know the "R. B." Maybe you will find civil records in still another community.

To assist you in using gazetteers, consult the pamphlet of the Genealogical Society of Utah: "Gazetteers-The German Empire (1871-1918)." It is available at most family history centers of the LDS Church. Each center has at least one gazetteer on permanent loan. The film numbers for *Meyers Orts-und-Verkeras-Lexicon* are: 0496640 (localities A-K) and 0496641 (localities L-Z).

At the Newberry Library, the *Meyers Orts-und-Verkeras-Lexicon* is found on the open shelves and *Ritter's Geographisch-Statistiches Lexicon* is under call number fg 005. 741. If you need to convert the German name of a village east of the Oder/Niese River to the current Polish name, the mechanics of how to use the family history centers' collection to make the conversion are found in *Poland-Prussia: How to Locate Vital Records of Former Prussian Areas of Poland in the Mormon Genealogical Library* by Daniel M. Schlyter. This seven page booklet is available from Genealogy Unlimited, Inc. One of the tools suggested by Schlyter is *Mueller's*

Directory of Localities Across the Oder-Niese Under Foreign Administration. This 1958 publication is found as LDS microfilm #1045448. While utilizing the collection of an family history center, remember to check the *International Genealogical Index* (IGI).

As with other genealogical research, German research information can be found in the major Chicago area libraries. Information on fraternal organization information is limited. Consult the Chicago Historical Society Library and the Newberry Library. To flesh out the genealogical skeleton of a German workingman in a Cook County, consider:

Keil, Hartmut, and John B. Jentz, eds. *German Workers in Industrial Chicago, 1850-1910: A Comparative Perspective.* DeKalb, IL: Northern Illinois University Press, 1983).

> This book describes the everyday life of the ancestors of most of us, the German workingman and woman, doing their best to raise a family and to enjoy life.

Greek Sources

Abbott, Grace. "A Study of the Greeks in Chicago." *The American Journal of Sociology,* (November 1909): 379-93.

Burgess, Thomas. *Greeks in America. An Account of Their Coming, Progress, Customs, Living, and Aspirations.* American Immigration Collection, Series #2. New York: Arno Press, 1970.

Chicago Board of Education. *Greek American.* Ethnic Studies Process. Chicago, 1972.

Diacou, Stacy, ed. *Hellenism in Chicago.* Chicago: The United Hellenic American Congress, 1982.

Kopan, Andrew T. *The Greeks of Chicago and the Great Fire.* Chicago, 1971. mimeographed.

Kopan, Andrew Thomas. "Education and Greek Immigrants in Chicago, 1892-1973: A Study in Ethnic Survival." Master's thesis, University of Chicago, 1974.

Kourvetaris, George A. *First and Second Generation Greeks in Chicago.* Athens, 1971.

Mistaras, Evangeline. "A Study of First and Second Generation Greek Out-Marriage in Chicago." Master's thesis, University of Chicago, 1950.

Petrakis, Harry Mark. "Chicago's Greeks, the Warmth of Halsted Street." *Chicago Tribune Magazine,* (August 4, 1974).

Saloutos, Theodore. *The Greeks in the United States.* Cambridge, 1964.

> Contains a large amount of information related to Chicago.

Yeracaris, Constantine A. "A Study of the Voluntary Associations of the Greek Immigrants of Chicago from 1890 to 1948 with Special Emphasis on World War II and the Post War Period." Master's thesis, University of Chicago, 1950.

Irish Sources

The following information was extracted from an article titled "The Irish in Chicago" by Kyle J. Betit and Thomas M. Cook, written for periodical *The Irish At Home and Abroad,* Salt Lake City, 1994 (P. O. Box 521806, Salt Lake City, 84152).

In large part, the Great Potato Famine of the late 1840s in Ireland was responsible for the great numbers of Irish Catholic immigrants who sought a new life, and settled in three specific parts of the Chicago area: on the westside, between Halsted Street and the Chicago River from Lake Street south to Harrison Street; on the northside, along Market Street and Indiana Street (now Grand Avenue); and on the southside beyond the city limits, along the south branch of the Chicago River and the area between the river and Archer Avenue. Three Catholic parishes grew out of these three areas: St. Patrick's on the westside; Holy Name on the northside; and St. Bridget's on the southside.

Another large wave of Irish Catholic immigrants, particularly from the Irish counties of Mayo and Galway, reached Chicago in the 1880s. By the end of the nineteenth century, half of the Irish Catholics lived on the southside.

Around the turn of the century, the Irish began leaving the old neighborhoods of central Chicago for the suburbs. There were recognizable patterns to this migration. Westside Irish families tended to move farther west and north along the elevated railways built to link the westside with downtown. Southside Irish families generally moved farther south and southwest along similar elevated rail lines.

Irish American Heritage Center
    4626 North Knox Avenue, Chicago, IL 60630
    (312-282-7035)
Irish Interest Group
    Contact the Chicago Genealogical Society.

Irish Personal Name Index

Biographies and obituaries of the Chicago Irish are the sources of an extensive index compiled by John Corrigan. Information has been extracted principally from *The Chicago Inter Ocean, The Chicago Citizen, The South Side Sun, Lake Vindicator, The Sun,* and t*he New World* (Chicago Archdiocese) newspapers. Additional data has been extracted from published Chicago sources and personal research. Send a self-addressed, stamped envelope for more information and fee schedules to:

John Corrigan
    1669 West 104th Street
    Chicago, IL 60643.

Irish Studies Collection

DePaul University
    Lincoln Park Campus Library
    2323 North Seminary
    Chicago, IL 60614
The Irish studies collection housed in the library includes educational materials pertaining to the history, literature, and culture of Ireland.

Selected Bibliography

Betit, Kyle J., and Thomas M. Cook. "The Irish in Chicago." *The Irish At Home and Aboard* 2, no. 2 (1994-95): 46-53.

The Irish At Home and Aboard is a quarterly (P. O. Box 521806, Salt Lake City, UT 84152).

Cross, Robert. "Chicago's Irish: Swimming in the Mainstream." *Chicago Tribune Magazine*, (September 17, 1978): 38-.

Duff, John B. *The Irish in the United States. Minorities in American Life Series*. Belmont, CA: Wadsworth Publishing Company, Inc., 1971.

Falley, Margaret Dickson. *Irish and Scotch-Irish Ancestral Research*. Evanston, IL: Margaret Dickson Falley, 1962.

Fallows, Marjorie R. *Irish Americans. Identity and Assimilation. Ethnic Groups in America Series*. Englewood Cliffs, NJ: Prentice Hall, Inc., 1979.

Ffrench, Charles, ed. *Biographical History of the American Irish in Chicago*. Chicago, 1897.

Funchion, Michael F. *Chicago's Irish Nationalists, 1881-1890*. New York, 1976.

Griffin, William D. *A Portrait of the Irish in America*. New York: Charles Scribner's Sons, 1981.

Heraldic Artists, Ltd. *Handbook on Irish Genealogy*. Dublin: Heraldic Artists, Ltd., 1978.

Hoobler, Dorothy, and Thomas Hoobler. *The Irish American Family Album*. New York: Oxford University Press, 1994.

Maguire, John F. *Irish in America*. American Immigration Collection, Series #1. New York: Arno Press, 1971.

Maylone, R. Russell. "Irish-American Falley Collection." *Illinois Libraries* 74, no. 5 (November 1992).

McCaffrey, Lawrence J., Ellen Skerrett, Michael Funchion, and Charles Fanning. *The Irish in Chicago*. Chicago: University of Illinois Press, 1987.

O'Day, Edward J. "Tracking Irish Immigrant Ancestors."

Illinois State Genealogical Society Quarterly 16, no. 4 (Winter 1984).

———"From Irish-American to Irish Ancestry." *Illinois Libraries* 74, no. 5 (November 1992).

O'Grady, Jospeh P. *How The Irish Became Americans. The Immigrant Heritage of America Series.* Boston: Twayne Publishers.

Piper, Ruth M. *"The Irish in Chicago 1848 to 1871."* Master's thesis, University of Chicago, 1936.

Ryan, James G. *Irish Records Sources for Local & Family History.* Salt Lake City: Ancestry, 1988.

———. *Tracing Your Dublin Ancestors.* Dublin, Ireland: Flyleaf Press, 1988.

Wittke, Carl. *The Irish in America. Localized History Series.* New York: Teachers College Press, 1968.

Yurdan, Marilyn. *Irish Family History.* Baltimore: Genealogical Publishing Co., 1990.

Italian Sources

Italian-American Heritage Center
  263 North York Road
  Emhurst, IL 60126
Italians in Chicago Project
  Department of History
  University of Illinois at Chicago
  Box 4348
  Chicago, IL 60680
  (312-996-3144)

The Italians in Chicago Project traveling exhibit was created from 5000 items from 300 donors. The material suggests the variety and texture of Italian-American culture, creating a feeling of nostalgia for the warm family lives of the hard-working immigrants, their children, and the Chicago experience. Copies of all collected materials, and the oral history tapes and transcriptions, are on file at the Manuscripts Department of the library at the University of Illinois at Chicago. A permanent version of the exhibit is at the Italian Cultural Center.

Selected Bibliography

Chicago Board of Education. *"Italian Americans."* Ethnic Studies Process. Chicago, 1972.

Candeloro, Dominic. "Suburban Italians: Chicago Heights, 1890-1975". In *Ethnic Chicago*, edited by Peter d'A. Jones and Melvin G. Holli. Grand Rapids, MI: William B Eerdman's Publishing Company, 1981.

———. *Villa Scalabrini: Citadel of Italian American Ethnicity.* unpublished paper, 1984.

———. *Chicago's Italians: A Survey of the Ethnic Factor 1850-1985.* unpublished paper, 1985.

———."Making History: A Handbook for Italian-American Social History Projects." *Illinois Libraries* 74, no. 5 (November 1992).

Cole, Trafford R. *Italian Genealogical Records: How to Use Italian Civil, Ecclesiastical & Other Records in Family History Research.* Salt Lake City: Ancestry, 1995.

Graham, Jory. "The Italians." *Chicago* 6, no. 4 (Winter 1969): 72-78.

Hoobler, Dorothy, and Thomas Hoobler. *The Italian American Family Album.* New York: Oxford University Press, 1994.

Lopreato, Joseph. *Italians Americans. Ethnic Groups in Comparative Perspective.* New York: Random House, 1970.

Lord, Eliot. *The Italians in America.* San Francisco: R & E Research Associates, 1970.

Nelli, Humbert S. *Italians in Chicago, 1880-1930.* New York, 1970.

Quaintance, Ester Crockett. "Rents and Housing Conditions in the Italian District of the Lower North Side of Chicago, 1924." Master's thesis, University of Chicago, 1925.

Sager, Gertrude E. "Immigration: Based Upon a Study of the Italian Women and Girls of Chicago." Master's thesis, University of Chicago, 1914.

Schiavo, Giovanni E. *The Italians in Chicago: A Study in Americanization.* Chicago, 1928.

Vecoli, Rufolph John. "Chicago's Italians Prior to World War I: A Study of Their Social and Economic Adjustment." Ph. D. diss., University of Wisconsin, 1962.

Wright, Caroll D. *The Italians in Chicago.* NY: Arno Press, 1970.

Zaloha, Anna. "A Study of the Persistence of Italian Customs among 143 Families of Italian Descent, Members of Social Clubs at Chicago Commons." Master's thesis, Northwestern University, 1937.

Japanese Sources

Nagata, Kiyoshi. "A Statistical Approach to the Study of Acculturation of an Ethnic Group Based on Communication Oriented Variables: The Case of Japanese-Americans in Chicago." Ph. D. diss., University of Illinois, Urbana, 1969.

Nakane, Kenji. *History of the Japanese in Chicago.* Chicago, 1968. (In Japanese).

Nishi, Setsuko Matsunaga. "Japanese American Achievement in Chicago: A Cultural Response to Degradation." Master's thesis, University of Chicago, 1947.

Osako, Masako M. "Japanese-Americans: Melting into the All-American Pot?" In *Ethnic Chicago,* edited by Peter d'A. Jones and Melvin G. Holli. Grand Rapids, MI: William B Eerdman's Publishing Company, 1981.

Uyeki, Eugene Shigemi. "Process and Patterns of Nisei Adjustment in Chicago." Ph. D. diss., University of Chicago, 1953.

Jewish Sources—See section 11.

Lithuanian Sources

Balzekas Museum of Lithuanian Culture
  6500 South Pulaski
  Chicago, IL 60629
  (312-582-6500)

This museum and library has folk art, handicrafts, memorabilia, weapons, costumes, and houses approximately 10,000 volumes on Lithuanian history and humanities. You can also obtain genealogical society information from the museum.

Selected Bibliography

Consulate General of Lithuania. *Lithuanians in Chicago.* Chicago.

Daraska, Jessie L. "The Immigration History and Genealogy Department of the Balzekas Museum of Lithuanian Culture." *Illinois Libraries* 74, no. 5 (November 1992).

Fainhauz, David. *Lithuanians in Multi-Ethnic Chicago, Until World War II.* Chicago: Lithuanian Library Press, Inc., 1977.

Kezys, Algim. *A Lithuanian Cemetery.* Chicago: Loyola University Press, 1976.

Krisciumas, Joseph. "Lithuanians in Chicago." Master's thesis, DePaul University, 1935.

Raece, Helen. "A Dream of Freedom." *Chicago Tribune Magazine,* (April 30, 1978): 23-30.

Mexican Sources

De Curutchet, Marta Isabel Kollman. "Localization of the Mexican and Cuban Population of Chicago." Ph. D. diss., University Of Chicago, 1967.

Hoobler, Dorothy, and Thomas Hoobler. *The Mexican American Family Album.* New York: Oxford University Press, 1994.

Jordan, Lois B. *Mexican Americans.* Littleton, CO: Libraries Unlimited, Inc., 1973.

Pacyga, Dominic A., and Ellen Skerrett. *Chicago City of Neighborhoods: Histories and Tours.* Chicago: Loyola University Press, 1986.

Ropka, Gerald W. "The Evolving Residential Pattern of the Mexican, Puerto Rican and Cuban Population in the City of Chicago." Ph. D. diss., Michigan State University, 1973.

Sussman, Sue. "The Mexicans." *Chicago* 6, no. 3 (Fall 1969).

Norwegian Sources

Andersen, A. W. *The Norwegian-Americans.* The Immigrant Heritage of America Series. Boston: Twayne Publishers, 1975.

Blegen,T. C. *Norwegian Migration to America: The American Transition.* Northfield, MN: 1940.

Qualey, Carlton C. *Norwegian Settlement in the United States.* American Immigration Collection, Series 2. New York: Arno Press, 1970.

Strand, Algot E., comp. *A History of the Norwegians of Illinois.* Chicago: J. Anderson Publishing Co., 1905.

Contains much information about Chicago and its Norwegian community.

Wellauer, Maralyn A. *Tracing Your Norwegian Roots.* Milwaukee, WI: Maralyn A. Wellauer, 1979.

Polish Sources

Polish Museum of America
  984 N. Milwaukee Avenue
  Chicago, IL 60622
  (312-384-3352)

Free admission

Hours: Monday thru Saturday 1:00 to 4:00 P.M.

Sunday from 12 noon to 5:00 P.M.

Closed Good Friday and Christmas Day

Library open: 10:00 A.M. to 4:00 P.M. week days only.

Researchers should call the library in advance to specify their requirements.

Exhibits of Polish art, costumes, religious artifacts, and memorabilia of Polish leaders.

The library houses approximately 15,000 volumes on Poland and Poles of Chicago. The library also contains: a newspaper microfilm collection, geographical dictionaries of Poland, histories of churches and villages, Polish heraldry, Polish biographical dictionaries, Polish Army Daily Order Books, family histories, Chicago Polish telephone directories, and anniversary books of Chicago parishes.

Polish Genealogical Society of America
  984 N. Milwaukee Ave.
  Chicago, IL 60622
    The Polish Genealogical Society was organized in 1978 to promote interest in Polish genealogy, and to provide an exchange of information among researchers. The society publishes the semiannual PGS Newsletter, the PGS Bulletin, and has a number of excellent Polish research reference volumes available for sale. It holds quarterly meetings and workshop sessions. Members and non-members are invited to submit ancestor index cards for inclusion in a master index of Polish ancestors.

Polish National Alliance Library—Archives
  1520 West Division Street
  Chicago, IL 60622
  (312-276-0700)
    A circulating library of approximately 18,000 books in English and Polish; archival materials; rare books from Poland; and information on Poles of Chicago.

Selected Bibliography

Ames, Mary Boczon, *How to Research Your Personal Polish Family History*. New Carrollton, MD: Mary Boczon Ames, 1976.

Andrea, M. "The Societies of St. Stanislaw Kosta Parish, Chicago." *Polish American Studies* 9, nos. 1-2 (January-June 1952).

Chorzempa, Rosemary A. *Polish Roots*. Baltimore: Genealogical Publishing Company, 1993.

Emmons, Charles Frank. "Economic and Political Leadership in Chicago's Polonia: Some Sources of Ethnic Persistence and Mobility." Ph. D. diss., University of Illinois, Chicago, 1971.

Fox, Paul. *Poles in America*. American Immigration Collection, Series 2. New York: Arno Press, 1970.

Franzin, Judith R. *A Translation Guide to 19th Century Polish Language Civil Registration Documents (Birth, Marriage and Death Records)*. Niles, IL: The Jewish Genealogical Society, 1985.

Gnacinski, Jan, and Len Gnacinski. *Polish and Proud: Tracing Your Polish Ancestry*. West Allis, WI: Janlen Enterprises, 1979.

Golembiewski, Thomas E. *Index to Polish American Family Biographies Found in Jubilee Books of St. Stanislaus Kostka Parish, and Holy Trinity Parish*. Chicago: The Polish Genealogical Society, 1982.

———. *The Study of Obituaries as a Source for Polish Genealogical Research*. Chicago: The Polish Genealogical Society, 1984.

Hollowak, Thomas L., and William F. Hoffman. *Index to the Obituaries and Death Notices Appearing in the Dziennik Chicagoski*. Chicago: Polish Genealogical Society.

Hollowak, Thomas L., ed. *Polish Directory for the City of Chicago 1903*. Chicago: The Polish Genealogical Society, 1981.

Inviolata Ficht, Sister M. "Noble Street in Chicago: Socio-Cultural Study of Polish Residents within Ten Blocks." Master's thesis, DePaul University, 1952.

Kantowicz, Edward R. *Polish-American Politics in Chicago 1888-1940.* Chicago: The University of Chicago Press, 1975.

Konrad, J. *Polish Family Research.* Munroe Falls, OH: Summit Publications, 1982.

Kowallis, Otto K. *A Genealogical Guide and Atlas of Silesia.* Logan, UT: Everton Publishers, Inc., 1976.

Lagodzinska, Adela. *The Polish Heritage and the Future of Chicago.* Chicago: Polish Women's Alliance of America, 1953.

Lewanski, Richard C. *Guide to Polish Libraries and Archives.* Irvington, NY: Columbia University Press, 1974.

Lopata, Helena Znaniecki. *Polish Americans: Status Competition in an Ethnic Community.* Ethnic Groups in American Life Series. Chicago: Claretian Publications, 1972.

Lopata, Helena Znaniecki. "The Function of Voluntary Associations in an Ethnic Community: 'Polonia'." In *Contributions to Urban Sociology,* edited by Ernest W. Burgess and Donald J. Bogue. Chicago, 1964.

Magierski, Louis. "Polish American Activities in Chicago 1919-1939." Master's thesis, University of Illinois, Urbana, 1940.

Michalski, Diane Marie. "The Family in a Polish-American Community in Chicago." Master's thesis, University of Chicago, 1942.

Nowosielski, Janina Eugenia. "The Changes in the Residential Patternof the Polish Population in Chicago, Illinois as a Measure of Acculturation." Master's thesis, Northeastern Illinois State College, 1971.

Obal, Thaddeus J. *A Bibliography for Genealogical Research Involving Polish Ancestry.* Hillsdale, NJ: Thaddeus J. Obal, 1978.

Ortell, Gerald A. *Polish Parish Records of The Roman Catholic Church.* Astoria, NY: Gerald A. Ortell, 1979.

Ozog, Julius John. "A Study of Polish Home Ownership in Chicago." Master's thesis, University of Chicago, 1942.

Parot, Joseph John. *Polish Catholics in Chicago, 1850-1920: A Religious History.* DeKalb, IL: Northern Illinois University Press, 1981.

Pawlowski, Eugene Joseph. "The Polish American Element in the Politics of Chicago." Master's thesis, Northwestern University, 1970.

Peckwas, Edward A. *Collection of Articles on Polish Heraldry.* Chicago: Edward A. Peckwas, 1978.

------. "Genealogical Resources of the Polish Museum Library." *Illinois Libraries* 74, no. 5 (November 1992).

Poles of Chicago, 1837-1937: A History of One Century of Polish Contribution to the City of Chicago, Illinois. Chicago: Polish Pageant, 1937.

Slowiak, Walter J. "A Comparative Study of the Social Organization of the Family in Poland and the Polish Immigrant Family in Chicago." Master's thesis, Loyola University, 1950.

Tobiasiewicz, Maryellen. *Poles in Chicago* 15, nos. 2, 3 & 4 (Winter 1983, Spring & Summer 1984).

Wellauer, Maralyn A. *Tracing Your Polish Roots.* Rev. ed. Milwaukee, WI: Maralyn A. Wellauer, 1979.

Russian Sources

Hall, Thomas Randolph. "The Russian Community of Chicago." *Papers in Illinois History* 44, 1937.

Hall, Thomas Randolph. "Russians in Chicago." *Pierce Papers*, Regenstein Library, University of Chicago. Photocopy.

Mehr, Kahlile B., and Daniel M. Schlyter. *Sources for Genealogical Research in the Soviet Union.* Buffalo Grove, IL: Genun Publishers, 1983.

Scottish Sources

Cory, Kathleen B. *Tracing Your Scottish Ancestry.* Baltimore: Genealogical Publishing Co., 1990.

MacMillan, Thomas C. "The Scots and Their Descendants in Illinois." *Illinois State Historical Society,* vol. 26, (Springfield, IL, 1919): 31-85.

McLeod, Dean L. "Success In Tracing Your Scottish Ancestors." *The Genealogical Helper* (January-February 1980).

Stuart, Margaret. *Scottish Family History: A Guide to Works of Reference on the History and Genealogy of Scottish Families.* Buffalo Grove, IL: Genealogy Unlimited, Inc.

Address of Genealogy Unlimited, Inc. : 789 Buffalo Grove, IL 60089 (312-541-3175). This guide lists several titles and maps for Scottish research.

Tracing Your Scottish Ancestry. Northwest Orient Airlines, 1983.

Swedish Sources

Swedish-American Historical Society
    5125 North Spaulding Avenue
    Chicago, IL 60625
    (312-583-5722)

The purpose of this society is to stimulate and promote interest in Swedish-American contributions to the history and growth of the United States, collect and preserve documents and other valuable material, encourage historical research, and sponsor publications that will keep this heritage alive and strong. The society publishes a quarterly known as the *Swedish Pioneer Historical Quarterly,* a respected, frequently quoted journal, available in university and other libraries throughout the United States and abroad. The Swedish-American Archives of Greater Chicago are located on the campus of North Park College, but the society is not affiliated with the college.

The archives, established in 1968, contain a rich documentary record of the Swedish-American experience. Emphasis is given to records of the Swedish-American experience in Chicago, once known as "the world's second largest Swedish city." These holdings have provided a resource for scholars, students, genealogists, and American and Swedish journalists, among others. Materials include letters, diaries, family histories, organization records, newspapers, periodicals, pamphlets, music, photographs, books, oral histories and reference files.

The North Park campus is also the home of the Covenant Archives and Historical Library. The library contains books about the Covenant Church and other Swedish-American denominations. Timothy J. Johnson has written a concise overview of the archives.

Both archives are open Monday through Thursday (by appointment) and are located at Foster and Kedzie Avenues in Chicago. For additional information and appointments call 312-583-2700, ext. 5267.

Another center for conducting Swedish-American genealogical research is the Swenson Swedish Immigration Research Center (Augustana College, Box 175, Rock Island, IL 61201). The Center is located on campus in the Denkmann Memorial Hall (the former college library building), and is considered one of the premier facilities for conducting Swedish genealogical research; refer to the Kermit B. Westerberg article for more detailed information about the Center and its collections.

Selected Bibliography

Beijbom, Ulf. *Swedes in Chicago: A Demographic and Social Study of the 1846-1880 Immigration*. Stockholm, 1971.

Beijbom, Ulf. "Chicago's Swede Town—Gone But Not Forgotten." *The Swedish Pioneer Historical Quarterly* (October 1964): 144-158.

————. "Scandinavians in Chicago 1850-1860." *The Swedish Pioneer Historical Quarterly* (January 1963): 163-174.

Hemdahl, Reuel G. "The Swedes in Illinois Politics: An Immigrant Group in an American Political Setting." Ph. D. diss., Northwestern University, 1940.

Johansson, Carl-Erik. *Cradled in Sweden: A Practical Help for Genealogical Research in Swedish Records.* Rev. ed. Logan, UT: Everton Publishers, 1977.

Johnson, Timothy J. "Swedish-American Genealogy and the Archives at North Park College." *Illinois Libraries* 74, no. 5 (November 1992).

Nelson, Helge. *The Swedes and the Swedish Settlements in North America.* Lund, 1943.

Olson, Ernst W. *History of the Swedes of Illinois.* 2 vols. Chicago: Engberg-Homberg Publishing Company, 1908.

Volume 2 contains biographical sketches.

————. *The Swedish Element in Illinois. Survey of the Past Seven Decades.* Chicago: Swedish American Biographical Publishers, 1917.

Olsson, Nils William. "Tracing Your Swedish Ancestry." *Swedish Pioneer Historical Quarterly* 13 (1962). Reprint, Stockholm: Royal Swedish Ministry of Foreign Affairs, 1965.

————."First Swedes in Chicago (1838-50)." *American Swedish Monthly* 42, no. 6 (June 1948): 81-82.

Scott, Eleanor Torell. "The Influence of Swedish Settlers on a Community in Greater Chicago." *The Swedish Pioneer Historical Quarterly* (January 1954): 13-19.

Stephenson, George M. *The Stormy Years of the Swedish Colony in Chicago Before the Great Fire.* Illinois State Historical Society, vol. 36, (Springfield, IL, 1929): 166-184.

Westerberg, Kermit B. "Genealogical Research and Resources at the Swenson Swedish Immigration Research Center." *Illinois Libraries* 74, no. 5 (November 1992).

This article provides an excellent overview of the Center, and the resources available.

Ukrainian Sources

Ukrainian National Museum
  2453 W. Chicago Avenue
  Chicago, IL 60622
  (312-276-6565)
Hours: Sunday 12:00 P.M.—3 P.M. (4:30 P.M. when Culture Bus is in service)

Selected Bibliography

Kochman, Thomas, and Miroslav Semchyshyn. *Ukrainians in Illinois*. Chicago: Ukrainian Bicentennial Committee, 1976.

Pleshkewych, Dan. *Ukrainians in Chicago: Immigration and Assimilation.* Northeastern Illinois University, 1975. Photocopy.

SECTION SIXTEEN

Family History Library of The Church of Jesus Christ of Latter-day Saints

The Genealogical Society of Utah of The Church of Jesus Christ of Latter-day Saints (LDS Church; "The Mormons") was incorporated in 1894, and serves as an umbrella organization for the different LDS Church organizations involved in the collection, storage, and distribution of genealogical information. Over the years, the names of the member organizations and the structure of the collective have changed. However, for the purpose of negotiations, acquisitions, and microfilming records, the name Genealogical Society of Utah has been retained.

Family History Library

The Family History Library (FHL) was the organization created to act as a repository for the collected genealogical information; it began preserving records on microfilm in 1938. Trained specialists throughout the world are microfilming a variety of records including land grants, deeds, probate, marriage, cemetery, parish registers of all religious denominations, and passenger lists. It is the most active and comprehensive genealogical program in the world. More than 1.7 million rolls of microfilm and approximately 325,000 microfiche have been accumulated thus far. These microfilm and microfiche records are available for public use at the FHL. Many of the resources at the FHL can be found or accessed at a local family history center.

A booklet is available from the FHL (for a nominal fee) that provides information to help orient you on the basic steps of research, and how to use the FHL or family history centers. The FHL is located at 35 North West Temple Street, Salt Lake City, UT 84150 (801-240-2331).

Family History Centers

A system of family history centers was established in 1964. There are now over 1,600 of these centers operating in 57 countries and territories. The family history centers provide genealogical researchers access to many of the resources at the FHL. A family history center can obtain, on loan, most of the FHL microfilm and microfiche holdings if you make a request in person at one of the centers. All of the family history centers are staffed by volunteers, and have limited research hours during the week. The staff would prefer you call, rather than write, for information about the operations of a center.

Family History Centers in Chicago Area

The family history centers currently operating in the Chicago area are:

Chicago Heights Family History Center
  402 Longwood Drive
  (708-754-2525)
Naperville Family History Center
  Ridgeland & Naperville Roads
  (708-505-0233)

Orland Park Family History Center
  13150 South 88th Avenue
  (708-361-5474)
Schaumburg Family History Center
  1320 West Schaumburg Road
  (708-882-9889)
Wilmette Family History Center
  2801 Lake Avenue
  (708-251-9818)

Genealogical Resources

Besides the microfilm and microfiche collection, there are many other resources developed by the Genealogical Society of Utah to help you find and use the information at the FHL. Examples of some of these resources are:

Family History Library Catalog

The *Family History Library Catalog* is a list of the holdings at the FHL, and was a standard card catalog until 1969 when computerization of the catalog was begun. The conversion was completed in 1987, and a computer printout of the catalog is available on microfiche. You can search the catalog by author; locality; locality, foreign-language (geographic headings and categories are in the native language); subject; surname; or title.

The catalog is also available on a CD-ROM, and allows you to search by film number, locality, and surname. Use the catalog to determine the microfilm, microfiche, or book numbers you need to find, or request, specific records.

International Genealogical Index

The *International Genealogical Index* (IGI) lists the names of over 150 million deceased persons, and includes information (if available) on birth, christening, marriage, and LDS temple ordinance dates. It is organized by country and then by state or province within that country. Each state, or province, contains an alphabetical list of names and supporting birth and marriage information. The IGI is available on CD-ROM and microfiche at the FHL and family history centers.

Social Security Death Index

The *Social Security Death Index* is available only on CD-ROM, and contains 39 million Social Security Administration records of deaths from 1962 forward.

FamilySearch

FamilySearch is a computer program developed as an aid in searching genealogical records. Originally, you could use *FamilySearch* only at the FHL or at a family history center equipped to run the program. However, it was recently licensed to a commercial distributor who is selling and installing the program in local libraries around the country. *FamilySearch* provides computer access to many sources of information including: Ancestral File, IGI, Family History Library Catalog, Social Security Death Index, and Military Index.

Ancestral File

Ancestral File is used with *FamilySearch* to link individuals into families and pedigrees. The file is available only on CD-ROM. Information of interest can be printed or copied to a computer diskette if the necessary hardware (printer or diskette drive) is available on the computer you are using.

SECTION SEVENTEEN

Gazetteer of Cook County Towns and Townships

In 1795, an act of Congress required that a survey of the Northwest Territory be made in preparation for offering public lands for sale. With meridians as reference lines, land was marked off in squares six miles on each side. These Congressional, or survey, townships have never been units of government, but their boundaries have been used as the basis for school districts, civil townships, road districts, election districts, and statistical reports. Most civil townships within Cook County are based on these Congressional District lines.

Early settlers from the East brought the concept of New England, where the town was the general purpose unit of government. As a result, 85 township counties, including Cook County, and 17 commission counties, were established in Illinois in 1848. Thirty-eight civil townships were established as political divisions of Cook County. The eight civil townships within Chicago's boundaries are inactive, but Congressional township lines remain.

Alsip—Worth Township; Zip Code 60658. South of Chicago on the Calumet Sag Channel; Incorporated in 1927.

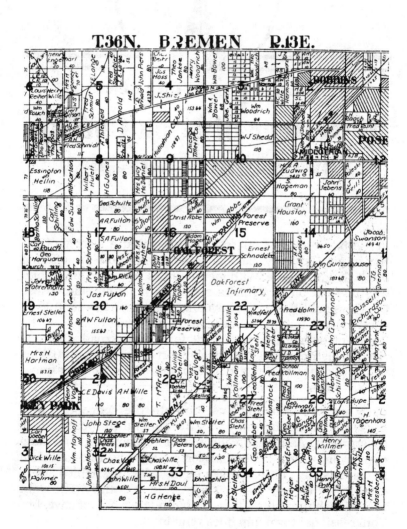

Figure 11: Bremen Township, Cook County—ca. 1880

Arlington Heights—Elk Grove, Palatine and Wheeling Townships; Zip Code 60005. Located northwest of Chicago. Settled in the 1830s and incorporated in 1887.

Auburn—Town of Lake.

Avondale—Jefferson Township.

Bandow—Jefferson Township.

Barrington—Barrington and Palatine Townships, Cook-Lake County line; Zip Code 60010. Located 32 miles northwest of Chicago, and founded in 1845. Early pioneers in Barrington included Quakers; Some came from Great Barrington, Massachusetts from which it derives its name. Main Street in Barrington is the dividing line of Cook and Lake counties.

Barrington Hills—Barrington Township; encompasses 30 sq. miles of Cook, Lake, McHenry, and Kane counties; Zip Code 60010; Incorporated in 1959.

Barrington Township—Presently comprised of: Barrington (part); Barrington Hills (part); Hoffman Estates (part); Inverness (part); and South Barrington.

Bartlett—Hanover Township; Cook-DuPage County lines; Zip Code 60103. Located 31 miles west of the Chicago Loop. Founded in 1873 by Luther Bartlett, the first postmaster, who also bought the land in 1844. Incorporated in 1891.

Bensenville—Leyden Township; Zip Code 60106.

Bedford Park—Lyons and Stickney Townships; Zip Code 60638. Located west of Chicago, and incorporated as a village in 1940.

Bellwood—Proviso Township; Zip Code 60104. Located 13 miles west of Chicago. The first enterprise in town was a blacksmith shop (1870). Incorporated in 1900.

Berkeley—Proviso Township; Zip Code 60163. Located west of Chicago, and named for Berkeley, California. Incorporated in 1924.

Berwyn—Berwyn Township; Zip Code 60402. Located 10 miles west of Chicago, and named for a town in Pennsylvania. Chartered in 1908.

Berwyn Township—Presently comprised of Berwyn City.

Bloom—See Chicago Heights.

Bloom Township—Presently comprised of: Chicago Heights; East Chicago Heights; Flossmoor (part); Glenwood (part); Homewood (part); Lansing (part); Lynwood; Olympia Fields (part); Park Forest (part); Sauk Village; South Chicago Heights; and Steger.

Blue Island—Bremen, Calumet, Thornton and Worth Townships; Zip Code 60406. Located south of Chicago on the Calumet Sag Canal. Blue Island was first settled in 1835 by German and Italian pioneers and was named for the ridge upon which it grew. The ridge is a glacial remnant on the otherwise flat Chicago lake plain. At times a blue haze could be seen enveloping the densely wooded ridge which rose like an island from the surrounding marshlands. Blue Island became incorporated in 1872.

Bremen Township—Presently comprised of: Blue Island (part); Country Club Hills (part); Crestwood (part); Harvey (part); Hazel Crest (part); Homewood (part); Markham (part); Midlothian; Oak Forest; Orland Park (part); Posen (part); Robbins (part); and Tinley Park (part).

Bridge View—Lyons, Palatine, Stickney and Worth Townships; Zip Code 60455. Located southwest of Chicago, Bridge View was incorporated in 1947.

Brighton Park—Town of Cicero.

Broadview—Proviso Township; Zip Code 60153. Located west of Chicago. Incorporated as a village in 1910.

Brookfield—Lyons, Proviso, and Riverside Townships; Zip Code 60513. Located west of Chicago. Founded in 1893 following extensive land purchases by members of the Ogden, Armour, McCormick, and Rockefeller families. Originally called Grossdale, the name was changed to Bookfield in 1905.

Buffalo Grove—Wheeling Township; Zip Code 60090. Located 15 miles northwest of Chicago, at the Lake County and Cook County line, in an agricultural area noted for feed-grains.

Burbank—Stickney Township; Zip Code 60459.

Burnham—Thornton Township; Zip Code 60633. At the Indiana line just north of Calumet City.

Burr Oak—Calumet Park.

Burr Ridge—Lyons Township.

Caldwell's Reserve—Jefferson Park and Niles Townships.

Calumet City—Thornton Township; Zip Code 60409. Located 20 miles south of Chicago on the Indiana border. Calumet City was platted in 1833, but owed much of its growth to the real estate boom of the 1920s. The city developed as part of the residential-industrial complex of Gary-South Chicago-Hammond. It was called West Hammond until 1924 when it gained its present name (derived from the French word for "peace-pipe of the Indians").

Calumet Park—Calumet and Thornton Townships; Zip Code 60643. Located south of Chicago. Originally known as Burr Oak, the name was changed to Calumet Park in 1925.

Calumet Township—Until March 5, 1867, Calumet Township was part of what is now Hyde Park. The township originally had within its limits the villages of Blue Island, Washington Heights, and Morgan Park. Presently comprised of: Blue Island (part); Calumet Park; Riverdale (part); and Chicago (part).

Chicago—Seat of Cook County.

Canfield—Maine Township.

Central Park—Cicero.

Cheltenham Beach—Hyde Park.

Chicago Heights—Bloom Township; Zip Code 60411. Located south of Chicago. The city was settled at the junction of the historic Sauk and Old Vincennes trails in the 1830s, and has been known respectively as Thorn Grove, Bloom, and Chicago Heights (1892). It developed independently of Chicago's influence, and became the area's first steel-producing city.

Chicago Ridge—Worth Township; Zip Code 60415. Located southwest of Chicago.

Cicero—Cicero Township; Zip Code 60650. Located east of Chicago. Cicero was founded in 1857 on a swampy lowland. It grew slowly until the Civil War when the rich bottom lands around the settlement were perceived to be agriculturally productive. The community developed steadily as settlers from the East poured into the area. Incorporation came in 1867 as agriculture and the nearness of the area to Chicago spurred industrial growth. Fifty miles of swamp lands were drained and put into crops. Cicero eventually became economically independent of its great neighbor. The city gained notoriety in Prohibition days (until 1931), as being the headquarters of gangland leader Al Capone.

Cicero Town—Lies immediately west of Chicago. Bounded on the north by Jefferson, on the east by Chicago, on the south by Lake and Lyons and on the west by Proviso. Presently comprised of the town of Cicero.

Clyde—Town of Cicero.

Colehour—Hyde Park.

Cook County—Established in 1830 and located in northeast Illinois; Chicago is the county seat. The county is the major population center of the state, and is cut through by the Illinois and Des Plaines Rivers. The eastern border is formed by Lake Michigan and the Indiana state line. Governmental organization is based on township and county system, with ten commissioners from Chicago and five from outlying townships serving on the county board. See section 1 for historical information.

Country Club Hills—Bremen and Rich Townships; Zip Code 60477. Located south of Chicago.

Countryside—Lyons Township; Zip Code 60525. Located west of Chicago.

Cragin—Jefferson Park Township.

Crestwood—Bremen and Worth Townships; Zip Code 61445. Located southwest of Chicago in an agricultural and industrial region.

Cummings—Hyde Park.

Deerfield—Northfield Township.

Des Plaines—Elk Grove, Maine and Wheeling Townships; Zip Code 60016. Located northwest of Chicago. Des Plaines was founded in the 1830s as Rand in honor of its first settler, Socrates Rand. It is located on the Des Plaines River, for which it was renamed in 1869. It flourished early as a lumber center whose main mill produced timbers for a plank road between Jefferson Park and Chicago and ties for the railroad built in 1853.

Dixmoor—Thornton Township; Zip Code 60406. Located south of Chicago, and incorporated in 1922.

Dolton—Thornton Township; Zip Code 60419. Located 17 miles South of Chicago. Dolton was incorporated in 1892.

Dutchman's Point—Niles Township.

East Chicago Heights—Bloom Township; Zip Code 60411.

East Hazelcrest—Thornton Township; Zip Code 60429. Located south of Chicago, and incorporated in 1918.

Egandale—Hyde Park.

Elgin—Cook-Kane County line; Hanover Township; Zip Code 60120. Located 36 miles west-northwest of Chicago. Founded in 1835. Land was cleared along the Fox River, and a road was built to Belvidere which became part of the Chicago-Galena stage route. The stage route was partially responsible for Elgin's rapid settlement. A dam was built to provide power for the grist and sawmills, and the river has since been a link to the city's business. Elgin shipped milk to Chicago as early as 1832; a task which became sufficiently easier when the Galena and Chicago Union

Railroad laid its tracks there in 1847. Gail Borden patented the condensed milk process in Elgin in 1856. The Elgin Watch Company, established in 1866, became a great rival to the flourishing dairy industry, and essentially initiated Elgin's rise as an industrial center.

Elk Grove Township—Presently comprised of: Arlington Heights (part); Des Plaines (part); Elk Grove Village (part); Mount Prospect (part); Rolling Meadows (part); and Schaumburg (part).

Elk Grove Village—Elk Grove Township; Zip Code 60007. Located northwest of Chicago.

Elmwood Park—Leyden Township; Zip Code 60635. Located west of Chicago, and incorporated in 1914.

Englewood—Town of Lake.

Evanston—Evanston Township; Zip Code 60201. Located north of Chicago. Evanston existed as a settlement as early as 1674 when Father Pere Marquette and his Indian companions landed in the harbor on Lake Michigan. Temporary encampments were used until 1826 when the first permanent dwelling was built. Evanston proper was not platted until 1854, the year before the opening of Northwestern University. The university became the focus of the new town, and Evanston remained small for the next 25 years as it channeled all its energies into the development of the school. Cheap transportation eventually made Evanston one of Chicago's leading commuter suburbs. Of historic interest is the Grosse Pointe Lighthouse, built in the 1800s on a high bluff overlooking the lake.

Evanston Township—Until Cook County was organized into townships in 1850, the territory now comprising Evanston was included in the Grosse Point District, a tract of the county which was of somewhat uncertain dimensions, but supposedly existed for the convenience of voters. In 1850 when the township of Ridgeville was organized, it included the towns of Evanston and Lake View. The Wilmette Reservation was added later, and Evanston Township was formed in 1857. Evanston Township is presently comprised of the City of Evanston.

Evergreen Park—Worth Township; Zip Code 60642. Located southwest of Chicago, and incorporated in 1893.

Flossmoor—Bloom and Rich Townships; Zip Code 60422. Located south of Chicago, and incorporated in 1924. The name of the village is of Scottish derivation, and means "gently rolling countryside."

Forest Glen—Jefferson Park Township.

Forest Park—Proviso Township; Zip Code 60130. Located west of Chicago and on the Des Plaines River. Forest Park was founded in 1835, and was originally the site of an historic Indian burial ground. Nearly half of its corporate area is occupied by cemeteries.

Forest View—Stickney Township; Zip Code 60638. Located west of Chicago, and primarily a commuter suburb. Incorporated in 1924.

Forestville—Hyde Park.

Franklin Park—Leyden Township; Zip Code 60131. Located west-northwest of Chicago on the Des Plaines River. The area around the village was inhabited in the 1670s after Father Pere Marquette and Louis Joliet declared the Des Plaines River valley suitable for settlement. Incorporated in 1892.

Galewood—Jefferson Township.

Garfield—Jefferson Township.

Glencoe—New Trier and Northfield Townships; Zip Code 60022. Located 22 miles north of Chicago. Founded in 1836 and incorporated as a village in 1869. The name is a composite of "glen" suggestive of the site, and "coe" the maiden name of the wife of one of the founders, Walter S. Gurnee.

Glenview—Maine, New Trier, Niles, and Northfield Townships; Zip Code 60025. Located 18 miles north-northwest of Chicago, and site of a U. S. Naval Air Station.

Glenwood—Bloom and Thornton Townships; Zip Code 60425. Located south of Chicago.

Golf—Niles Township; Zip Code 60029, located north of Morton Grove and Chicago.

Grand Crossing—Hyde Park.

Grossdale—Brookfield.

Grayland—Jefferson Township.

Grosse Pointe—Evanston.

Hanover Park—Hanover and Schaumburg Townships; Zip Code 60103. Located 27 miles west-northwest of Chicago, near Bartlett, and incorporated in 1958.

Hanover Township—Presently comprised of: Bartlett (part); Elgin (part); Hanover Park (part); Hoffman Estates (part); South Barrington (part); Streamwood (part).

Harvey—Bremen and Thornton Townships; Zip Code 60426. Located 18 miles south of Chicago and 6 miles west of the Illinois-Indiana line. Founded in 1890 by Turlington W. Harvey, a Chicago land developer. Incorporated in 1894.

Harwood Heights—Norwood Park Township, Zip Code 60656. A northwest suburb of Chicago, three miles east of O'Hare Airport. Name contrived from the "Har" of Harlem and the "wood" of Norwood Park Township. Incorporated in 1947.

Hawthorne—Town of Cicero.

Hazel Crest—Bremen, Rich, and Thornton Townships; Zip Code 60429. Located 23 miles south of Chicago Loop, and incorporated in 1912.

Hazel Green—Iincluded with Alsip; Zip Code 60482. Located near Worth.

Hegewisch—Hyde Park.

Hickory Hills—Lyons and Palos Townships; Zip Code 60457. Located 15 miles southwest of Chicago, near Bridgeview and Justice. Incorporated in 1951.

Hillside—Proviso Township; Zip Code 60162. Located west-southwest of Oak Park, and 14 miles west of the Chicago Loop. Settled by German farmers in 1837, and named by railroad 1905.

Hinsdale—Lyons Township; Zip Code 60521.

Hodgkins—Lyons Township; Zip Code 60525. Located 15 miles Southwest of the Loop between the Des Plaines River and Joliet Road. Explored by Father Pere Marquette and Louis Joliet (1673), settled by laborers who dug a canal from local tributary of the Mississippi to Lake Michigan, 1836-48. Major producer of dolomite limestone from a 500-acre quarry. Incorporated 1896.

Hoffman Estates—Barrington, Hanover and Palatine Townships; Zip Code 60172.

Holbrook—Zip Code 60411. Located near Chicago Heights.

Hometown—Worth Township; Zip Code 60456. A southwest suburb of Chicago, and a village in the northwest corner of Oak Lawn between Cicero Avenue and Pulaski Road. Developed in 1948 as a subdivision. Incorporated in 1953.

Homewood—Bloom, Bremen, and Rich Townships; Zip Code 60430. Located 22 miles southeast of Chicago. Settled in 1834 by German, Dutch, and Yankee homesteaders. Incorporated 1893.

Humbolt Park—Jefferson Park.

Hyde Park—The act of incorporation, approved February 20, 1861, separated the town of Hyde Park (which extended from 39th to 63rd Streets and included the settlements of Oakland, Egandale, Forestville, Kenwood, and South Park) from the town of Lake. Lake was the district bounded by 39th Street on the north, Grand Boulevard (South Park Avenue) on the west, Lake Michigan on the east, and by 87th Street on the south. Under an amended charter of March 5, 1867 the town of Hyde Park embraced the portion of the township bounded by Lake Michigan and the Indiana state line on the east, 39th Street on the north, 138th Street and the Indian boundary line on the south, and State Street on the west. By an ordinance approved on June 1, 1874, the village of Hyde Park included all the territory bounded by 39th Street on the north, Lake Michigan and the Indiana State line on the east, State Street to the Calumet River, then the Calumet to the center line of 130th Street, then to the eastern line of the Illinois Central Railroad Company's right of way to the Calumet River and then Indiana Avenue to 138th Street, the Calumet River, from Indiana Avenue to the Illinois Central Railroad bridge on the south. The government of Hyde Park was initially merged with the government of the Town of Lake. In 1889, the village of Hyde Park was annexed to Chicago.

Indian Head Park—Lyons Township, Zip Code 60525.

Inverness—Barrington and Palatine Townships; Zip Code 60067. An exclusive real estate development since 1847. Incorporated 1962.

Irving Park—Jefferson Park.

Jefferson Township—Bounded by Norwood Park, Niles, and Evanston on the north, Lake View and Chicago on the east, Chicago and Cicero on the south; and on the west by Leyden and Norwood Park. Jefferson Park was annexed to Chicago in 1889.

Justice—Lyons Township; Zip Code 60458.

Kenilworth—New Trier Township; Zip Code 60043. Located 17 miles northwest of Chicago. Founded 1890, and incorporated 1896.

Kensington—Hyde Park.

Kenwood—Hyde Park.

La Grange—Lyons Township; Zip Code 60525. A suburb 13 miles west of Chicago. Settled 1862 when the Burlington Railroad was extended westward across the Des Plaines River. Chartered 1879, and named for LaGrange, Tennessee.

La Grange Park—Proviso Township; Zip Code 60525. A western suburb of Chicago immediately north of the older town of La Grange. Founded in 1871 from 5 farms on Salt Creek 15 miles southwest of the Loop by refugees from the Great Fire. Incorporated 1892.

Lake—Town of Lake.

Lake View Township—The history of the early settlement of North Chicago and the southern portion of the town of Lake View are intimately connected. Lakeview was annexed to Chicago in 1889.

Lansing—Bloom and Thornton Townships; Zip Code 60438. Located 24 miles south of Chicago on the Indiana border. Founded 1864 by brothers John and Henry Lansing.

Lemont—Cook and DuPage counties; Lemont Township; Zip Code 60439. Located on the Illinois River 25 miles southwest of Chicago. The name is the French word meaning "mountain." A post office was established May 30, 1850. Lemont is an industrial city served by the Chicago Sanitary and Ship Canal, the Calumet Sag Channel, and it has long been known for the limestone quarries. Incorporated June 9, 1873.

Lemont Township—First settled in 1833, the history of Lemont is closely connected to the building of the Illinois and Michigan Canal and the rock quarries. Presently comprised of the village of Lemont.

Leyden Township—Presently comprised of: Bensenville (part); Elmwood Park; Franklin Park; Melrose Park (part); Norridge (part); Northlake (part); Park Ridge (part); River Grove; Rosemont; and Schiller Park.

Lincolnwood—Niles Township; Zip Code 60645. Located north of Chicago. Founded by German farmers and wood haulers for the Chicago and Northwestern Railway, and at onetime called Tessville. Incorporated 1911.

Littlefort—New Trier Township.

Lynwood—Bloom Township; Zip Code 60411.

Located near Chicago Heights, and incorporated 1959.

Lyons—Lyons and Riverside Townships; Zip Code 60534. Located 8 miles west of Chicago at an old portage between the Des Plaines River and the Chicago River. A post office was established February 29, 1848. It is the site of Hofmann Tower, on a dam built in 1908 by George Hofmann to generate electricity for a beer garden. Incorporated July 18, 1888.

Lyons Township—Bounded on the east by the township of Lake, on the south by the townships of Worth and Palos, on the west by DuPage County, and on the north by the townships of Proviso and Cicero. Lyons Township is presently comprised of: Bedford Park (part); Bridgeview (part); Brookfield (part); Burr Ridge (part); Countryside; Hickory Hills (part); Hinsdale (part); Hodgkins; Indian Head Park; Justice; La Grange; Lyons (part); McCook; Riverside (part); Summit; Western Springs (part); Willow Springs (part).

Lyttleton's Point—Niles Township.

McCook—Lyons Township; Zip Code 60525.

Maine Township—The first settlement in the township was made in 1832 by Captain Wright. Presently comprised of: Des Plaines (part); Glenview (part); Morton Grove (part); Mount Prospect (part); Niles (part); Park Ridge (part); and Rosemont (part).

Maplewood—Jefferson Park.

Markham—Bremen and Thornton Townships; Zip Code 60426. A southern suburb of Chicago. Incorporated October 23, 1925, and named for a former president of the Illinois Central Railroad.

Matteson—Rich Township; Zip Code 60443. Located 26 miles south of Chicago. Founded by German settlers in the 1850s. A post office was established November 29, 1856. Incorporated March 20, 1889, and named for Governor Joel A. Matteson.

Maywood—Proviso Township; Zip Code 60153. Located 12 miles west of Chicago on the west bank of Des Plaines River. Founded in 1860s by a group of New Englanders headed by Col. W. T. Nichols, who named the settlement for his daughter, May. A post office was established April 29, 1870. Incorporated October 31, 1881.

Melrose Park—Leyden and Proviso Townships; Zip Code 60160. An industrial suburb 12 miles west of Chicago with a large Italian population. Founded in 1860 when a road was built from Chicago northwest toward Galena. A post office was established in January 28, 1893. Incorporated March 13, 1893.

Merrionette Park—Worth Township; Zip Code 60655. A residential subdivision located 16 miles southwest of the Loop. Incorporated February 18, 1947.

Midlothian—Bremen Township; Zip Code 60445. Located 18 miles south of Chicago. Received its name from a golf club built in the area in 1898 by George R. Thorne, then head of Montgomery Ward. The golf club was named for a shire in Scotland.

Mont Clare—Jefferson Township.

Montrose—Jefferson Township.

Moreland—Town of Cicero.

Morgan Park—Calumet and Worth.

Morton Grove—Maine and Niles Townships; Zip Code 60053. Located 15 miles north of Chicago on the north branch of the Chicago River. First settled in 1831 by immigrant farmers from England. A post office was established July 2, 1874. Named for Levi Parsons Morton, an official of the Chicago, Milwaukee, and St. Paul Railroad when it was built in 1872. Morton later became Vice-President of the United States under President Benjamin Harrison. Primarily rural area until after WWII. Incorporated September 24, 1895.

Mount Forest—Lyons Township.

Mount Prospect—Elk Grove, Maine, and Wheeling Townships; Zip Code 60056. Located 21 miles northwest of Chicago. Settled by Busse family, descendants of Friedrich Busse, a German immigrant who came here in 1848. A post office was established December 31, 1885. Incorporated February 3, 1917.

New Trier Township—Presently comprised of: Glencoe (part); Glenview (part); Kenilworth; Northfield (part); Wilmette (part); and Winnetka. In 1829, the United States made a treaty with the Potawatomi Indians at Prairie du Chien. As a result of this treaty, 1,280 acres of land located approximately fourteen miles from Chicago, and on the shore of Lake Michigan, were ceded to Antoine Ouilmette, a Frenchman who had married a Potawatomi woman of royal blood. After the Black Hawk War most of the Native Americans migrated to the Green Bay area, but among those who stayed behind on reservations was Ouilmette, or Wilmette.

Niles—Maine Township; Zip Code 60648. Located 14 miles north of Chicago. Once called Dutchman's Point and Lyttleton's Point, it derived its present name from pioneer newspaper owner William Ogden Niles. A post office was established May 23, 1850. Niles was once the site of a Civil War gristmill on the north branch of the Chicago River. Incorporated August 24, 1899.

Niles Center—Niles Township. Settled in the 1850s.

Niles Township—First settled in 1831. Presently comprised of: Glenview (part); Golf; Lincolnwood; Morton Grove (part); Niles (part); and Skokie.

Normalville—Town of Lake.

Norridge—Leyden, and Norwood Park Townships.

Northbrook—Northfield and Wheeling Townships; Zip Code 60062. A northwest suburb of Chicago, and at one time, called Shermerville. The first settlers of Northbrook were French traders and trappers, then Germans. A post office was established in February 1, 1923. Incorporated January 8, 1923.

Northfield—New Trier and Northfield Townships. Zip Code 60093.

Northfield Township—Presently comprised of: Deerfield (part); Glencoe (part); Glenview (part); Northbrook (part);

Northbrook (part); Northfield (part); Prospect Heights (part); Wilmette (part).

Northfield Woods—Zip Code 60025. Located near Glenview.

Northlake—Leyden and Proviso Townships, Zip Code 60164. Located northeast of Chicago astride North Avenue and Lake Street and west of Mannheim Road. Incorporated April 23, 1949.

North Pullman—Hyde Park.

North Riverside—Proviso and Riverside Townships; Zip Code 60546.

Norwood Park Township—Located northwest of Jefferson Township and northeast of Leyden Township. Parts of Jefferson, Leyden, Niles, and Maine townships were taken in 1872 to form Norwood Park Township. Presently comprised of: Harwood Heights; Norridge (part); and Park Ridge (part).

Norwood Park Village—Norwood Park Township. The first settlement was in 1869 by George Dunlap.

Oak Brook—DuPage and Cook counties; Proviso Township; Zip Code 60521. Located 16 miles west of Chicago. Incorporated February 21, 1958.

Oak Forest—Bremen Township; Zip Code 60452. Located 20 miles south of Chicago. A post office was established November 21, 1912. Incorporated May 10,1947.

Oakland—Hyde Park.

Oak Lawn—Worth Township; Zip Code 60453. Located 12 miles southwest of Chicago, and one of the largest suburbs of Chicago in Cook County. Settled 1842; a post office was established March 22, 1895. Bounded by 87th Street on the north, 111th Street on the south, Pulaski on the east, and Harlem Avenue on the west. Incorporated 1909.

Oak Park—Oak Park Township; Zip Code 60302. Located 10 miles west of Chicago, and founded 1833. A post office was established in March 6, 1866. Initially called Oak Ridge because of a slight, tree covered rise which has since disappeared due to grading and building. The first settler was Joseph Kettlestrings, who came from Maryland in 1833. Oak Park is noted for the 25 structures, public and private, designed by Frank Lloyd Wright, including his own home and studio, and the Unitarian Universalist Church. Incorporated November 13, 1901. Also known as the town of Cicero in Andreas' *History of Cook County.*

Oak Park Township—Presently comprised of the Village of Oak Park.

Oak Ridge—Oak Park.

Olympia Fields—Bloom and Rich Townships; Zip Code 60461. Located south of Chicago. A residential community developed in 1926.

Orland Park—Bremen, Orland Park and Palos Townships; Zip Code 60462.

Orland Township—Presently comprised of: Orland Park (part); Tinley Park (part); and Westhaven.

Palatine—Palatine Township; Zip Code 60067. A Chicago suburb named for a division in Germany by that name.

Palatine Township—Presently comprised of: Arlington Heights (part); Barrington (part); Hoffman Estates (part); Hoffman Estates (part); Inverness (part); Palatine; Rolling Meadows (part); Schaumburg (part); and South Barrington (part).

Palos Heights—Palos and Worth Townships; Zip Code 60463.

Palos Hills—Palos Township; Zip Code 60465.

Palos Park—Palos Township; Zip Code 60464.

Palos Township—Situated in the southwestern portion of Cook County. Bounded on the north by Lyons, on the east by Worth, on the south by Orland, and on the west by Lemont Township and Downer's Grove in DuPage County. Presently comprised of: Bridgeview (part); Hickory Hills (part); Orland Park (part); Palos Heights (part); Palos Hills; Palos Park; Willow Springs (part); and Worth (part).

Park Forest—Bloom and Rich Townships; Zip Code 60466.

Park Forest South—Rich Township.

Park Ridge—Leyden, Maine and Norwood Park Townships; Zip Code 60068.

Peck Place—New Trier Township.

Pennock—Jefferson Township.

Phoenix—Thornton Township; Zip Code 60426.

Posen—Bremen and Thornton Townships; Zip Code 60469. Located 20 miles south of Chicago.

Prospect Heights—Northfield and Wheeling Townships

Proviso Township—The township lies in western part of Cook County. Bounded on the north by Leyden, on the east by Cicero and Riverside, on the south by Riverside and Lyons, and on the west by DuPage County. It originally contained 36 sections, but in 1870 the township of Riverside, consisting of the four southeastern sections were set off as a separate township. Presently comprised of: Bellwood; Berkeley; Broadview; Brookfield (part); Forest Park; Hillside; La Grange Park; Maywood; Melrose; Northlake (part); North Riverside (pt); Oak Brook (part); Stone Park; Westchester; Western Springs (part).

Pullman—Hyde Park.

Rand—Des Plaines.

Rich Township—Presently comprised of: Country Club Hills (part); Flossmoor (part); Hazel Crest (part); Homewood (part); Matteson; Olympia Fields (part); Park Forest (part); Park Forest South (part); Richton Park; and Tinley Park (part).

Richton Park—Rich Township; Zip Code 60471.

Ridgeville—Evanston Township.

Riverdale—Calumet and Thornton Townships; Zip Code 60627.

River Forest—River Forest Township; Zip Code 60305.

River Forest Township—Presently comprised of River Forest.

River Grove—Leyden Township; Zip Code 60171. A northwest suburb of Chicago, and located on the Des Plaines River.

Riverside—Lyons and Riverside Townships; Zip Code 60546. Designed as a Chicago residential suburb, 1866.

Riverside Township—Presently comprised of: Brookfield (part); Lyons (part); North Riverside (part). Riverside (part).

Robbins—Bremen and Worth Townships; Zip Code 60472. A Chicago suburb near Blue Island.

Rolling Meadows—Elk Grove, Palatine and Wheeling Townships; Zip Code 60008.

Roselle—Schaumburg Township; Zip Code 60172.

Roseland—Hyde Park.

Rosemont—Leyden and Maine Townships; Zip Code 60018.

Sag Station—Lemont.

Sauk Village—Bloom Township; Zip Code 60411.

Schaumburg—Elk Grove, Palatine and Schaumburg Townships; Zip Code 60194.

Schaumburg Township—Presently comprised of: Elk Grove Village (part); Hanover Park (part); Hoffman Estates (part); Rolling Meadows (part); Roselle (part); Schaumburg (part); and Streamwood (part).

Schiller Park—Leyden Township; Zip Code 60176.

Shermerville—Northbrook.

Skokie—Niles Township, Zip Code 60001. Located 15 miles north of Chicago, and established in 1922. The site of the Hebrew Theological Seminary.

South Brighton—Town of Lake.

South Chicago—Hyde Park.

South Englewood—Town of Lake.

South Holland—Thornton Township; Zip Code 60473. Located 10 miles south of Chicago. Originally settled in 1840 by Dutch farmers.

South Lawn—Thornton Township.

South Lynn—Town of Lake.

South Park—Hyde Park.

Steger—Bloom Township, Zip Code 60465.

Located 30 miles south of Chicago.

Stickney—Stickney Township.

Stickney Township—Bedford Park (part); Bridgeview (part); Burbank; Forest View; and Stickney.

Stone Park—Proviso Township.

Streamwood—Hanover and Schaumburg Townships; Zip Code 60103.

Summit—Lyons Township; Zip Code 60501. Located 12 miles southwest of Chicago on the Des Plaines River at the crest of the watershed divide between the Great Lakes and Mississippi River. Important corn refining area.

Tessville—Lincolnwood.

Thorn Grove—Chicago Heights.

Thornton—Thornton Township; Zip Code 60476.

Thornton Township—Presently comprised of: Blue Island (part); Burnham; Calumet City; Dixmoor; Dolton; East Hazel Crest; Glenwood (part); Harvey (part); Hazel Crest (part); Homewood (part); Lansing (part); Lansing (part); Markham (part); Phoenix; Posen (part); Riverdale (part); South Holland and Thornton.

Tinley Park—Bremen, Orland and Rich Townships; Cook and Will Counties; Zip Code 60477. A suburb of Chicago.

Town of Lake—The township, or village of Lake, was bounded on the north by 39th Street, on the east by State Street, on the south by 87th Street, and on the west by the township of Lyons. It was incorporated with these boundaries in February 1865. The Illinois Legislature amended the charter in 1867, and gave enlarged and special powers to village officers to govern the entire territory embraced within the congressional township. The Town of Lake was annexed to the City of Chicago in 1889.

Union Stock Yards—Town of Lake.

Upwood—Calumet and Worth Townships.

Washington Heights—Calumet and Worth Townships.

Westchester—Proviso Township; Zip Code 60153.

Western Springs—Lyons and Proviso Townships; Zip Code 60558. A residential area located 15 miles south of the Chicago Loop. Incorporated by Quakers in 1866, and named for local mineral springs (now dry) believed to have medicinal properties.

West Hammond—Calumet City.

Westhaven—Orland Township; Zip Code 60477.

Wheeling—Wheeling Township; Zip Code 60090. Located 20 miles northwest of Chicago. Originally settled in 1830 as a country store.

Wheeling Township—First settled in 1833. Presently comprised of: Arlington Heights (part); Buffalo Grove (part); Des Plaines (part); Mount Prospect (part); Northbrook (part); Prospect Heights (part); Rolling Meadows (part); and Wheeling (part).

Wildwood—Hyde Park.

Willow Springs—Lyons and Palos Townships; Zip Code 60480.

Wilmette—New Trier and Northfield Townships; Zip Code 60091. A suburb of Chicago located on the shores of Lake Michigan. Originally settled in 1829, and named for the settler, Antoine Ouilmette, a French Canadian whose Potawatomi wife gained land under a government treaty.

Wilmette Reservation—Evanston Township.

Winnetka—New Trier Township, Zip Code 60093. A residential town located on the shores of Lake Michigan 20 miles north of Chicago. Incorporated in 1869.

Worth—Palos and Worth Townships; Zip Code 60482. Located south of Chicago.

Worth Township—Presently comprises: Alsip; Blue Island (part); Bridgeview (part); Chicago Ridge; Crestwood (part); Evergreen Park; Hometown; Merrionette Park; Oak Lawn; Palos Heights (part); Robbins (part); and Worth (part).

Genealogical Societies Serving the Chicago Metropolitan Area

The African-American Genealogical and Historical Society of Chicago

P.O. Box 3772651

Chicago, IL 60637

Offers genealogy classes and workshops and publishes a monthly newsletter.

The Chicago Genealogical Society

P.O. Box 1160

Chicago, IL 60690-1160

Call 312-725-1306 for membership and any other information; call 708-834-7491 for an appointment to use the library.

Meetings: First Saturday of each month at 1:30 p.m. (September through June), at Newberry Library. Publishes a monthly newsletter and the *Chicago Genealogist* (quarterly publication). Sponsors genealogical publications, programs, and annual workshops.

The Chicago Genealogical Society also has the 381 page book, *Chicago Ancestor File: 1974-1984*, available for purchase. This book contains records of over 10,000 individuals who were residents of Chicago. The records, which show dates and locations of births, marriages and deaths, were contributed by over 1,200 of their descendants. The names and addresses of the contributors make it possible to exchange surname information.

Chicago Irish Interest Group

Contact the Chicago Genealogical Society.

Council of Northeastern Illinois Genealogical Societies

3629 West 147th Place
Midlothian, IL 60445
(708-389-1627)

The Council coordinates a calendar of events for genealogical societies in northeastern Illinois. It also sponsors a clearinghouse, workshops, and meetings for area genealogical society leaders. Cooperates with the Genealogical Society of Utah in preserving and microfilming records of genealogical and historical importance. The Council also works closely with the Illinois State Genealogical Society.

DeKalb County Historical-Genealogical Society

DeKalb County Courthouse
P.O. Box 295
Sycamore, IL 60178-0295
(815-756-1048)

Joiner History Archives: Thursday—1:00 P.M.—4:00 P.M.

Local history of DeKalb County families.

Des Plaines Genealogical Questors

Des Plaines Historical Society
789 Pearson
Des Plaines, IL 60016-4506
(708-391-5399)

Meetings: First Tuesday of the month (October through

May). Promotes research into family and local history.

Dunton Genealogical Society

Arlington Heights Memorial Library
500 North Dunton
Arlington Heights, IL 60004-5966
(708-392-0100)

Society has information on immigration trails to northern Illinois.

DuPage County, Illinois, Genealogical Society

P.O. Box 133
Lombard, IL 60148-0133

Meetings: Third Wednesday (September, November, January, March and May). Publishes *The Review*, a bimonthly newsletter with special Summer and Winter issues. Sponsors projects, publications, and workshops of genealogical and historical interest. Maintains a genealogy library collection (that can be used only on the premises) at the:

Wheaton Public Library
225 N. Cross Street
Wheaton, IL

Elgin Genealogical Society

P.O. Box 1418
Elgin, IL 60121-0818
(708-742-1692)

Meetings: First Tuesday (9:30 A.M.) and third Thursday (7:30 P.M.) of the month (January through December) at the:

Gail Borden Public Library
200 North Grove Avenue
Elgin, IL 60121

There are no evening meetings in June, July, August, and December. Publishes a newsletter quarterly, and sponsors projects, publications, and workshops of genealogical and historical interest.

Federation of Genealogical Societies

An international genealogical organization that sponsors projects, publications, and conferences of genealogical and historical interest. Publishes bi-monthly newsletter (*FORUM*). Address correspondence regarding newsletter to:

Federation of Genealogical Societies FORUM
    Editorial Office
    P.O. Box 271
    Western Springs, IL 60558-0271

Fox Valley Genealogical Society

705 North Brainerd Street
Naperville, IL 60563-3132
(708-355-4370)

Meetings: Second Thursday of the month at 7:00 p.m. in John Green Realty Building on Washington Street in Naperville. Publishes the *Fox Tales* quarterly and special occasional publications of genealogical and historical interest. Preserves genealogies of Naperville's early families. The Society works with Kane, DuPage, Will, and Grundy counties to preserve artifacts.

Genealogical Forum of Elmhurst

120 East Park Avenue
Elmhurst, IL 60126-3420
(708-832-2600)

Holds five meetings each year on the first Sunday in September, November, January, March, and May.

German Interest Group

Contact the Chicago Genealogical Society.

Grayslake Genealogical Society

c/o Grayslake Historical Municipal Museum
164 Hauley Street
P.O. Box 185
Grayslake, IL 60030-0185
(708-223-4978)

The focus of this group is on Grayslake history and

artifacts from the 1895 era and later.

Green Hills Genealogical Society

c/o Green Hills Library
8611 West 103rd Street
Palos Hills, IL 60465

Illinois State Genealogical Society

P.O. Box 10195
Springfield, IL 62791-0195
Business office: 2nd floor, Archives Building, Springfield, IL. Hours: Monday through Friday— 8:00 A.M.—4:30 P.M.

The Illinois State Genealogical Society was established in 1968 as a non-profit, non-sectarian, educational organization with the following purposes:

* To stimulate an interest in people who contributed to the establishment and development of the State of Illinois.

* To seek, preserve, and make available all data pertaining to individuals, families, and groups who lived in Illinois and to incidents and events which took place therein.

* To inform people of the value of and need to pre- serve family and local history for posterity.

* To encourage the formation of local genealogical societies and to coordinate and disseminate infor- mation.

Individuals, libraries and societies may apply for membership. Each member receives one volume (four issues) of the quarterly publication and a monthly newsletter. The Society holds an annual Fall Conference, with business meetings, and a Spring Conference.

Jewish Genealogical Society of Illinois

P.O. Box 515
Northbrook, IL 60065-0515
Meetings: Last Sunday of month at library at 3:00 P.M.

Library:

North Shore Congregation Israel
  (1185 North Sheridan Road, Glencoe, IL 60022)
Computer Interest Group meets on last Sunday of month at 2:00 P.M. Jewish genealogy and history is the main focus of the group.

Publishes the *Search* quarterly and sponsors projects, workshops, and occasional publications of genealogical and historical interest.

Jewish Genealogical Society, South Suburban Branch

c/o Ellen Kahn
3416 Ithaca
Olympia Fields, IL 60461

Kane County Genealogical Society

P.O. Box 504
Geneva, IL 60134-0504
(708-695-5893)
  Publishes the *Kane County Chronicle* quarterly. Interests are in Kane County historical and genealogical materials.

Kankakee Valley Genealogical Society

P.O. Box 442
Bourbonnais, IL 60914-0442
(815-933-5529)
  Has a library; focus is on genealogy and Illinois history.

Lake County, Illinois, Genealogical Society

Cook Memorial Library
P.O. Box 721
Libertyville, IL 60048-0721
(815-675-9306)
  Hours: Monday through Thursday—9:00 A.M.—9:00 P.M. (September through May); Friday and Saturday—9:00 A.M.—5:00 P.M.; Sunday—1:00 P.M.—2:00 P.M. (June through August). Sponsors educational programs and supports library's genealogical holdings.

Lithuanian Genealogical Society

c/o Balzekas Museum of Lithuanian Culture
6500 South Pulaski Road
Chicago, IL 60629-5136
(312-582-6500)

Emphasis is on Lithuanian culture. Supports research center, library, archives, children's museum, and art gallery. Sponsors programs, lectures, and workshops.

McHenry County, Illinois, Genealogical Society

P.O. Box 184
Crystal Lake, IL 60039-0184
(815-385-0686)

Meetings: Second Thursday of each month at McHenry County Library.

North Suburban Genealogical Society

c/o Winnetka Public Library
768 Oak Street
Winnetka, IL 60093-2583
(708-251-4891)

Publishes a newsletter, maintains a genealogical reference collection at the Winnetka Library, and sponsors programs throughout the year.

Genealogical Project Committee volunteers on duty at library: Monday through Saturday from 9:15 A.M.—12:00 P.M. and 1:15 P.M.—4:00 P.M.; Monday and Thursday from 7:15 P.M.—9:00 P.M.; Sunday from 1:15 P.M.—4:00 P.M.

Northern Will County Genealogical Society

121 Cypress Drive
Bolingbrook, IL 60439

Northwest Suburban Council of Genealogists

P.O. Box AC
Mt. Prospect, IL 60056-9019
(708-394-3897)

Meetings: 7:30 P.M. on the third Thursday of month

(except December) at:

John Hersey High School, Room 124C
1900 East Thomas
Arlington Heights

Publishes a bimonthly newsletter, *News from the Northwest*, and maintains surname and locality files. The Council also sponsors projects and programs which are of interest to genealogists. Library:

Mt. Prospect Public Library
10 South Emerson Street.
Hours: Monday through Friday—9:00 A.M.—9:00 P.M.; Saturday—9:00 A.M.—5:00 P.M.; Sunday—12:00 P.M.—5:00 P.M.; volunteer on duty: Monday and Friday—9:00 A.M.— 12:00P.M.

Polish Genealogical Society of America

Polish Museum of America
984 North Milwaukee Avenue
Chicago, IL 60622
(312-384-3352)
Publishes a newsletter and sponsors occasional projects and publications which are of interest to genealogists and historians. Meetings held at the Polish Museum of America. Annual Workshop is held in the Fall. The collection in the Polish Museum Library includes: local history, genealogy, Polish pioneers, archives, seven books on Polish genealogy, and Chicago Daily News indexes (1890-1929).

Poplar Creek Genealogical Society

200 Kosan Circle
Streamwood, IL 60103

Schaumburg Genealogical Society

c/o Schaumburg Public Library
32 West Library Lane
Schaumburg, IL 60194

South Suburban Genealogical and Historical Society

320 East 61st Place
P.O. Box 96
South Holland, IL 60473-0096
(708-333-9474)

Meetings: Second Saturday of the month (September to June) at 1:30 P.M. at:

Roosevelt Center
    161st Place and Louis Avenue
    South Holland, IL

Publishes a monthly newsletter and the quarterly, *Where the Trails Cross*. Sponsors projects, occasional publications, and an annual workshop of interest to genealogists and historians. Maintains a library of over 2000 genealogical and historical volumes with an especially good collection of south suburban local histories and a surname index. Local history, genealogy, pioneers, American history, library, special collections.

Library Hours: Monday—10:00 A.M.—4:00 P.M.; Tuesday—1:00 P.M.— 9:00 P.M.; Wednesday—10:00 A.M.—11:30 A.M. and 12:30 P.M.—4:00 P.M.; Friday—10:00 A.M.—4:00 P.M.; Saturday—11:00 A.M.—4:00.P.M.

Tinley Moraine Genealogical Society

P.O. Box 521
Tinley Park, IL 60477-0521

Meetings: First Thursday of each month at 7:00 P.M.

No meetings are held in July or August. All meetings are open to the public. Meetings held at:

Tinley Park Public Library
    17101 South 71st Avenue
    Tinley Park, IL

Publishes newsletter, *Relatively Speaking*.

Western Springs Genealogical Society

c/o Western Springs Historical Society
Grand Avenue School
4211 Grand Avenue
P.O. Box 139
Western Springs, IL 60558-0139
(708-246-7073)

Supports museum, historic site preservation, genealogy, library, local history, archives activities. Hours: Saturday—10:00 A.M.—2:00 P.M.; and by appointment (summer: 7:00 P.M.—9:00 P.M.). Archives: Tuesday—9:00 A.M.—12:00 P.M.

Will/Grundy Counties Genealogical Society

P.O. Box 24,
Wilmington, IL 60481-0024
(815-634-2518)

Interests are in genealogy and local history.

Zion Genealogical Society

c/o Zion Benton Public Library
2400 Gabriel Avenue
Zion, IL 60099-2296
(708-623-3501)

Assists individuals with their research. Genealogical workshop: Thursday—7:00 P.M.—9:00 P.M.

Historical Libraries and Museums in Cook County

This section contains a list of historical libraries and museums located in Cook County.

AASR Valley of Chicago

915 North Dearborn Street
Chicago, IL 60610
(312-787-7605 ext. 9)

Emphasis is on Free Masonry, art, and history.

American Camping Association—Chicago Section

67 East Madison, Suite 1406
Chicago, IL 60603-3010
(312-332-0833)

Has collection of historic camp artifacts and information on: architecture, landscapes, archaeology, and oral history.

American Police Center and Museum

1717 South State Street
Chicago, IL 60616-1215
(312-431-0005)

Has police related materials; objective is the education of civilians about police work in order to promote a better understanding.

Ancient Egyptian Museum

3849 South Michigan Avenue
Chicago, IL 60653-1513
(312-268-3700)

Has artifacts related to gods and lifestyles; paintings by ancient Egyptians.

Arlington Heights Memorial Library

500 North Dunton
Arlington Heights, IL 60004-5910
(708-303-1080)

Has information about Illinois, Midwest states, German ancestry, and genealogy.

Arlington Heights Historical Museum

110 W Fremont
Arlington Heights, IL 60004-5912
(708-255-1225)

Has artifacts, a library, and information about historic structures and local history.

Art Institute of Chicago

Michigan at Adams
Chicago, IL 60603
(312-443-3511)

Has numerous collections: American and European painting, sculpture, decorative arts from Medieval and Classical through Contemporary; Asian arts; prints; drawings; African; Oceania; the Americas; architecture; textile; photography; arms and armor.

Avalon Branch of Chicago Public Library

8828 South Stony Island
Chicago, IL 60617
(312-747-5234)

Focus is on African-American history (particularly Chicago history). Collections include archival material, photographs, artifacts, art. A main function is to collect, document, preserve, and disseminate information about African-American history and culture, and to help interpret the experiences and contributions of African-Americans past and present.

Balzekas Museum of Lithuanian Culture

6500 South Pulaski Road
Chicago, IL 60629-5136
(312-582-6500; FAX: 312-582-5133)

Emphasis is on Lithuanian culture; there is a library, archives, children's museum, art gallery, and research center.

Blue Island Public Library

2433 York Street
Blue Island, IL 60406-2094
(708-388-1078)

Has information on Blue Island history.

Bridgeview Public Library

7840 West 79th Street
Bridgeview, IL 60455-1496
(708-458-2880)

Calumet City Historical Society Museum

760 Wentworth Avenue
Calumet City, IL 60409-3515
(708-862-8662)

Has information on Calumet City history.

Calumet Memorial Park District Museum

521 Garfield
Calumet City, IL 60409-2604
(708-862-6440)

Contains artifacts and memorabilia related to the park district in the area of Calumet City and Burnham.

Center to Commemorate U.S. Constitution in Illinois

633 North East Avenue
Oak Park, IL 60302-1715
(708-383-9724)
   Monday through Friday—9:00 A.M.—5:00 P.M.

Chicago Heights Public Library

15th Street and Chicago Road
Chicago, IL 60411
(708-754-0323)
   Monday through Thursday—9:00 A.M.—9:00 P.M.; Friday and Saturday—9:00 A.M.—5:00 P.M.;

   Winter: also Sunday—1:00 P.M.—5:00 P.M.

   Has information on Chicago Heights history.

Chicago Historical Society Museum

Clark Street at North Avenue
Chicago, IL 60614-6099
(312-642-4600)
   Research collections: Tuesday through Saturday—9:30 A.M.—4:30 P.M.;

   Museum: Monday through Saturday—9:30 A.M.—4:30 P.M., Sundays 12:00 P.M.—5:00 P.M.

   Has Chicago and Illinois, Civil War, and urban history. There is also information about the decorative and industrial arts.

Chicago Lawn Library

6120 Kedzie Avenue
Chicago, IL 60629-4638
(312-580-2020)
   Collects memorabilia and information on the history of Chicago Lawn. There is an annual meeting for the community to display materials old and new.

Crabtree Nature Center

Forest Preserve District of Cook County
536 North Harlem
River Forest, IL 60305-1872
(708-366-9420)

Provides the natural and man-made history of the region, and historic trails of the area.

Crossing Trails Square Dance Heritage Society

631 West Richton Road
Steger, IL 60475-1328
(708-748-3406)

Has square dancing memorabilia and history; collects information about square dancing.

Czechoslovak Heritage Museum, Library and Archives

CSA Fraternal Life
122 W. 22nd Street
Oak Brook, IL 60521
(708-795-5800)

Houses fraternal records, Czechoslovakian artifacts, cut glass, literature, porcelain, folk costumes, and instruments.

Des Plaines Historical Museum/Library

789 Pearson
Des Plaines, IL 60016-4506
(708-391-5399)

Monday through Friday—9:00 A.M.—4:00 P.M.; Sunday —1:00 P.M.—4:00 P.M.; and by appointment.

Emphasis is on local history.

Donald E. Stephens Museum

Lobby of Rosemont/O'Hare Expo Center
5555 North River Road
Mail to: 9301 West Bryn Mawr
Rosemont, IL 60018-5201
(708-692-4000)

Monday through Friday—8:00 A.M.—4:00 P.M.; Saturday— 8:00 A.M.—12:00 P.M.

Has M.I. Hummel and European folk art.

East Side Historical Society Museum

9801 Avenue G,
Calumet Park Fieldhouse
(312-721-7948)
Wednesday—1:00 P.M.—4:00 P.M., Saturday—9:00 A.M.
—12:00 P.M., and by appointment.

Has historical items for the East Side, Hegewisch, South Chicago, South Deering.

Elmwood Park Library

2823 North 77th Avenue
Elmwood, IL 60635-1408
(708-453-1133)
Monday through Friday—9:00 A.M.—6:00 P.M.;
Saturday—9:00 A.M.—5:00 P.M.; Sunday—1:00 P.M.—
5:00 P.M.

Houses historic photographs, publishing artifacts, village Who's Who, and holds meetings and provides local tours.

Evanston Historical Society Museum/Library

225 Greenwood Street
Evanston, IL 60201-4713
(708-475-3410)
Monday, Tuesday, Thursday, Friday and Saturday—
1:00 P.M.—5:00 P.M.

Emphasis is on local history; has archives.

Field Museum of Natural History

Roosevelt Road at Lake Shore Drive
Chicago, IL 60605-2496
(312-922-9410)
Open daily 9:00 A.M.—5:00 P.M.

This is a public research museumwith collections on varied topics including: evolutionary biology, environment, cultural understanding and change, anthropology, botany, geology, and zoology.

Flagg Creek Historical Museum

Pleasantdale Park District
7425 South Wolf Road
Burr Ridge, IL 60525
(708-246-4142)

Emphasis is on local history. There is a restored 1856 farm house that is used as a learning center and museum.

Frank Lloyd Wright Home/Studio Foundation Research Center

951 Chicago Avenue
Oak Park, IL 60302-2007
(708-848-1976)

Museum: Monday through Friday tours—11:00 A.M., 1:00 P.M., 3:00 P.M.;

Saturday and Sunday tours—11:00 A.M., 4:00 P.M.

Research Center: Wednesday through Saturday—1:00 P.M.— 4:00 P.M.; closed in August.

This historic house museum contains archives and a collection of decorative art objects.

Glencoe Historical Museum

999 Green Bay Road
Glencoe, IL 60022-1263
(708-835-4935)

September through April: Sunday—2:00 P.M.—4:00 P.M.

May: Third Sunday of month—2:00 P.M.—4:00 P.M.; and by appointment.

Emphasis is on Glencoe history; museum contains archives.

Glenview Area Historical Museum and Library

1121 Waukegan Road
Glenview, IL 60025-3036
(708-724-2235)

Farm Home Museum: Sunday 1:00 P.M.—4:00 P.M.; and by appointment.

Research Library: Wednesday—1:00 P.M.—3:00 P.M.; and by appointment.

This is an 1864 farmhouse furnished with nineteenth and twentieth century furnishings. There is a founders room and the coach house is a research library for the Glenview area.

Grove National Historic Landmark

1421 Milwaukee Avenue
Glenview, IL 60025-1436
(708-299-6096)
Kennicott House—The Grove: Sunday—1:00 P.M.—4:00 P.M.

Interpretative Center and Grounds: Monday through Friday—8:00 A.M.—4:30 P.M.; Saturday and Sunday—9:00 A.M.—5:00 P.M.

Contains items related to the Kennicott family: library, history of site, manuscripts. There is a museum and a nature center.

Hartung's License Plate and Auto Museum

3623 Westlake
Glenview, IL 60025
(708-724-4354)
Open daily—hours vary.

Museum has antique autos, motorcycles, trucks, tractors, license plate history from all states and Canada, police badges, old bicycles, and toys.

Hedrich-Blessing

11 West Illinois Street
Chicago, IL 60610 (312-321-1151)

Hellenic Museum and Cultural Center

400 North Franklin Street
Chicago, IL 60610-4403

Historical Society of Oak Park and River Forest Museum

217 Home
P.O. Box 771
Oak Park, IL 60303-0771
(708-848-6755)

Museum room: Thursday through Sunday—1:00 P.M.—4:00 P.M.

Office and research room: Tuesday and Thursday—1:00 P.M.—5:00 P.M.

A library and museum with an emphasis on local history.

Hofmann Tower

Berry Point Road at Joliet Avenue
c/o Lyons Historical Commission
P.O. Box 392
Lyons, IL 60534
(708-447-5815)

First Sunday of month- 2:00 P.M.—5:00 P.M.

Has information about the history of Lyons (museum), and about historic site preservation.

Homewood Historical Museum

2035 West 183rd Street
Homewood, IL 60430-1044
(708-799-1896)

Tuesday and Saturday—1:00 P.M.—3:00 P.M.; and by appointment.

Emphasis is on local history.

Illinois Association for the Preservation of Historic Arms and Armaments, Inc.

1800 Western Avenue
Flossmoor, IL 60422-0339
(708-798-1109)

By appointment.

Interests are in acquiring and preserving Civil War armaments, artifacts, and living histories.

International Museum of Surgical Science

1524 North Lake Shore Drive
Chicago, IL 60610-1607
(312-642-6502)
Medically oriented collection and library.

International Polka Music Hall of Fame and Museum

4145 South Kedzie Avenue
Chicago, IL 60632-2442
(312-254-7771)
Houses material related to polka music (old sheet music, old instruments, etc.).

Irish-American Heritage Center Museum and Art Gallery

4626 North Knox Avenue
Chicago, IL 60630-4030
(312-282-7035)
Has various collection: Irish Belleek parian ware; Books of Kells, works of Irish-American artists, artifacts of Chicago Irish history. A room is available for rental by social groups; sponsors activities for Irish-American community.

Italian Cultural Center

1621 North 39th Avenue
Stone Park, IL 60165-1105
(708-345-3842)
Monday through Saturday—10:00 A.M.—4:00 P.M.

Collects information on local history, and has art gallery, library, and museum.

Jacob Hostert Log Cabin and Bernard Hostert Log Cabin

West Avenue and 147th Street
Mail to: 14228 Union Avenue
Orland Park, IL 60462-2011
(708-349-0046)

Sunday—2:00 P.M.—4:00 P.M. (seasonal); and by appointment.

These former dwellings contain pre-1860 furniture (primitive), the Bernard Hostert cabin has primitive farm equipment and other exhibits that deal with the local history, genealogy, early settlers, historic preservation, and archaeology. There is also a library.

James P. Fitzgibbons Historical Museum

9800 Avenue G
Calumet Park Fieldhouse
(mailing address: 3558 East 106th Street
Chicago, IL 60617)
(312-721-7948)

Contains materials related to the history of East Side, Hegewisch, South Chicago, and South Deering neighborhoods, and has artifacts and memorabilia donated by residents and friends.

Jane Addams' Hull House Museum at University of Illinois-Chicago

800 South Halsted Street
Chicago, IL 60607-7017
(312-413-5354)

Monday through Friday—10:00 A.M.—4:00 P.M.; Sunday—12:00 P.M.—5:00 P.M.

A historic structure containing a museum and information about local history and women's history.

Kenilworth Historical Museum and Library

415 Kenilworth Avenue
(mailing address: P.O. Box 181
Kenilworth, IL 60043-1134)
(708-251-2565)

Monday—9:00 A.M.—4:30 P.M.; Thursday—9:00 A.M.—12:00 P.M.; and by appointment.

Subject matter is: local history, pioneers, historic preservation, and costumes.

LaGrange Area Historical Museum and Library

444 South LaGrange Road
LaGrange, IL 60525-2448
(708-482-4248)
Wednesday—9:00 A.M.—12:00 P.M.; last Sunday
of month—1:00 P.M.—4:00 P.M.

Subject matter is: local history, genealogy, pioneers, and military.

Lansing Historical Museum

2750 Indiana Avenue
Lansing, IL 60438-0633
(708-474-6160)
Monday—6:00 P.M.—8:00 P.M.; Wednesday—10:00 A.M.
—12:00 P.M.; Saturday—10:00 A.M.—12:00 P.M. except
June through August; and as announced.

Has special exhibits, oral history materials, museum tours, and educational, programs.

Latvian Folk Art Museum

4146 North Elston Avenue
Chicago, IL 60618-1828
(312-588-2085)
Daily from 10:00 A.M.—1:00 P.M.; and by appointment.

Collection includes textiles, ceremonial costumes, ceramics, and ancient musical instruments.

Lemont Area Historical Museum

306 Lemont Street
Lemont, IL 60439-0126
(708-257-2972)
Sunday—1:00 P.M.—4:00 P.M.; Tuesday through Saturday—10:00 A.M.—2:00 P.M.

Subject matter is: local history, genealogy, and photos. There are archives and a library; the museum also sponsors educational programs, building restoration projects, and tourist attractions.

Malcolm X College

1900 West Van Buren Street
Chicago, IL 60612-3145
(312-738-5845)
    Monday through Friday—9:00 A.M.—5:00 P.M.

    Emphasis is on African-American culture, and has collections of artifacts, fine art by African-American artists, and items representative of African culture; there are also archives.

Mary and Leigh Block Gallery

Northwestern University
1967 South Campus Drive
Evanston, IL 60201-2410
(708-491-4000)
    Tuesday and Wednesday—12:00 P.M.—5:00 P.M.; Thursday through Sunday—12:00 P.M.—8:00 P.M.

    Subject matter is the history of the arts and humanities.

Matteson Historical Museum

813 School Avenue
Matteson, IL 60443
(708-748-3033)
    Monday and Tuesday—9:00 A.M.—5:00 P.M.; tours and programs by appointment.

    Subject matter is local history, genealogy, and oral history.

Mexican Fine Arts Center Museum

1852 West 19th Street
Chicago, IL 60608-2706
(312-738-1503)
    Tuesday through Sunday—10:00 A.M.—5:00 P.M.

    Collection includes elements of the arts and culture of Mexico and the Mexican communities in the U.S.

Mitchell Indian Museum at Kendall College

2408 Orrington Avenue
Evanston, IL 60201-2899
(708-866-1395)

> Monday through Friday—9:00 A.M.—4:30 P.M.; Sunday—1:00 A.M.—4:00 P.M.

> Museum contains artifacts and examples of North American Indian art; there is also a library.

Morton B. Weiss Museum of Judaica

K.A.M. Isaiah Israel Congregation
100 East Hyde Park Boulevard
Chicago, IL 60615-2899
(312-924-1234)

> Monday through Thursday—9:00 A.M.—5:00 P.M.; Friday—9:00 A.M.—4:00 P.M.; Sunday—9:30 A.M.—12:00 P.M.

Morton Grove Historical Museum

(Haupt-Yehl House)
Harrer Park—6240 Dempster Street
P.O. Box 542
Morton Grove, IL 60053-2946
(708-965-7185)

> Sunday—2:00 P.M.—4:00 P.M.; Wednesday—11:00 A.M.—3:00 P.M.

> This is an 1888 Victorian farm house furnished in the early 1900s decor; there is a museum on the lower level that has changing exhibits.

Motorola Museum of Electronics

1303 East Algonquin Road
Schaumburg, IL 60196-1065
(708-576-5304)

Mt. Greenwood Public Library

11010 South Kedzie Avenue
Chicago, IL 60655-2222
(312-239-2805)

> Emphasis is local history.

Mt. Prospect Historical Society Museum

1100 South Linneman Road and 101 South Maple
P.O. Box 81
Mt. Prospect, IL 60056-0081
(708-392-9006)

1100 South Linneman: by appointment.

101 South Maple: Tuesday and Thursday—1:30 P.M.—4:30 P.M.; Sunday—1:00 P.M.—3:00 P.M.

Subject matter is related to Mt. Prospect at the turn of the century.

Museum of Broadcasting Communications

78 East Washington Street
Chicago, IL 60602-3407
(312-987-1500)

Wednesday—12:00 P.M.—5:00 P.M.; Thursday, Friday, and Sunday—12:00 P.M.—5:00 P.M.

Saturday—10:00 A.M.—5:00 P.M.

Museum has archives (radio, T.V., advertising-tape) and Midwestern contributions to broadcasting.

Newberry Library

60 West Walton Street
Chicago, IL 60610-3305
(312-943-9090)

General Reading Room: Tuesday through Thursday—10:00 A.M.—6:00 P.M.

Friday and Saturday—9:00 A.M.—5:00 P.M.

Special Collections Reading Room: Tuesday through Saturday—11:00 A.M.—5:00 P.M.

Collections at the Newberry Library include: history, humanities, western European and American civilization, Middle Ages to 20th century.

Niles Historical Society Museum

8970 Milwaukee Avenue
Niles, IL 60714-1737
(708-390-0160)
Wednesday through Friday—10:30 A.M.—4:00 P.M.

First and third Sundays of month—2:00 P.M.—4:00 P.M.;
and by appointment.

Museum emphasizes local history.

Olde Country Store

8420 West Brookfield Avenue, Brookfield
213 Herrick Road, Riverside, IL 60546-2016
(708-863-8979)
One side of the building fronts Brookfield, but Riverside
is official address. The grocery museum is housed in an
original building from 1893; collectibles are on display.

Oriental Institute Museum

University of Chicago
1155 East 58th Street
Chicago, IL 60637-1569
(312-702-9520; FAX: 312-702-9853)
Tuesday and Thursday through Saturday—10:00 A.M.—
4:00 P.M.

Sunday—12:00 P.M.—4:00 P.M., Wednesday—10:00 A.M.
—8:30 P.M.

Collections emphasize the history, art, and archaeology
of the ancient Near East.

Paarlberg Farmstead Homestead

172nd Place and Paxton Avenue
P.O. Box 48
South Holland, IL 60473-0048
(708-596-2722)
Saturday—1:00 P.M.—4:00 P.M.

The Homestead has historical farm house and barn,
local memorabilia, and items related to Dutch culture.

Palatine Park District/Clayson House Museum

224 East Palatine Road
P.O. Box 134
Palatine, IL 60078-0134
(708-991-6460)
   Tuesday and Thursday—9:00 A.M.—4:30 P.M.; Sunday
   —1:30 P.M.—4:30 P.M.

   Group tours available Monday through Friday

   An 1870s restored Victorian home that has collections
   and information related to: architecture, furnishings,
   local history, genealogy, and historic preservation.

Pleasant Home

217 Home Avenue
Oak Park, IL 60302-3101
(708-383-2654)
   Thursday through Sunday—1:00 P.M.—4:00 P.M.;
   groups by appointment.

   George W. Maher designed this prairie style home which
   is under restoration. Tours highlight the architectural
   style and the turn-of-the-century lifestyle.

Polish Museum of America

984 North Milwaukee Avenue
Chicago, IL 60622-4101
(312-384-3352)
   Daily—11:00 A.M.—4:00 P.M.

   Contains items of Polish and Polish-American culture
   and art.

Poplar Creek Public Library District

1405 South Park Avenue
Streamwood, IL 60107-2997
(708-837-6800)
   Monday though Thursday—9:00 A.M.—9:30 P.M.;

   Friday and Saturday—9:00 A.M.—5:00 P.M., Sunday—
   12:00 P.M.—5:00 P.M.

Prairie House Museum

1800 South Prairie Avenue
Chicago, IL 60604-2507
(312-326-1480)

Museum in historic house features items related to: architecture, social history, and decorative arts.

Printers Row Printing Museum

731 South Plymouth Court
Chicago, IL 60605-1847
(312-987-1059)

Saturday—9:00 A.M.—5:00 P.M., Sunday—10:00 A.M.—3:00 P.M., and by appointment.

Has a working nineteenth century print shop. Emphasis is on teaching and nineteenth century graphic arts design.

Riverdale Library

208 West 144th Street
Riverdale, IL 60627-2788
(708-841-3311)

Tuesday—10:00 A.M.—2:00 P.M.; Monday and Thursday —9:30 A.M.—8:00 P.M.; Friday—9:30 A.M.—6:00 P.M.; Saturday—9:30 A.M.—4:00 P.M.; Sunday—11:00 A.M.—3:00 P.M.

Has items related to Riverdale history.

Riverside Historical Museum

Longommon and Pine Roads (beside historic water tower)
27 Riverside Road
Riverside, IL 60546-2264
(708-442-0711)

Saturday—10:00 A.M.—2:00 P.M.; groups by appointment three weeks in advance.

Museum has information about the area and its importance in U.S. history; supports education programs.

Romanian Folk Art Museum

2526 Ridgeway
Evanston, IL 60201-1160
(708-328-9099)
 Saturday—2:00 P.M.—6:00 P.M.; and by appointment.

 Contains Romanian items of folklore and fine art; has a Romanian resource center; rugs, tapestries, arts, and crafts available for purchase; A/V presentations available.

South Holland Historical Society Museum

16250 Wausau Avenue
South Holland Public Library
Lower Level
P.O. Box 48
South Holland, IL 60473-0048
(708-596-2722)
 Saturday—1:00 P.M.—4:00 P.M.

 Houses artifacts of community culture.

South Suburban Genealogical and Historical Society Library

320 East 61st Place
P.O. Box 96
South Holland, IL 60473-0096
(708-333-9474)
 Library: Monday—10:00 A.M.—4:00 P.M.; Tuesday—1:00 P.M.—9:00 P.M.

 Wednesday—10:00 A.M.—11:30 A.M. and 12:30 P.M.—4:00 P.M.; Friday—10:00 A.M.—4:00 P.M.; Saturday—11:00 A.M.—4:00 P.M.

 Has special collections in addition to those that deal with local history, genealogy, pioneers, and American history; library also available for research.

Spertus Museum

618 South Michigan Avenue
Chicago, IL 60605-1901
(312-922-9012; FAX: 312-922-6406)

Sunday through Thursday—1:30 A.M.—4:30 P.M.

Museum houses archives and a library; subjects of collections and displays include fine art, decorative art, history, ethnography, and ceremonial items. Also has a hands-on archaeology gallery.

Spring Valley Nature Sanctuary

1111 East Schaumburg Road
Schaumburg, IL 60194
(708-980-2100)
  Grounds: daily—8:00 A.M.—sunset

  Natural History Museum: daily 9:00 A.M.—5:00 P.M.

Emphasis is on natural history and 1880s agricultural lifestyles of Schaumburg township.

St. Peter Lutheran Church Museum

208 East Schaumburg Road
Schaumburg, IL 60194
(708-843-0799)

Streamwood Historical Society Museum

777 West Bartlett Road
Streamwood, IL 60107-1394
(708-289-3276)
  By appointment.

Emphasis is on local history, the history of education, and agriculture.

Swedish-American Museum Center

5211 North Clark Street
Chicago, IL 60640-2101
(312-728-8111)
  Tuesday through Friday—11:00 A.M.—4:00 P.M.; Saturday and Sunday—11:00 A.M.—3:00 P.M.

The importance of Swedish immigrants in building Chicago is illustrated by collections that include tools, art objects, handicrafts, and Bibles.

Swedish-American Historical Society Library

5125 North Spaulding Avenue
Chicago, IL 60625-4816
(312-583-2700; ext. 5267)

Located is located on the campus of North Park College; contains records for various associations, personal papers, family histories, photographs, and other items of genealogical interest.. The Swedish-American Archives and the Covenant Archives are located here. The archives and library are open Monday through Thursday, but access is limited. You need to call to make an appointment.

Tinley Park Historical Society Museum

6727 West 174 Street
P.O. Box 325
Tinley Park, IL 60477-0325
(708-429-4210)

Wednesday—10:00 A.M.—2:00 P.M.; and by appointment.

Museum is in a former prairie gothic church building (1884). Emphasis is on the history of New Bremen and Tinley Park area.

Trailside Museum

738 Thatcher Avenue
River Forest, IL 60305
(708-366-6530)

Ukrainian National Museum

2453 West Chicago Avenue
Chicago, IL 69622-4633
(312-276-6565)

Thursday through Sunday—11:00 A.M.—4:30 P.M.; Monday through Wednesday by appointment.

Museum features Ukrainian folk art: Easter eggs ("Pysanka"), weaving, embroidery, carving, ceramics, necklaces ("Herdan") done with beads.

University Gallery/President's Gallery

Chicago State University
95th at King Drive
Chicago, IL 60628-1598
(312-995-3985)

Monday through Friday—9:00 A.M.—5:00 P.M. when exhibits on display.

Various categories of art are exhibited: modern paintings and sculpture, 18th and 19th century prints, photographs, and ceramic pieces.

Urban Traditions

55 East Jackson, Suite 1880
Chicago, IL 60604-4106
(312-663-5400)

Monday through Friday—9:00 A.M.—5:00 P.M.

Features Chicago area ethnic arts and cultural documentation.

Van Oostenbrugge Home

444 East 157th Street
P.O. Box 48
South Holland, IL 60473-0048
(708-596-2722)

May though October: Saturday—1:00 P.M.—4:00 P.M.; and by appointment.

This is the former home of a local Dutch pioneer.

Village of Thornton Historical Society Library and Museum

208 Schwab Street
P.O. Box 34
Thornton, IL 60476-0034
(708-877-9394)

May through October: Saturday—1:00 P.M.—4:00 P.M.; and by appointment.

Emphasis is on local history.

Village of Franklin Park Historical Museum

Franklin Park Public Library
9545 West Belmont
Franklin Park, IL 60131-2706
(708-455-6016)
> Monday through Thursday—9:00 A.M.—9:00 P.M.
>
> Friday and Saturday—9:00 A.M.—5:00 P.M.; Sunday—1:00 P.M.—5:00 P.M.
>
> Houses historical artifacts and records.

Western Electric Hawthorne Works Museum

Historical Society of Cicero
2423 South Austin Boulevard
Cicero, IL 60650-2695
(708-652-8305)
> Open by appointment.
>
> Exhibits of telephones and telephone switchboards; also Cicero artifacts and memorabilia.

Western Springs Historical Society Museum

Grand Avenue School
4211 Grand Avenue
P.O. Box 139
Western Springs, IL 60558-0139
(708-246-7073)
> Saturday—10:00 A.M.—2:00 P.M.; and by appointment.
>
> Summer: Thursday—7:00 P.M. —9:00 P.M.
>
> Archives: Tuesday—9:00 A.M.—12:00 P.M.
>
> Museum has a library and archives; emphasis is on historic site preservation, genealogy, local history.

Wheeling Historical Museum

251 North Wolf Road
P.O. Box 3
Wheeling, IL 60090-0003
(708-537-0327)
> Sunday—2:00 P.M.—4:00 P.M.; and by appointment.

Has changing exhibits; collections include early Wheeling artifacts and genealogical records.

Willard House

1730 Chicago Avenue
Evanston, IL 60201-4585
(708-864-1397)
Monday through Friday by appointment.

An historic house with collection of furniture and other memorabilia.

Wilmette Historical Museum

565 Hunter Road
Wilmette, IL 60091-2209
(708-256-5838)
September through mid-June: Tuesday through Thursday—9:30 A.M.—12:00 P.M. and 1:30 P.M.—4:00 P.M.

Saturday and Sunday—2:00 P.M.—5:00 P.M.

Emphasis is on Wilmette and Gross Point history and costume history.

Winnetka Historical Museum and Library

1140 Elm Street
Mail to: 510 Green Bay Road
Winnetka, IL 60093-2563
(708-501-6025)
Tuesday, Thursday and Saturday—1:00 P.M.—4:00 P.M.; and by appointment.

Focus is on the history of Winnetka and environs, period costumes; houses the Carleton Washburn Memorial Library.

Wood Library—Museum of Anesthesiology

520 North Northwest Highway
Park Ridge, IL 60068-2573
(708-825-5586)
Monday through Friday—9:00 A.M.—4:45 P.M.

Subject of collection is the history of anesthesiology in medicine.

Woodlands Native American Indian Museum and Art Gallery

6384 West Willow Wood Drive
Palos Heights, IL 60463-1847
(708-614-0334)
Monday through Saturday—9:00 A.M.—5:00 P.M.; Sunday and Holidays—12:00 P.M.—5:00 P.M.

Collections are education with focus on Native American cultures, beliefs, spirituality,and lore. Features Potawatomi and Lakota Sioux cultures. Gift shop on site has original works of art.

SECTION TWENTY

Historical Societies, Archives, and Manuscript Collections

Libraries, repositories, and information centers included in this section were chosen because of the type, access, and usefulness of their collections for genealogical or historical research. Though considered an important resource, corporation archives were not included as they are more readily found by consulting current directories.

Some historical societies that were contacted indicated they did not have archives or a manuscript collection. Some of the larger and more important archives or manuscript collections are described in more detail in separate sections of this book.

A useful reference containing the addresses and some descriptive information about various organizations (museums, historical research, etc.) is:

Association of Illinois Museums and Historical Societies. *Historical and Cultural Agencies and Museums in Illinois.* Springfield, IL: Phillips Brothers, 1993.

Alexian Brothers Hospital Archives

600 Alexian Way
Elk Grove Village, IL 60007
(312-640-7550)

American Medical Association Library & Archives

535 North Dearborn
Chicago, IL 60610
(312-645-4846)

Art Institute of Chicago-Ryerson & Burnham Libraries

Michigan at Adams Street
Chicago, IL 60603
(312-443-3511)

Barrington Area Historical Society

212-218 West Main Street
Barrington, IL 60010
(708-381-1730)

Bartlett Historical Society

P.O. Box 8257
Bartlett, IL 60103-8257
(708-837-0800 or 708-289-2024)

Berwyn Historical Society

P.O. Box 479
Berwyn, IL 60402-0479
(708-484-0020)

Blue Island Historical Society

c/o Blue Island Public Library
2433 York Street
Blue Island, IL 60406-2094
(708-371-8546)

Calumet City Historical Society

P.O. Box 1917
Calumet City, IL 60409-3515
(708-862-8662)

Chicago & Northwestern Historical Society & Archives

1812 Hood Avenue
Chicago, IL 60660
(312-743-1159)
A specific contact is:
Craig Pfannkuche
8612 Memory Trail
Wonder Lake, IL 60097
(815-653-9459)

Chicago & Northwestern Historical Society

8703 North Olcott Avenue
Niles, IL 60648-2023
(312-794-5633)

Chicago Architecture Foundation

224 South Michigan Avenue
Chicago, IL 60604-2507
(312-326-1480)

Chicago Area Women's History Conference

c/o P. Hunter & Associates
8928 South Paxton Avenue
Chicago, IL 60617-3009
(312-984-2809)

Chicago Heights Historical Society

15th Street & Chicago Road
Chicago Heights, IL 60411
(708-754-0323)

Chicago Historical Society

Clark Street at North Avenue
Chicago, IL 60614-6099
(312-642-4600)

Chicago Jewish Historical Society

618 South Michigan Avenue
Chicago, IL 60605
(312-580-2020)

Chicago Lawn Historical Society

4043 West 63rd Street
Chicago, IL 60629-4638
(312-582-8778)

Chicago Public Library

Special Collections Department, Floor 9
Harold Washington Library Center
400 South State Street
Chicago, IL 60605
(312-747-4876 or 4875)
Reference Desk: Tuesday &
Thursday—12:00 P.M.—
6:00 P.M.

Wednesday, Friday & Saturday—12:00 P.M.—
4:00 P.M.

The collection includes material related to the Civil War, Chicago history, Chicago theater, Chicago authors, and book arts.

Chicago Sun-Times Public Service Bureau

401 North Wabash
Room 110
Chicago, IL 60611
(312-321-2031)

Chicago Tribune Archives

Tribune Tower, Room 1231
435 North Michigan Avenue
Chicago, IL 60611
(312-222-3026)

City of Chicago-Department of Planning

City Hall, Room 1000
121 North LaSalle Street
Chicago, IL 60602
(312-744-4160)

City of Chicago-Department of Public Works, Bureau of Engineering

320 North Clark Street
Room 700
Chicago, IL 60610
(312-744-3544)

City of Chicago-Commission on Chicago Landmarks

320 North Clark Street
Room 516
Chicago, IL 60610
(312-744-3200)

Cook County Hospital Archives

Health Science Library
Nurses Residence
1900 West Polk Street
Chicago, IL 60612
(312-633-7538)

Croation Ethnic Institute, Inc.
4851 South Drexel Blvd.
Chicago, IL 60615
(312-373-2248)

De Paul University Archives
2323 North Seminary
Chicago, IL 60614
(312-341-8088)

Des Plaines Genealogical Questors
789 Pearson
Des Plaines, IL 60016-4506
(708-391-5399)

DuSable Museum of African-American History
740 East 56th Place
Chicago, IL 60637-1408
(312-947-0600)

DuSable Museum Archives
740 East 56th Place
Chicago, IL 60637-1495
(312-947-0600)

East Side Historical Society
3658 East 106th Street
Chicago, IL 60617-6611
(312-721-7948)

Edgewater Historical Society
1112 West Bryn Mawr
Chicago, IL 60660-4410
(312-334-5609)

Elk Grove Historical Society
399 Biesterfield Road
Elk Grove, IL 60007-3625
(708-439-3994)

Elmhurst Historical Museum
120 East Park Avenue
Elmhurst, IL 60126-3420
(312-833-1457)

Episcopal Diocese of Chicago
Archives and Historical Collections
St. James Cathedral
65 East Huron
Chicago, IL 60611
(312-787-6410)

Evangelical Covenant Church of America
Archives & Historical Library
5125 North Spaulding Ave.
Room 25
Chicago, IL 60637
(312-583-2700, ext. 287)

Evanston Historical Society
225 Greenwood Street
Evanston, IL 60201-4713
(708-475-3410)

Evergreen Park Historical Society
3538 West 98th Street
Evergreen Park, IL 60642

Filipino-American Historical Society
5462 South Dorchester Ave.
Chicago, IL 60615-5309
(312-752-2156)

Flagg Creek Historical Society

P.O. Box 227
Western Springs, IL 60558
(708-246-4142)

German-American Heritage Institute

7824 West Madison Street
Forest Park, IL 60130-1485
(708-366-0017)

Glencoe Historical Society

999 Green Bay Road
Glencoe, IL 60022-1263
(708-835-4935)

Glenview Area Historical Society

1121 Waukegan Road
Glenview, IL 60025-3036
(708-724-2235)

Grove Heritage Association

P.O. Box 484
Glenview, IL 60025-0484
(708-299-6096)

Hazel Crest Historical Trust Fund

3102 West 175th Street
Hazel Crest, IL 60429-1623
(708-335-0929)

Historic Preservation Commission of Oak Park

1 Village Hall Place
Oak Park, IL 60302-4295
(708-383-6400)

Historic Pullman Foundation, Inc.

11111 S. Forrestville Avenue
Chicago, IL 60628-4649
(312-785-8181)

Historical Pictures Service, Inc.

17 North State Street
Chicago, IL 60602
(312-346-0599)

Historical Society of Elmwood Park

c/o Elmwood Park Library
2823 North 77th Avenue
Elmwood Park, IL 60635-1408
(708-453-1133)

Historical Society of Cicero

2423 South Austin Boulevard
Cicero, IL 60650-2695
(708-652-8305)

Historical Society of Oak Park & River Forest

P.O. Box 771
Oak Park, IL 60303-0771
(708-848-6755)

Historical Society of Arlington Heights

110 West Fremont
Arlington Heights, IL 60004-5912
(708-255-1225)

Historical Society of Forest Park

519 Jackson Boulevard
(mailing address)
Forest Park, IL 60130-1896
(708-771-7716)

Holocaust Memorial Foundation of Illinois
4255 Main Street
Skokie, IL 60076
(708-677-4640)

Homewood Historical Society
2035 West 183rd Street
P.O. Box 1144
Homewood, IL 60430-1044
(708-799-1896)

Hyde Park Historical Society
5529 South Lake Park
Chicago, IL 60637-1916
(312-493-1893)

Illinois Institute of Technology Archives
31 Perlstein Hall
10 West 33rd Street
Chicago, IL 60616
(312-567-3039)

Illinois Labor History Society
28 East Jackson Boulevard
Chicago, IL 60604-2215
(312-663-4107)

Illinois Postal History Society
P.O. Box 1513
Des Plaines, IL 60017-1513
(312-443-4442)

Illinois State Archives
Archives Building
Springfield, IL 62756-0001
(217-782-4682)

Irving Park Historical Society
4122 North Kedvale
Chicago, IL 60641-2245
(312-736-2143)

K & S Photo Graphics
180 North Wabash Avenue
8th Floor
Chicago, IL 60601

LaGrange Area Historical Society
444 South LaGrange Road
LaGrange, IL 60525-2448
(708-482-4248)

Landmarks Preservation Council
53 West Jackson Boulevard
Suite 752
Chicago, IL 60604-3699
(312-922-1742)

Lansing Historical Society
P.O. Box 1776
Lansing, IL 60438-0633
(708-474-6160)

Lemont Area Historical Society
P.O. Box 126
Lemont, IL 60439-0126
(708-257-2972)

Leyden Historical Society
P.O. Box 506
Franklin Park, IL 60131
(708-678-1929)

Loyola University Archives
6525 Sheridan Road
Chicago, IL 60626
(312-274-3000 ext. 791)

Lutheran Church in America Archives
1100 East 55th Street
Chicago, IL 60615
(312-667-3500)

Lyons Historical Commission
P.O. Box 392
Lyons, IL 60534-0392
(708-447-7907)

MAC (Midwest Archives Conference) Archives
Northwestern University
Library Archives
Evanston, IL 60201
(312-491-3136)

Maine West Historical Society
Maine West High School
1755 South Wolf Road
Des Plaines, IL 60018-1994
(708-827-6176)

Marquis Who's Who
200 East Ohio Street
Chicago, IL 60611
(312-787-2008 ext. 253)

Matteson Historical Society
813 School Avenue
Matteson, IL 60443
(708-748-3033)

Max Epstein Photography Archive
The Joseph Regenstein
Library, Room 420
The University of Chicago
1100 East 57th Street
Chicago, IL 60637
(312-753-2887)

Maywood Historical Society
202 South 2nd Avenue
Maywood, IL 60153-2304
(708-344-4282)

Melrose Park Historical Society
P.O. Box 1453
Melrose Park, IL 60160

Midlothian Historical Society
14609 Springfield
Midlothian, IL 60445
(708-389-5066)

Midwest Nursing History Research Center
College of Nursing
Room 1042
845 South Damen Avenue
Chicago, IL 60612
(312-996-8005)

Moody Bible Institute Library
820 North La Salle Street
Chicago, IL 60610
(312-329-4140)

Morton Grove Historical Society

P.O. Box 542

Morton Grove, IL 60053-2946

(708-965-7185)

Mt. Greenwood Historical Society

11010 South Kedzie Avenue

Chicago, IL 60655-2222

(312-239-2805)

Mundelein College Archives-Chicago

6363 Sheridan Road

Chicago, IL 60660

(312-262-8100)

National Archives-Great Lakes Region

7358 Pulaski Road

Chicago, IL 60629

(312-581-7816)

National Baha'I Archives

Wilmette, IL 60091

(312-869-9039)

National Railway Historical Society—Chicago Chapter

P.O. Box 53

Oak Park, IL 60303-0053

(708-386-2809)

National Trust of Historic Preservation

53 West Jackson Boulevard, Suite 1135

Chicago, IL 60610-3701

(312-939-5547; FAX: 312-939-5651)

Newberry Library Modern Manuscripts

60 West Walton

Chicago, IL 60610-3305

(312-943-9090)

North Eastern Illinois Historical Council

7007 Fargo Avenue

Niles, IL 60714-3719

(708-647-0185)

Northbrook Historical Society

1776 Walters Avenue

P.O. Box 2021

Northbrook, IL 60065

(708-998-1322)

Northeastern Illinois University Library

5500 North St. Louis

Chicago, IL 60625

(312-583-4050 ext. 479)

Northwestern Memorial Hospital Group

329 West 18th Street

Suite 901

Chicago, IL 60616

(312-649-3090)

Northwestern University Library

Special Collections-Archives

Evanston, IL 60201

(312-492-3635)

Norwood Park Historical Society
5624 North Newark Avenue
Chicago, IL 60631-3137
(312-631-1496)

Oak Forest Historical Society
15440 South Central Avenue
Oak Forest, IL 60452-2104
(708-687-4050)

Oak Lawn Historical Society
9526 South Cook Avenue
Oak Lawn, IL 60453
(312-425-3424)

Oak Park Public Library
834 Lake Street
Oak Park, IL 60301
(312-383-8200)

Old Edgebrook Historical Society
6173 North McClellan
Chicago, IL 60646-4013
(312-631-2854)

Orland Historical Society
P.O. Box 324
Orland Park, IL 60462-0324
(708-349-3216)

Palatine Historical Society
P.O. Box 134
Palatine, IL 60078-0134
(708-991-6460)

Palos Heights Historical Society
7607 College Drive
Palos Heights, IL 60463

Palos Historical Society
12332 Forest Glen Boulevard
Palos Park, IL 60464-1707
(708-448-1410)

Park Forest Historical Society
400 Lakewood Boulevard
Park Forest, IL 60466-1684
(708-748-3731)

Park Ridge Historical Society
41 West Prairie Avenue
Park Ridge, IL 60068

Park Ridge Heritage Committee
35 South Prospect
Park Ridge, IL 60068-4031
(708-318-9400)

Ravenswood-Lake View Historical Society
4455 North Lincoln Avenue
Chicago, IL 60625-2192
(312-744-7616)

Ridge Historical Society
10621 South Seely Avenue
Chicago, IL 60643-2618
(312-445-5806)

Riverdale Historical Society
c/o Riverdale Library
208 West 144th Street
Riverdale, IL 60627-2788
(708-841-3311)

Robbins Historical Society
P.O. Box 1561
Robbins, IL 60472-1561
(708-389-5393)

Rogers Park Historical Society
2555 West Farwell (mailing address)
Chicago, IL 60645-4617
(312-764-2401)

Rush Presbyterian-St. Luke Medical Center
1753 W. Congress Parkway
Chicago, IL 60612
(312-942-7214)

Schiller Park Historical Society
4501 North 25th Avenue
Schiller Park, IL 60176
(708-678-2550)

Skokie Historical Society
8031 Floral
Skokie, IL 60077
(708-675-3674)

Society of American Archivists
600 South Federal, Suite 504
Chicago, IL 60605-1898
(312-922-0140)

South Holland Historical Society
P.O. Box 48
South Holland, IL 60473-0048
(708-596-2722)

South Shore Historical Society
7566 South Shore Drive
Chicago, IL 60649
(312-375-1699)

South Side Irish Archives Project
South Side Irish Parade and Heritage Foundation
10926 South Western Ave.
Chicago, IL 60643
(312-238-1969)

South Suburban Genealogical & Historical Society
P.O. Box 96
South Holland, IL 60473-0096
(708-333-9474)

South Suburban Heritage Association
P.O. Box 716
Tinley Park, IL 60477-3450
(708-614-8713)

Stone Park Historical Association
Village Hall
1629 North Mannheim Road
Stone Park, IL 60165-1118
(708-345-2272)

Streamwood Historical Society
777 West Bartlett Road
(mailing address)
Streamwood, IL 60107-1394
(708-289-3276)

Swedish-American Historical Society
5125 North Spaulding Avenue
Chicago, IL 60625-4816
(312-583-2700)

The John Crerar Library
35 West 33rd Street
Chicago, IL 60616
(312-225-2526)

Thornton Township Historical Society
154 East 154th
Harvey, IL 60426-3326
(708-331-4247)

Tinley Park Historical Society
P.O. Box 325
Tinley Park, IL 60477-0325
(708-429-4210)

Triton Community History Organization
Triton College
2000 5th Avenue
River Grove, IL 60171-1995
(708-456-0300 ext. 245)

University of Illinois Medical Center Archives
1750 West Polk Street
Chicago, IL 60612
(312-996-8977)

University of Chicago Library Special Collections
1100 East 57th Street
Chicago, IL 60637
(312-962-8705)

University of Illinois at Chicago Library
P.O. Box 8198
801 South Morgan
Room 220
Chicago, IL 60607
(312-996-2756)

Village of Thornton Historical Society
P.O. Box 34
Thornton, IL 60476-0034
(708-877-9394)

West Side Historical Society
115 S. Pulaski Rd.
Chicago, IL 60624

Westchester Historical Society
10332 Bond Street
Westchester, IL 60154-4361
(708-865-1972)

Western Springs Historical Society
P.O. Box 139
Western Springs, IL 60558-0139
(708-246-7073)

Wheeling Historical Society
P.O. Box 3
Wheeling, IL 60090-0003
(708-537-0327)

Wilmette Historical Society
565 Hunter Road
Wilmette, IL 60091-2209
(708-251-8092)

Winnetka Historical Society
P.O. Box 142
Winnetka, IL 60093-0142
(708-501-6025)

Illinois Regional Archives Depository (IRAD)

The Illinois Regional Archives Depository (IRAD)-Chicago Branch, is a repository of primary sources on Chicago history, particularly for information on local government, and genealogical information for Cook County. The research collections of the IRAD are open to the public weekdays from 9:00 A.M.—4:00 P.M. The IRAD is located at:

Northeastern Illinois University
  Ronald Williams Library, Lower Level
  5500 North St. Louis
  Chicago, IL 60625
  (312-794-6279)

The IRAD collections include:

Probate Records (1872-1895; 1921-1923). Partial volumes; no index.

Records of Bonds and Letters of Administration & Wills (1877-1922). No index.

Records of Foreign Wills (1880-1908; 1904-1913; 1915-1922). Partial volumes; no indexes.

Grants of Guardianship (1877-1923). Partial volumes; no index.

Burned Record Files (for dates after 1871).

> Available on microfilm, and indexed by surnames of plaintiffs and defendants. Documentation to re-establish property ownership for reissuance of deeds lost in the Chicago fire in 1871, accomplished by court proceedings requiring witnesses to testify to prior ownership. The files cover the years 1873 through 1904, but some years are not included.

Naturalization—Cook County records available on microfilm:

> Circuit Court Declarations of Intention (1874-1912). No indexes.
>
> Circuit Court Alien Index (1871-1903).
>
> Circuit Court Naturalization Records (1871-1925). Index to 1912.
>
> Circuit Court Naturalization Petition Records (1906-1929). Most volumes indexed.
>
> Criminal Court Declarations of Intention (1878-1886). No index.
>
> Superior Court Naturalization Records Indexes (1871-1906).
>
> Superior Court Naturalization Petitions and Records—Indexes: 1906-1929.
>
> Superior Court Declarations of Intention (1871-1906; partial volumes). No index.
>
> Superior Court Declarations of Intention Indexes (1906-1929; 1915; 1926-1929).

Minors and Old Soldiers Index, 1871-1903.

Marriage Record Index 1830-1900. Microfiche; Cook County not included.

Federal Records at The Illinois State Archives (microfiche)

Cook County Historic Records Survey (HRS), 1936-1942. Microfiche.

Federal Land Surveyors' Field Notes, 1804-1856. Microfilm.

Public Domain Land Tract Records, 1814-1873. Microfiche.

State Sources at The Illinois State Archives

Descriptive Inventory of the Archives of the State of Illinois, by Victoria Irons and Patricia Brennan, under the direction of Dr. John Daly, Director, Illinois State Archives, 1978 (book) and *Index*, 1990 (book).

Laws of Illinois, 1818-1969. Microfiche.

The Atlas Collection

The collection at IRAD consists of approximately 100 Chicago atlases and atlases that include the towns and villages eventually annexed to Chicago. They constitute a rare and highly valuable collection, with original plat books dating as far back as 1872.

Sources for Chicago and the Towns Annexed

The Chicago City Council Proceedings Files, 1833-1942.

> The proceedings are the working papers of the Chicago City Council. They include: committee reports; orders; assessment rolls; appointments; official oaths and bonds; ordinances and resolutions; poll books and tally sheets; licenses; communications; citizen petitions and remonstrances.

Bailey, Robert and Evans, Elaine Shemoney. *Chicago City Council Proceedings Files, 1833-1871: An Inventory.* and *Chicago City Council Proceedings Files, 1833-1871: An Index.*

> A microfiche set that categorizes the Chicago pre-fire documents by subject.

The Chicago City Council Minutes, 1853-1855; 1857-1858; 1859-1860; 1863-1907.

> These records summarize the actions detailed in the City Council Proceedings. The records of the city of Chicago, and those of various towns and villages, total 551 volumes. A significant portion of the accession pre-dates the Great Fire of 1871, and because these records were previously believed to have been destroyed, they are of particular interest and value.

Record and Index of Persons Registered and of Poll List of Voters, Chicago Election Commission, 1888; 1888-1890; 1892.

> Microfilm. Lists voters, their addresses, years in precinct, county and state, place of birth, and if naturalized, their country of origin, and date and court where naturalized.

Chicago Streets—History. Two 3-ring binders.

Chicago Street Name Changes—An Index. Six 3-ring binders.

Film Board Censorship Files, 1912-1982.

Liquor Licenses, 1934-1969.

Clipping File

The IRAD houses an extensive clipping file which includes pamphlets and small books. Some of the clippings come from newspapers and others from *Chicago History* (published by the Chicago Historical Society).

Town Documents

These documents include the proceedings and/or minutes of 15 towns and villages before they were incorporated into the city of Chicago. Documents concern all town business and government, including petitions, bids and contracts, ordinances and resolutions, and town records that touch on many aspects of everyday life.

Additional Sources—Suggested References

Eakle, Arlene, and Johni Cerny, eds. *The Source: A Guidebook of American Genealogy.* Salt Lake City: Ancestry, 1984.

Illinois State Archives. *A Summary Guide to Local Government Records in the Illinois Regional Archives.* Springfield, IL: Illinois State Archives, 1992.

   Available from the Illinois State Archives, Springfield, IL.

The Library—A Guide to the LDS Family History Library, 1988.

Turnbaugh, Roy C., Jr. *A Guide to County Records in the Illinois Regional Archives,* Illinois State Archives, 1983.

Clabaugh, Chas. W., Randy De Villez, and John William Martin. *Township School Trustees and Treasurers in Illinois, 1819-1980,* 1980.

SECTION TWENTY-TWO

Illinois State Sources for Cook County

By Sandra Hargreaves Luebking

Two repositories and two societies offer holdings and publications which are of interest to Cook County genealogy researchers. The repositories are the Illinois State Archives and the Illinois State Historical Library, both located in Springfield, Illinois and the societies are the Illinois State Genealogical Society and the Illinois State Historical Society. Both societies have helpful publications, and have news and articles about Chicago.

Illinois State Archives

Several record groups created, administered, or simply deposited at the state level have specific application to research activity in Cook County. The records discussed in this section are held by the Illinois State Archives.

The categories of records include: Name Index to Early Records; Sales of Public Domain Land; War Indexes and Veteran's Burial Lists; Civil War Military Enrollments; Muster Rolls; World War I Draft Registration and State Council of Defense Records; Supreme Court of Illinois Case

Files; Criminal Records; and the Illinois Historical Records Survey of the WPA (Work Projects Administration). A publication essential to understanding both the characteristics and organization of Illinois archival material is the *Descriptive Inventory of the Archives of the State of Illinois*, by Victoria Irons and Patricia C. Brennan (Springfield, IL: Illinois State Archives, 1978). This may be purchased from the Illinois State Archives. There is also a pamphlet titled *Genealogical Records and Mail Research Policy of the Illinois State Archives* available without charge upon request.

Limit mail inquiries or search requests to one or two specific items at a time. Designate the specific record to be searched, and provide the complete name(s) of the person(s) sought. Submit no more than two names per request, and do not send a second request until you have received an answer to the first. Personal visits are encouraged. The State Archives building is located south of the Capitol, west is the Centennial Building, and north of the Illinois State Museum in Springfield. The hours vary.

Most of the descriptions of the holdings at the Illinois State Archives include numbers preceded by the letters RG. These are "record group" numbers to help you find the particular set of records described.

Name Index to Early Illinois Records

This is a cumulative card file, sorted by individual name, of all extant Illinois and U.S. Census records from 1810 through 1855. Also included are names from early house and senate journals, the governor's executive records, election returns and other state documents. The file contains well over a half million index cards.

Northeastern Land District Office

The Northeastern Land District Office was established in Chicago by an Act of Congress on June 26, 1834 and operated through 31 July 1855. The area was originally contained in the Danville district, and was comprised of part of those lands lying north of the line separating townships thirty and thirty-one north of the baseline for the second and third principal meridians.

The Illinois State Archives holds receipt entries, correspondence, account books for the Receiver of the General Land Office, and original tract books and abstracts of the surveyor's field notes.

To find details about the first purchase of land from the federal government, search of the Archives Public Domain Computer Conversion project microfiche. Be aware that preemption prevented some individuals from making original purchases, and their names will not appear in this source. A search of the ledgers concerning preemption claims (RG 952. 326; RG 952. 327; RG 952. 328 and RG 952. 329) might reveal evidence of disputes involving another individual's right to own or purchase a specific tract of land. The preemption claims ledgers are not indexed and are best searched in person. The collection consists of fewer than three volumes and 2½ cubic feet of declaration statements, the latter being RG 952. 327.

Public Domain Computer Conversion Project

The first purchases of land in Illinois from the federal government are indexed alphabetically by the purchaser's name in this statewide finding aid. In addition, purchases of school lands sold by the state government and some county swamp lands sales are also indexed. Two other sources in the Illinois State Archives reference room may be of interest: an alphabetical list of Cook County purchasers (by surname), and a list of Cook County property by township, range, section, and purchaser's surname.

War Indexes and Veteran's Burial Lists

There are separate indexes for the Indian, Black Hawk, Mexican, Civil and Spanish-American Wars. *The Honor Roll of Veterans Buried in Illinois* lists veterans of all wars who were buried in Illinois. The file is incomplete and contains errors, but it is the single most comprehensive source to burials. On request, the Illinois State Archives will search the three-volume 1956 edition for Cook County.

For the names and death dates of soldiers, sailors, and marines from the Revolutionary War through World War I who were buried in Cook County, refer to an index of a 1929 edition of the *Honor Roll of Veterans Buried in Illinois.*

Index to Roll of Honor, Cook County, Illinois Salt Lake City, Markham Publications.

> Markham Publications
> P.O. Box 521018
> Salt Lake City, Utah, 84152-1018

Civil War Military Enrollments

On May 3, 1861, the Illinois legislature approved an act requiring county assessors to list all able-bodied male citizens between the ages of 18 and 45 who were subject to militia duty. Information in these enrollment registers is limited to names and classification as volunteer or reserve.

In August of 1862, General Order No. 99, issued by the U.S. War Department, required state governors to prepare lists of able-bodied male citizens between 18 and 45. Although Illinois was already preparing similar lists, the decree added requirements to list age, occupation, and a remarks section regarding possible exemption from duty.

The federal lists are not indexed, and most Cook County entries appear to be missing. Remaining entries are listed by town and are found on roll #1012407. Additional names are mixed randomly with entries for adjacent DuPont and Will Counties.

When requesting a search of these enrollments, you must indicate a specific township location.

Military Muster Rolls

The Indian Wars muster rolls for Illinois units contain only the names of men who served. The muster rolls for the

Black Hawk War (RG 301. 7) and Mexican War (RG 301. 8) include names, county of residences, and occasional remarks. Civil War and Spanish-American War rosters will provide a physical description, residence, nativity, and service dates; muster-out rolls for the Spanish-American War (RG 301. 89) provide the name of next-of-kin.

World War I Draft Registration and State Council of Defense Records

Draft registration was required of all able-bodied males by the Selective Service Act of May 18, 1917. These records are on microfilm at the Illinois State Archives. The lists include name, address, date and place of birth, occupation, and a brief physical description. Cook County names are not indexed, but arranged alphabetically under draft board number. Lists are extant for ninety-five Cook County draft boards. You need to provide the Illinois State Archives with the full name, 1917 address, and city ward number.

The Military Affairs Committee Administrative Files go through 1919 (RG 517. 13), and include correspondence between committee officials and Illinois Volunteer Training Corps (IVTC) officers. Among other topics are the development of Polish and Bohemian corps units, a list of IVTC units in Cook County and their officers, and a list of all IVTC commissioned officers.

The Cook County Members' Register (RG 517. 21) is a one-volume alphabetical register of members of several Committees of the State Council of Defense listing each member's name, address, occupation, and committee affiliation.

The Cook County Neighborhood Committee and Volunteers files (RG 517. 39) lists the name, address, and occasionally the telephone number of the chairman, vice chairman, secretary, treasurer and volunteers.

The Cook County Neighborhood Committee Entertainers Files (RG 517. 41) lists names, addresses, and telephone numbers of musicians, singers, and music teachers; the instrument or the specialty of each is also shown.

Supreme Court of Illinois Case Files

Record Group 901 (RG 901. 1) consists of case files for every case heard before the Supreme Court of Illinois between 1820 and 1936. These cases are primarily appeals. However, original jurisdiction is assigned to this Court in cases relating to revenue, cases of mandamus, and impeachment cases required to be tried before it (original jurisdiction for impeachment was withdrawn in 1870). Cases are indexed by appellant or petitioner, and occasionally the index provides genealogical information.

Criminal Records

A comprehensive list of registers, petitions, and other records maintained by the Department of Corrections appears in an article by Robert S. Johnston (see bibliography). Access to some criminal records is restricted by the Freedom of Information Act (Public Act 83-1013) and the Unified Code of Corrections (Revised Statues of the State of Illinois, chapter 38).

Illinois Historical Records Survey of the WPA

Record Group 954 contains data and inventory work sheets from unpublished inventories compiled by field workers as part of the Illinois Historical Records Survey by the WPA. This survey sought to locate and describe federal, state, county, municipal and church archives in Illinois. The inventories for Cook County have not been published but are available in manuscript form at the Illinois State Archives. While there is no genealogical information in these inventories, they serve to establish the presence and location of a particular record at the time of inventory.

The Cook County archives were inventoried by record title, dates, quantity, arrangement, type of indexing, contents, and location by field workers between 1936 and 1942 (RG 954. 7). In addition, research material and preliminary essays include drafts of historical sketches of Cook County and Chicago and legal essay material on county officials and county courts (RG 954. 9).

A list of Cook County municipal archives inventoried includes: Bellwood, Berwyn, Blue Island, Brookfield, Chicago, Cicero, Crestwood, Des Plaines, Dixmoor, Evanston, Forest Park, Franklin Park, La Grange, Lyons Township, Maywood, Melrose Park, Oak Park, Park Ridge, River Forest, Riverside, Summit, Tinley Park, Westchester, and Westmont. The information provided on each form includes title and creation or inclusive dates of items inventoried, description and form of recording, size and condition, and location at the time of inventory.

Illinois State Historical Library

An estimated four million manuscript items, consisting of 200 large collections and over 2,000 smaller ones, are housed in the Illinois State Historical Library rooms in the lower level of the Old State Capitol in Springfield. Most items date from 1818, the year of Illinois statehood, and relate to all phases of Illinois history. The library is known particularly for its fine holdings relating to Abraham Lincoln, papers of political leaders and other state officials, and military collections from the Black Hawk War and the Civil War. Of particular interest to Chicago area genealogy researchers is the fine collection of Cook County newspapers on microfilm. More than 300 titles, ranging from the November 26, 1833 *Democrat* to the present are available for Chicago. Holdings include scattered issues for more than three dozen Chicago ethnic newspapers. An excellent finding aid can be found in the March, 1985 issue of *Illinois Libraries*, available from the Illinois State Library, Springfield, IL 62756.

The Library is open to the public from 8:30 A.M.—5:00 P.M., Monday through Friday.

Illinois State Genealogical Society

There are more than 2,500 members of the Illinois State Genealogical Society which was organized in 1968. Each year the Society publishes ten issues of a newsletter and four issues of a quarterly. Membership information is available from the Illinois State Genealogical Society, P.O. Box 157, Lincoln, IL 62656.

Illinois State Historical Society

The Illinois State Historical Society is a private, not-for-profit corporation organized in 1899 to collect, preserve, and disseminate information concerning the history of Illinois. Members receive a discount on publications sold by the society, the quarterly *Illinois Historical Journal*, and a bimonthly newsletter, *The Dispatch*. The quarterly often contains book reviews and articles of historical interest concerning Chicago. Contact the Illinois State Historical Society, Old State Capitol, Springfield, IL 62701.

Bibliography

Irons, Victoria, and Patricia C. Brennan. *Descriptive Inventory of Archives of the State of Illinois*. Springfield: Illinois State Archives, 1978.

Johnston, Robert S. "Criminal Records of Illinois in the Illinois State Archives." *Illinois State Genealogical Quarterly* 18, no. 1 (Spring 1986).

> Provides titles and record group numbers; lists of "Convicts in the Illinois State Prison Who Have Been Pardoned, Died or Escaped 1 January 1855 to 31 December 1856." Forty-seven percent of these convicts were from Cook County.

Stark, Sandra M. "Newspapers in the Illinois State Historical Library." *Illinois Libraries* 67, no. 3 (March 1985).

Volkel, Lowell M., "Genealogical Sources in the Illinois State Archives." *Illinois Libraries* 68, no. 4 (Spring 1986).

SECTION TWENTY-THREE
Land and Property Records

Land records contain a variety of genealogical and historical data and can help your research in different ways. They are a major source of information for many family history studies, and provide primary source material for local history as well. They are closely related to probate and other official court records, and should be investigated in connection with them. Land and property are leading issues in estate settlements, and the majority of civil cases in the courts deal with real and personal property. Although land records rarely yield vital statistics, in many instances they provide the only proof of family relationships. Often they include the names of heirs of an estate (including a daughter's married name and a widow's subsequent married name), and refer to related probate and other court cases by number and court name; such information can open up other areas of research. In Cook County, where other sources are information are sometimes scarce, the land records take on extra importance. Occasionally these documents will disclose former residences, and frequently provide the new addresses of the grantors or heirs at the time of the sale of the property.

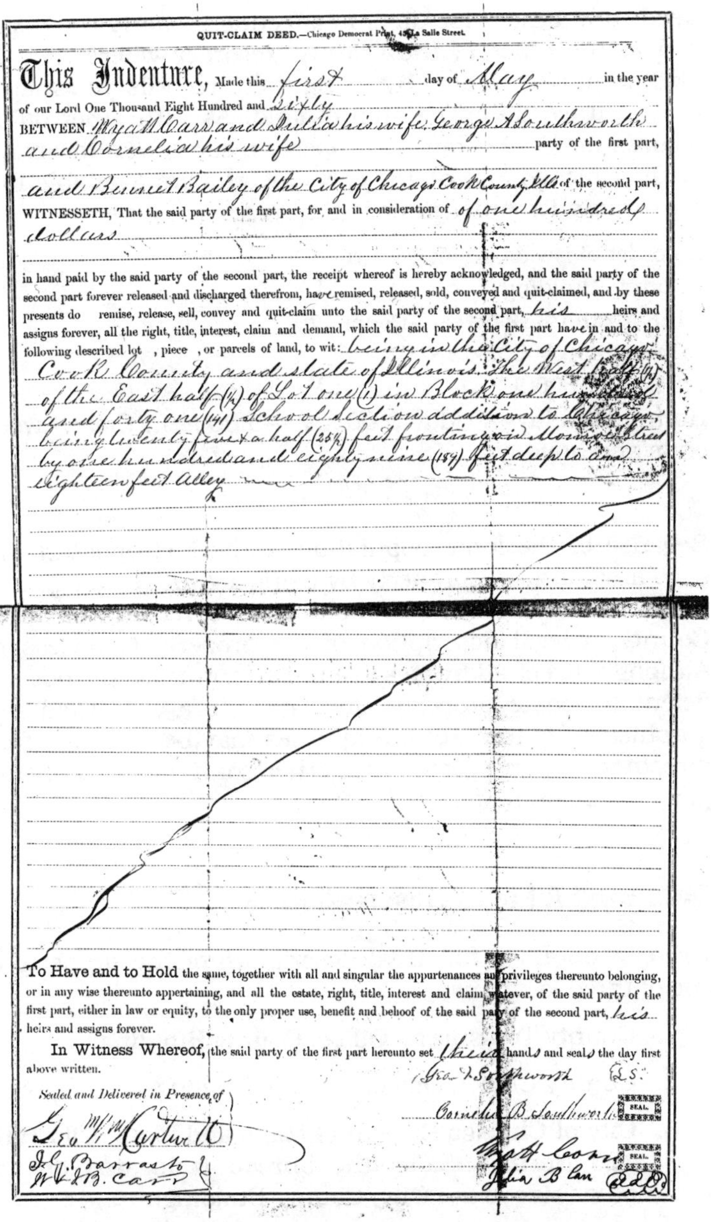

QUIT-CLAIM DEED.—Chicago Democrat Print, 45 La Salle Street.

This Indenture, Made this first day of May in the year of our Lord One Thousand Eight Hundred and Sixty BETWEEN Wyatt Carr and Julia his wife George A Southworth and Cornelia his wife party of the first part, and Bennet Bailey of the City of Chicago Cook County Ills of the second part, WITNESSETH, That the said party of the first part, for and in consideration of of one hundred dollars

in hand paid by the said party of the second part, the receipt whereof is hereby acknowledged, and the said party of the second part forever released and discharged therefrom, have remised, released, sold, conveyed and quit-claimed, and by these presents do remise, release, sell, convey and quit-claim unto the said party of the second part, his heirs and assigns forever, all the right, title, interest, claim and demand, which the said party of the first part have in and to the following described lot, piece, or parcels of land, to wit: being in the City of Chicago Cook County and state of Illinois. The West half (½) of the East half (½) of Lot one (1) in Block one hundred and forty one (141) School Section addition to Chicago, being twenty five & a half (25½) feet fronting on Monroe Street by one hundred and eighty nine (189) feet deep to an eighteen feet Alley

To Have and to Hold the same, together with all and singular the appurtenances and privileges thereunto belonging, or in any wise thereunto appertaining, and all the estate, right, title, interest and claim whatever, of the said party of the first part, either in law or equity, to the only proper use, benefit and behoof of the said party of the second part, his heirs and assigns forever.

In Witness Whereof, the said party of the first part hereunto set their hands and seals the day first above written.

Sealed and Delivered in Presence of

Geo W McCarter

I. G. Barrasto

W. B. Carr

Geo A Southworth L.S.

Cornelia B Southworth SEAL.

Wyatt Carr SEAL.

Julia B Carr L.S.

Figure 12: Ante-fire Chicago Deed
(personal papers)

Deeds and other instruments affecting property are deposited in the office of the County Recorder where they are filed as public record. By using these records you may be able to trace the ownership of land. As with other official records for Cook County, property records were destroyed in the Chicago Fire of 1871. No records are available from the County Recorder prior to that year.

Recorder of Deeds, Cook County
  County Building
  118 North Clark Street—Room 120
  Chicago, IL 60602-1387
  (312-443-5060)
Hours: Monday—Friday 9:00 A.M.—5:00 P.M.; Closed weekends and holidays.

Because of the large population of the Metropolitan Chicago area, locating property by using a grantee and grantor index is impractical. To obtain land records in Cook County, a legal description of the property is necessary. Although street addresses are important, they are not sufficient to locate property since records are indexed geographically by township. Addresses may be obtained from directories, from probate and other court cases, and from personal documents.

Obtaining A Legal Description

You can obtain a full legal description of the property at one of three locations:

1. County Treasurer's Office, County Building.

2. County Clerk's Office, County Building.

3. City of Chicago Bureau of Maps and Plats, City Hall, 121 North LaSalle (the bureau is located on the other side of the City/County Building).

There is a minimal charge for the address/legal description conversion.

Finding Recorded Documents

Locating property records can be tricky, and there are several steps you need to follow to improve your chances for success. These steps should be followed carefully; one number copied incorrectly can throw off the entire process. The recommended steps are:

1. If you do not have a legal description of the property, go to the County Treasurer's Office, Room 112, (or one of the other locations listed) and obtain one. Give the person at the counter the address or permanent tax index number.

2. Present a legal description of the property to the Tract Department at the Recorder of Deeds, Cook County located in the County Building on Clark Street. A clerk at the desk just inside the door will translate the legal description and provide the number of the ledger to be consulted in the Tract Department. Tract books contain information dating from 1871 to October 1, 1985 and are divided by section, township and range. These identifiers will enable you to locate any property in the county to the nearest square mile. Records after October 1, 1985 are searched using a computer.

   Transactions are filed chronologically. If you scan several pages of a tract book, your should be able to trace the history of ownership of a property. When the correct tract book is located, look under the section and block number. For each document, the following information is posted: document number, grantor, grantee, type of instrument, date of instrument, date of filing and description.

3. Copy the document number from the tract book, and go to the microfilm library in the south concourse of the basement. You will need to use a paging book to locate the microfiche of the original document. The first digit (or digits) of the document number refer to the book number, the middle numbers to the page, and the last numbers to the line.

The numbers recorded in the paging books refer to another book and page. Record the numbers in the paging book(s) on a slip of paper, and use the numbers to order the microfiche(s) you want to search from the clerk. You can use one of several microfiche readers in that same room to examine the microfiche(s).

4. Once a document is identified on the microfiche, you can order a copy. Since these documents are typically copied for legal purposes, they are certified which makes it a rather expensive proposition if many pages are requested. Most deeds are two to four pages in length. With proper authorization, copies can be made without the extra expense of certification. The clerk will price the copies and give you a statement.

5. Take the statement to the cashier's cage on the first floor, Room 120 and get a paid receipt. Take the receipt to counter 6 where you will receive a copy of the order receipt. Additional charges are added if documents are to be mailed. Documents ordered can be picked up 48 hours after the order is placed at Counter 6.

Abbreviations Used in Cook County Recorder's Tract Indexes

The following is a list of abbreviations generally used in describing the instruments posted in the Cook County Recorder's tract indexes:

Accpt	As Trustee
Aff'd	Affidavit
Bill	Suit filed in Circuit or Superior Court
Ch'cy	Suit filed in Circuit or Superior Court
C. M.	Chattel Mortgage
C of I	Certificate of Incorporation

STATE OF ILLINOIS)
) SS:
COUNTY OF COOK   )

IN THE CIRCUIT COURT OF COOK COUNTY.

TO THE ᵣ MARCH TERM A.D. 1915.

TO THE HONORABLE
    THE JUDGES OF SAID CIRCUIT COURT OF COOK COUNTY
              IN CHANCERY SITTING:

Your petitioner, ELSA MADLENER, of the City of Chicago, in the County of Cook and State of Illinois, respectfully represents unto Your Honors that she is the owner, in fee simple, of the following described real estate situated in the City of Chicago, in the County of Cook and State of Illinois, to-wit:

> Lot Forty-two (42) in E. K. Rogers' Subdivision of Lots One (1) and Two (2) in Block Five (5) in Duncan's Addition to Chicago, together with Block One (1) in the Canal Trustees' Subdivision of the West half (W½) and the West half (W½) of the Northeast quarter (NE¼) of Section Seventeen (17), Township Thirty-nine (39) North, Range Fourteen (14) East of the Third Principal Meridian.

Your petitioner further represents that she acquired her title to the said premises in the manner following:

That said premises, together with other lands, were selected by the commissioner of the general land office, under the direction of the President of the United States, as a portion of those lands intended to be granted by the United States to the State of Illinois by act of the Congress of the United States, approved March 2, 1827 entitled: "An Act to grant a quantity of land to the State of Illinois for the purpose of aiding in opening a canal to connect the waters of the Illinois River with those of

Figure 13: Burnt Record Series, Cook County Circuit Court

C of R	Certificate of Redemption
Consent	(Generally by Trustee)
D	Deed
Dec'd	Deceased (Probate Court Case # in document column)
Ded	Dedication of alley
D in T	Deed in Trust
Div	Divorce Proceedings
D of T	Deed of Trust (Trust Deed)
Extn	Extension of Mortgage
Invty	Inventory of Estate
Judgmt	Judgement
LR	Land Registration under Torrens System
Grant	Form U. S. Government
MD or Mast. D.	Master in Chancery Deed
MS or Mast S	Master in Chancery Sale
Mtg.	Mortgage
Petn	Petition (County Clerk or Treasurer to collect back taxes or Declaration of Bankruptcy)
QC	Quit Claim
R or Rel	Release Deed
Resgn	Resignation (As Trustee, Receiver, etc.)
Satis	Satisfaction of Lien or Judgement
Schedule	An instrument in Bankruptcy
Sub or Subdvn	Plat of Subdivision
SWD	Special Warranty Deed
TD	Trust Deed (Mortgage)
Tx D	Tax Deed
Tx S	Tax Sale
TR D	Trustees Deed
WD	Warranty Deed

The Chicago Fire and Property Records

At the time of the Chicago Fire of 1871, the Cook County
Courthouse was on the same site as the present combina-

tion county courthouse and city hall (often called the County Building). The land, owned entirely by the county, is bounded on the north by Randolph Street, on the east by Clark Street, on the south by Washington Street, and on the west by LaSalle Street. The burned courthouse was constructed in 1853, enlarged in 1858, and again enlarged in 1870. The offices of the mayor of Chicago and other city officials, then as now, occupied the west portion. It has been suggested that the records of the recorder's office were not removed from the courthouse at the time of the fire because they weighed tons, and there was not sufficient time to remove them after it became apparent that the "fireproof" courthouse was doomed for almost immediate destruction.

Shortly after the fire, the county recorder secured a new set of maps and tract books, and was ready to record (and re-record) deeds and other instruments. However, many of the property owners had no deeds to record because their documents were destroyed by the fire; the recorder was comparatively helpless.

Emergency legislation was needed. Accordingly, on April 9, 1872, the state legislature enacted a law known as the "Burnt Record Act" which provided methods for the re-establishment of property records. The act stipulated, among other things, that the owner of a property whose deed had not been destroyed could re-record the document, that copies of court orders of transfer could be accepted by the recorder as valid, and that the county board might purchase from abstract companies any existing maps, tract books, or other official entries and have them recorded on behalf of the property owner.

The most important provision, however, was the one stipulating that in cases of destroyed records, the claimant of a property could go into any court in the county having chancery (court of record) jurisdiction, present whatever evidence could be mustered to support a claim, and the presiding judge (if satisfied with the evidence) issue whatever order was necessary to proclaim ownership. The court order then could be recorded with the county recorder.

The best evidence of ownership proved to be the records kept by private abstract and title guarantee companies, of which there were three in operation in Chicago. These records, kept in books similar to tract books, were compiled through the years as properties changed hands and new deeds were recorded. A sworn statement by the abstractor, certifying that a person was shown to be the owner of a certain parcel of property by an entry in the abstractor's books, would satisfy the court.

The Burnt Record Series

The Genealogical Society of Utah has microfilmed the *Burnt Record* book series 1871-1932, (created as a result of the Burnt Records Act) with indexes on 49 microfilm reels. The original records, available through the Law Division of the Circuit Court (Room 1201), must be ordered from the warehouse where they are stored.

Ante-Fire Records for Cook County

Everett Chamberlin described in his book, *Chicago and Its Suburbs* (Chicago: T. A. Hungerford & Co, 1874) the preservation of some of the records by the abstract companies.

Chase Brothers

"At the time of the fire this was still the leading abstract firm in town, employing a force of 25 men, and having accumulated a collection of 300 volumes of indexes, 230,000 pages of letterpress copies of abstracts-in all, some three tons of manuscripts. The fire came, and destroyed a portion of these books, but fortunately the most valuable parts saved from the flames by other conveyances mentioned below."

Shortall & Hurd

"Mr. Shortall arrived at the place where his precious books were stored at midnight . . . . Observation already told him that the safeguards which had been thrown around his property were not, as had been supposed, sufficient. The only safety lay in removing the books beyond the district likely to be burned over. What to do for a means of conveyance?

For Shortall, though versed in all manner of legal conveyances, was not equal to this emergency without help from a conveyancer of a more literal or physical type. But the carters were the greatest men in town that night, and in the vicinity of Larmon block none could be got, for love or money, to move those books. The only other resort was in the rear pocket of Shortall's trowsers. He drew it forth—a revolver! and requested the nearest carter to come alongside and anchor while his craft could be filled with books from upstairs.

By keeping this instrument carefully trained upon the commander of the unknown craft, Shortall was able to hold him there while the boys of the office brought down most of the books, and while the flames roared and the walls toppled around them. A friend came to the rescue after a while, with a wagon more commodious and a driver more trustworthy than the one whom Shortall had impressed into his service.

The latter was, therefore, honorably discharged and reasonably paid. The friend's wagon was driven off in the direction of safety, and the books were saved. A great many loose crannies in our land titles were thereby made snug and tight, and Shortall's fortune was made. The exertions by which the other sets of abstract books were saved were scarcely less brave and praiseworthy."

Jones & Sellers

"The books of Messrs. Jones & Sellers which were also contributed to the joint library of archives from which the most of our land titles are now verified, were started at a later period than either of the two sets referred to above. These books, like those of the other firms named, were rescued by dint of great exertion from the consuming element, hardly any portion being lost in any case except those least valuable, viz., copies of abstracts.

Alliance Formed

"The fire over, and every scrap of the public records gone up in the fiery whirlwind, the abstract men were not long in perceiving that they held the key to the land title situation. It was found that by combining their books a record could be made up which would afford not only a complete chain of title of every tract in Cook county, but would also furnish very full evidence relative to the effect of all judgments—in fact a thoro inquest could be made by means of these books into all the strong and weak points of possession, claim, or conveyance. The three firms therefore lost no time in forming an alliance, and in making themselves ready to serve the public."

Chicago Title Insurance Company Records

The combined books of the three firms described by Chamberlin were leased on December 1, 1872 to Messrs. Handy, Simmons and Company. In 1879, this firm became Handy and Company, and in 1887 was succeeded by Title Guarantee and Trust Company who became the owner of all the ante-fire records of Cook County. In 1901, through further consolidations, the records became the property of Chicago Title and Trust Company (now Chicago Title Insurance Company).

Chicago Title Insurance Company
   171 North Clark
   Chicago, IL 60602
   (312-223-2000)

The Chicago Title Insurance Company is one of the largest title insurers in the country. The downtown Chicago office

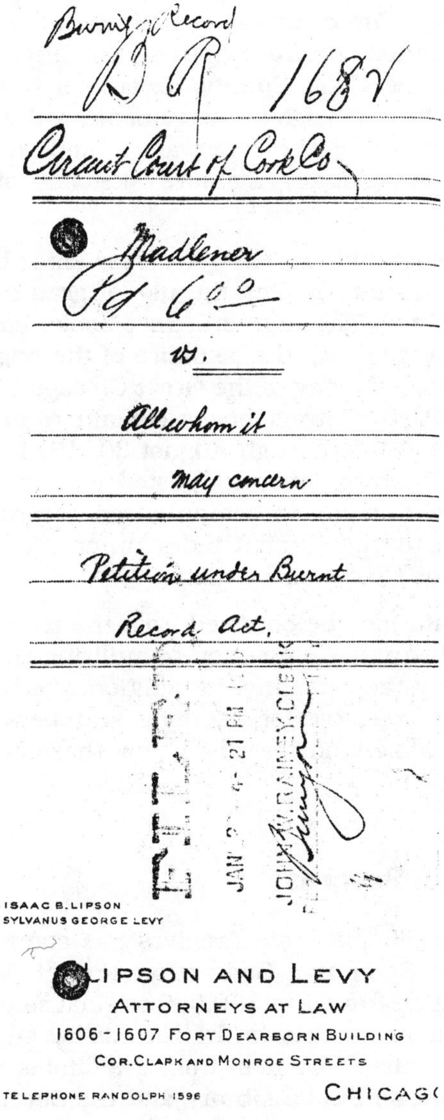

Burnt Record

B R 168

Circuit Court of Cook Co

Madlener

Pd 6.00

vs.

All whom it

may concern

Petition under Burnt

Record Act.

FILED

JAN 2 4-21 PM

JOHN W. RAINEY CLERK

ISAAC B. LIPSON

SYLVANUS GEORGE LEVY

LIPSON AND LEVY

ATTORNEYS AT LAW

1606-1607 FORT DEARBORN BUILDING

COR. CLARK AND MONROE STREETS

TELEPHONE RANDOLPH 1596

CHICAGO

Figure 14: Burnt Record Series, Cook County Circuit Court

holds records for some 1,600,000 parcels of land in Cook County, including the only surviving sets of ante-fire tract and copy books. The company's collection of copy books contain information abstracted from the original documents filed in the Cook County Recorder's Office. Copy books summarize the original instruments listing grantor, grantee, description of the conveyances and the encumbrances, and occasionally includes sketches of the recorded plats.

Tract books (geographic indexes) are used since the population of Cook County makes the use of grantor/grantee indices impractical. The ante-fire tract books contain recorded data starting with the issuance of the original government patent to the day of the Great Chicago Fire (October 8, 1871). Post-fire tract books contain recorded data from October 9, 1871 through August 30, 1974. The data from recorded instruments was posted into the Chicago Title Insurance Company's computerized record keeping system against the permanent index number assigned to real estate by the Cook County Clerk.

All recorded data may be obtained from the records of the Chicago Title Insurance Company by utilizing the various searches sold by the company. In addition, the company's tract books are available for use by researchers who are well versed in using land records; use of these documents is by appointment only.

Public Domain Records

The staff of the Illinois State Archives has completed the Public Domain Computer Conversion Project which includes information from over 550,000 original sales of public lands in Illinois. Access to the records by surname of purchasers is available by mail from the Illinois State Archives. The Chicago Public Library and the South Suburban Genealogical Society also have copies of the index for Cook County. It should be noted that these records cover only the original purchases from the federal government.

The original sales records were entered in over 100 large bound volumes. These records were acquired by the Illinois State Archives in the 1950s from the Auditor of Public Accounts who held them since the 1870s when the federal government gave the records to the state.

Information entered for each sale includes the name of the purchaser, identification number, type of sale, description of land purchased, number of acres, price per acre, total price, sex of purchaser, date of purchase, county or state of residence of purchaser, and volume and page of original land record.

After a name is located, land purchases can be found on a map of Illinois. For a small fee, Illinois State Archives staff can provide photocopies of printout listings along with a map on which to locate the purchase. Individuals requesting land purchase information should address inquiries to: Information Service/Reference, Illinois State Archives, Archives Building, Springfield, IL 62756.

National Archives—Great Lakes Region

The National Archives-Great Lakes Region has some records of land purchases which cover only the initial transfer from the federal government. The land records include those for Illinois, Indiana, Ohio, and Wisconsin, and are in the form of cash receipts, certificates, and credit applications. The records were entered by date, and you will need the name of the land office and certificate of purchase number to access them.

A Selected Bibliography of Sources of Land Information

Eakle, Arlene, and Johni Cerny. *The Source: A Guidebook of American Genealogy.* Salt Lake City: Ancestry, 1984.

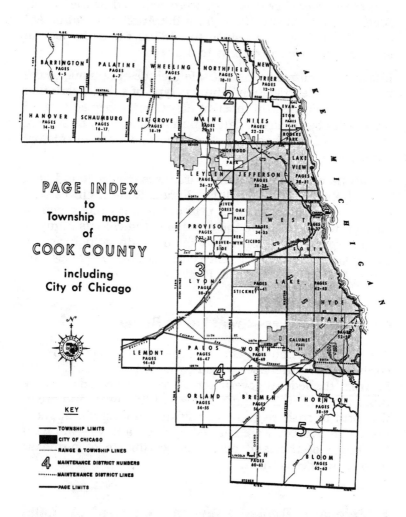

Figure 15. Township Map of Cook County

Greenwood, Val D. *The Researchers Guide to American Genealogy.* Baltimore, MD: Genealogical Publishing Co. 1975.

Hammersmith, Mary P. "Those Menacing Metes and Bounds Surveys." *Genealogy* (October 1978), published by the Indiana Historical Society, Genealogy Section.

Oran, Daniel. *Law Dictionary for Non-Lawyers.* St. Paul, MN: West Publishing Co., 1975.

Smith, Clifford Neal. "Reconstructing Chicago's Early Land Records." *Illinois State Genealogical Society Quarterly* 5, no. 4 (Winter 1973): 217-21.

White, Elizabeth P. "Early Land-Entry Records." *Illinois State Genealogical Society Quarterly* 8, no. 1 (March 1976): 19-22.

White, Elizabeth P., and Henry G. R. White. "Land Records Revisited." *Illinois State Genealogical Society Quarterly* 10, no. 4 (Winter 1978): 181-93.

SECTION TWENTY-FOUR

Libraries in Cook County—
Outside of Chicago

Acorn Public Library District
15624 South Central Ave.
Oak Forest 60452
(708-687-3700)

Alsip-Merrionette Park Public Library
11960 South Pulaski 60658
(708-371-5666)

Arlington Heights Memorial Library
500 North Dunton Avenue 60004
(708-392-0100)

Barrington Public Library District
505 North Northwest Highway 60010
(708-382-1300)

Bartlett Public Library District
302 Railroad Avenue 60103
(708-837-2855)

Bedford Park Public Library District
7816 West 65th Place 60501
(708-458-6826)

Bellwood Public Library
600 Bohland Avenue 60104
(708-547-7393)

Berkeley Public Library
1637 Taft Avenue 60163
(708-544-6017)

Berwyn Public Library
3400 South Oak Park Avenue 60402
(708-484-6655)

Blue Island Public Library
2433 York Street 60406
(708-388-1078)

Bridgeview Public Library
7840 West 79th Street
60455
(708-458-2880)

Broadview Public Library
2226 South 16th Avenue
60153
(708-345-1325)

Brookfield Free Public Library
3609 Grand Boulevard
60513
(708-485-6917)

Buffalo Grove (See Indian Trails Public Library District)

Burbank (See Prairie Trails Public Library District)

Calumet City Public Library
660 Manistee, 60409
(708-862-6220)

Calumet Park Public Library
1500 West 127th Street
60643
(708-385-5768)

Chicago Heights Public Library
15th and Chicago Road
60411
(708-754-0323)

Chicago Ridge Public Library
6301 West Birmingham
60415
(708-423-7753)

Cicero Public Library
5225 West Cermak Road
60650
(708-652-8084)

Clarendon Hills Public Library
7 North Prospect Avenue
Clarendon Hills 60514
(708-323-8188)

Cook Memorial Public Library District
413 North Milwaukee
Avenue 60048
(708-362-2330)

Crestwood Public Library District
13838 South Cicero Avenue
60445
(708-371-4090)

Des Plaines Public Library
841 Graceland Avenue
60016
(708-827-5551)

Des Plaines Valley Public Library District
121 East 8th Street
Lockport 60441
(815-838-0755)

Dolton Public Library District
14037 Lincoln Avenue
60418
(708-849-2385)

East Chicago Heights Public Library District

941 East 14th Street 60411

(708-758-3230)

Eisenhower Public Library District

4652 North Olcott 60656

(708-867-7828)

Elgin (See Gail Borden Public Library District)

Elk Grove Village Public Library

101 Kennedy Boulevard 60007

(708-439-0447)

Elmhurst Public Library

211 Prospect
Emhurst, IL 60126

(708-279-8696)

Elmwood Park Public Library

4 Conti Parkway 60635

(708-453-7645)

Evanston Public Library

1703 Orringotn Avenue 60201

(708-866-0300)

Evergreen Park Public Library

9400 South Troy Avenue 60642

(708-422-8522)

Flossmoor Public Library

2801 School Street 60422

(708-798-4008)

Forest Park Public Library

7555 West Jackson Boulevard 60130

(708-366-7171)

Franklin Park Public Library District

9618 Franklin Avenue 60131

(708-455-6016)

Gail Borden Public Library District

200 North Grove Avenue
Elgin 60120

(708-742-2411)

Glencoe Public Library

320 Park Avenue 60022

(708-835-5056)

Glenview Public Library

1930 Glenview Road 60025

(708-724-5200)

Glenwood-Lynwood Public Library District

315 Glenwood-Lansing Road 60425

(708-758-0090)

Grande Prairie Public Library District

3479 West 183rd Street
Hazel Crest 60429

(708-598-8446)

Green Hills Public Library District

8611 West 103rd St
Palos Hills 60465

(708-598-8446)

Hanover Township Library
204 Jefferson Street 61041
(815-591-3517)

Hanover Park (See
Schaumburg Township Public
Library and Poplar Creek
Public Library District)

Harvey Public Library
155th and Turlington
Avenue 60426
(708-331-0757)

Harwood Heights (See
Eisenhower Public Library
District)

Hazel Crest (See Grande
Prairie Public Library District)

Hickory Hills (See Green Hills
Public Library District)

Hillside Public Library
405 North Hillside Avenue
60162
(708-449-7510)

Hinsdale Public Library
20 East Maple Street
Hinsdale 60521
(708-986-1976)

**Hodgkins Public Library
District**
6500 Wenz Avenue 60525
(708-579-1844)

Hoffman Estates (See
Schaumburg Township Public
Library)

Hometown Public Library
4331 Southwest Highway
60456
(708-636-0997)

Homewood Public Library
17917 Dixie Highway
60430
(708-798-0121)

**Indian Trails Public Library
District**
355 South Schoenbeck
Road 60090
(708-459-4100)

**Justice Public Library
District**
7641 Oak Grove Avenue
60458
(708-496-1790)

La Grange Public Library
10 West Cossitt Avenue
60525
(708-352-0576)

Lansing Public Library
2750 Indiana Avenue
60438
(708-474-2447)

Lemont Public Library
800 Porter Street 60439
(708-257-6541)

**Lincolnwood Public Library
District**
4000 West Pratt 60646
(708-677-5277)

Lockport (See Des Plaines
Valley Public Library District)

Lynwood (See
Glenwood-Lynwood Public
Library District)

Lyons Public Library
4209 Joliet Avenue 60534
(708-447-3577)

**McCook Public Library
District**
50th Street and Glencoe
Avenue 60525
(708-442-1242)

Markham Public Library
16640 South Kedzie 60426
(708-331-0130)

Matteson Public Library
801 South School Avenue
60443
(708-748-4431)

Maywood Public Library
121 South 5th Avenue
60153
(708-343-1847)

Melrose Park Public Library
801 North Broadway 60160
(708-343-3391)

Merrionette Park (See
Alsip-Merrionette Park Public
Library)

Midlothian Public Library
14701 South Kenton 60445
(708-535-2027)

Morton Grove Public Library
6140 Lincoln Avenue 60053
(708-965-4220)

Mt. Prospect Public Library
10 South Emerson 60056
(708-253-5675)

Niles Public Library District
6960 Oakton Street 60648
(708-967-8554)

Norridge (See Eisenhower
Public Library District)

North Chicago Public Library
1645 Lincoln Avenue 60064
(708-689-0125)

**North Riverside Public
Library**
2501 South Des Plaines
North Riverside 60546
(708-447-0869)

**North Suburban District
Library**
6340 North Second Street
Loves Park 61111
(815-633-4247)

Northbrook Public Library
1201 Cedar Land 60062
(708-272-6224)

Northfield (See Winnetka
Public Library District)

**Northlake Public Library
District**
231 North Wolf Road 60164
(708-562-2301)

Oak Forest (See Acorn Public
Library District)

Oak Lawn Public Library
9427 South Raymond
Avenue 60453
(708-422-4990)

Oak Park Public Library
834 Lake Street 60301
(708-383-8200)

Orland Park Public Library
14760 Park Lane 60462
(708-349-8138)

**Palatine Public Library
District**
500 North Benton Street
60067
(708-358-5881)

Palos Heights Public Library
12501 South 71st Avenue
60463
(708-448-1473)

Palos Hills (See Green Hills
Public Library District)

Palos Park Public Library
12350 Forest Glen 60464
(708-448-1530)

Park Forest Public Library
400 Lakewood Blvd. 60466
(708-748-3731)

Park Ridge Public Library
20 South Prospect Avenue
60068
(708-825-7083)

**Poplar Creek Public Library
District**
1405 South Park Blvd
Streamwood 60103
(708-837-6800)

**Prairie Trails Public Library
District**
8449 South Moody Avenue
Burbank 60459
(708-430-3688)

**Prospect Heights Public
Library District**
12 North Elm Street 60070
(708-259-3500)

**Richton Park Public Library
District**
4045 Sauk Trail 60471
(708-481-5333)

River Forest Public Library
735 Lathrop Avenue 60305
(708-366-5205)

**River Grove Public Library
District**
8638 West Grand Avenue
60171
(708-453-4484)

**Riverdale Public Library
District**
208 West 144th Street
60627
(708-841-3311)

Riverside Public Library
1 Burling Road 60546
(708-442-6366)

Robbins Public Library District
13822 Central Park 60472
(708-597-2760)

Rolling Meadows Library
3110 Martin Lane 60008
(708-259-6050)

Sauk Village Public Library District
1909 Sauk Trail 60411
(708-757-4771)

Schaumburg Township Public Library
32 West Library Lane 60194
(708-885-3373)

Schiller Park Public Library
4200 Old River Road 60176
(708-678-0433)

Skokie Public Library
5215 Oakton Street 60077
(708-673-7774)

South Holland Public Library
16250 Wausau Avenue 60473
(708-331-5262)

Steger-South Chicago Heights Public Library
54 East 31st
Steger 60475
(708-755-5040)

Stickney-Forest View Library District
6800 West 43rd Street
Stickney 60402
(708-749-1050)

Streamwood (See Poplar Creek Public Library District)

Summit-Argo Public Library
6209 South Archer Road
Summit 60501
(708-458-1545)

Thornton Public Library
115 East Margaret Street 60476
(708-877-2579)

Tinley Park Public Library
17101 South 71st Avenue 60477
(708-532-0160)

University Park Public Library
1100 Blackhawk Drive
University Park 60466
(708-534-2580)

Westchester Public Library
10700 Canterbury 60153
(708-562-3573)

Western Springs-Thomas Ford Memorial Library
800 Chestnut Street
Western Springs
(708-246-0520)

Wheeling (See Indian Trails Public Library District)

Wilmette Public Library District
1242 Wilmette Avenue 60091
(708-256-5025)

Winnetka Public Library District
768 Oak Street 60093
(708-446-7220)

Woodridge Public Library
3 Plaza Drive
Woodridge 60517
(708-964-7899)

Worth Public Library District
6917 West 111th Street 60482
(708-448-2855)

Allen County Public Library
P.O. Box 2270
900 Webster Street
Fort Wayne, IN 46801
(219-424-7241 ext. 3315)

Although this library is in Indiana, it is only a couple of hours' drive from Chicago. The Fred J. Reynolds Historical Genealogy Department in the library has the second largest genealogical collection in the U. S.

Federal Depository Libraries in Cook County

In Chicago

Chicago Public Library
Harold Washington Library Center
Government Publications Department, Floor 5
400 South State Street
Chicago 60605
(312-747-4500)

Chicago State University
Paul and Emily Douglas Library
95th Street at King Drive
Chicago 60628
(312-995-2284)

DePaul University Law Library
25 East Jackson Blvd.
Chicago 60604
(312-321-7710)

Field Museum of Natural History Library
Roosevelt Road at Lake Shore Drive
Chicago 60605
(312-992-9410 ext. 281)

Illinois Institute of Technology
Chicago-Kent College of Law Library
77 South Wacker Drive
Chicago 60606
(312-567-5968)

Illinois Institute of Technology
Kemper Library
3300 South Federal Street
Chicago 60616
(567-6844)

John Crerar Library
Documents Dept.
35 West 33rd Street
Chicago 60616
(312-225-2526)

John Marshall Law School Library
315 South Plymouth Court
Chicago 60604
(312-427-2737 ext. 484)

Loyola University of Chicago
E. M. Cudahy Memorial Library
6525 North Sheridan Road
Chicago 60626
(312-274-3000 ext. 791)

Loyola University School of Law Library
1 East Pearson Street
Chicago 60611
(312-670-2950)

Northeastern Illinois University
Documents Dept.
5500 North Street Louis Avenue
Chicago 60625
(312-583-4050 ext. 8178)

Northwestern University School of Law Library
357 East Chicago Avenue
Chicago 60611
(312-649-7344)

University of Chicago Law Library
1121 East 57th Street
Chicago 60637
(753-3423)

University of Chicago Documents Section
1100 East 57th Street
Chicago 60637
(753-3475)

University of Illinois at Chicago Circle
Library Documents Department
Box 8198,
Chicago 60680
(312-996-2738)

Outside Chicago

Oakton Community College
Learning Resource Center
1600 East Golf Rd
Des Plaines 60016
(312-635-1645)

Northwestern University Library
Government Publications Department
Evanston 60201
(312-492-5290)

Mount Prospect Public Library

Documents Department
10 South Emerson Street
Mount Prospect 60056
(312-398-6460)

Oak Park Public Libary

834 Lake Street
Oak Park 60301
(312-383-8200)

Moraine Valley Community College Library

10900 South 88th Avenue
Palos Hills 60465
(312-974-4300 ext. 221)

Governors' State University Library

Park Forest South 60465
(312-534-5000 ext. 2232)

Rosary College

Rebecca Crown Library
7900 West Division Street
River Forest 60305
(312-366-2490 ext. 303)

Poplar Creek Public Library

1405 South Park Blvd
Streamwood 60103
(312-837-6800)

Maps and Geographical Finding Aids

A solid knowledge of the geography of the locality is essential to the success of any genealogical or historical research project. Contemporary maps are usually good initially, but they will not resolve the problems encountered in locating Cook County and Chicago towns, communities, neighborhoods, and street names that have changed since the nineteenth century. To add to the confusion, street numbering and ward boundaries have changed, and villages were incorporated at different times.

A critical factor in Chicago genealogy research is the street numbering change which took place in 1909. Ignorance of that change can completely alter the results of research.

Old and New Numbers Street Numbers

A new street numbering plan was passed by the City Council on June 22, 1908. The specifics of the plan were made retroactive to September 1, 1900. Madison Street, between Lake Michigan to the east and the city limits to the west, became the baseline for numbering all north and south streets (and for streets running in a northerly or southerly direction). State Street, between the city

numbering all north and south streets (and for streets running in a northerly or southerly direction). State Street, between the city limits to the south and North Avenue to the north, became the baseline for east and west streets; the actual baseline was State Street and an imaginary line that extended the street through Lincoln Park and Lake Michigan.

The street numbers on each north-south street increase by 100 per block, and eight blocks equal one mile. Numbering begins with 1 at Madison Street. The numbering for east-west streets follows the same pattern (beginning with 1 at State Street).

Before the change in street numbering, the situation was very confusing since physical boundaries, for example, the branches of the Chicago River, were used to determine street numbers. *Moran's Dictionary of Chicago* (1892) provides a detailed explanation of the old numbering system.

The Chicago Historical Society and the Chicago Public Library have guides which convert old and new street numbers.

Street Name Changes

Many Chicago streets, and portions of streets, have undergone name changes. Other streets have completely disappeared when expressways were built over them. The Chicago Historical Society has a street name file which gives the origins of Chicago street names, street name changes, and dates when street name changes took effect. There is also a notebook with several thousand street name changes listed.

Current Maps

There are several sources for current maps:

Telephone Directories

Chicago and suburban telephone directories have detailed sectional maps.

County Clerk

The County Clerk's office has the most complete set of Cook County maps.

Cook County Clerk
  Maps and Tax Redemption Department
  County Building
  118 North Clark Street
  Chicago, IL 60602
  (312-443-5640)

City of Chicago

The city has a bureau of maps and plats which has all of the city maps, a street name change file, and a cross-reference index to old and new house numbers.

City of Chicago
  Department of Public Works—Bureau of Maps and Plats
  121 North LaSalle Street—Room 803
  Chicago, IL 60602
  (312-744-4996)

Chicago Convention and Tourism Bureau, Inc.

Chicago Convention and Tourism Bureau, Inc.
  McCormick Place-on-the-Lake,
  Chicago, IL 60616
  (312-225-5000)

Rand McNally Map Store

This store has a number of Cook County and Chicago maps and detailed atlases. Call or visit for map descriptions.

Rand McNally Map Store
  23 East Madison Street
  Chicago, IL 60602-4497
  (312-267-6868)

Old Maps and Geographical Finding Aids

Chicago Historical Society

The Chicago Historical Society has the most extensive collection of old Chicago and Cook County maps. A map note-book (*A Listing of Maps of the City of Chicago*) is on the open-shelves in the society library. Maps in the notebook are arranged by the following subject order:

* By date—139 entries for the years 1812-1975
* Prehistory and geology—53 entries
* Fire of 1871—3 entries
* World's Columbian Exposition—34 entries
* Annexation and accretion—11 entries
* Cemeteries—8 entries
* Fort Dearborn—27 entries
* General (political, postal, real estate, etc.)—45 entries
* Communities (alphabetically by name, from Albany Park to Woodlawn)—163 entries
* Ward maps (1851-1975)—23 entries
* Historical and pictorial Maps—47 entries
* Industries—46 entries
* Maps of individual wards (showing election precincts)—12 pages of entries (about 60 entries per page)
* Institutions (schools, churches, hospitals, etc.)

Other subject headings include parks, population, sociology, portage, transportation, waterworks, and sanitation. Not included in the notebook, but at the society and of considerable importance, are the fire insurance maps for Chicago. The Sanborn Map Company produced some 700,000 sheets of detailed maps for 12,000 cities and towns in North America from 1867 to the present. These maps were used by insurance agents to determine hazards and risk in underwriting specific buildings. Each map is produced on a large over-size sheet in pastel colors: olive drab for adobe, pink for stone; blue for brick, yellow for wood, gray for iron. Among other details indicated are: size, shape and construction of homes, businesses, farm buildings; locations of windows, doors, firewalls, roof types; widths and names of streets; property boundaries; ditches, water mains, sprinkling systems. The names of residents do not appear on the maps, although specific addresses are shown. Businesses appear by name. Once you find an address for your ancestor or subject of interest in the census or city directory, you can determine precisely what house or business the family lived or worked in.

Chicago Historical Society
Clark at North Avenue
Chicago, IL 60614-6099
(312-642-4600)

Library of Congress

The Library of Congress also has a large collection of fire insurance maps due to the requirement for depositing all copies of materials submitted for copyright.

Maps for Census Searching

The Newberry Library, the Chicago Public Library, and the National Archives-Great Lakes Region all have some maps to aid in locating addresses in census years. Of these, the Newberry Library map collection is the most complete.

Bibliography

Cummings, Kathleen Roy. *Architectural Records in Chicago*. Chicago: The Art Institute of Chicago, 1981.

Kirkham, E. Kay. *A Handy Guide to Record Searching in the Larger Cities of the United States*. Logan, UT: Everton Publishers, 1974.

   Includes an 1850-55 and an 1878 map and street guide for Chicago.

Sherwood, Arlyn. "Cartographic Materials for Genealogical Research: An Overview of Resources at the Illinois State Library." *Illinois Libraries* 68, no. 4 (April 1986): 267-72.

Styx, Sherrie A. *Chicago Ward Maps, 1837-1970*. Eugene, OR: Styx Enterprises, 1988.

SECTION TWENTY-SIX
Military Records

In July of 1803, a detachment of United States infantry soldiers under the command of Captain John Whistler and Lieutenant James Swearingen built and established Fort Dearborn at the mouth of the Chicago River. Thus began Chicago's recorded military history. Many of Cook County's earliest settlers were Revolutionary War veterans who had been anxious to own land and brought their families from the eastern states to settle here. From its very inception, Chicago and Cook County have contributed great numbers of men and women to serve in the armed forces, and this involvement has generated many useful records which are available for research. Military personnel records often supply the most genealogically valuable information, and, as with other federally created records, these records are generally more reliable than most other sources.

The term "military records" refers to all records of all branches of the armed services. These records fall into two general categories: military service records and veteran's benefits. Like other record categories, there is little uniformity in military records. Although some indexes do exist, identifying persons from Chicago, and the heavily populated metropolitan area, who served in the armed forces is more complicated. Most pre-World War I military service and related records are kept at the National Archives in Washington, D.C.; those from World War I andafter are at the National Personnel Records Center in St. Louis, Missouri.

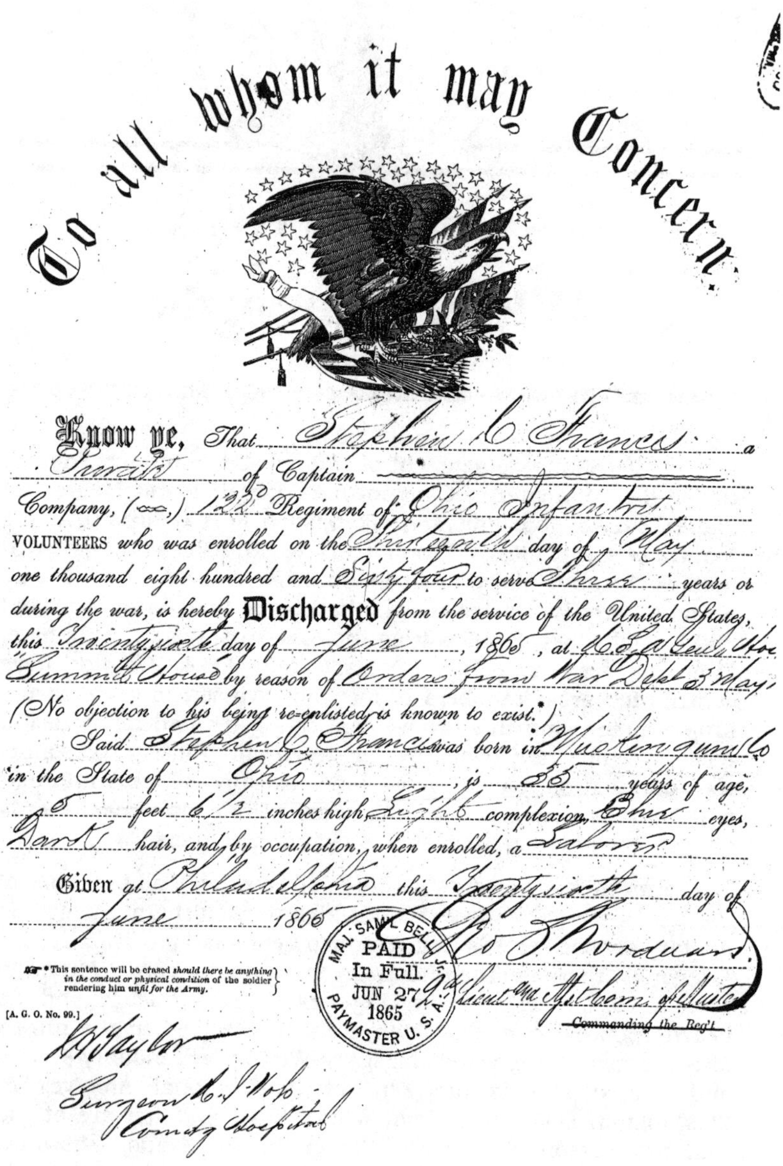

To all whom it may Concern.

Know ye, That Stephen C. Francis a Private of Captain ——— Company, (——) 122d Regiment of Ohio Infantry VOLUNTEERS who was enrolled on the Thirteenth day of May one thousand eight hundred and Sixty four to serve Three years or during the war, is hereby **Discharged** from the service of the United States, this Twentysixth day of June, 1865, at U.S.A. Genl. Hos. Summit House by reason of Orders from War Dept. 3 May. (No objection to his being re-enlisted is known to exist.*)

Said Stephen C. Francis was born in Muskingum Co in the State of Ohio, is 35 years of age, 5 feet 6 1/2 inches high Light complexion, Blue eyes, Dark hair, and by occupation, when enrolled, a Laborer

Given at Philadelphia this Twentysixth day of June 1865

MAJ. SAM'L BELL, Jr. PAID In Full. JUN 27 1865 PAYMASTER U.S.A.

R. S. Woodward
2d Lieut. and Asst. Com. of Muster
~~Commanding the Reg't.~~

* This sentence will be erased should there be anything in the conduct or physical condition of the soldier rendering him unfit for the Army.

[A. G. O. No. 99.]

W. Taylor
Surgeon U.S. Vols.
Comdg Hospital

Figure 16: Civil War Discharge Papers of a Chicagoan
(personal papers)

Archives in Washington, D.C.; those from World War I and after are at the National Personnel Records Center in St. Louis, Missouri.

These two facilities hold the bulk of military records, but there are many references (microfilms and books) available locally which can provide the necessary foundation to begin research for an individual's military history.

The Chicago Public Library has the Civil War and American History Research Collection, a major resource in the Special Collections Department of the library.

General References

For detailed descriptions of military records, their content and use, these general references are suggested:

Eakle, Arlene, and Johni Cerny. *The Source: A Guidebook of American Genealogy.* Salt Lake City: Ancestry, 1984.

Greenwood, Val D. *The Researcher's Guide to American Genealogy.* Baltimore: Genealogical Publishing Co., Inc., 1975.

National Archives and Records Service. *Guide to Genealogical Research in the National Archives.* Washington, DC: National Archives Trust Fund Board, 1982.

National Archives and Records Administration. *Military Service Records: A Select Catalog of National Archives Microfilm Publications.* Washington, DC: National Archives Trust Fund Board, 1986.

Neagles, James C. *U.S. Military Records: A Guide to Federal & State Sources: Colonial America to the Present.* Salt Lake City: Ancestry, 1994.

Military Service and Pension Records

You must submit all requests for copies of military service records held by the National Archives in Washington, DC on NATF Form 80. The National Archives and Records Administration will research the request, prepare copies of any records located, and hold the copies for three weeks or until payment is received, whichever is sooner. As soon as records are located and copied, you will be sent a bill and instructions for making a remittance.

You should submit a separate NATF Form 80 for each pension, bounty-land, or compiled military service record desired. Copies of NATF Form 80 may be obtained by writing to Reference Services Branch (N—R), National Archives and Records Administration, Washington, DC 20408.

General Sources for Chicago and Cook County

Andreas, Alfred T. *History of Chicago*. 3 vols. Chicago: A.T. Andreas, 1884-86. Provides a good general history of military-related activity in Chicago, especially for regiments that served during the Civil War.

Andreas, Alfred T. *History of Cook County, Illinois*. Chicago: A.T. Andreas, 1884. Good general history of military-related activity in Cook County.

Revolutionary War

Revolutionary War Pension and Bounty-Land-Warrant Application Files and Compiled Service Records of Soldiers Who served in the American Army During the Revolutionary War. These are available on microfilm at the National Archives-Great Lakes Region.

DAR Directory—Illinois. Information is compiled by member's name. This source includes a veteran's index, but is difficult to use unless the submitting member's name is known. It is available at the Newberry Library and some other area libraries.

DAR Patriot Index, 2 vols. Washington, DC: Daughters of the American Revolution, Vol. 1, 1966; Vol. 2, 1979. These volumes include the name of the patriot, amd any available information on dates of birth, death, marriage (and to whom), residence, and type of service rendered. The set is available at the Newberry Library.

DAR Index of the Rolls of Honor, 4 vols., 1916-40 Washington DC: Daughters of the American Revolution. There are four volumes combined into two available at the Newberry Library.

Meyer, Virginia M. *Roster of Revolutionary War Soldiers and Widows Who Lived in Illinois Counties.* Chicago: Virginia M. Meyer, 1962.

Schweitzer, George K. *Revolutionary War Genealogy.* Knoxville, TN: George K. Schweitzer, 1982.

War of 1812

Elliot, Isaac H., Adjutant General. *Record of Services of Illinois Soldiers in the Black Hawk War, 1831-32, and in the Mexican War, 1846-48. With an appendix of the Illinois Militia, Rangers, and Riflemen in Protecting the Frontier from the Ravages of the Indians from 1810-13.* Springfield: Illinois Adjutant General, 1882.

The Index to Compiled Service Records of Volunteer Soldiers Who Served During the War of 1812. Available at the National Archives-Great Lakes Region.

Matheny, Willard R., comp. *Illinois Index, Soldiers of 1812, Illinois.* Springfield, 1947. Typescript. Available at the Newberry Library.

Schweitzer, George K. *War of 1812 Genealogy.* Knoxville, TN: George K. Schweitzer, 1982.

U.S. General Land Office. *Lands in Illinois to Soldiers of the Late War. (War of 1812).* 26th Cong., 1st sess. House Doc. 262; Washington, DC, 1840.

Walker, Homer. A. *Illinois Pensioners List of the Revolution, 1812, and Indian Wars.* Washington, DC, 1955. Contents include the names of soldiers, widows, and heirs.

War of 1812 Military Bounty Land Warrants, 1815-58. Available on microfilm at the National Archives-Great Lakes Region.

Mexican War

The Index to Compiled Service Records of Volunteer Soldiers Who Served During the Mexican War. This index is available on microfilm at the National Archives-Great Lakes Region.

The Army Record of *Stephen O. Francis*
during the Civil War, 186*4* to 186*5*

GEORGE G. MEADE POST, No. 444
DEPT. OF ILLINOIS, G. A. R. CHICAGO

I was born at *Muskingum Co Ohio*, on the *23rd*
day of *June*, 18*32*; Enlisted on the *13th* day of
May, 1864, at the age of *32*, as a *Private*
in the *122nd Ohio Infantry*

Company _____, for a period of *Three years*

I served in the Army of the *"Potomac"*

under Generals *U S Grant. & Others*

I took part in the following battles and skirmishes _____

I was _____ wounded at the battle of _____

Figure 17: Chicago G.A.R. Post Application
(personal papers)

Civil War

The Chicago Public Library. *One Hundred Important Additions to the Civil War and American History Research Collection.* Chicago: The Chicago Public Library, 1978.

Chicago Public Library, Special Collections Department. *The Black Soldier in the Civil War.* Chicago: Chicago Public Library, 1986. A three page checklist and bibliography are available from the Chicago Public Library.

Civil War Centennial Commission of Illinois. *Illinois Units in the Civil War.* Springfield: State of Illinois, 1962.

Index to Compiled Service Records of Volunteer Union Soldiers Who Served in Organizations from the State of Illinois. This is available on microfilm at the National Archives-Great Lakes Region. The index gives soldier's name, rank, and unit in which he served. With this information, additional military records may be obtained by writing to the National Archives in Washington.

Schweitzer, George K. *Civil War Genealogy.* Knoxville, TN: George K. Schweitzer, 1982.

Szucs, Loretto D., Kathryn Bobko, John Stoddard, and Sharon Murdoch, comps, *List of Pensioners—Chicago & Cook County, Illinois—January 1, 1883.* Chicago: Chicago Genealogical Society, 1985. Most of the pensions are for Civil War service. The name of each pensioner is given, together with the reason for the pension, the post office address, the rate of pension per month, and the date of the original allowance. The publication is available from the Chicago Genealogical Society.

Vandenberg, Kirk. *Research Series Volume 2: Able Bodied Men, Military Census 1861-1862.* South Holland, IL: South Suburban Genealogical and Historical Society, 1991. Lists the names of able-bodied men (ages 18-45 years) from the Cook County Townships: Bloom, Bremen, Calumet, Cicero, Hyde Park, Jefferson, Lake, Lakeview, Lemont, Lyons, Orland, Palos, Proviso, Rich, South Chicago, Thornton, West Chicago and Worth.

Common names are frequently a special problem, especially when a statewide index is being used. To narrow a search, and identify individuals who served from Cook County, the following list may be useful:

Cook County Regiments—Infantry

12th Reg.-Co. A,D,I,K	69th Reg.-Co. C,E
19th Reg.-Co. -A,D,E,G,I,K	72nd Reg.-Co. A,B,C,D,E,F,H,K
23rd Reg.-Co. B,C,F,G,H,I,K	82nd Reg.-Co. A,B,C,D,E,G,H,I
24th Reg.-Co. A,C,D,E,F,G,H	88th Reg.-Co. A,B,C,D,E,F,G,H,I,K
37th Reg.-Co. D,G,I	89th Reg.-Co. C,K
39th Reg.-Co. F,G	90th Reg.-Co. C,E,F,G,H,I
42nd Reg.-Co. B,C,E,F,G,H,I,K	113th Reg.-Co. A,C,E,G
43rd Reg.-Co. D	127th Reg.-Co. B,G,H
44th Reg.-Co. E,K	132nd Reg.-Co. B,G,H,I,K
51st Reg.-Co. A,K	134th Reg.-Co. A,C,D,E,F,G,I,K
55th Reg.-Co. B	142nd Reg.-Co. A
57th Reg.-Co. C,E,G	147th Reg.-Co. D,H
58th Reg.-Co. A,B,D,E,F,H	153rd Reg.-Co. F,G,I
59th Reg.-Co. K	156th Reg.-Co. A,C,E,I,K
65th Reg.-Co. D,H,K	Sturgis Rifles
67th Reg.-Co. B,D,E,G,I	

Cook County Cavalry Units

4th Reg.-Co. A,B	13th Reg.-Co. A,B,C,D,E
9th Reg.-Co. D,F,L	Thielman's Cavalry-Co. A,B
10th Reg.-Co. D	29th Reg. U.S.Colored- Co. B,C,D
12th Reg.-Co. A,D,H,I	

Cook County Artillery

1st Reg.-Batteries A,B,E,H,L,M	Chicago Board of Trade Battery
2nd Reg.-Batteries L,M	Chicago Mercantile Battery

Draft Records

Civil War

In 1863, the federal draft system was created. Men between the ages of twenty-five and forty, both citizens and aliens who had declared their intent to naturalize, were eligible for the Civil War draft. Males who were twenty to thirty-five, and unmarried, were required to serve unless physically disabled. Males who were seventeen to twenty could serve with the permission of a parent or guardian. The draft applied to men residing in the states under Union control. The lists which were created are arranged by state, then by county. To obtain records, it is necessary to provide the name of the individual, the state from which he served, the county and the Congressional district for the county in which a man lived, the city (including the ward number which can sometimes be found by using the 1860 census) or the town name if it is outside of Chicago. Requests must be submitted to:

Navy and Old Army Branch
National Archives and Records Administration
Washington, D.C. 20408

The Congressional district number can be obtained by consulting the Congressional Directory for the Second Session of the 38th Congress of the U.S. (Washington, D.C.: For the Joint Houses of Congress, 1865).

World War I Selective Service Records

When the United States became involved in World War I in 1917, all males between the ages of 18 and 45 were required to register for the draft. More than 24 million of these selective service records are on file at the National Archives-Atlanta Region. They are filed by state and then by draft board. To obtain a copy of the Selective Service records, you must supply the full name of the individual and the city or county in which they were living at the time of registration. Street addresses (available from the *1917 Chicago Directory*) must also be supplied for those who were resident of the city. Requests may be made to:

National Archives-Atlanta Region
1557 St. Joseph Avenue
East Point, GA 30344.

A check for $5.00 made out to the National Archives Trust Fund must accompany each request. The Illinois State Archives also has a set of these draft registrations.

The Illinois State Archives
Archives Building
Springfield, IL 62756-0001

World War II Selective Service Records 1942-1947 (RG 147)

Draft registration cards were issued for men born on or after April 28, 1877 and on or before February 16, 1897, who resided in Illinois, Indiana, Michigan, Ohio, and Wisconsin. The cards are arranged alphabetically by surname within each state, except for Michigan. The Michigan cards are arranged by draft board and county. There are also Michigan and Illinois Selective Service records that relate to the personal histories of aliens, and applications for exemption from military service.

Illinois Selective Service 1940-1947

Kleber, Col. Victor. *Selective Service in Illinois 1940-1947.* Springfield: State of Illinois, 1949.

A complete history of the operation of the Selective Service System in Illinois from its inception on September 16, 1940 to its termination March 31, 1947. The volume includes a list of individuals serving on each of the local boards in Illinois with several hundred from Chicago and Cook County. A copy is available at the National Archives-Great Lakes Region.

Illinois Soldiers and Sailors Home

The Illinois Soldiers and Sailors Home in Quincy, Illinois was established in 1885 by an act of the General Assembly of Illinois to provide subsistence and a home for honorably discharged and disabled veterans of the Mexican and Civil Wars. In later years, Illinois veterans of all wars became eligible for admission, and since 1903, wives of veterans are also eligible for admission. These records have been indexed and are available at the Illinois State Archives and in a book by Lowell M. Volkel.

Volkel, Lowell M. Illinois *Soldiers and Sailors Home at Quincy 1887-1898.* Indianapolis: N.p., 1980.

The book gives the individual's name, registry number, rank, company regiment, length of service, amount of pension, age, disability, county admitted from, birthplace, occupation, marital status, literacy, date of admission, and status in some cases. Also included is information on getting copies of the soldier's complete file.

American Battle Monuments Commission

Upon request, the American Battle Monuments Commission (Washington, DC 20314) will search its Department of the Army, Veteran's Administration, and Department of the Interior files for the place of permanent internment of WWI and WWII war dead. It will also provide information concerning the place of commemoration of the missing in action and the lost or buried at sea of WWI, WWII, Korea, or Vietnam.

In addition, the commission will provide relatives, upon request, with a photograph of either the grave site in the American Battle Monuments Commission cemetery or the section of the *Tablets of the Missing* where an individual is commemorated by name. The photograph is mounted on a color lithograph of the cemetery or memorial concerned, and a booklet describing the cemetery, or memorial, in detail accompanies the lithograph.

National Archives—Great Lakes Region

Genealogical Resources at the National Archives—Great Lakes Region

One of the thirteen regional archives of the National Archives and Records Administration is located in Chicago, and is known as the National Archives—Great Lakes Region. It has more than 62,000 cubic feet of historical records dating from 1800 to the 1980s, including textual records and nontextual records such as maps and photographs. These records were created or received by federal courts and agencies in Illinois, Indiana, Michigan, Minnesota, Ohio, and Wisconsin, and were transferred to the archives in accordance with federal law. The National Archives-Great Lakes Region also is a depository for selected National Archives microfilm publications.

Location and Hours

You can contact or visit the Archives at this address:

National Archives—Great Lakes Region
7358 South Pulaski Road
Chicago, IL 60629
(321-581-7816)

The National Archives-Great Lakes Region is open:

Monday and Wednesday through Friday, 8:00 A.M.—4:15 P.M. ; Tuesday, 8:00 A.M.—8:30 P.M.

Closed Saturday, Sunday, and federal holidays.

Records

Federal records at the National Archives-Great Lakes Region document the impact of federal government policies and programs for a six state region, and are unique. The records are preserved because of their permanent historical, fiscal, or legal value, and their importance to the continuing work of the U. S. Government. They are available to both private individuals and public officials. Citizens settling legal claims, genealogists researching family history, history scholars, and federal employees working on government projects will find resources of encyclopedic diversity at the National Archives-Great Lakes Region.

Among subjects covered by the records are: the Great Lakes and inland waterways, Native Americans, the environment, immigration and naturalization, inventions and technology, railroads, the automotive industry, the labor movement, organized crime, domestic conditions during World Wars I and II, sedition and treason, and nuclear energy research.

Access to Records

Records in the National Archives-Great Lakes Region are arranged by record group, and each group is identified by an RG number. Within each record group are the records from an agency, bureau, or the federal courts. A descriptive *Guide to the Records in the National Archives-Great Lakes Region* is available upon request. *The Archives: A Guide to the National Archives Field Branches* by Loretto Dennis Szucs and Sandra Hargreaves Luebking (Salt Lake City: Ancestry, 1988) provides additional details on the holdings of the Great Lakes Region (formerly called the Chicago

Branch), as well as ten other regional archives.

If you want to use original records you should schedule your visits to the archives in advance. The staff will arrange copying of records for a fee. In addition, copies can be certified for legal purposes.

Textual Records Pertaining to Genealogy

The dates included in the following record group descriptions represent the period of time covered by the records. Be aware that there are gaps and incomplete files.

Bureau of Indian Affairs Records—RG 75

Contain tribal censuses, Indian trust fund accounts, and land and timber allotments. Arranged by reservation and thereunder chronologically:

Iowa 1896-1947

Michigan 1892-1948

Minnesota 1878-1912

Wisconsin 1870-1960.

Bureau of Marine Inspection Records—RG 41

Contain certificates of enrollment and licensing of commercial vessels and yachts, oaths taken by owners and masters, records of mortgages and bills of sale of vessels, correspondence regarding vessel documentation. Arranged chronologically by type of record and port:

Illinois 1865-1952

Indiana 1865-1968

Iowa 1865-1939

Michigan 1831-1973

Ohio 1850-1967

Wisconsin 1853-1954

General Land Office Records—RG 49

Contain cash and credit certificate books denoting completed purchase of land from the federal government. Arranged by land office and thereunder chronologically:

Illinois 1814-1885

Indiana 1808-1876

Ohio 1801-1828

Immigration and Naturalization Service Records—RG 85

Index 1840-1950

This index covers final naturalizations filed with courts (local, county, or federal) in eastern Iowa, eastern and southern Wisconsin, northwest Indiana, and northern Illinois for the period 1840-1950. For Chicago-Cook County, the index covers the period 1871-1950.

Copies of Cook County, Illinois Final Naturalizations 1871-1906

These copies of Cook County naturalizations represent only petitions; the original documents are held by the Cook County Circuit Court in Chicago.

Chinese Exclusion Casefiles

Records are for Chicago, Illinois 1899-1939 and St. Paul, Minnesota 1893-1942.

Internal Revenue Service Records—RG 58

Contain tax assessment records. Arranged by district and thereunder chronologically:

Illinois 1867-1873, 1905-1919

Indiana 1867-1873

Michigan 1867-1928

Minnesota 1867-1874

Ohio 1867-1874, 1899-1919

Wisconsin 1867-1919

Selective Service Board Records, 1917-1919—RG 163

Included in the records for Illinois, Indiana, Michigan, Minnesota, Ohio, and Wisconsin are:

* Indexes to delinquent and deserter forms (incomplete for some states).

* Indexes to docket books of registrants.

The indexes are arranged within each state by county and division.

Selective Service System Records, 1942-1947—RG 147

Contain draft registration cards for men born on or after April 28, 1877 and on or before February 16, 1897, who resided in Illinois, Indiana, Michigan, Ohio, and Wisconsin. The cards are arranged alphabetically by surname within each state, except for Michigan. The Michigan cards are arranged by draft board and county. There are also Michigan and Illinois Selective Service records that relate to the personal histories of aliens, and applications for exemption from military service.

U. S. District Court Records—RG 21

Bankruptcy, civil, criminal, and naturalization case files. Arranged by court, by type of record, and thereunder numerically:

Illinois 1819-1982

Indiana 1819-1974

Michigan 1815-1970

Minnesota (third division-St. Paul, fifth division-Duluth, sixth division-Fergus Falls) 1861-1979

Ohio 1803-1967

Wisconsin 1842-1979

Microfilm Publications

Many National Archives records have been published on microfilm to facilitate their preservation and distribution. The National Archives-Great Lakes Region has extensive holdings of National Archives microfilm publications, containing basic documentation for the study of history, economics, public administration, political science, law, ethnology, genealogy, and other subjects.

A catalog, *Microfilm Publications in the National Archives-Great Lakes Region,* is available upon request. The self-service microfilm reading room operates on a reservation system. You should call in advance to reserve a microfilm reader. A coin-operated reader-printer is available for making paper copies from microfilm.

Microfilm Publications of Genealogical Interest

The categories of microfilm publications that are of particular interest to genealogical researchers include:

* Census and related records including Federal Population Census for all states (1790-1920).

* Immigration records including selected passenger arrival records and indexes for vessels arriving at New York and other U.S. ports.

* Naturalization index covering parts of Illinois, Indiana, Iowa, and Wisconsin.

* Military records including some military service and pension records, and bounty land warrant applications.

* Miscellaneous records including Illinois public domain land sales and freedman records.

Census and Related Records

Federal Population Census Schedules, 1790-1920 (except 1890). All states.

Soundex Indexes: 1880 census, all states (families with children 10 and under only); 1900 and 1920 censuses, all states; 1910 census, 21 states only.

Descriptions of 1900 Census Enumeration Districts.

Descriptions of Census Enumeration Districts, 1830-1890, 1910, and 1920.

Cross Index to Selected Cities' Streets and Enumeration Districts, 1910 Census (microfiche). Arranged by city.

Nonpopulation Census Schedules for Illinois, 1850-1880.

Nonpopulation Census Schedules for Ohio, 1850-1880.

Special Schedules of the 1890 Census Listing Union Veterans of the Civil War. Kentucky-Wyoming (including District of Columbia). Arranged by state and thereunder by county.

Federal Mortality Schedules, 1850-1880, and Related Indexes. Selected states only. Arranged alphabetically by state.

Indian Census Rolls, 1885-1940. Schedules for American Indian agencies in Michigan, Minnesota, and Wisconsin only. Arranged by name of agency and thereunder by year.

City Directories: Chicago, 1871, 1880, 1890, 1900, 1910, 1917, New York City, 1909-1910; Brooklyn, NY, 1910-1911.

Immigration Records

Passenger lists are usually arranged chronologically by date of a ship's arrival, and indexes are alphabetically arranged by passenger surnames. Exceptions are noted.

Index to Passenger Lists of Vessels Arriving at New York, 1820-1846.

Passenger Lists of Vessels Arriving in New York, 1846-1897. No index available.

Index to Passenger Lists of Vessels Arriving at New York, June 16, 1897-June 30, 1902.

Registers of Vessels Arriving at the Port of New York from Foreign Ports, 1789-1919.

Copies of Lists of Passengers Arriving at Miscellaneous Ports on the Atlantic and Gulf Coasts and at Ports on the Great Lakes, 1820-1873. Arranged alphabetically by port.

Index to Passenger Lists of Vessels Arriving at Galveston, Texas, 1896-1906.

Index to Passenger Lists of Vessels Arriving at Galveston, Texas, 1906-1951.

Passenger Lists of Vessels Arriving at Galveston, Texas, 1896-1948.

Alphabetical Index to Canadian Border Entries through Small Ports in Vermont, 1895-1924.

Soundex Index to Entries into the St. Albans, Vermont District through Canadian Pacific and Atlantic Ports, 1924-1952. Surnames arranged by Soundex.

Manifests of Passengers Arriving in the St. Albans, Vermont District through Canadian Pacific Ports, 1929-1949. Arranged chronologically.

Card Manifests of Entries through the Port of Detroit, Michigan, 1906-1954. Arranged alphabetically by surname.

Passenger and Alien Crew Lists of Vessels Arriving at the Port of Detroit, Michigan, 1946-1957. Arranged chronologically.

Records of Imperial Russian Consulates in the United States, 1862-1922. Only records of the Russian Consulate in Chicago, 1906-1920. Arranged by record type (visa applications, cancelled passports, individual files, etc.).

Naturalization

Soundex Index to Naturalization Petitions for the United States District and Circuit Courts, Northern District of Illinois, and Immigration and Naturalization Service District 9, 1840-1950.

U. S. Military Service

Revolutionary War, 1775-1783

General Index to Compiled Military Service Records of Revolutionary War Soldiers. Arranged alphabetically by surname.

Compiled Service Records of Soldiers Who Served in the American Army during the Revolutionary War. Arranged under the designation "Continental Troops" or a state name, then by organization, and thereunder alphabetically by surname.

Index to Compiled Service Records of American Naval Personnel Who Served in the Revolutionary War. Arranged by surname.

Compiled Service Records of American Naval Personnel & Members of the Departments of the Quartermaster General and the Commissary General of Military Stores Who Served during the Revolutionary War. Arranged by department and thereunder by surname.

Revolutionary War Pension and Bounty Land Warrant Application Files. Arranged alphabetically by surname.

Revolutionary War Bounty Land Warrants in the Military District of Ohio and Related Papers (Acts of 1788, 1803, 1806). Arranged numerically by warrant number. Indexes.

Revolutionary War Rolls. Arranged by state and thereunder by organization.

War of 1812, 1812-1815

Index to Compiled Service Records of Volunteer Soldiers Who Served during the War of 1812. Arranged alphabetically by surname.

War of 1812 Military Bounty Land Warrants, 1815-1858. Arranged numerically by warrant number. There are indexes.

Patriot War, 1838-1839

Index to Compiled Service Records of Volunteer Soldiers Who Served from the State of Michigan during the Patriot War, 1838-1839. Arranged alphabetically by surname.

Index to Compiled Service Records of Volunteer Soldiers Who Served from State of New York during the Patriot War, 1838. Arranged alphabetically by surname.

Mexican-American War, 1846-1848

Index to Compiled Service Records of Volunteer Soldiers Who Served during the Mexican War. Arranged alphabetically by surname.

Civil War, 1861-1865

Indexes to Compiled Service Records of Volunteer Union Soldiers Who Served in Organizations from Illinois, Indiana, Michigan, Minnesota, Ohio, and Wisconsin. Arranged alphabetically by surname.

Index to Compiled Service Records of Volunteer Union Soldiers Who Served with U. S. Colored Troops.

Compiled Records Showing Service of Military Units in Volunteer Union Organizations. United States Colored Troops. Arranged by type of unit (cavalry, artillery, or infantry) and thereunder numerically by unit designation.

Special Schedules of the 1890 Census Listing Union Veterans of the Civil War. Kentucky-Wyoming (including District of Columbia). Arranged by state and thereunder by county.

List of Photographs and Photographic Negatives Relating to the War for the Union.

The Matthew B. Brady Collection of Civil War Photographs.

Records of the Fifty-Fourth Massachusetts Infantry Regiment (Colored), 1863-1865. Arranged by type of records (letters, musters, etc.) and thereunder chronologically.

Wars With Indian Nations

Senate 37A-F3, trial transcript and other records relating to Sioux-Dakota Indians and atrocities in Minnesota, 1862.

Index to Compiled Service Records of the Volunteer Soldiers Who Served During the Indian Wars and Disturbances, 1815-1858.

Letters Received by the Office of Adjutant General (Main Series), 1871-1880.

Spanish-American War, 1898

General Index to Compiled Service Records of Volunteer Soldiers Who Served During the War with Spain.

Philippine Insurrection, 1899-1902

Index to Compiled Service Records of Volunteer Soldiers Who Served During the Philippine Insurrection.

World War I, 1917-1918

Selective Service registration cards for men residing in Illinois, Indiana, Michigan, Minnesota, Ohio, and Wisconsin.

General Military Records and Reports

Registers of the Records of the Proceedings of the U. S. Army General Courts-Martial, 1809-1890.

Historical Information Relating to Military Posts and Other Installations, ca. 1700-1900.

The Negro in the Military Service of the United States, 1639-1886.

Miscellaneous Records

Internal Revenue Assessment Lists for Illinois, 1862-1866. Arranged by collection district, thereunder alphabetically.

Registers and Letters Received by the Commissioner of the Bureau of Refugees, Freedmen, and Abandoned Lands, 1865-1872.

Registers of Signatures of Depositors in Branches of the Freedman's Savings and Trust Company, 1865-1874.

Indexes to Deposit Ledgers in Branches of the Freedman's Savings and Trust Company, 1865-1874.

Record of Appointment of Postmasters, 1832-1971. Arranged by state, then county, and thereunder by post office name.

Letters of Application and Recommendation for Federal Offices, 1797-1869. Arranged by presidential administration and thereunder by surname of applicant or person recommended.

Enrollment Cards of the Five Civilized Tribes, 1898-1914. Arranged by Indian tribe (Cherokee, Chickasaw, Choctaw, Creek, Seminole), then by tribal subdivision, and thereunder by census card number.

Final Rolls of Citizens and Freedmen of the Five Civilized Tribes in Indian Territory, 1907, 1914. Arranged by Indian tribe (Cherokee, Chickasaw, Choctaw, Creek, Seminole), then tribal subdivision, and thereunder by roll number.

Indexes to Illinois Public Domain Land Sales (microfiche, compiled by the Illinois State Archives).

Illinois State Archives Marriage Index (microfiche; ongoing compilation of surname index for marriages, ca. 1818-1900. Only portions of 27 counties, not including Cook County).

City of Chicago—Board of Election Commissioners, Voter Registration Lists 1888-1892.

SECTION TWENTY-EIGHT

Naturalization Records

Although naturalization (citizenship) records are considered a valuable resource for genealogy research, the information in these records varies significantly depending on when and where they were created. Most naturalization records prior to 1906 contain little information of genealogical value because the naturalizations were done in local and state courts not federal courts. With some exceptions, the most information you can get from pre-nineteenth-century naturalization documents is: name, native country, date and place of naturalization, and a mark or signature (if the applicant was literate).

The first naturalization act, passed by Congress on March 26, 1790 (1 Stat. 103), allowed any free, white alien over the age of twenty-one to petition for citizenship after a two year residency in the United States. The applicant was required to visit any common court of record, where the presiding judge would rule on the petition and evidence of good moral character. If the judge approved the petition, the applicant swore an oath of allegiance to the Constitution. Married women derived citizenship from their husbands; children under the age of twenty-one derived citizenship their fathers. Children of unsuccessful applicants could apply for citizenship in their own right upon attaining the age of twenty-one.

Congress repealed the 1790 act, and passed a more stringent law on January 29, 1795 (1 Stat. 414). Except for a brief period (1798-1802), the new law established the eligibility and procedural requirements that have been the foundation of United States naturalization policy and legislation since. The 1795 act increased the residency requirement to five years and stipulated that one year be spent in the state or territory where the court of petition was located. The naturalization process was increased from a one-step to a two-step procedure. The applicant was required to file a declaration of intention (frequently called the "first paper") at least three years before filing a petition for admission to citizenship (frequently called the "second" or "final" paper). The 1795 act also required the applicant to renounce any title of nobility.

The undeclared naval war with France, from 1798 to 1802, played a   significant role in the passage of the Alien and Sedition Act of 1798. This act increased the waiting period between filing the declaration of intention and filing the petition from three years to five years. It also extended the residency requirement to fourteen years, including five years in the state where the court of petition was located (1 Stat. 566). The act also required court clerks to forward copies of declarations of intention to the United States Secretary of State. Due to strong complaints about the law, Congress supplanted it with another law on April 14, 1802 (2 Stat. 153), which basically reverted to the 1795 act, but retained the 1798 requirement of registry.

The 1802 act was the last major change in naturalization law until 1906. Minor revisions made after 1798 reduced the waiting period between filing the declaration of intention and the naturalization petition from three years to two years, and required petitioners to attest they were not anarchists.

An 1862 act for the U.S. Army (12 Stat. 597) and an 1894 act for the U.S. Navy and Marine Corps (28 Stat. 124) waived the requirement for aliens to file a declaration of intention if they were honorably discharged from a branch of the United States military.

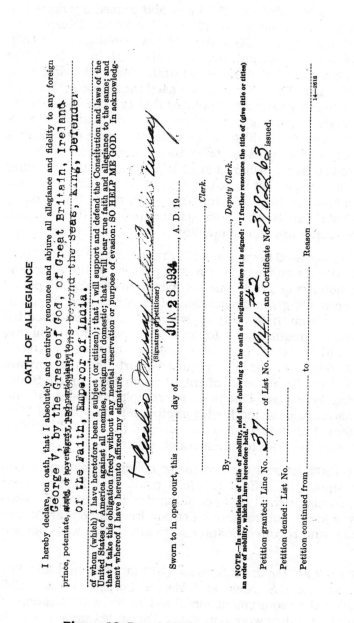

Figure 18: Post-1906 Naturalization Oath
(*courtesy National Archives—Chicago Branch*)

TRIPLICATE   No. 86925

UNITED STATES OF AMERICA

DECLARATION OF INTENTION
(Invalid for all purposes seven years after the date hereof)

UNITED STATES OF AMERICA | In the _____ DISTRICT _____ Court
NORTHERN DISTRICT OF ILLINOIS } ss: THE UNITED STATES at CHICAGO

CECELIA MURRAY - - Sister Cecelia Murray

I, _____
now residing at ____6337 Harvard Avenue, Chicago, Illinois,____ (Number and street) (City or town) (State)
occupation ___nun___, aged ___51___ years, do declare on oath that my personal description is:
Sex ___female___, color ___white___, complexion ___fair___, color of eyes ___grey___
color of hair ___brown___, height ___5___ feet ___1___ inches; weight ___130___ pounds; visible distinctive marks
___none.___
race ___Irish___; nationality ___British___
I was born in ___Brewers Mills, Canada,___ on ___May 16, 1880___
(City or town) (Country) (Month) (Day) (Year)
I am ___not___ married. The name of my wife or husband is _____; she or he was
we were married on _____, at _____
(Month) (Day) (Year) (City or town) (State or country)
born at _____ on _____ entered the United States
(City or town) (State or country) (Month) (Day) (Year)
at _____, on _____, for permanent residence therein, and now
(City or town) (State) (Month) (Day) (Year)
resides at _____ I have _____ children, and the name, date and place of birth,
(City or town) (State or country)
and place of residence of each of said children are as follows:

I have ___not___ heretofore made a declaration of intention: Number _____, on _____
(Date)
at _____
(City or town) (Name of court)
my last foreign residence was ___Kingston, Canada,___
I emigrated to the United States of America from ___Kingston, Canada,___
(City or town) (Country)
my lawful entry for permanent residence in the United States was at ___Port Huron, Michigan,___
(City or town) (State)
under the name of ___Sister Cecelia Murray___, on ___July 15, 1908___
(Day) (Year)
on the vessel ___G. T. RR___
(If other than by vessel, state manner of arrival)
I will, before being admitted to citizenship, renounce forever all allegiance and
fidelity to any foreign prince, potentate, state, or sovereignty, and particularly,
by name, to the prince, potentate, state, or sovereignty of which I may be at
the time of admission a citizen or subject; I am not an anarchist; I am not a
polygamist nor a believer in the practice of polygamy; and it is my intention in
good faith to become a citizen of the United States of America and to reside
permanently therein; and I certify that the photograph affixed to the duplicate
and triplicate hereof is a likeness of me: So HELP ME GOD.

Cecelia Murray, Sister Cecelia Murray
(Original signature of declarant without abbreviation, also alias, if used)
Subscribed and sworn to before me in the office of the Clerk of said Court,
at ___Chicago, Illinois___ this ___28___ day of ___Oct.___
anno Domini 19.31. Certification No.11 30394 from the Commissioner of Naturalization showing the lawful entry of the declarant for permanent
residence on the date stated above, has been received by me. The photograph
affixed to the duplicate and triplicate hereof is a likeness of the declarant.

Sister (Mrs) Cecelia Murray

[SEAL]

Charles E. Bates,
Clerk of the U.S. District Court.
By _____, Deputy Clerk.
14-2623 U. S. GOVERNMENT PRINTING OFFICE 19JS

Form 2202-L-A.
U. S. DEPARTMENT OF LABOR
NATURALIZATION SERVICE

Figure 19: Post-1906 Declaration of Intention
(courtesy National Archives—Chicago Branch)

Steady increases in the number of immigrants entering the
United States increased the workload of court clerks who
did most of the documentation associated with obtaining
citizenship. To relieve the court clerks, and courts, of the
processing burden, and to standardize the naturalization
procedure, Congress passed an act on June 29, 1906 (32
Stat. 596), which established a Bureau of Immigration and
Naturalization. Although court judges retained a degree of
independence, the findings and recommendations of the
Bureau of Immigration and Naturalization were the basis
for the final determinations of the courts regarding admission, denial, or continued investigation of petitioners. The
1906 statute established the requirement that the names
of minor children be included on petitions, and duplicate
records be furnished to the bureau.

An act passed on September 22, 1922 (42 Stat. 1021) required married women to be naturalized in their own right,
and eliminated derivative citizenship for women. The residency requirement was reduced to one year, and the declaration of intention was waived for alien wives of United
States citizens.

Most naturalization proceedings after September 26, 1906,
were conducted in federal courts according to Bureau of
Immigration and Naturalization standards, and many of
those federal records and indexes have been preserved in
various National Archives regional offices.

National Archives-Great Lakes Region

National Archives-Great Lakes Region
7358 South Pulaski Road
Chicago, IL 60629

The National Archives-Great Lakes Region houses the original card *Soundex Index to Naturalization Petitions for the
United States District and Circuit Courts Northern District of
Illinois and Immigration and Naturalization Service District
#9—1840-1950.* The Soundex index, brings together more
than 150 million names that were recorded in naturaliza-

tion indexes generated by several courts. These include both civil and military petitions from the United States District Court, Northern District of Illinois, Eastern Division; the circuit, county, criminal, and superior courts of Cook County; and several county and municipal courts in the old Immigration and Naturalization Service (INS) District #9 (at one time called District #14). District #9 was comprised of northwestern Indiana, southern and eastern Wisconsin, and eastern Iowa. Because the Great Chicago Fire of October 1871 destroyed local and federal court records in the city, the naturalization index entries pertaining to Chicago and Cook County do not begin until 1871.

The naturalization index consists of 162-cubic feet of 3- by 5-inch cards indexed in the Russell-Soundex order, then arranged alphabetically by given (first) name. To search for a particular surname you must first convert it to its Soundex form. The index has been microfilmed by the Genealogical Society of Utah.

While the National Archives-Great Lakes Region retains the major index (also available at the Family History Library in Salt Lake City), it does not have the original records created by Cook County courts as described in the card index. However, the National Archives has dexograph (negative photostat) copies of naturalizations from 1871 to 1906 for the local courts.

To inquire about original Cook County records for the years 1871 to December 1929, when the local courts lost jurisdiction, contact:

Cook County Clerk of Court, Naturalizations
    Room 1201 Daley Center
    50 West Washington Street, Chicago, IL 60602.

Illinois Regional Archives Depository (IRAD)

The Illinois Regional Archives Depository at Northeastern Illinois University in Chicago has microfilm copies of natural-ization records for Cook County.

United States District Court—Chicago

The U.S. District Court—Chicago maintains an index to all naturalizations which took place in the court from 1871 to the present.

Calumet City Court Naturalization Index

Nine volumes of Calumet City naturalizations, which were temporarily stored in a local library basement in the 1980s, were donated to the South Suburban Genealogical and Historical Society in South Holland, Illinois. The records dating from about 1906 to 1952, were indexed by Joan Alguire, a member of the society. Although the majority of entries in this index are for Polish and Italian immigrants, other nationalities are represented.

Most of the declarations of intention of individuals included in the collection were not registered in Illinois, but completed their final papers in the Calumet City Court after arriving from other states where they may have settled initially.

The alphabetically arranged card index and the original papers are available for use at the:

South Suburban Genealogical and Historical Society Library
P.O. Box 96
161st Place and Louis Avenue
South Holland, IL 60473

Chicago Heights Naturalizations

Original naturalization records for nearly four thousand individuals who completed citizenship requirements in Chicago Heights are currently held by the Chicago Heights Public Library. The declaration of intention and petition books, which cover the time period between 1907 and 1954, have been indexed by the South Suburban Genealogical and Historical Society. The Chicago Heights Library will photocopy naturalization records for a nominal fee. For further information, contact:

The Chicago Heights Public Library
15th Street and Chicago Road
Chicago Heights, IL 60411
(708-754-0323)

The U.S. Immigration and Naturalization Service

The U.S. Immigration and Naturalization Service (Washington, DC 20536) has duplicate records of all naturalizations that occurred after September 26, 1906.

SECTION TWENTY-NINE
Newberry Library

The Newberry Library, a landmark on the city's near north side, extends along Walton between Dearborn and Clark Streets, and is a mecca for scholars, students, and genealogists. Named for Walter Loomis Newberry, pioneer Chicago real estate speculator and philanthropist, its awesome collection consists of roughly 1.5 million volumes and 5 to 6 million manuscripts. It is a reference library for history and the humanities, and specializes in several areas including: local and family history, the history of cartography, the American Indian, printing, music, and the Renaissance.

The library's treasures are world-famous. Over two thousand of its books were printed before 1500. Its European manuscripts date from the ninth century. Brahms, Mozart, Wagner, and Mendelssohn are among composers whose manuscripts are in the library's possessions, and its music collection is particularly strong in Renaissance items.

Notable, also, are materials collected by Edward E. Ayer on archaeology and ethnology of the North American Indian and the native races of the Philippines, Hawaii, and Mexico. The John M. Wing Foundation provided the library with a comprehensive collection on the history of book-making. The Midwest Manuscript Collection is relatively new and includes the personal papers of Sherwood

Anderson, Victor Lawson, and Graham Taylor.

At a very early point in the Newberry Library's history, the emphasis was on the acquisition of local and family history materials; this emphasis continues to this day. The library is, perhaps, best known for this strength and probably fifty to sixty percent of its patrons are genealogy researchers. The book, *Guide to Local and Family History at The Newberry Library* (Salt Lake City: Ancestry, 1987) by Peggy Tuck offers a well organized presentation of the holdings of the library as they relate to family history research.

The Newberry Library is not affiliated with the Chicago Public Library system and receives no tax support. No fees are charged for the use of the collection. To receive a library card, you need to show some form of current identification and fill out a short registration form. This is a non-circulating, closed stack library.

Location and Hours

You can contact or visit the library at this address:

The Newberry Library
  60 West Walton Street
  Chicago, IL 60610-3305
  (312-943-9090)

The library is not open on Sundays or Mondays. Since library hours can change often, you should call before you visit the library to be sure the sources you wish to search are available during the time you are there.

Geographical Scope of the Collection

The geographical scope of the local and family history collection is not limited to Chicago, the State of Illinois, or even the Midwest, although it is certainly strong in these areas. The library collects local history (county, town, church, etc.) for the United States and Canada. As for published record transcriptions (vital records, cemetery inscriptions, court abstracts, etc.), the library collects such material for the entire United States and Canada. Some vital records and indexes are on microform.

The British Isles collection of printed materials is also strong, consisting primarily of local histories and published county record series, for example, the Yorkshire Parish Register series. Basic sources and guides are also available for continental European research. Most of the materials that can be used for continental research are confined to a treatment of nobility and heraldry.

The primary collection at the library consists of books, although many of the newer acquisitions are on microfilm. The collections do not include original records such as vital statistics or manuscripts found at a county clerk's office or in state archives. Also missing are microfilmed copies of original records like the ones you might find at a family history center. What is available depends, in general, on what has been printed. If your ancestors came from a county or town which has a genealogical or historical society that publishes information, there is a good chance the library will have something for you.

Genealogies and Vital Records

A collection of 16,000 family genealogies comprises an important segment of the local and family history holdings. The collection of New England genealogies of the late nineteenth and early twentieth centuries is especially extensive.

As with any collection of published genealogies, the longer a family has been in the country, the more likely you will find a published genealogy.

Census Records

The library does not have all of the microfilmed Federal Population Census Schedules; only the 1810, 1820, and 1850 schedules are complete for all states and territories.

All extant microfilm and indexes to federal censuses through 1850 are available. Census holdings for the years 1860 through 1900 are especially strong for the Midwest and most southern and border states. Census holdings for the twentieth century are almost exclusively for Illinois. Only population schedules for Illinois are available as a complete set to 1920; the 1900 and 1920 Soundex, but not the 1910 Miracode, for Illinois is also available.

In connection with Chicago census work, the library has developed its own specialized finding aids. These are in the form of maps which are designed to locate Chicago residents in census schedules based on address alone. The obvious strategy is to obtain the address by consulting the Chicago directory for the corresponding year; a complete set of directories is on file. The Local and Family History Section of the library can respond to correspondence requesting information, but requests are limited to three addresses at a time.

The library also has some agricultural and mortality schedules. A few state censuses for Illinois, and others, are available on microfilm. Although state census schedules for other states are incomplete, there are substantial holdings. For example:

* The 1855, 1875, 1905 and 1925 census for New York.

* The complete 1905 census for Wisconsin.

* The 1915 census for Iowa.

* A near-complete collection of Canadian censuses for Ontario and the Maritime Provinces (through 1871) and Quebec (through 1881).

Local Histories

Probably one of the greatest strengths of the library collection is in local history. It is still regarded as one of the best in the country. Volumes should be accessed by searching for the name of the county in both the card and computer catalogs. For New England and Mid-Atlantic states, you should also look up the name of the town. City directories are available from all over the United States, mostly from 1870 to 1920.

Biographical Sources

An ongoing project of the Local and Family History Section at the library is the creation of a card index to all the biographical sketches appearing in several selected Chicago, Cook County, and Illinois histories. The purpose is to provide a way to search the bibliography and industry file once, and eliminate the need to search the seventeen indexed titles individually. Historical sketches of industries are also included in this file, but the bulk of the entries (over 6,000) refer to individuals. Library patrons are free to consult the file in person. Multi-volume biographical and genealogical works such as the *Dictionary of American Biography, Cyclopedia of American Biography*, and the *American Genealogical Index* are also available.

Maps, Atlases and Gazetteers

The Newberry Library is renowned for its collection of maps, atlases, and gazetteers. Although not a part of the local and family history collection per se, the map collection is significant to genealogists. There is an extensive collection of United States county land ownership maps and atlases in original editions as well as facsimile. The collection also contains important nineteenth and twentieth century maps for Europe; the most complete sets are for Ireland, Germany, and the Austro-Hungarian Empire.

Military Records

Military records of the American Revolution, War of 1812, and the Civil War are available in the form of published roster, pension records, and regimental histories.

Additional Sources

The library has many other sources of interest to a genealogist:

* Lineage books, rosters, annual reports, periodicals and year books from patriotic and hereditary societies.

* Passenger lists and indexes to passenger lists, some on microfilm and some in print. Patrons with specific interests should contact the library in advance.

* The *Genealogical Index of the Newberry Library*, which is available at many libraries, is a massive compilation of family names taken from selected volumes in the library. It is not a catalogue of the library's holdings, but is useful as a clue finder for family history research. The index was created between the years 1896 and 1918, and therefore, contains no reference to any book published after 1918.

Newspapers

If you ignore newspaper sources during your research, you may miss finding a piece of valuable information. Newspapers are an excellent source for family and local history because they provide accounts of events from a contemporary point of view. Old newspapers take on added importance when official public records have been destroyed, as they were in the Great Chicago Fire of 1871. They became essential in reconstructing the history of Chicago. A great number of newspapers have come and gone, and some collections are missing or not accessible. However, many newspapers, defunct and contemporary, have been microfilmed, and are available as an important resource. This section includes a list of the most important collections for the Cook County area, but it is sometimes necessary to seek out the needed issues in specialized libraries, museums, or at the original publishing company.

All of the libraries listed in this section have additional newspaper holdings which extend to other interests and geographical areas. The Newspapers and General Periodicals Center at the Chicago Public Library, for example, has a wide selection of contemporary American, ethnic, and foreign newspapers, but only the names of major indexes and newspaper collections considered relevant to research in the Cook County area are provided.

Newspapers at The Chicago Historical Society

Aftonbladet Skandia Sept. 17, 1890 to June 1, 1891.

(Chicago) American July 17, 1840 to Oct. 19, 1842.

Arlington Heights Herald Sept. 21, 1961 to Oct. 12, 1961.

Broad Ax Aug. 31, 1895 to Sept. 10, 1927.

Centennial of the North-Western Territory Nov. 1793 to June 1796.

Citizen Jan. 14, 1882 to May 16, 1914.

Clipper Apr. 9, 1870 to Mar. 24, 1877; Dec. 31, 1881 to Jan. 6, 1883; Apr. 1884 to Oct. 1884; Apr. 1892 to Mar. 9, 1893.

Conservator 1882 to 1883; 1886.

(Chicago) Daily News Dec. 1, 1875 to Mar. 4, 1978.

Defender 1909 to the present.

(Chicago Daily) Democrat Feb. 27, 1840 to Jan. 18, 1842; June 30, 1847 to Dec. 25, 1852; loose issues for: 1853 to 1855; Feb. 26, 1856 to Dec. 27, 1856; Mar. 11, 1857 to July 24, 1861.

(Weekly Chicago) Democrat Nov. 26, 1833 to Dec. 14, 1842; Jan. 25, 1843 to Dec. 30, 1845; Jan. 5, 1847 to Nov. 2, 1847; Jan. 4, 1848 to July 27, 1861.

Egyptian Republican Jan. 1939 to Dec. 1948.

(Chicago) Express July 12 and Aug. 2, 1881 to Nov. 29, 1881; Dec. 13, 1881 to Dec. 27, 1881; 1882 to 1886 (missing: Sept. 5 and Sept. 12 to Sept. 19, 1885); Dec. 13, 1890 to Dec. 20, 1890; 1891; Jan. 2, 1892 to Jan. 30, 1892.

Faderneslandet Jan. 4, 1879 to Jan. 31, 1880.

(La) Fiaccola Sept. May 1912 to Feb. 10, 1921.

Fosterlandet Nov. 4, 1891 to Sept. 25, 1907.

Framat Jan. 8, 1890 to Oct. 28, 1891.

Gem of the Prairies May 29, 1844 to 1852.

Genius of Universal Emancipation Feb. 26, 1839 to Sept. 13, 1839.

Hemfrid Nov. 21, 1889 to Dec. 29, 1892.

Chicago Herald Mar. 1, 1859 to Oct. 21, 1859; May 10, 1881 to Dec. 31, 1889; May 1, 1893 to Feb. 28, 1901; Apr. 1901 to Dec. 1932.

Hyde Park Herald Apr. 29, 1882 to Aug. 7, 1886; Jan. 5, 1884 to June 28, 1884; Aug. 14, 1886 to Mar. 29, 1889; Sept. June 1918 to Dec. 28, 1934; Apr. 16, 1936 to Dec. 27, 1940; Feb. 2, 1941 to Apr. 15, 1953.

Illinois Gazette Sept. 25, 1819 to 1830 (incomplete).

Illinois State Journal Jan. 2, 1856 to June 30, 1860.

Illinois Swede & Nya Verlden Apr. 24, 1869 to Jan. 5, 1874.

Inter Ocean Mar. 27, 1872 to May 7, 1914.

(L') Italia Apr. 28, 1886 to May 27, 1889; Jan. 1, 1901 to Dec. 25, 1909; Jan. 1, 1910 to Dec. 29, 1918.

(Chicago Daily and Chicago Evening) Journal Aug. 31, 1844 to Apr. 21, 1845; Sept. 30, 1845 to Dec. 31, 1845; June to Sept. and Nov. to Dec. 1847; Jan. 1848 to Dec. 1849; Jan. 3, 1853 to June 27, 1854; Oct. 2, 1854 to Mar. 31, 1855; Jan. 3, 1856 to Mar. 31, 1856; Oct. 1, 1856 to June 30, 1857; Jan. 2, 1858 to Sept. 1867; July 1, 1868 to Dec. 31, 1897; July 1, 1898 to Dec. 30, 1916; June 1, 1921 to Aug. 21, 1929.

Labor Enquirer Feb. 23, 1887 to Aug. 18, 1888.

(Chicago) Labor News May 1919 to Mar. 2, 1923.

Liberator Sept. 3, 1905 to Apr. 15, 1906.

Little Fort Porcupine and Lake County Visiter Mar. 4, 1845 to Oct. 2, 1847.

Chicago Evening Mail July 1, 1885 to Dec. 1895.

Messaggiere Italiano Dell 'Ouest Oct. 1, 1867 to Feb. 10, 1869.

Mormon newspapers (Illinois)—No dates given.

North Shore News Sept. 20, 1902 to July 7, 1911.

(Chicago Evening) Post Apr. 29, 1890 to Oct. 29, 1932.

(Il) Proletario 1905 to Aug. 1921.

Republican Jan. 1, 1916 to Oct. 21, 1922.

Rights of Labor 1886 to 1893.

Sentinel Nov. 15, 1883 to Dec. 6, 1883; Dec. 20, 1883 to Dec. 27, 1883; Jan. to Oct., 1884.

Skandia June 11, 1890 to June 24, 1891.

(Chicago) Socialist Mar. 11, 1899 to Apr. 6, 1907.

Sporting and Theatrical Journal Mar. 1, 1884 to Sept. 20, 1884; June 20, 1885.

Steel Labor 1936 to 1941.

(Chicago) Sun May 2, 1884 to Mar. 21, 1909; Dec. 4, 1941 to Jan. 31, 1948.

(Chicago) Sun Times Feb. 1, 1948 to present.

Svenska Arbetaren Dec. 30, 1882 to Nov. 1, 1884.

Svenska Nyheter Oct. 1, 1901 to June 26, 1906.

Svenska Tribunen Sept. 20, 1877 to Dec. 26, 1889.

Svenska Varlden Mar. 11, 1904 to Feb. 28, 1908.

(Weekly Chicago and Daily Chicago) Times Jan. 16, 1855 to July 20, 1859; Aug. 20, 1857 to June 30, 1858; Oct. 1, 1858 to Dec. 1858; Apr. 1, 1859 to Mar. 31, 1860; Mar. 9, 1861 to Dec. 31, 1861; Jan. 1, 1871 to Dec. 1894.

(Chicago) Tribune Apr. 23, 1849 to July 13, 1853; Sept. 1, 1853 to Sept. 30, 1854; Jan. 11, 1855 to Sept. 20, 1856; Jan. 7, 1857 to the present.

Watchman of the Prairies Aug. 10, 1847 to Feb. 22, 1853.

Western Citizen July 26, 1842 to July 19, 1855.

Western Herald Apr. 1, 1846 to Aug. 1, 1849.

Western Pioneer and Baptist Standard Bearer July 1835 to Dec. 13, 1838.

(Chicago) Whip June 24, 1919 to Dec. 30, 1922.

Woodlawn Booster July 13, 1932 to Dec. 30, 1959.

Worker's Digest Sept. 27, 1935 to Sept. 25, 1936.

(Chicago Evening) World 1906 to Oct. 25, 1907; 1908 to 1912.

The Chicago Public Library

These resources are located in the Newspapers and General Periodicals Center:

Microfilm

Chicago American 1950 to 1969.

Chicago Daily American April 1839; Jan to Apr, 1840; 1841 to 42.

Chicago Daily News 1876 to 1978.

Chicago Daily Times 1929 to 1948.

Chicago Defender (daily edition) 1956+.

Chicago Defender (weekly edition) 1909+.

Chicago Democrat 1833 to 1839.

Chicago Democratic Press 1852 to 1858.

Chicago Evening Post 1890 to 1932.

Chicago Express Oct 1842 to Sept. 1843.

Chicago Foreign Language Press Survey (approx.) 1861 to 1938.

Chicago Herald 1914 to 1918; May 1893 to Mar. 1895.

Chicago Herald-American 1939 to 1969.

Chicago Herald and Examiner 1919 to 1938.

Chicago Inter-Ocean 1872 to 1914.

Chicago Journal 1846 to 1929.

Chicago Mail 1885 to 1895.

Chicago Maroon July 1970 to June 1971.

Chicago Reader Oct. 1971-.

Chicago Record 1881 to 1901.

Chicago Record-Herald 1901 to 1914.

Chicago Sun Dec 1941 to Jan 1948.

Chicago Sun Times 1855 to 1894.

Chicago Times Herald 1895 to 1901.

Chicago Today April 1969 to Oct.1974.

Chicago Tribune 1849-.

Indexes and Newspaper-Related Sources

Current Newspaper Directories

Ayer Directory of Publications. Philadelphia: Ayer Press. (Annual).

National Directory of Weekly Newspapers. New York: American Newspaper Representatives, Inc. (Annual).

Union Lists of Newspapers

Newspapers in Microform 1948-1972. 2 vols. Washington, D.C.: Library of Congress. 1973.

Gregory, Winifred, ed. *American Newspapers 1821-1936.* New York: Reprint Corp. 1967.

Bringham, Clarence S. *History and Bibliography of American Newspapers 1690-1820.* Westport, Conn.: Greenwood Press, 1976.

Newspaper Indexes, 1972 and Later

Newspaper Index. Wooster, OH: Bell & Howell.

Includes indexing for the *Chicago Tribune, The Los*

Angeles Times, The Times-Picayune (New Orleans), and *The Washington Post.*

Newspaper Index to The Chicago Sun-Times. 1979-1982. Wooster, OH: Bell & Howell.

Newspaper Indexes, Pre-1972

Chicago Democratic Press Index. 1855.

Chicago Record-Herald Index. 1904-1912.

New York Times Index. 1851. New York: New York Times Co.

Palmer's Index to The Times Newspaper. (London). 1790-1905. Vadus Kraus Reprint Ltd.

Official Index to The Times (London). 1906-. London: The Times Publishing Co.

Miscellaneous Newspaper Indexing

New York Times Obituaries Index 1858-1968. New York: New York Times Co., 1970.

Personal Name Index to The New York Times Index' 1851-1974. Succasunna, NJ: Roxbury Data Interface.

Newspapers at The Newberry Library

Advance 1876 to 1889.

Chicago Arbeiter Zeitung May 1879 to Dec. 1889.

Chicago Daily Democratic Press 1855 Index.

Chicago Daily News Jan. 1879 to Dec. 1935.

Chicago Daily News—Morning Edition Mar. 21, 1881 to Mar. 1901.

Chicago Daily Times (see *Chicago Times*).

Chicago Evening Journal (see *Chicago Journal*).

Chicago Evening Post June 15, 1894.

Chicago Evening Post- Friday Literature Review Mar. 1909 to Feb. 28, 1913.

Chicago Journal (also titled *Chicago Evening Journal*) 1854 to 1890.

Microfilm available at Chicago Historical Society; bound volumes in Special Collections.

Chicago Overseas Tribune 1943 to 1946.

The Chicago Record (title varies) Mar. 21,1881 to Mar.27, 1901.

Chicago Republican May 30, 1865 to Mar. 23, 1872.

Chicago Sun Book Week Nov. 1942 to Sept. 1947.

Chicago Times (also titled *Chicago Daily Times*) 1857 to 1884.

Microfilm available at Chicago Historical Society; bound volumes in Special Collections.

Chicago Tribune 1876 to 1884; Feb to Mar. 1914; 1928 to 1939.

Chicago Tribune 1940 to 1964.

Chicago Tribune Book World Sept. 1967 to Dec. 1970, Indexes.

Chicago Weekly Journal 1878 to 1894.

Chicagoer Arbeiter Zeitung May 1879 to Dec.1889.

Die Freie Presse 1872 to 1898.

Illustrated Graphic News 1885 to 1887.

Illinois Staats-Zeitung 1861 to 1901.

Interocean Jan. 1880 to May 7, 1914 (closed).

Ipavia Independent 1896 to 1898 (missing: Nov.4, 11, and 18, 1896; Feb. 10 to 17, Mar. 3 to 17, Aug. 25, 1897).

Lockport Telegraph May 6 to Nov. 6, 1850.

Der Volksfreund June 19 to Sept. 8, 1878; Aug. 14 to 28, 1879.

Weekly Chicago Times Jan. 16, 1855 to July 20, 1859.

College and University Newspaper Collections

All of the area colleges and universities have some kind of newspaper collection in their library, and most have micro-film copies of the *Chicago Tribune* and the *New York Times.* Besides the major dailies, these libraries generally have special collections which often include smaller local news-papers serving the community in which the school is lo-cated.

An example of the type of newspaper collection you may find at one of these libraries in the Chicago area is the one at Governors State University.

Governors State University Newspaper Holdings
   Governors State University
   Park Forest South, IL 60466
   (312-534-5000)

Billboard 1894 to 1940.

Chicago Daily News 1971 to 1973.

Chicago Defender City Edition 1909 to 1967.

Chicago Defender 1921 to 1967.

Chicago Sun Times 1971-.

Chicago Today 1971 to 1974.

Chicago Tribune 1849 to the present.

Christian Science Monitor 1908 to the present.

The Era Jan. 1851 to Sept. 1939.

Illinois State Journal 1971 to 1973.

London Times 1900 to 1974.

London Times Educational Supplement 1960 to 1976.

New York Times 1851 to the present.

Park Forest Star 1961 to the present.

Variety 1940 to 1972.

Wall Street Journal 1958 to the present.

The Governors State University Library also has *The Chicago Tribune Index* and *The New York Times Index.*

Newspapers in The Illinois State Historical Library

The Illinois State Historical Library has acquired over 60,000 reels of newspaper microfilmsince 1959. Back files of newspapers are acquired from various sources, microfilmed, and added to the library's collection. Current newspapers are received on subscription, either in original form or on microfilm. A list of their holdings for Chicago and Cook County may be found in "Newspapers in the Historical Library" (*Illinois State Library Special Report Series* 1,no. 1, 1994) published by the Office of the Secretary of State/Illinois State Librarian. There 297 newspaper titles for Chicago alone and the rest of Cook County is also well represented. Some of the newspapers, such as *Happy Hours* (Oct. 11,1871), are a single issue, some exist for a few years, and others like the *Chicago Tribune* are almost complete runs. There are several ethnic publications including the *Illinois Staats-Zeitung*, for the German readership, and the *Citizen* which catered to the Irish. Neighborhood papers, such as the *Beverly Review* and the *Logan Square Herald*, also appear in limited numbers. Argo-Summit, Barrington, Blue Island, Lemont, Melrose Park, Midlothian, Niles, Oak Lawn, Western Springs, and Wilmette are among other Cook County towns included in newspaper listings.

The microfilmed titles are available on interlibrary loan to any library in the U.S. with microfilm viewing capabilities. If you want your library to borrow a film, request that it contact:

Illinois State Historical Library
Newspaper Microfilm Section
Old State Capitol
Springfield, IL 62701
(217-785-7941)

Obituary Sources

These libraries and historical societies have indexed obituaries:

Arlington Heights Public Library

Balzekas Museum of Lithuanian Culture

Chicago Historical Society

Evanston Historical Society

Evanston Public Library

Illinois State Historical Society

Oak Park Public Library

South Suburban Genealogical and Historical Society

Winnetka Public Library

There are probably other collections in the area, and it is worth inquiring about obituary resources at any library or historical society not listed. These are unpublished sources and do not appear in major obituary references. Some libraries maintain separate obituary files, for example the one at the South Suburban Genealogical and Historical Society, and some obituary sources are intermixed with the general card catalog entries (as is the case at the Chicago Historical Society).

Irish Obituaries

Biographies and obituaries of Chicago Irish are the source of an extensive index compiled by John Corrigan. Information has been extracted principally from the *Chicago Inter-Ocean, The Chicago Citizen, The South Side Sun, Lake Vindicator, The Sun* and *The New World* (Catholic Archdiocese newspaper). Additional data has been extracted from published Chicago sources and personal research. Send a self-addressed, stamped envelope for more information and a fee schedule to: John Corrigan, 1669 West 104th Street, Chicago, IL 60643.

Published Cook County Obituaries

Carlock, Mabe. *Obituaries: Attorneys and Physicians, Cook County, Illinois, January-September 1952*. (Copied from *Chicago Tribune*.) Oak Park, IL, 1952.

Chicago Genealogical Society. Newspaper Research Committee. *Vital Records from Chicago Newspapers, 1833-1839*. Chicago: Chicago Genealogical Society, 1971.

——. *Vital Records from Chicago Newspapers, 1840-1842*. Chicago: Chicago Genealogical Society, 1972.

——. *Vital Records from Chicago Newspapers, 1843-1844*. Chicago: Chicago Genealogical Society, 1974.

——. *Vital Records from Chicago Newspapers, 1845*. Chicago: Chicago Genealogical Society, 1975.

——. *Vital Records from Chicago Newspapers, 1846*. Chicago: Chicago Genealogical Society, 1976.

Chicago Sun Times. Newspaper Index. Wooster, Ohio: Bell and Howell Company, 1979 -1982 (monthly).

Chicago Tribune. Newspaper Index. Wooster, Ohio: Bell and Howell Company, 1972—(monthly).

Daily Democratic Press. *The Chicago Daily Democratic Press Index for the Year 1855*. Chicago: Works Project Administration, 1940.

Cook County Genealogical Records, 4 vols. Chicago: Daughters of the American Revolution, 1972.

Volume 1 contains obituaries from *Oak Leaves* (Oak Park, IL) July-Nov. 1943. Volume 4 contains obituaries from the *Evanston Index* (Evanston, IL) 1873-1875, 1880-1887.

Epstein, Francis James. *Decet Meminisse Fratrum: A Necrology of the Diocesan Priests of the Chicago Archdiocese, 1844-1936.* Chicago, IL: J.F. Higgins Printing Co., 1937.

Fergus, Robert. "Obituary Compiled by Robert Fergus Before 1900: Names, Places, Dates and Ages at Death of Some of Chicago's Old Settlers Prior to 1843, and Other Well-Known Citizens Who Arrived After 1843, Together With Others Prominently Connected With Illinois History." *Chicago Genealogist* 7, no. 3 (Spring 1975): 96-101.

Grimes, Marilla R. "Items from Oneida County, New York Newspapers Having an Illinois Reference (1860)." *Illinois State Genealogical Society Quarterly* 7, no. 2 (1976).

Hollowak, Thomas L., and William F. Hoffman. *Index to the Obituaries and Death Notices Appearing in the Dziennik Chicagoski.* Chicago: Polish Genealogical Society.

Knights of Columbus, Chicago Council No. 182. *Obituary Sketches.* Chicago, 1921.

Koss, David. "Chicago Obituaries in Der Christliche Botschafter, 1844-1971." *Chicago Genealogist* (Summer 1979).

Newbill, Leona Hopper. *Early Settlers of LaGrange, Illinois and Vicinity.* 2 vols. LaGrange, IL: 1941.

Bibliography of Newspaper Sources

Ayer Directory of Publications. (Published Annually, Without Interruption since 1869).

The Professional's Directory of Print Media. Chicago.

> Published annually in the United States and contains: Economic Descriptions of the States, Provinces, Cities and Towns in Which all Listees are Published; 15 Separate, Classified Lists; 69 Custom Made Maps on Which All Publication Cities and Towns are Indicated.

Center for Research Libraries. The Center for Research Libraries: *Catalogue: Newspapers.* Chicago: The Center, 1978.

Ryan, George H., Secretary of State and State Librarian of Illinois. *Newspapers in the Historical Library.* Illinois State Library Special Report Series, 1, issue 1, 1994.

Szucs, Loretto Dennis. "Newspapers," In *The Source: A Guidebook of American Genealogy.* Edited by Arlene Eakle, and Johni Cerny. Salt Lake City: Ancestry, 1984.

——."Newspapers," In *Source Book.* South Holland, IL: The South Suburban Genealogical and Historical Society, 1983.

University of Chicago. Library. *Newspapers in Libraries of Chicago, a Joint Checklist.* Chicago: University of Chicago, Document Section, 1936.

Occupational and Business Resources

The Chicago Historical Society is the best starting place to search professional records. Subject headings (by business or occupation) in the card catalog include many entries for publications and manuscripts. The general sources listed represent some of the more commonly requested and most available occupational and business references for the Cook County area. Original records, archives, and published sources exist for others.

General Sources

Album of Genealogy and Biography , Cook County, Illinois. Chicago: Calumet Book & Engraving Co., 1897.

Appleton, John B. *The Iron and Steel Industry of the Calumet District.* Urbana, IL, 1927.

Barnett, Femont O. *Politics and Politicians of Chicago, Cook County, Illinois. Memorial Volume 1787-1887.* Chicago: Blakely Printing Company, 1886.

Bate, Phyllis A. "The Development of the Iron and Steel Industry of the Chicago Area, 1900-1920." Ph.D. diss., University of Chicago, 1948.

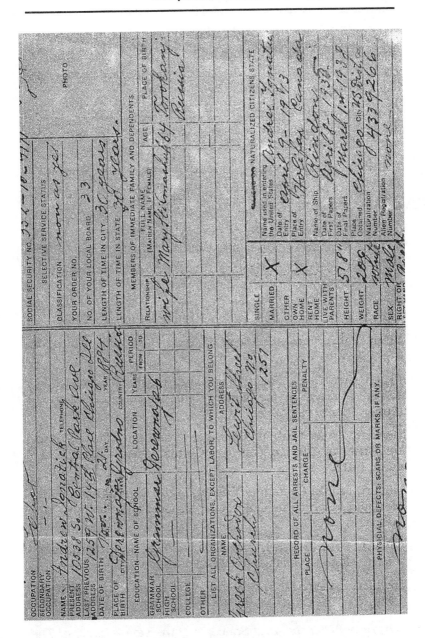

Figure 20: Employment record
(courtesy South Suburban Genealogical & Historical Society)

Biographical Sketches of the Leading Men of Chicago. Chicago: Wilson & St. Clair, 1868.

Biographical Sketches of the Leading Men of Chicago. Chicago: Wilson, Pierce & Co., 1876.

Chicago Historical Society. *Chicago Photographers 1847-1900 as Listed in Chicago City Directories.* Chicago: Chicago Historical Society, 1958.

Currey, Josiah Seymour. *Manufacturing and Wholesale Industries in Chicago.* Chicago: Thomas B. Poole Co., 1918.

Darling, Sharon. *Chicago Metalsmiths.* Chicago: Chicago Historical Society, 1978.

———. *Chicago Furniture: Art, Craft & Industry 1833-1983.* Chicago: Chicago Historical Society in association with W.W. Norton & Company, New York/London, 1984.

Fleming, I.A. *Chicago Stock Exchange: An Historical Sketch with Biographies of Its Leading Members.* Chicago, 1894.

Flinn, John J. *Handbook of Chicago Biography.* Chicago, 1893.

Frueh, Erne Rene. "Retail Merchandising in Chicago, 1833-1848." *Journal of the Illinois State Historical Society* 2 (June 1939): 149-72.

German Press Club of Chicago. *Prominent Citizens and Industries of Chicago.* Chicago: German Press Club of Chicago, 1901.

Gilbert, Frank. *Centennial History of the City of Chicago: Its Men and Institutions.* Chicago: Inter Ocean Publishing Co., 1905.

Gilbert, Paul Thomas, and Charles Lee Bryson. *Chicago and Its Makers.* Chicago: F. Mendelsohn, 1929.

Heckler, Edwin L. *The Meat Packing Industry.* Boston, 1944.

History of Chicago, and Souvenir of the Liquor Interest: The Nation's Choice for the Great Columbian Exposition, 1893. Chicago: Belgravia Publishing Co, 1891.

James, Frank Cyril. *The Growth of Chicago Banks*. 2 vols. New York, 1938.

Jewell, Frank. *Annotated Bibliography of Chicago History*. Chicago: Chicago Historical Society, 1979.

Monchow, Helen C. *Seventy Years of Real Estate Subdividing in the Region of Chicago*. Chicago, 1939.

Mosher, Charles D. *Centennial Historical Album, 1876*.

Nash, Jay Robert. *People to See: An Anecdotal History of Chicago's Makers and Breakers*.

Piscataway, NJ: New Century Publishers, Inc., 1981.

O'Grady, R. P. *Chicago and Cook County Official Republican Directory and Sketch Book, 1900*. Chicago: R.P. O'Grady, 1900.

Parkhurst, M.S. *History of the Yards, 1865-1953*. Chicago, 1953.

Pfannkuche, Craig L. "Genealogical Data Available in Railroad Historical Society Archives: The Chicago & Northwestern Historical Society. *Chicago Genealogist* 15, no. 2 (Winter 1992-93): 35-38.

Rice, Wallace. *The Chicago Exchange: A History*. Chicago, 1923.

Rothermel, Charles T., and Co. *Portraits and Biographies of Fire Underwriters of the City of Chicago*. Chicago: Monarch Printing and Binding Company, 1895.

Schoff, S. *The Glory of Chicago—Her Manufactories*. Chicago: Knight and Leonard, 1873.

Schroder, H. L., and C. W. Forbrick. *Men Who Have Made the Fifth Ward*. Chicago, 1895.

"Sketches of Manufacturers, Memoirs of Business Men." In *Industrial Chicago*. Chicago, 1894.

Taylor, Charles Henry. *History of the Board of Trade of the City of Chicago*. Chicago: Robert O. Law Co., 1917.

Who's Who in Chicago and Illinois. Chicago: A.N. Marquis Company, 1905, 1911, 1917, 1926, 1931, 1936, 1941, 1945.

Wood, David Ward. *Chicago and Its Distinguished Citizens*. Chicago, 1881.

World's Columbian Exposition Souvenir. Chicago: North American Engraving and Publishing Co., 1895.

Physicians

The American Medical Association (A.M.A.), headquartered in Chicago, has a card file of more than a million entries about American physicians. Membership in the A.M.A. was not a prerequisite for inclusion in the index. Information on the individual cards may include an obituary, history of the individual's education, places of practice, and dates of birth and death. Original cards are not currently available for research, but they are being microfilmed by the Genealogical Society of Utah. The microfilming project is expected to be completed during 1997, when the original cards will be sent to the National Genealogical Society; the microfilmed copies will become available at and through the Family History Library in Salt Lake City. See also Arthur W. Hafner, ed., *Directory of American Deceased Physicians, 1804-1929,* 2 vols. (Chicago: American Library Association, 1996).

The American Medical Directory has been published by the A.M.A. since 1906. It was not published annually, but is very useful for the years it was.

Chicago Medical Society. *History of Medicine and Surgery and Physicians and Surgeons of Chicago 1803-1922.* Chicago: Biographical Publishers Corp., 1922.

Sperry, I.M. *Distinguished Physicians & Surgeons of Chicago. A Collection of Biographical Sketches of Many of the Eminent Representatives Past & Present of the Medical Profession of Chicago.* Chicago: Beers Publishers, 1904.

University of Illinois Medical School. *Student Records from Medical School, M.S. and Ph. D. Thesis Reports, 1905-1975.* Chicago, 1976.

American Medical Association
  515 North State Street
  Chicago, IL 60610
  (312-464-5000)

Firemen

Bushnell, George D. "Chicago's Rowdy Firefighters." *Chicago History* 2, no. 4 (Fall/Winter 1973): 232-41.

Little, Kenneth. *Chicago Fire Department Engines: Sixty Years of Motorized Pumpers, 1912-1972.* Chicago, 1972.

McQuade, James S. *A Synoptical History of the Chicago Fire Department.* Chicago, 1908.

The Retirement Board of the Firemen's Annuity and Benefit Fund of Chicago

   180 North LaSalle Street, Suite 701
   Chicago, IL 60601
   (312-726-5823)

Law

Caton, John Dean. *Early Bench and Bar of Illinois.* Chicago: Legal News Company, 1922.

Crossley, Frederic B. *Courts and Lawyers of Illinois.* Chicago: The American Historical Society, 1916.

Linder, Usher F. *Reminiscences of the Early Bench and Bar of Illinois.* Chicago: Chicago Legal News Company, 1879.

Wilke, Franc Bangs. *The Chicago Bar.* Chicago, 1872.

Chicago Bar Association
   29 South LaSalle Street
   Chicago, IL 60603
   (312-782-7348)

Police

Flinn, John Joseph. *History of the Chicago Police.* New York, 1973.

   Biographical sketches included.

The Secretary
 The Police Pension Fund
 221 North LaSalle Street Room 1626
 Chicago, IL 60601
 (312-744-4149)

Pullman Records

Over one million documents for Pullman Standard workers
are at the South Suburban Genealogical and Historical
Society (P.O. Box 96, South Holland, IL 60473). The records date from the late 1800s to the mid-1950s, and cover
the shops located on 111th Street and Cottage Grove in
Chicago, and those in Indiana (two shops in Hammond and
others in Michigan City). The personnel records vary in
content, but most have considerable information of genealogical and historical value. Some files list only birth dates;
others give physical descriptions, family relationships,
educational background, previous employment, and include birth certificates or other proofs of age. Immigrant
files frequently include the date of arrival in the U.S., ship
name, naturalization information, and documents. Historically, the collection reflects the nationality, race, sex, and
working conditions of a labor force before government reg-
ulation and scrutiny. The collection is closed to the public,
but the Pullman Committee will search the index of approximately 152,000 Pullman employees for a fee.

The Newberry Library has yet another group of Pullman
records. The organization of the Newberry collection also
makes retrieval of information for individuals difficult.

Railroad

The Railroad Retirement Board began operations in the
mid-1930s, and its records are limited to individuals who
were associated with the rail industry or were receiving a
private rail pension since that time. In 1937, the Railroad
Retirement Board assumed responsibilities for rail pensions. The records are arranged by the railroad employee's

social security number making it extremely difficult to locate a record by name only. For further information refer to:

Poulos, Bill. "Genealogical Research and the U. S. Railroad Retirement Board." *Ancestry Newsletter* 3, no. 5 (September-October 1985).

Railroad Retirement Board
844 Rush Street
Chicago, IL 60611

There are several railroad archives in the Chicago area, but most of these manuscript collections are not organized for retrieval of information regarding individuals.

Other References

Eakle, Arlene H. "How to Find Business and Employment Records." In *The Source: A Guidebook of American Genealogy.* edited by Arlene Eakle and Johni Cerny. Salt Lake City: Ancestry, 1984.

> Provides lists of places to write for employment records, some background on record keeping practices, suggestions on how to get desired information, and what to expect from these collections.

Jackson, Elisabeth Coleman, and Carolyn Curtis. *Guide to the Burlington Archives in the Newberry Library, 1851-1901.* Chicago: The Newberry Library, 1949.

Meyerink, Kory L. "Business and Employment Records." In *The Source: A Guidebook of American Genealogy.* edited by Arlene Eakle and Johni Cerny. Salt Lake City: Ancestry, 1984.

Mohr, Carolyn Curtis. *Guide to the Illinois Central Archives in The Newberry Library, 1851-1906.* Chicago: The Newberry Library, 1951.

Sinko, Peggy Tuck. *Guide to Local and Family History at The Newberry Library.* Salt Lake City, Ancestry, 1987.

SECTION THIRTY-TWO

Passenger Lists and Maritime Records

Passenger Lists

Among the records cherished by family historians, perhaps none are as symbolic as passenger lists—the records of arrivals of passengers at American ports. To know when, and where, ancestors first set foot on the soil of this continent becomes a piece of personal Americana. Passenger lists, in addition to adding an historical dimension the family, frequently open several other avenues for further research. While there is nowhere in the Chicago area where passenger lists will be found for all ports, some important microfilm sources are noted here. Keep in mind that microfilm collections are often expanded, and because of their popularity, additional passenger lists may be acquired by the institutions listed.

National Archives—Great Lakes Region

The National Archives—Great Lakes Region has the largest collection of microfilmed passenger lists in the Chicago area. The Port of New York arrivals (1820—1897) form the greatest number of films since New York City was the most used port by individuals coming into this country. The collection of passenger lists at the National Archives has continued to grow during the 1990s, and these films are currently available:

Index to Passenger Lists of Vessels Arriving at New York 1820—1846.

Passenger Lists of Vessels Arriving at New York, 1846—1897 (arranged chronologically by year). No comprehensive index available at this time for this series.

Index to Passenger Lists of Vessels Arriving at New York June 16, 1897—June 30, 1902.

Registers of Vessels Arriving at the Port of New York, New York from Foreign Ports, 1789—1919.

Copies of Lists of Passengers Arriving at Miscellaneous Porets on the Atlantic and Gulf Coasts and at Ports on the Great Lakes, 1820—1873.

Index to Passenger Lists of Vessels Arriving at Galveston, Texas, 1896—1906.

Index to Passenger Lists of Vessels Arriving at Galveston, Texas, 1906—1951.

Passenger Lists of Vessels Arriving at Galveston, Texas, 1896—1951.

Alphabetical Index to Canadian Border Entries through Small Ports in Vermont, 1895—1924.

Soundex Index to Entries into the St. Albans, Vermont District through Canadian Pacific and Atlantic Ports, 1924—1952.

Manifests of Passengers Arriving in the St. Albans, Vermont District through Canadian Pacific Ports, 1929—1949.

Card Manifests (Alphabetical) of Individuals Entering through the Port of Detroit, Michigan, 1906—1954.

Passenger and Alien Crew Lists of Vessels Arriving at the Port of Detroit, Michigan, 1946—1957.

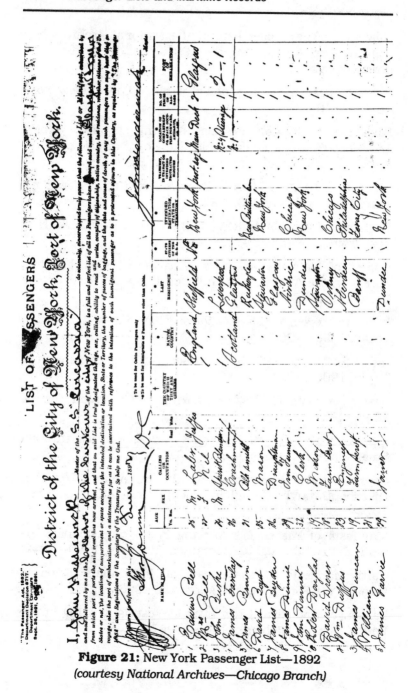

Figure 21: New York Passenger List—1892
(*courtesy National Archives—Chicago Branch*)

The National Archives—Great Lakes Region also has some passenger list indexes, such as the *Famine Irish,* available in book form.

The Chicago Public Library

The Chicago Public Library has some microfilm copies of passenger lists for the ports of Baltimore, Boston, and Philadelphia, as well as a few passenger list indexes in book form. The most important to researchers are:

Index to Passenger Lists of Vessels Arriving at Baltimore, Maryland, 1833—1866.

Index to Passenger Lists of Vessels Arriving at Baltimore, Maryland, 1820—1897.

Index to Passenger Lists of Vessels Arriving at Boston, Massachusetts, 1849—1891.

Index to Passenger Lists of Vessels Arriving at Philadelphia, Pennsylvania, 1800—1906.

Newberry Library

Index to Passenger Lists of Vessels Arriving at New York, NY, 1902—1943.

Index to Passenger Lists of Vessels Arriving at New Orleans, 1820—1902.

Family History Centers

The family history centers of The Church of Jesus Christ of Latter-day Saints have available a catalog including a large number of passenger lists and indexes on microfilm that may be ordered from the Family History Library in Salt Lake City through a family history center (for Chicago area locations see section 16).

Maritime Records

Chicago Historical Society

The Chicago Historical Society has a great number of publications cataloged which provide a sound basis for maritime research.

The Chicago Historical Society
Clark Street at North Avenue
Chicago, IL 60614-6099
(312-642-4600)

National Archives—Great Lakes Region

The National Archives-Great Lakes Region has the records of the Bureau of Marine Inspection for Illinois, 1865-1952. Certificates of enrollment and licensing of commercial vessels and yachts; oaths taken by owners and masters; records of mortgages and bills of sale of vessels; and correspondence regarding vessel documentation are arranged chronologically.

Records of shipwrecks were indexed by a volunteer (Don Reilly) to make these records more accessible. His "Index to Records of Wrecks and Other Casualties, 1908-1941" was based on records from the Chicago Office of the Bureau of Customs (RG 36).

National Archives—Great Lakes Region
7358 Pulaski Road
Chicago, IL 60629
(312-581-7816)

Suggested References

Conzen, Michael P., and Kay J. Carr, eds. *The Illinois & Michigan Canal: National Heritage Corridor: A Guide to its History and Sources.* DeKalb, IL: Northern Illinois University Press, 1988.

Feltner, Charles E., and Jeri Baron Feltner. *Great Lakes Maritime History: Bibliography and Sources of Information.* Dearborn, MI: Seajay Publications, 1982.

This bibliography is a valuable source for anyone interested in Great Lakes maritime history. There are over one thousand entries organized in twelve categories which include: Reference Works; Great Lakes History; Ship History; Directories and Registers; Shipbuilding and Ship Construction; Shipwreck History; U. S. Government Organizations; Charts, Maps and Cartography; Newspapers and Periodicals; Photographic Collections; Special Topics; Archives, Societies and Museums.

SECTION THIRTY-THREE

Societies: Fraternal, Social, and Patriotic

By Linda Stone Lamberty

After you have searched the more conventional sources without success, you may need to try fraternal, social, and patriotic society records. Locating these records and examining them can be a complicated and time-consuming process. However, with patience and perseverance you may unearth enough information to keep going.

Societies are formed for many reasons. Some are job-oriented, and many are ethnic. Some are social groups, perhaps with philanthropic aspects, and vice versa; others form for some mutual benefit, but may have a social purpose too. The information they record varies. Excluding groups with a genealogical or historical focus, they have one thing in common: their records are not for the benefit of outsiders doing personal research.

The individuals who maintain records for an organization have many duties. Receive graciously whatever information you glean from the kind souls who help. In the past, Masonic Grand Secretaries have generously responded to numerous inquiries.

Your initial step is to determine whether the individual you are researching was associated with some society. If family members cannot help, clues may be found in a death notice, an obituary, a biographical note, a probate record, a headstone, or among personal possessions. In early years, a death notice might not provide much information, but under "Fraternal Notices" in the classified section of an old newspaper, you might find a reference to a deceased "brother" (and probably the name of the organization). Personal papers or jewelry may bear an insignia containing initials or words. You should examine old photographs closely for previously unnoticed rings, medallions, watchfobs, or other items that could provide a clue to membership in some organization. Painstaking research may be necessary to merely identify the social organization represented by an item. Bear in mind, the individual could have belonged to more than one organization. Within any organization there might be subgroups, and each subgroup might have its own records. Research an organization to improve your chances of getting useful information.

Many libraries and historical societies list a variety of printed sources under headings like: associations, clubs, fraternities, lodges, organizations, and societies. Some of these sources are devoted to specific organizations. Check the sources for the organization you are interested in, including any printed histories and directories of the time. The *History of Chicago* by A.T. Andreas gives detailed histories of organizations in the city, and his *History of Cook County, Illinois* provides much of the same information for the suburbs prior to 1885. Encyclopedias are another source of information about established national or international organizations (for example, the Masons and the Oddfellows). An understanding of the history and functions of such complex organizations sometimes leads to records otherwise ignored. Current organization directories that provide addresses are available. The *Yellow Pages* include many, but the organization might be listed under a different (but similar) name.

If the organization you seek no longer exists, you must determine where its records, if any, were stored. A fraternal lodge may merge with another, but its records are often retained by the lodge it joined. Records of an organization may have been stored in a local library, historical society, or an individual's home. Many records were discarded, and fires and floods have destroyed records intended for posterity. However, if you can identify significant dates in the history of an organization, examine the local newspapers, especially nostalgia columns, for more information. The organization may have published a newsletter, magazine, or its own history; copies may be on file somewhere. These types of publications can be a good source for obituaries, biographical notes on milestone birthdays, or anniversaries of individual members.

Ancient Free and Accepted Masons

Freemasonry originated centuries ago as a stonecraft. Craftsmen travelled the countryside to work, and they felt it necessary to develop some secret means (word or handshake) to differentiate Apprentices and Fellows of the Craft from cowans (workmen who had not been apprenticed or had been poorly taught). The lodge in their home jurisdiction was a workshop as well as a place to relax and speak freely, thus necessitating a bond of secrecy between fellows to protect themselves from employers and non-masons.

With the decline of cathedral building in the seventeenth century, many of the stonecraft groups became purely social organizations. They began to admit men who had not worked in stonecraft (called Speculative Masons). As the numbers of non-craftsmen members increased, these gentlemen Masons became known as Accepted Masons. Between 1737 and 1907, about 16 English princes of royal blood had joined the brotherhood, and over the years many of the world's elite in government and society have been members of the Masonic fraternity.

In Illinois, the first Masonic Blue Lodge (so called because of the official color, and comprising Masons having achieved the first three degrees) was formed in 1805 at Kaskaskia. A Grand Lodge was formed in Vandalia in December of 1822, but was discontinued in about 1828 because of controversy about the order. Out of this controversy was born the Anti-Masonic party which helped to form the Whig party in 1834. The Masonic society dispersed, and the remaining Masonic factions survived underground until about 1835 when they began to regroup.

In April of 1840, an Illinois Masonic Grand Lodge was again established by 127 members of six lodges in the state. Certainly Masons lived in Chicago before the creation of lodges in the city, and while degrees could still be conferred by the required number of Masons of appropriate degree and standing, without lodges there would have been no records of their actions as Masons.

In 1846 an anti-Masonic society was organized in Illinois. Politically driven, this group chose to warn voters by publishing names of known Masons. In 1850, only two of the Chicago Blue Lodges chartered in the early 1840s remained (LaFayette #18 & Oriental #33; the number following the name of a lodge is the sequence in which charters were granted by the state Grand Lodge). By 1875, the number of Blue Lodges had risen to 34 in the city and 10 in surrounding Cook County.

Note that, unless the lodge surrendered it or the lodge merged with another, the lodge number remains the same, even if the name of a particular lodge was changed.

Organization

Though Masonic lodges existed during the colonial years, they were governed by provincial Grand Lodges whose grand masters were under the Masonic authority in Great Britain. After the Revolutionary War, the provincial grand bodies declared themselves independent, each confining itself within state boundaries where they remained supreme in Masonic matters. Thus in each state a Grand Lodge governs the Blue Lodges with no nationwide or worldwide authority above it.

Upon receipt of the 3rd degree (Master Mason), a Blue Lodge Mason has the option to earn additional degrees in the York Rite or Scottish Rite (not mutually exclusive). With each degree, the Mason is eligible for membership in other (appendant) Masonic societies.

The York Rite is a name for the Capitular, Cryptic (optional), and Templar Rites. Each of these rites comprises named and numbered degrees culminating in the 33rd degree, or Knight Templar. The Templar Rite is exclusively Christian. The Capitular chapters, Cryptic councils and Templar commanderies each come under the authority of a state Grand Body, which in turn answers to a nationwide general Grand Body. These grand bodies do not retain records on individual members of the subordinate groups.

In the Scottish Rite, the lodges, councils, chapters and consistories progressively confer the 4th through the 32nd degrees. These bodies are governed by a Supreme Council. The 33rd degree is an honorary degree bestowed on individuals by the governing Supreme Council in recognition of outstanding service; the degree may not be requested.

The first Supreme Council of the Scottish Rite was established at Charleston, South Carolina in 1801. A Supreme Council is a parent body composed of active 33rd degree Masons, which elects its own members. Each country is entitled to only one Supreme Council, but due to difficulties of travel in colonial times in the United States, a second Supreme Council (northern jurisdiction) was established. It governs all states (termed "orients") north of the Ohio River and east of the Mississippi River; the first Supreme Council in Charleston (southern jurisdiction) governs all remaining states and territories. For information pertaining only to 33rd degree Masons of the Scottish Rite in the northern jurisdiction contact:

Supreme Council of the Scottish Rite
  P.O. Box 519
  Lexington, MA 02173

The Blue Lodges and the York and Scottish Rites groups are the foundation of Masonic society. There are more than one hundred other independent Masonic organizations. These organizations are especially prevalent in the United

States. Among the most notable are the Order of the Eastern Star (includes women), Imperial Council of the Ancient Arabic Order of Nobles of the Mystic Shrine (known as the Shriners; 32nd degree Masons or Knights Templar), the Order of DeMolay (boys), and the Order of Job's Daughters (girls). The National League of Masonic Clubs has chartered many of the hundreds of such local organizations. English Masons are forbidden to affiliate with these extra-curricular appendant orders.

Records

The Blue Lodge records of the state Grand Secretary is the best initial source. Beyond that, your research is limited to individual lodge records and proceedings, which usually give little relevant information. Many of these records suffered from fires and floods, even recently. But, if you are desperate for clues, you may want to search these records.

When examining records, note that a member who is listed as *dimitted*, requested that his name be removed (usually a date is given). A member often did this to join another lodge. A member listed as *suspended* was removed from the roster by the lodge, perhaps for not paying his dues.

The Illinois Grand Secretary has records for every Mason in Illinois since 1840. When a Blue Lodge disbands its records are usually taken over by the office of the Grand Secretary. However, fires in 1850 and 1870 left only the records of annual Grand Lodge proceedings for research. In records after 1871, some dates and places of birth and death are available. The individual records system did not originate until about 1930.

Illinois Grand Secretary
  Grand Lodge A.F. & A.M.
  Box 4147
  Springfield, IL 62708

By 1883, most of the fraternal organizations that existed in the country were represented in Chicago. At least 570

lodges were listed in the city directory. A general history of
many of these groups can be found in:

Fraternal Directory. San Francisco: The Bancroft Co., 1889.

Chicago Directory of Lodges for the Year 1883. Chicago: C.
F. Lichtner & Bro.

> Contains a list of the lodges in Chicago for 1883,
> including memberships of many.

The Calumet Club

The history of the Calumet Club and accounts of its receptions make interesting research and reading. Chartered by
the state in 1878, the Calumet Club was organized on the
near South Side of Chicago as a gentlemen's social club
that was open to early and distinguished settlers of the
city.

As early as the 1850s, and again in 1871, unsuccessful
attempts were made to organize an old settlers' society. In
May of 1879, the Calumet Club finally achieved a measure
of success when it extended an invitation to a reception to
settlers who had come to Chicago as adults before 1840.
This reception became an annual event under the direct
supervision of qualifying old settlers who were members of
the Calumet Club. Information about those who attended
the first reception in 1879 can be found in *Reception to the
Settlers of Chicago Prior to 1840 by the Calumet Club of
Chicago,* and on pages 394 to 397 in Volume 3 of the *History of Chicago* by Alfred T. Andreas. In May of 1885, the
invitations to this event numbered almost 450, and the
collection of relics and records of pioneers grew to significant proportions. Unfortunately, much of the collection
was destroyed by a fire in 1893.

Membership in 1885 numbered 581 regular and 28 non-
residents, and eventually rose to 800, but declined to approximately 100 by 1917. In November of that year, the
Calumet Club closed as a social institution forever.

Patriotic Societies

Sons of The American Revolution—SAR

In anticipation of the centennial celebrations in 1876, a state society, Sons of the American Revolution was proposed in San Francisco, California in 1875. Organized there on July 4, 1876, it was the first of many SAR groups that formed in other states. A national society was not organized until 1889, at which time efforts were made to create an SAR society in Illinois. As a result of receptions at the Iroquois and Union League Clubs in Chicago, the Illinois SAR was organized in January of 1890.

The objectives of the SAR were patriotic and social. Applicants were required to be male, 21 years of age, a citizen of good repute, and lineally descended from an active, recognized soldier or patriot of the American Revolution.

Daughters of the American Revolution—DAR

With eligibility requirements similar to those of the SAR, the Daughters of the American Revolution (DAR) was organized in 1890 after a motion to admit women into the SAR was voted down. Within a year, the first chapter in Chicago was organized. In 1895, the DAR created the Children of the American Revolution (C.A.R.).

In addition to its many charitable, educational, and historic preservation activities, one ongoing project of the DAR is the acquisition of transcripts of old Bible records, regardless of whether or not they apply to a patriotic family. These are maintained at the DAR library in Washington, DC. Numbered *DAR Lineage Books* and *Lineage and Revolutionary Record Books* (containing lineages of members), as well as *The Patriot Index* which lists Revolutionary War patriots, are bound and indexed periodically. These can be found on the open shelves at the Newberry Library. Documentation cited in earlier membership applications, is a good source of information.

The excellent DAR Library (1776 D. Street, N.W., Washington, DC 20000) is open to the public year round except for the month of April. The library staff does not do research in response to requests, but it will send you a list of individuals who will (for a fee). The library staff will send photocopies of up to 30 specified pages, per day, by mail for a copy fee per page. Recent catalogues of the contents of the library have been published by the DAR.

Illinois Athletic Club—IAC

The Illinois Athletic Club was founded and organized by Chicago Mayor William Hale "Big Bill" Thompson and a small group of friends and businessmen who desired a place to exercise, relax and entertain. The IAC was chartered by the State of Illinois in 1904. Their only assets were a box of cigars, an architect's plan, and sketch (done in good faith). This ingenious group led the press to believe that something big was in the works. With the ensuing publicity, the needed applicants for membership began showing up. Ground was broken for a club facility in February, 1905. Construction of an impressive 12-story building was completed in November, 1907, and is still standing at 112 S. Michigan Avenue. With facilities to accommodate quite a variety of sports, the IAC sponsored many accomplished athletes, including some Olympic champions.

After many years of making a name and a place for itself in the history of the city and the nation, the IAC encountered financial difficulties and sold out to the Charlie Fitness Club chain. The Charlie Fitness Club and Hotel subsequently went out of business. The Chicago Historical Society Library has quite an extensive run of the IAC magazine: June 1912-1925, Aug 1927, 1933-1955, and 1957-1965.

Bibliography

Encyclopedia of Associations. Annual, 19th ed., 5 vols. Detroit: Gale Research Company, 1985.

Volume 1 lists addresses and other information for National Organizations of the United States.

SECTION THIRTY-FOUR

Vital Records

Vital records, regardless of where they are found, are documents which officially mark the significant events of life: birth, marriage and death. Vital statistics, as considered here, are compiled from the official records of birth, marriage and death created and maintained by governmental agencies (local, state, or federal). Whether found in a county clerk's office or in newspapers, vital records are prime sources for documenting individuals' lives.

Compulsory recording of vital statistics did not begin until January 1, 1916 in Illinois, however, a large percentage of births, deaths, and marriages were registered with Cook County in earlier years.

The Chicago Fire of 1871 destroyed the Cook County Court House and the official documents which were recorded and filed prior to that date. For verification of events which were registered before the fire, or for information on events not officially registered, alternative solutions are often available. You may find birth, marriage, or death information in church records, histories, biographies, Bible records, newspapers, employment records, military records, and cemeteries. Approximate birth dates can be obtained from census and school records.

Cook County Bureau of Vital Statistics

The Cook County Clerk is legally responsible to preserve the orginal, and provide copies of, birth, death, and marriage records generated within the county limits. It is the job of the Bureau of Vital Statistics to receive, process, and store these vital records. Because of the huge volume of records created by a large metropolitan population (over 40 million), it is impractical to search the birth, marriage, and death indexes. Cook County exercises home rule, and does not allow the free access to records taken for granted in some less-populated counties in the state. On a typical day, a thousand vital statistics requests are processed by the Office of the County Clerk, giving it the distinction of being the world's busiest vital statistics office.

Obtaining birth, death, or marriage records from the Cook County Vital Statistics office in Chicago was seldom a problem in years past. With correct identification, you could request a search of indexes, and the clerks were almost always able to provide the certificates within an hour.

Then a major newspaper broke the story of a few unscrupulous individuals who were buying and selling records for the purpose of obtaining false identification. The well-meaning, Cook County Clerk moved quickly to avert any such criminal activity in his own office. Without advance notice, access to birth and death records in Cook County was essentially denied starting in July, 1991. This action brought immediate protests from many individuals who needed records for legitimate, and often urgent, reasons.

Asked to review the matter, the State Attorney determined that in allowing "open access" to birth and death records, Cook County had not been in compliance with the Illinois Vital Records Act. After hearing from a number of family historians, professional genealogists, and genealogical societies, Illinois State Senator John Cullerton (Chicago) sponsored a bill to remedy the situation. Attorney, and genealogist, Ronald Otto assisted in drafting Senate Bill 2062, which was introduced by Senator Cullerton, and signed by Governor Jim Edgar on September 11, 1992.

The bill that became law on January 1, 1993 applies to all Illinois counties. It allows county clerks to issue copies stamped "For genealogical purposes only" of birth records 75 years or older and death records 20 years or older. Marriage records are open to the public and are not restricted.

A fee of $7.00 is required for a three-year search of each vital record (birth, marriage, or death). The current fee includes one certified copy of the record if it is found. Additional copies are $2.00 each. A certified notice that a particular search has been made will be issued if a record cannot be found. Under Illinois State law, search fees are not refundable, even when a vital record is not located. All fees are subject to change.

Bureau of Vital Statistics
  Cook County, Lower Concourse
  118 North Clark Street
  Chicago, IL 60602
  (312-443-7790)

Hours: Monday-Friday 8:30 A.M.—5 P.M.; closed Saturday, Sunday and holidays.

Cook County vital records are available at suburban locations also, but you cannot get a death record in person the same day you request it. The following suburban offices are open from 9 A.M.—5 P.M. Monday through Friday and 9 A.M.—12:00 P.M. on Saturday:

  10220 South 76th Avenue, Bridgeview

  16501 South Kedzie Avenue, Markham

  1311 Maybrook Square, Maywood

  5600 West Old Orchard, Skokie

  2121 Euclid Avenue, Rolling Meadows

The increased use of vital records for fraudulent purposes has necessitated more vigilant enforcement of Illinois state statutes, and these changes are reflected in the forms used to request vital records in Cook County. Although the newer restrictions may seem inconvenient, they serve to protect us from those who would use our records for false identification. The more information you supply when requesting a record will improve your chances of getting positive results. It is generally understood that genealogists do not always have all the information requested on the forms that must be filled out to secure a certificate, and some exceptions are made. In early years, a baby that was unnamed at the time of the birth was registered with "Baby" as a first name. Often a baby's name was changed after due reflection on the part of the parents, and a name used later in life will not be the name registered with the county. As in any other records, clerical errors and careless handwriting make searches more difficult, if not impossible.

Birth Records

Birth records and other official vital statistics were destroyed in the Chicago Fire. To further complicate matters, fewer births were registered in early years because many babies were born at home with only a midwife in attendance.

Cook County Birth Records

A typical Cook County birth certificate in the 1870s provided: the child's name; number of children of the mother; race and sex; date and place of birth; nationality, place of birth, and age of each parent; full and maiden name of mother and her residence; full name of father and his occupation; name and address of the medical attendant; and the date of birth registration. Information provided on birth certificates changed little over the years until about 1920 when more questions (mostly of a medical nature) were added to city and county forms.

The Genealogical Society of Utah has microfilmed the following birth records:

Cook County (Illinois). County Clerk. *Chicago birth registers, 1871-1922.*

> These are microfilmed versions of original records at the Cook County Courthouse in Chicago, and ar-

STANLEY T. KUSPER, JR., County Clerk

Form CB

REQUEST FOR PHOTOSTATIC COPY OF

BIRTH RECORDS

Before Filling Out Application Be Certain BIRTH Occurred in Cook County

Name _____

First Name   Middle Name   Last Name

Date of Birth _____

Place of Birth _____

Name of Father _____

Maiden Name of Mother _____

First Name   Middle Name   Last Name

I, the undersigned do hereby certify that as the person whose record is sought, or as the parent, guardian, or legal representative of the person, am legally entitled according to the Illinois State Statute [Chap. 111-1/2, Sec. 73-25(4)(b)] to receive the requested certified copy.

_____
Name of Person Requesting Copy

_____
Signature of Person Requesting Copy

_____
Address

_____
City

_____
Relationship of Person Requesting Copy

Please Enclose Self Addressed
Stamped Envelope

Kindly Mail Certificate to:

Name _____

Address _____

City_____ **State** _____ **Zip Code** _____

Statutory Fee for All Searches is $5,.00 for each 3 Year period searched.
If Record is Found a Certified Copy Will Be Mailed Free of Charge.
Additional copies are $2.00 each.

Make Remittance by Money Order or Check, Payable to:

STANLEY T. KUSPER, JR., County Clerk

Bureau of Vital Statistics (Lower Randolph Street Concourse)
118 North Clark Street, Chicago, Illinois 60602

Figure 22: Application for Birth Record
(may be photocopied)

ranged by certificate number within each year (906 microfilm reels).

For indexes to Cook County births on microfiche, check the Family History Card Catalog locality fiche or the author-title indexes under Cook County (Illinois) County Clerk. *Birth record indexes 1871-1916.*

Cook County (Illinois). County Clerk. *County birth records, 1878-1894.*

Microfilmed versions of original records at the Cook County Courthouse in Chicago (31 microfilm reels).

For indexes to Cook County births on microfiche, check the Family HIstory Card Catalog locality fiche or the author-title indexes under Cook County (Illinois) County Clerk. *Birth record indexes 1871—1916.* Arranged by certificate number within each year.

Northwestern University Hospital Archives Birth Records

The Northwestern University Hospital Archives have the records of several older hospitals; some of them are now defunct. The Genealogical Society of Utah has microfilmed part of the hospital collection which included birth records. The archives are open Monday through Friday from 8:30 A.M.—5:00 P.M. Call for further information regarding holdings, finding aids, and access to collections. Photocopy and microform copies are available for materials not restricted.

Hospital Information
  The Northwestern University Group Archives
  329 West 18th Street, Suite 901
  Chicago, IL 60616
  (312-908-3090)

Additional information about the archives may be found in an article by Rima Schultz in the newsletter (*Origins*) of the Local & Family History Section and the Family & Community History Center at the Newberry Library:

Schultz, Rima. "Discoveries in the Stacks." *Origins* 1, no.3 (April 1985): 6-7.

The Genealogical Society of Utah has microfilmed thousands of birth records and case records of the Chicago Maternity Center, 1896-1933. The records include those of the Maxwell Street Dispensary, the Newberry Clinic, Chicago Lying-In Hospital, and the Stockyards Clinic.

The records contain the only copies of birth certificates of a number of persons born in the area. Because Chicago did not require registration of babies born at home prior to 1915, Northwestern Memorial has the only record of thousands of births during the thirty-five-year period.

Chicago (Illinois) birth records, 1896-1933.

These are microfilmed versions of original records in the Northwestern University Hospital, Chicago (14 microfilm reels).

Cook County (Illinois). County Clerk. *County birth registers, 1916-1922* (34 microfilm reels).

For indexes to Cook County births on microfiche, check the Family History Card Catalog locality fiche or author-title indexes under Cook County (Illinois) County Clerk, *Birth record indexes 1871-1916.*

Cook County (Illinois). County Clerk. *Chicago delayed birth indexes, 1871-1948* (7 microfilm reels).

These are microfilmed versions of original records at the Cook County Courthouse in Chicago; not listed in strict alphabetical order.

Cook County (Illinois). County Clerk. *Birth corrections and indexes, 1871-1915* (17 microfilm reels).

Microfilm of original records at the Cook County Courthouse, in Chicago; not in strict alphabetical order. Includes some actual birth records.

Cook County (Illinois). County Clerk. *Birth corrections and delayed births 1916-1918* (21 microfilm reels) .

Microfilm of original records at the Cook County Courthouse, Chicago, Illinois.

Marriage Records

Cook County Marriage Records

Marriage records begin in 1871 in Cook County. Upon completion of a request form, a copy of the marriage license (if found) will be furnished. Information provided on marriage licenses has not changed significantly over time. The names of the bride and groom, their respective towns or cities of residence, and their ages are given. Some of the most helpful information often comes from the information provided by the individual who officiated at the marriage. By linking the name of the minister, priest, or rabbi with the congregation to which he belonged, you may find additional religious records that will lead to other family relationships. The exact address of the person officiating was added to the licenses in the 1920s. Unfortunately, the addresses of brides and grooms were not furnished. Marriages which were performed by a justice of the peace present a more difficult problem; any records that were kept would have remained in the possession of the justice. (*Note: The author has not been successful in locating any of these collections.*)

Unlike other Illinois counties, the marriage applications in Cook County are not any more complete than the marriage licenses. It was not until the 1920s when the exact birth dates of brides and grooms were added. In 1962 marriage applications changed, and specific addresses of brides and grooms were provided. It was not until January 2, 1968 that a Cook County marriage application asked for birthplaces and the names of the applicant's parents.

Marriages in Cook County were indexed from 1871 to 1878 by the name of the groom. Unless you know his name, a long and tedious page-by-page search must be made to locate a record. In some cases, the ink in the old ledgers has faded to the extent that microfilming is impossible.

Sources for Cook County Marriage Records

The Genealogical Society of Utah has microfilmed these marriage records:

STANLEY T. KUSPER, JR., County Clerk

Form CM

REQUEST FOR PHOTOSTATIC COPY OF

MARRIAGE RECORDS

Before Filling Out Application Be Certain MARRIAGE Occurred in Cook County

Name of Husband

_____

First Name   Middle Name   Last Name

Wife's Name at Time of Marriage

_____

First Name   Middle Name   Last Name

Date of Marriage _____

Date License Issued _____

Place of Marriage _____

City, Town or Village

I, the undersigned do hereby certify that I am a person, or a duly authorized agent of a person, who is legally entitled to the marriage certificate requested above, as specified by State Statute.

_____

Name of Person Requesting Copy

_____

Signature of Person Requesting Copy

_____

Address

_____

City   Relationship of Person Requesting Copy

Please Enclose Self Addressed
Stamped Envelope

Kindly Mail Certificate to:

Name _____

Address _____

City _____ **State** _____ **Zip Code** _____

Statutory Fee for All Searches is $5,.00 for each 3 Year period searched.
If Record is Found a Certified Copy Will Be Mailed Free of Charge.
Additional copies are $2.00 each.

Make Remittance by Money Order or Check, Payable to:

STANLEY T. KUSPER, JR., County Clerk

Bureau of Vital Statistics (Lower Randolph Street Concourse)
118 North Clark Street, Chicago, Illinois 60602

Figure 23: Application for Marriage Record
(may be photocopied)

Cook County (Illinois). County Clerk. *Marriage licenses, 1871-1920; index, 1871-1916.* (709 microfilm reels)

> Microfilmed versions of original records at the Cook County Courthouse in Chicago. Beginning in 1894, marriage licenses obtained in Chicago were segregated from other Cook County licenses. Within each sequence of one hundred numbers, the Cook County licenses come first, followed by licenses from Chicago. Licenses are arranged numerically and chronologically, but some that are in correct chronological order are misnumbered. A spade mark on a license indicates a numbering problem. Most years have out-of-order licenses indicated as "misc." Prior to 1894 licenses were held by the Clerk of the County Court. A few licenses are for the time prior to the Chicago Fire. Indexes for females did not begin until 1878.

Alternative sources include:

Alguire, Joan L. *Some Cook County Marriages Prior to the Fire.* South Holland, Ill.: The South Suburban Genealogical and Historical Society, 1981.

> Contains abstracts of 423 marriage licenses issued within the year before the 1871 Chicago Fire, and includes an index. Microfilmed by the Genealogical Society of Utah (1 microfilm reel).

The Illinois State Archives and the Illinois State Genealogical Society have collaborated for several years to index marriage records for all Illinois counties. To date, 38 counties are completed and 76 represented. Relatively few Cook County marriages have been entered into the statewide database thus far, but the index will be increasingly important to Cook County researchers in the future. Although it is a work in progress, a set of microfiche has been published and is available for use at the Illinois State Archives in Springfield, the South Suburban Genealogical and Historical Society Library, and various other repositories, mostly in Illinois. For further information, contact The

Illinois State Genealogical Society, P.O. Box 10195, Springfield, IL 62791-0195.

Newbill, Leona Hopper. *Cook County, Illinois Marriage License Records 1870-1880.*

A typescript with bride and groom index. Microfilmed by the Genealogical Society of Utah (1 microfilm reel).

Sam Fink's Chicago Marriage and Death Index

A microfilm copy of the typescript *Chicago Marriage and Death Index* compiled by Sam Fink, and in his custody, has been microfilmed by the Genealogical Society of Utah. The microfilm is available at family history centers (see section 16) and at the Newberry Library. The marriage portion of the index was duplicated and appears twice on the film (as it does in the original volume). Information for the marriage and death index originated in the *Chicago Tribune, Chicago Evening Journal, Chicago Democrat, Chicago Examiner, Chicago Evening Post, Chicago Record Herald, Chicago Daily News, Chicago Examiner,* and the *Inter-Ocean.*

The marriage index covers the years 1833-1871. The death index covers the years 1856-1889. The film is in the locality section of the Family History Library catalog under Illinois, Cook, Vital Records Indexes—Chicago Marriage and Death Indexes in the custody of Sam Fink—film #1321939.

Chicago Marriages in Crown Point, Indiana 1915-1940

By Herbert H. Post

An estimated 175,000 marriages, many of them couples from Chicago and environs, took place in Crown Point, Indiana during the period from 1915 to 1940. Four justices of the peace in Crown Point, not far from Chicago, advertised "quick, painless marriages" at minimal costs. They advertised in Chicago and other midwest city newspapers, and on Pathe News Service newsreels (the equivalent of today's television commercials). Elopement and marriage in Crown Point became the "in" thing to do, and thousands of

Chicagoans were attracted to Crown Point for marriage in what became known as the "Marriage Mills." Rudolph Valentino and the Mills Brothers are among the celebrities who were married at Crown Point in its heyday.

The years from 1937 to 1940 were the busiest. Illinois had passed a tough blood test law in 1937 and, with war clouds gathering in Europe, many Chicago area couples took advantage of the quick marriages available at nearby Crown Point. Crown Point was then accessible by trolley car, and the "Marriage Mills" operated twenty-four hours a day.

In 1940 Indiana passed a marriage law requiring blood tests and a three-day waiting period. The "Marriage Mills" ground to a sudden and permanent halt.

Crown Point is the county seat of Lake County, Indiana. The very early years of the "Marriage Mill" records can be readily accessed through the *Index to Marriage Records, Lake County, Indiana, 1805-1920 Inclusive*, done by the WPA in nine alphabetically arranged volumes. Locations where these volumes can be found include:

The Allen County Public Library, 900 Webster Street, Fort Wayne, IN 46302.

The Lake County Public Library in the Indiana Room, 1919 W. Lincoln Highway, Merrillville, IN 46410.

The Newberry Library, 60 W. Walton, Chicago, IL 60610-6099.

Records from 1920 to 1940 can be obtained by writing to the Recorder's Office, Marriage Clerk, Lake County Government Center, 2293 North Main Street, Crown Point, IN 46307. These records are indexed by years, and they will make a three-year search of their index. They ask that you submit the name of both the bride and groom and the date of marriage.

Some related references include:

Index to Marriage Records, Lake County, Indiana 1850-1920 Inclusive. 9 vols. Works Progress Administration, 1939.

"The Marrying Squires of Crown Point." *The Lake County Star*, April 18, 1974. Feature article.

Swisher, Charles W., and Mable Wise, eds. *Crown Point, Indiana 1834-1984, The Hub City*. Crown Point, Ind., 1984.

_____, *Souvenir of Crown Point's Anniversary, 1834-1959, 125 Years*. Crown Point, Ind., 1959.

Death Records

Death records are available in Cook County from 1871. They are often the easiest to access because the date of death was recorded conscientiously, and the records are often found by locating the date in indexes. In many ways, death records are some of the most helpful. The information recorded on a death certificate, a mortician's record, a coroner's record, cemetery record, in a probate, an obituary, or a church record can provide details about the deceased and may identify other family members. There is no strict order to follow if you plan to search death records. Often you begin with the known facts and work toward the unknown. If an exact death date is known, a copy of a death certificate is the best starting point. It should provide important facts about the individual and place of burial. Cemetery research will often identify other family members who may be buried in the same plot. Probate records provide exact death dates, and often list the place of burial, widows, heirs, and previous marriages. For Cook County, they have the advantage of being indexed by year.

Chicago Deaths 1871-1933 is an index which makes it possible to find death dates for a large percentage of Chicagoans who died within that time period. Detailed discussion of mortician's records, coroner's records, cemetery records, probates, obituaries, and church records will be found under appropriate headings in this volume.

Death Certificates

A typical death certificate from Chicago or Cook County (both are issued from the Cook County Bureau of Vital Statistics) from the 1870s will provide: the full name, age, sex, marital status, occupation, date and hour of death, cause, and the duration of any disease which caused the death. Other information requested on the standard forms were: the street address and the ward; nationality and place of birth; and length of residence in the state. The place and date of burial and the name and address of the undertaker are other valuable items noted on a certificate of death. Not until 1910 were the names and birthplaces of the deceased's parents included on death certificates.

Microfilmed Death Records

The Genealogical Society of Utah has microfilmed the following death records:

Cook County (Illinois). County Clerk. *Chicago death certificates, 1878-1915* (655 microfilm reels).

These are microfilmed versions of original records in the Cook County Courthouse. The certificates are divided into four-month periods: January to April; May to August; and September to December. Numbering begins at "1" for each period. The early years may be divided into two periods of six months each. After obtaining a name and date from the microfiche index, you must look in the appropriate sequence of numbers. For example, John Doe died in June, 1911, and his certificate number is listed as being 1001. His death certificate would be found in the second numbering sequence for 1911 (May-August). Certificates are arranged numerically. Many certificates are missing or were filmed out of sequence. Certificates for some months are arranged alphabetically by first letter of surname, and some county certificates are filed with city certificates.

Cook County (Illinois). County Clerk. *Death record indexes, 1871-1916* (on 70 microfiches).

These are microfiche copies of the original indexes at the Cook County Courthouse in Chicago.

Cook County (Illinois). County Coroner. *Coroner's death records, 1879-1904.*

STANLEY T. KUSPER, JR., County Clerk

Form CD

REQUEST FOR PHOTOSTATIC COPY OF

DEATH RECORDS

Before Filling Out Application Be Certain DEATH Occurred in Cook County

Name _____

First Name   Middle Name   Last Name

Date of Death _____

Place of Death _____

City, Town or Village

I, the undersigned do hereby certify that I am a person, or a duly authorized agent of a person, who has a personal or property right interest in the death certificate, and am legally entitled to the certificate, as specifed by Illinois State Statute [Chap. 111-1/2, Sec. 73-25(4)(d)].

_____

Name of Person Requesting Copy

_____

Signature of Person Requesting Copy

_____

Address

_____

City

_____

Relationship of Person Requesting Copy

Please Enclose Self Addressed
Stamped Envelope

Kindly Mail Certificate of Death to:

Name _____

Address _____

City _____ **State** _____ **Zip Code** _____

Statutory Fee for All Searches is $5,.00 for each 3 Year period searched.
If Record is Found a Certified Copy Will Be Mailed Free of Charge.
Additional copies are $2.00 each.

Make Remittance by Money Order or Check, Payable to:

STANLEY T. KUSPER, JR., County Clerk

Bureau of Vital Statistics (Lower Randolph Street Concourse)
118 North Clark Street, Chicago, Illinois 60602

Figure 24: Application for Death Record

(may be photocopied)

Microfilmed versions of original records at the Cook
County Courthouse. The records for each month are
arranged alphabetically by first letter of surname.

Chicago (Illinois). Board of Health. *Chicago Deaths 1871-
1933* (13 microfilm reels).

An alphabetical listing of Chicago and Cook County
deaths obtained from documents returned to the clerk.
The information includes: name, address, date of
death, and register number. (A register number is no
longer used; do not include it when filling out a request form for a death certificate.) This is the quickest
means of finding a death date for individuals in Chicago. It is not all-inclusive but it does include some
Chicagoans who died out of town, and stillbirths.

The index was compiled by the Works Progress Administration, and is alphabetically arranged by surname. To find the appropriate microfilm reel, use the
film number in this list:

Chicago Deaths	A-Bou	Film #1295943
Chicago Deaths	Bou-Cul	Film #1295944
Chicago Deaths	Cul-Fol	Film #1295945
Chicago Deaths	Fol-Haw	Film #1295946
Chicago Deaths	Haw-J	Film #1295947
Chicago Deaths	K-Lap	Film #1295948
Chicago Deaths	Lap-McB	Film #1295949
Chicago Deaths	McC-OB	Film #1295971
Chicago Deaths	Obr-Rep	Film #1295972
Chicago Deaths	Rep-Sik	Film #1295973
Chicago Deaths	Sik-Ste	Film #1295974
Chicago Deaths	Ste-Wal	Film #1295975
Chicago Deaths	Wal-Z	Film #1295976

(The criteria for inclusion of deaths on this list remains unknown. It would seem that they are burial
permits and their respective registration numbers
with the Chicago Board of Health. This would explain
the fact that the numbers do not agree with death
certificate numbers. Additionally, it would provide a

reason for the inclusion of out-of-town deaths and the absence of some persons who died in Chicago but whose names do not appear in the index.)

Death certificates for persons who appear on the list with an out-of-town address cannot be obtained in the Cook County Bureau of Vital Statistics even though the names appear on the index, but must be ordered from the city or county listed after the name of the individual. Those included in the list with an out-of-town address are almost always found to be buried in a Chicago-area cemetery.

It has been estimated that by 1918, over 95 percent of all deaths in Illinois were registered each year. The Illinois Department of Public Health, Division of Vital Records, has published a microfiche index to Illinois death information filed from 1916 to 1943. The index is available for patron use at the Illinois State Archives in Springfield, South Suburban Genealogical and Historical Society Library in South Holland, and family history centers (microfiche 6016852).

The death certificates for this time period in Illinois are also available on several hundred rolls of microfilm. The Illinois State Archives has the microfilm copy of the death certificates and will provide photocopies upon request by mail. Do not send money with your request. They will invoice you for the amount per certificate.

For further information regarding the use of these microfilms at a family history center, consult their catalog under the heading: Illinois—Vital Records.

When checking the microfilmed death records, check also the Social Security Death Benefit Records index. Published on CD-ROM by Automated Archives, Inc., this index contains approximately 50 million names of individuals to whom a lump sum payment was made by the Social Security Administration. Although the records are from 1937-1993, many of the people listed were born in the late 1800s or early 1900s. This index is available for patron use at a family history center and at the South Suburban Genealogical and Historical Society Library in South Holland.

Mortality Schedules

Mortality schedules (see section 7) list deaths for the twelve months prior to the federal census.

Alternative Sources of Vital Records

Chicago Board of Health

The Chicago Board of Health, located in the lower level of the Daley Center, maintains vital statistics for Chicago only. Birth records from 1955 to the present and death records from 1961 to the present are available at the Chicago Board of Health office for $10.00 (subject to change).

Cook County Suburban Cities and Towns

Cook County suburban cities and towns outside of Chicago also maintain their respective sets of vital statistics, however, they are for relatively recent years.

State of Illinois

State of Illinois
    Office of Vital Records
    Illinois Department of Public Health
    Springfield, IL 62761

Chicago Genealogical Society

The records of over 10,000 individuals who were residents of Chicago were contributed by more than 1,250 of their descendants, and compiled and indexed by the Chicago Genealogical Society. The society published the collection in 1985 as the *Chicago Ancestor File: 1974-84.* Each entry has: the name of the ancestor; date and location of birth, death, or marriage; name of spouse; names of parents; dates of residency in Chicago; and the name and address of the person submitting the information. The 381-page volume can be purchased from:

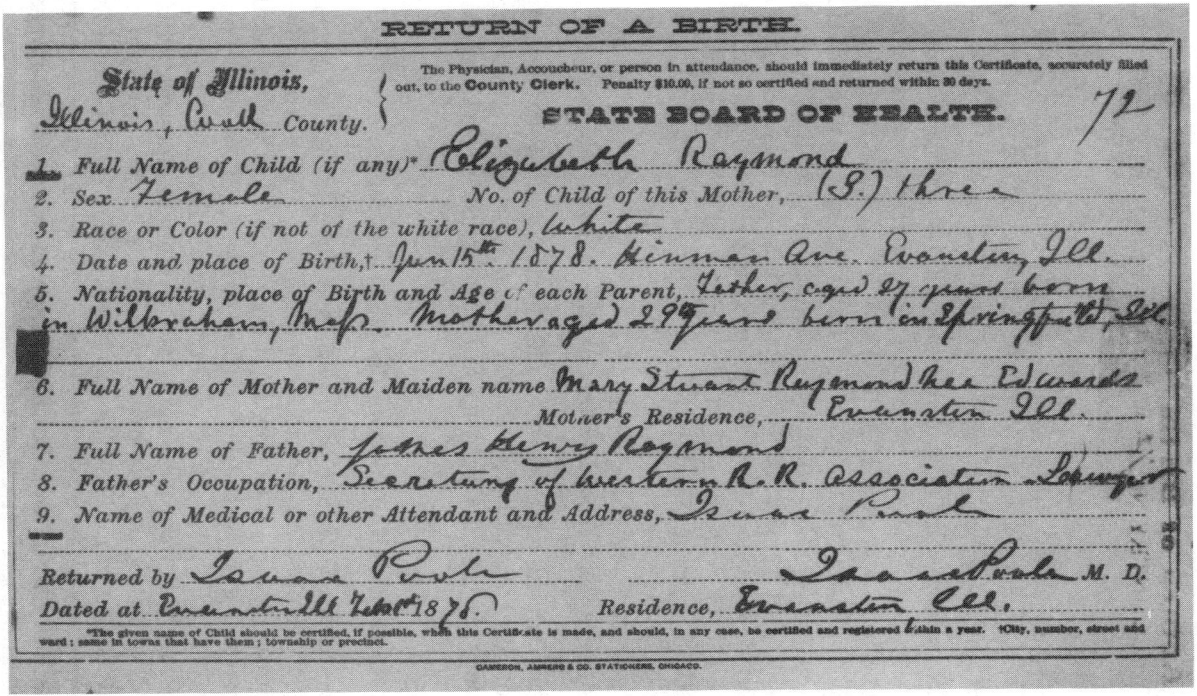

RETURN OF A BIRTH.

State of Illinois, Illinois, Cook County.

The Physician, Accoucheur, or person in attendance, should immediately return this Certificate, accurately filled out, to the County Clerk. Penalty $10.00, if not so certified and returned within 30 days.

STATE BOARD OF HEALTH. 72

1. Full Name of Child (if any)* Elizabeth Raymond
2. Sex Female No. of Child of this Mother, (3.) three
3. Race or Color (if not of the white race), White
4. Date and place of Birth,† Jan 15th 1878. Kinman Ave. Evanston, Ill.
5. Nationality, place of Birth and Age of each Parent, Father, aged 27 years born in Wilbraham, Mass. Mother aged 29 years born in Springfield, Ill.
6. Full Name of Mother and Maiden name Mary Stuart Raymond nee Edwards Mother's Residence, Evanston Ill.
7. Full Name of Father, James Henry Raymond
8. Father's Occupation, Secretary of Western R.R. Association Lawyer
9. Name of Medical or other Attendant and Address, Isaac Poole

Returned by Isaac Poole Isaac Poole M. D.

Dated at Evanston Ill Feb 1st 1878. Residence, Evanston Ill.

*The given name of Child should be certified, if possible, when this Certificate is made, and should, in any case, be certified and registered within a year. †City, number, street and ward; same in towns that have them; township or precinct.

CAMERON, AMBERG & CO. STATIONERS, CHICAGO.

Figure 25: Cook County Birth Record—1878

The Chicago Genealogical Society
  P.O. Box 1160
  Chicago, IL 60690-1160

Data collected since the publication of *Chicago Ancestor File 1974-1984* is being printed in the Chicago Genealogical Society quarterly publication, *The Chicago Genealogist.*

The society has also published vital statistics which appeared in Chicago newspapers. These are in seven volumes covering the years 1833 to 1848. The information in each of the books (sold separately) includes marriage and death information. This makes it possible to recreate the records destroyed by the 1871 Chicago Fire. All volumes are indexed. Volume 1 (1833-39); Volume 2 (1840-42); Volume 3 (1843-44); Volume 4 (1845); Volume 5 (1846); Volume 6 (1847); Volume 7 (1848).

Death Notices from Lithuanian Newspapers, 1900-1979

The Balzekas Museum of Lithuanian Culture in Chicago has the original index. The index is also on microfilm; check the Family History Card Catalog under Newspapers.

Index to Irish Names from Chicago Newspapers

An index of Chicago Irish names is being compiled primarily from personal sources, newspapers and other printed sources by John Corrigan. The index, which is constantly growing, consists of over 8,000 names and includes hundreds of death notices and obituaries. This is a valuable research tool because many of the names appearing in the index do not appear in other major sources. Newspapers covered in the index include: *The Chicago Inter Ocean, The New World, The Chicago Citizen, The South Side Sun* and *The Lake Vindicator.* For more information send a stamped, self-addressed envelope to:

John Corrigan
  1669 104th Street
  Chicago, IL 60643

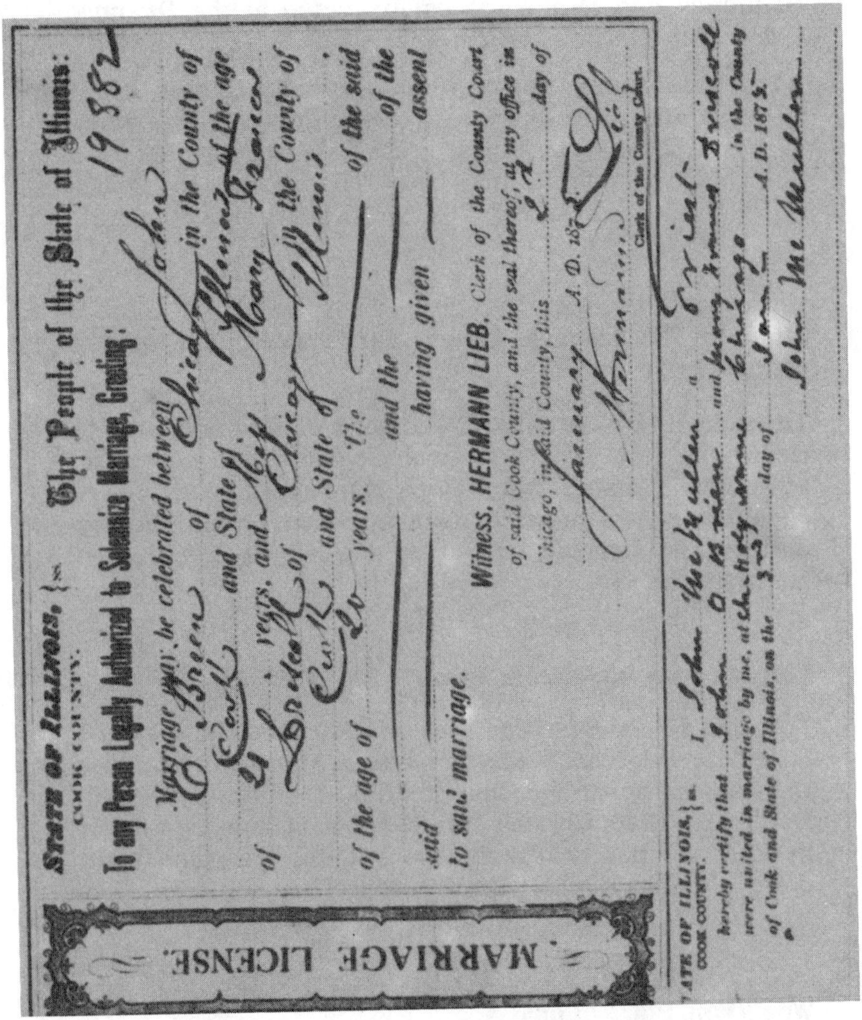
MARRIAGE LICENSE.

STATE OF ILLINOIS, } ss.
COOK COUNTY.

The People of the State of Illinois: 19582

To any Person Legally Authorized to Solemnize Marriage, Greeting:

Marriage may be celebrated between John O'Breen of Chicago in the County of Cook and State of Illinois of the age of 21 years, and Mary Driscoll of Chicago in the County of Cook and State of Illinois of the age of 20 years.

of the said
of the age of ——— and the ——— of the
said ——— having given ——— assent
to said marriage.

Witness, HERMANN LIEB, Clerk of the County Court of said Cook County, and the seal thereof, at my office in Chicago, in said County, this 2d day of January A. D. 187

Hermann Lieb
Clerk of the County Court.

STATE OF ILLINOIS, } ss.
COOK COUNTY.

I, John McMullen a Priest hereby certify that John O'Brien and Mary Driscoll were united in marriage by me, at ch. Holy name in the County of Cook and State of Illinois, on the 3rd day of Jan A. D. 1875.

John McMullen

Figure 26: Cook County Marriage License—1875

Index to Polish Obituaries and Death Notices

Hollowak, Thomas L., and William F. Hoffman. *Index to the Obituaries and Death Notices Appearing in the Dziennik Chicagoski.* Chicago: Polish Genealogical Society.

A multivolume work covering the years 1890 to 1929. It is an especially valuable tool since many of names included did not appear in English language newspapers. The volumes may be purchased from the Polish Genealogical Society, 984 North Milwaukee, Chicago, IL 60622.

Index to The Chicago Record Herald Daily and Sunday (1904-1912)

The index is by date, page, and column, and is alphabetized by subject. It does not include paid death notices or other vital statistics, but may pinpoint death dates of persons who gained notoriety for any reason, or who died by accident, fire, suicide, or murder. Available at the Chicago Historical Society.

Chicago Daily Democratic Press Index—1855

Prepared by the Omnibus Project, Division of Professional & Service Projects, Works Progress Administration under the sponsorship of The Chicago Public Library, Chicago, IL December, 1940, Volume 1. It does not include paid death notices or other vital statistics, but may pinpoint death dates of persons who gained notoriety for any reason, or who died by accident, fire, suicide, or murder.

Who's Who Publications

Who's Who and Blue Book publications contain biographical sketches of prominent Chicago area citizens, and provide birth dates, birthplaces, and names of parents.

STATE OF ILLINOIS
Department of Public Health - Division of Vital Statistics
STANDARD
CERTIFICATE OF DEATH

COUNTY CLERK'S RECORD

Registration Dist. No. 4261.
Primary Dist. No. 4261.

Registered No. 5

[If death occurred in a hospital or institution, give its NAME instead of street and number]

1. PLACE OF DEATH

County .... Cook ....
Township or Road-Dist. } Thornton
or Incorp.-Town or Village } Dollars.
or City

No. 137 .. Lincoln av. .... St.; .... Ward

2. FULL NAME .... Lydell McBehee ....

PERSONAL AND STATISTICAL PARTICULARS

3. SEX .... Female ....
4. COLOR OR RACE .... White ....
5. SINGLE, MARRIED, WIDOWED, OR DIVORCED (Write the word) .... Single ....

6. DATE OF BIRTH .... January .... 18 .... 1912 ....
(Month) (Day) (Year)

7. AGE .... yrs. .... 2 .... mos. .... 23 .... ds.
If LESS than 1 day .... hrs. OR .... min.?

8. OCCUPATION
(a) Trade, profession, or particular kind of work
(b) General nature of industry, business, or establishment in which employed (or employer)

9. BIRTHPLACE (State or country) .... Illinois ....

PARENTS
10. NAME OF FATHER .... Ellis McBehee ....
11. BIRTHPLACE OF FATHER (State or country) .... Alabama. ....
12. MAIDEN NAME OF MOTHER .... Annie Williams ....
13. BIRTHPLACE OF MOTHER (State or country) .... Tennessee, ...

14. THE ABOVE IS TRUE TO THE BEST OF MY KNOWLEDGE
(Informant) .... Ellis McBehee
(Address) .... 137 Lincoln av. ....

15. Filed .... April 12. .... 1920 .... North Dollon .... (Address of Registrar) Dollon Oak Glen Ill. .... Registrar

MEDICAL CERTIFICATE OF DEATH

16. DATE OF DEATH .... April .... 11 .... 1920 ....
(Month) (Day) (Year)

17. I HEREBY CERTIFY, That I attended deceased from .... April 1 .... 1920, to April 11 .... 1920.
that I last saw h... alive on .... April 10 1920,
and that death occurred, on the date stated above, at 5:30 A.M. .... m.

The CAUSE OF DEATH* was as follows:

.... Bronchitis Acuta ....

Contributory (Secondary) .... Bronchial Pneumonia ....
(Duration) .... yrs. .... mos. .... 10 .... da

(Signed) .... An. O. H. Thomas .... (Duration) .... yrs. .... mos. .... 2 .... ds .... M. D
(Address) .... Dollon, Illinois
Date .... April 12. .... 1920 Telephone Dollon 292.

18. LENGTH OF RESIDENCE (For Hospitals, Institutions, Transients, or Recent Residents)
At place .... yrs. .... mos. .... ds. In the State .... yrs. .... mos. .... ds.
of death
Where was disease contracted, if not at place of death?
Former or usual residence

19. PLACE OF BURIAL OR REMOVAL .... Oakland ....
20. UNDERTAKER .... P. W. Good ....

DATE OF BURIAL .... April 12. 1920
ADDRESS .... Dollon, Ill. ....

*State the DISEASE CAUSING DEATH, or, in deaths from VIOLENT CAUSES, state (1) MEANS OF INJURY; and (2) whether ACCIDENTAL, SUICIDAL, or HOMICIDAL.

Has decedent ever served in military or naval service of U. S.? .... no.

N. B.—Every item of information should be carefully supplied. AGE should be stated EXACTLY. PHYSICIANS should state CAUSE OF DEATH in plain terms, so that it may be properly classified. Exact statement of OCCUPATION is very important.

WRITE PLAINLY, WITH UNFADING INK. - - THIS IS A PERMANENT RECORD
MARGIN RESERVED FOR BINDING

V. S. No. 5
25M.—10-26-17

Figure 27: Cook County Death Record—1920

Church Vital Statistics

Guide to Church Vital Statistics Records in Illinois. Chicago, Illinois, 1942.

> This guide was prepared by the Illinois Historical Records Survey, Division for Community Service Programs, Works Projects Administration in 1942, and lists vital statistics which were found in churches in Illinois. It is available at The Newberry Library (Call # D2896.41).

Coroner's Inquest Records

By Patricia Kathryn Szucs

Coroner's inquest records are rarely mentioned and seldom used. When researching a violent, unknown or unnatural death, these records may contain a wealth of information that is not easily found in other sources. Inquest records in Cook County are available for 1878 to the present. Until 1910, these records were in bound ledgers. These ledgers are not as extensive as later records, but they do include some personal data. On December 6, 1976, the inquest records came under the jurisdiction of the first Cook County Medical Examiner. When this occurred, there was no longer a determination of guilt set or included in the record as was in the Coroner's verdict.

Beginning in 1911, individual inquest files were kept. These files usually include many personal details. If they were properly completed, the files include the individual's full name, the date of inquest, a list of names, addresses, and occupations of witnesses and jurors. A "Statistical History of the Deceased" included: the address of the individual, age, sex, color, marital status, birthplace, how long they were in the city and U.S., name and birthplace of father, maiden name and birthplace of mother, date of death, date of accident, hour of accident, mental and physical condition, height, weight, extent of education, religion, housing conditions, occupation, employer, past occupation, wages or salary due, amount of life insurance, value of personal and real estate property, military service, number and ages of dependents, cause of death, cause of accident or catastrophe, place of accident and death, name of company or persons involved in death, and more. The physician's statement, which is attached to the file, may in itself include several pages of physical details.

The testimony of a witness may give a detailed account of the death. A special insight into the character of the individual and lifestyle may be revealed when the witness happens to be a relative or someone who knew the decedent.

Some of the most notorious murder cases in the country are documented in the coroner's collection. Many times they provide the missing link to an unsolved police case. Among these records was found the John Dillinger autopsy report, which had been missing for decades.

Catastrophe records are grouped together by name of disaster (Our Lady of Angels Fire, railroad accidents, airplane crashes, etc.), and then by the individual names of persons involved. Records for early years are contained in single volumes for an entire year, but files for the last two years alone fill great bookcases in a large room.

Early ledgers and records have suffered water damage and crumble when they are touched. There are no other copies and no effort has been proposed to microfilm or otherwise preserve these documents.

When requesting a case file, the date of death or inquest must be known. Cases prior to 1974 are stored in a warehouse. Although the office tries to be accommodating, trips to the warehouse are not made on a regular basis for research purposes. If you make an appointment, you may be able to have a file brought to the Office of the Medical Examiner for viewing. Photocopies may be requested for a fee. If you are writing for information, please be patient with any delays.

The Office of the Medical Examiner
County of Cook
2121 W. Harrison
Chicago, IL 60612
(312-666-0500)

Cemetery Records

Cemetery records can be very useful for establishing death dates and for obtaining clues to other vital statistics. See the Cemetery Records section for more information.

Funeral Director's Records

Publications

The South Suburban Genealogical and Historical Society has several publications that are related to funeral and death records available for purchase from the Society:

* A report of a survey of 398 existing funeral homes in Cook County. The survey was conducted by Kirk Vandenburg of the South Suburban Genealogical and Historical Society. Every attempt was made to locate records of funeral homes that have been renamed or closed. The report is available for $6.00 postpaid.

* Obituaries of the *Blue Island Sun Standard*, published from 1919 to 1934, have been indexed by Res Reed of the South Suburban Genealogical and Historical Society. The index is available for $6.00 postpaid. The society plans to publish a second volume covering the years 1935 to 1942 in September 1996.

* A book on Bachelor's Grove Cemetery in Bremen Township, Cook County, compiled by Brad Bettenhausen, is available for $6.00 postpaid.

The address for the society is:

South Suburban Genealogical and Historical Society
 P.O. Box 96
 South Holland, IL 60473-0096
 (708-333-9474)

Funeral Home Records

The South Suburban Genealogical and Historical Society Library has the following funeral home records on microfilm; they are also available at the Illinois State Archives and at family history centers:

Carlson Funeral Home, 304-06 W. 119th Street, Chicago.

Alphabetical cards, 1937-1955. (ledger books: 1907-1936 and 1950-1975 have not been filmed).

Fedde-Heifrich Funeral Home, 112 Main Street. (Peotone ledger books, 1897-1915; 1915-1967. An index to the ledger books is in *Where the Trails Cross*, volume 23).

Otto Funeral Home, 10928 S. Michigan Avenue, Chicago.

Alphabetical cards, 1912-1949.

Phillips-Peterson Funeral Home, 10232 S. Michigan Avenue, Chicago.

Alphabetical cards, 1938-1973.

Burial Permits

The South Suburban Genealogical and Historical Society Library also has the Calumet City, Cook County, Illinois burial permits from ca. 1921 to ca. 1941. These were indexed by Kirk Vandenberg of the South Suburban Genealogical and Historical Society in 1994. The index can be found under 977. 2167 DCAL. The burial permits are not restricted to those who died or were buried in Calumet City.

Undertaker's Records

The Chicago Historical Society, Archives and Manuscripts Division, has the following undertaker's records:

Birren & Sons Funeral Home, 1868-1943.

C. H. Jordan & Company, 1866-1924.

Frederic Klaner, Undertaker and Embalmer, 1893-1898.

Gleason Funeral Home (formerly Martin Gleason & Son) 1916-1977.

Henry F. Schroeder, 1908-1928.

Voter Registration Lists and Tax Records

Voter Registration Lists

Original voter registration lists were thought to be unavailable for Chicago and Cook County. Most of the old lists, officials said, had been destroyed, and surviving lists were stored in warehouses, and could not be viewed by researchers. Except for the occasional lists of franchised citizens published in early Chicago newspapers, very little information was available in this area of research.

In the late 1980s, amateur genealogist Tom Burke found what was described in the Federation of Genealogical Societies publication the *Forum* (3, no. 2, Summer 1991) as the "discovery of the decade." In a back room of the Voter Registration department at the County Building, Burke noticed twenty bound ledgers in which were recorded the names of several hundred thousand voters for the years 1888, 1890, and 1892. The time period covered is very important because the 1890 federal census is not available. In addition to placing individuals in Cook County in those years, the neatly handwritten rosters included alphabetically arranged names of individuals and their: country of birth; date and place of naturalization; term of residence in precinct, county, and state; and current address.

Due, in large part, to the efforts of Tom Burke, and on the advice of Dr. John Daly of the Illinois State Archives, the *Record and Index of Persons Registered and Poll Lists of Voters* was microfilmed. The 1888, 1890, and 1892 voter lists may be viewed at the Illinois Regional Archives Depository-Chicago and the National Archives—Great Lakes Region.

Other lists that are available include:

"Cook County Voters—1826—A List of Cook County Voters of August 7, 1826." *Chicago Genealogist* 2, no. 2 (December 1969).

"Voters in the First City Election of Chicago—A List of Voters in the First City Election in Chicago." *Genealogical Sources in Chicago, Illinois 1835-1900.* Chicago: Chicago Genealogical Society, 1982.

Lurie Index of Chicago Voters—1937

> The Lurie Index was part of a private collection microfilmed by the Genealogical Society of Utah. It may be found in the *Family History Library Catalog* listed under "Illinois, Chicago," and is described as follows: "Lurie Index of people in Chicago in 1937 as well as all of the voters' registration for Chicago. Addresses are included. Microfilmed in Tucson, Arizona, 38 reels of microfilm, Nos. 0933501-0933538."

Most surviving voter registration lists for later years are especially difficult to use because they were arranged by voter precinct number, ward, and then by street address. Furthermore, they do not include the rich biographical information contained in earlier registers, only names of qualified voters.

Voter Lists—Voter Registration
  Cook County Clerk
  Election Department
  118 North Clark Street—Room 402
  Chicago, IL 60602
  (312-263-3163)

Tax Records

Cook County Assessor

The Cook County Assessor appraises Cook County property for tax purposes, and records dating from 1955 to the present are filed at the assessor's office. Appraisals of unimproved property and property with buildings, are filed by permanent real estate number. Older records are stored in a warehouse and are difficult to access.

Real Estate Tax
Cook County Assessor's Office
County Building
118 North Clark Street Room 301
Chicago, IL 60602
(312-443-5306)

IRS

Internal Revenue Assessment Lists for Illinois, 1862-1866

The bound volumes of tax assessment lists for the 13 collection districts established for the State of Illinois (by Executive order dated August 25, 1862) are reproduced on 63 rolls of microfilm. The lists were created in the assessors of internal revenue offices during the period 1862-66.

The Internal Revenue Act of July 1, 1862 was intended to provide internal revenue to support the federal government, and pay interest on the public debt. Specific and *ad valorem* duties were placed each month on manufactures, articles, and products ranging from ale to zinc. Monthly taxes were levied on the gross receipts of transportation companies; on interest paid on bonds; on surplus funds accumulated by financial institutions and insurance companies; on gross receipts from auction sales; and on sales of slaughtered cattle, hogs, and sheep. Gross receipts from newspaper advertisements were subject to quarterly tax. Annual licenses were required for all trades and occupations, and annual duties were placed on carriages, yachts, billiard tables, and gold and silver plate. An annual tax was also levied on all income in excess of $600, and legacies and distributive shares of personal property were made taxable. Stamp duties were imposed on legal and business documents, medical preparations, playing cards, perfumery, and cosmetics.

The act also authorized the establishment of the Office of Commissioner of Internal Revenue in the Treasury Department to supervise the collection of taxes and prepare regulations, instructions, and forms used in assessing and collecting taxes.

All persons, partnerships, firms, associations, or corporations submitted, to the assistant assessor of their division, a list showing the amount of annual income, articles subject to the special tax or duty, and the quantity of goods made or sold in volume. Lists are not included for every division or every month.

These records are part of the Records of the Internal Revenue Service (record group 58) in the National Archives, and available at the National Archives—Great Lakes Region. Cook County is district 1, and the records are on microfilm rolls numbers 1 and 2.

Internal Revenue Service Records 1905-1919

The National Archives-Great Lakes Region has *Records of the Internal Revenue Service: Illinois, 1905-1919* (record group 58). These records are in bound volumes, and are arranged by district and thereunder chronologically.

National Archives-Great Lakes Region
  7358 Pulaski Road
  Chicago, IL 60629
  (312-581-7816)

Index